Copyright © J F Frost
2012

Printed in Great Britain

ISBN 978-0-9564871-3-1

Published by Wyvern Media Ltd
United Kingdom

www.wyvernmedia.co.uk

Front cover photograph

Author's first photograph, taken when he was two years old
at Maling's Studio, Victoria Road, Diss, (who gave him the doll to hold).

Acknowledgements

I would like to thank all the people who have helped me to write this book, given me permission to write about their families and also let me take photographs of the places I knew in those early years.

My gratitude to two lifelong friends, Tom Hughes (New Zealand) and Jess Atkinson. Both have helped me over the years.

My sincere thanks to all the following people, Mr and Mrs M Rash, Mr L Potter, Mr R Collins, Mr and Mrs D Grainge, Mrs J Trudgill, Mr R Jones, Mr J Doe, Mr D Sharman, Mr Driver, Mr R Howell, Mr and Mrs C Rainer, Mr and Mrs W Bartrum, Mr C Bartrum, Mr and Mrs B Cobb, Mrs M Dorkings, Mrs J Cobb and Mr and Mrs C Lond.

I would also like the following businesses to be acknowledged for their co-operation;

Mr Cyril Goodwin, Cannells Butchers, Diss.

Durrants, Market Hill, Diss and Pollard Tree Farmhouse, Wortham Ling.

Musker McIntyre, Mere Street, Diss and Beech Tree Barns, Wortham.

A special thanks to our two grandsons, Chris and Matthew Way, for contributing their computer skills.

Finally a very special thank you to my wife, Betty, for all the patience and understanding she has shown over the years I have spent on this book.

Family and the Early Years

1928-1954

At Ivy Cottage, Rectory Road, Wortham

Introduction

My grandparents and parents were all country people, living a life that had not changed much over the last hundred years, keeping alive traditions that had been handed down from past generations. Much has been told and written about bygone days and the way people lived and worked. Most of this is the same throughout the country but each and every one of us, as individuals, has a different tale to tell.

The memory of the past, the things did and the way we used to do them will never return. With the exception of a few trades still hanging on to the old ways and some people trying to recreate the past, not much now remains. There is also the memory of the people we lived and worked with and the local characters. Some we felt sorry for and some we were scared stiff of and then there were the school days (the best days of our lives if we had only known) also the war years and all the changes they made to peoples' lives.

During a conversation with a friend about the way of life that I had known and lived, it was suggested that it should be written and recorded for future generations. This is what I will try to do, as well as I can remember about those early years.

The name of Frost - and remembered details

There appear to have been Frosts in Norfolk and Suffolk for quite a long way back in time and the following are some I have come across but am not closely related to, as far as I know:

Henry Cory Frost - Docking, 1813
George Frost - Hingham, 1818
William Frost - Heighham, Norwich, 1822
Mary Frost - Hockering, 1835

The years shown are the years that they got married so they must have been born between 1793 and 1815, using as a guide an age of twenty when they were married.

Then there was Thomas Frost who lived in Rectory Cottage, Wortham (the cottage I was born in). He was born in 1840 and died in 1905, aged 65.

Frederick William Frost (my grandfather) was born in 1873 and died 26 February 1944, aged 71 years, and was buried in Wortham churchyard. Then there was Harriet Frost who lived in Diss - born 1842 and died 1926 aged 84 years whom I believe to be my grandfather's sister. Grandfather also had a brother, Thomas ,who lived in Mellis. My grandfather married Christina Joly who was born 1874, died 25 February 1930 aged 56 and was buried in Wortham churchyard. I think she had a sister who was known as aunt Flo but I never knew her. I cannot ever remember seeing my grandmother as I was one year and four moths old when she died.

My grandparents on the Frost side of my family had three children. The oldest was a girl who they named Kate but was always known as Kitty. She married a soldier named Alfred Downhams and they lived in a village called Rowstock, Berkshire. They never had any children. I think they are buried in the Rowstock or Chilton churchyard. I am not sure which.

The second was a boy, Ernest William, born 1899 and he married Grace.

Evelyn Potte, who was born in 1903 and died January 1962 aged 59 years. Ernest died 26 October 1967 aged 68; both are buried in Wortham churchyard. They did not have any children either.

The third was another boy, Robert Victor (my father), born on 3 September 1901, who married Eliza Mendham (my mother) at her village church in South Creake, Norfolk in August 1926. Robert died 13 November 1963 aged 62 years and Eliza died 25 August 1987 aged 82 years. Both died in Norfolk and Norwich Hospital and both are buried in Wortham churchyard in one single grave between my grandfather and grandmother and aunt Flo's graves.

A past generation

BACK ROW - Robert Frost (my father), Frederick Frost (my grandfather),
Ernest Frost (my uncle), B. Rice (my grandfather's cousin)
FRONT ROW - Christina Frost (my grandmother), Kate Frost (my aunt),
Flo Jolly (my father's aunt)

Next generation down

BACK ROW - Robert Frost (my father), Me, Ernest Frost (my uncle)
FRONT ROW - Eliza Frost (my mother), Grace Frost (my aunt)

Me aged 14

My family, taken 15 October 1942

Grandfather and Grandmother with
their cycles, gas lamps and all.

This is a mystery photo. On the back is written '536 Oxford Street Dad and
Mum. With love from Ethel and Kate.' Kate was my Father's sister.
But who is Ethel? And whose Mum and Dad was it?

The Rice family, Cousins and half
Cousins of the Frost's

My Father in the garden

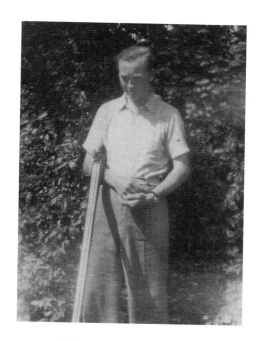

Me with 12 Bore shotgun

My Mother in the same garden

c o l o g n e 1919

The Army side of the Frost family
Ernest Frost my father's brother

The other side of my family, my mother's side, the Mendhams, when I knew them, lived at South Creake near Fakenham in Norfolk, about six miles away from Wells Next Sea. My grandfather, James Mendham (always called Jimmy), was born in the village of Kentford near Newmarket, Suffolk. He was aged 27 years in the 1901 national census records, where he was shown as a bricklayer, but was then living at Little Walsingham, Norfolk. There appears to be some contradiction here as I was always lead to believe that he was in the army when he left Kentford and was posted to barracks at North Creake during the 1914 - 1918 war. He was born in 1868 and died 20 July 1950 aged 82 years. It was during his time at North Creake that he met and married Louise Howell (my grandmother), a blacksmith's daughter from Walsingham, Norfolk. She was born about the same time 1869-70 and died 5 April 1952. Both are buried in the churchyard of St Mary the Virgin, South Creake. I have been told that for the first years of their married life they lived in a cottage at Walsingham, where the eldest of their large family was born, but later moved to where I spent my holidays with them, a semi-detached cottage just into Back Lane, South Creake, just over the river Burn next to the Fakenham-Wells road. They had a very large family. The girls were, May, Rose, Lucy, Eliza and Nellie and the boys were, Jimmy, Bob, Dick, Arthur, Fred, George, Ernie, Percy and John, a total of fourteen children in all. There was also another man who was a visitor to my grandparents. My mother called him Uncle Billy. I believe he was my grandmother's brother and I think he lived at Syderstone a village near Wells.

My mother was born at South Creake on 28 January and went to the village school till she left, aged 14 years, and was sent to work for a family by the name of Bambridge at Glebe Farm at North Creake as a live-in domestic servant (going into service as it was known those days). She walked home and back in what time she had off, a distance of about seven miles, sometimes in bad weather and on dark nights. Then she moved to Knightsbridge in London with a part of this family who besides having a big farm in Norfolk also had property there as well but more about this family later.

More about the Mendham's

I did not know too much about this family until I was about six or seven. We did have the odd day over there when I was very young which to me at that time did not mean very much. My mother and I a stayed there for a few days when I was six, getting there by train from Diss railway station after walking from home. I remember we had to change at Norwich Thorpe for the nearest station to South Creake which was Fakenham, where we were met by one of my uncles in a small van and taken to my grandparent's house. I did learn in later years that I had been there before I was a year old. As they had not got a cot for me to sleep in I was put in a big drawer from a chest of drawers and laid on the floor next to the bed where my mother was sleeping in the main bedroom. I can remember going up to my grandfather's allotment, walking beside him holding his hand and people would stop him for a chat and say to him "who have you got there today Jimmy?" and my grandfather would say, "That's Lisa's boy." At that time I had no idea who Lisa was, until I was old enough to find out.

I did find out that both my grandparents treated all of their grandchildren the same. They were very fair and I don't think they had any favourites. If they did nobody ever said about it. Myself and all my cousins who stayed at their house always got a halfcrown (2/6 in those days, 12½ p in today's money), when we left to go home. Now that must have been a lot for grandparents to give away as beer was 3 to 6 pence a pint so was worth at least five pints of beer and he certainly liked his beer. I had heard it said that on Sunday dinner times the pub was the meeting place for most of the menfolk of the village until 2 o clock in the afternoon. However one particular Sunday my Grandmother had cooked the dinner and 2 o clock came and went and no one came home so Grandmother dished up Grandfather's dinner on a plate and took it across to the Ostrich on a plate for him to eat. I don't think he let it happen again.

As nice as he was he was always ready to play a fast one on us if he had the chance. I went with him one night, after tea, to the Ostrich, which was only two or three hundred yards from their house. It was a summer's night and people were sitting outside drinking and he ordered a pint for himself and turned to me and said "Do you want a lemonade and a packet of crisps boy?" and my answer was. "I don't mind" and he said, "Neither do I" and I didn't get anything. So I thought to myself, this must not happen again. So a little while later while walking on a path around one of his many allotments fancying a nice young carrot, I selected one, pulled it up and cleaned it ready for eating. Well this was my downfall as, unknown to me, my grandfather was in a nearby shed and saw me do this. He then came out and said to me "Do you like raw carrots?". Then he went back into the shed and brought out the biggest carrot I had ever seen. "Would you like this one boy?", he said. Then my mind went back to the pub and the lemonade, not wanting the same thing to happen again I said, "Yes please granddad", and he gave it to me saying, "Sit you on the grass and eat it up." I am sure there was a sly smile under his moustache as he went back into the shed. What he didn't tell me was that these big carrots were grown for the sole purpose of food for pigs and cattle but not for people. Now with a quick brush of my hand it was ready for me to eat which I did and made my way home but something was telling me that all was not well. By the time I had been home a little while the pains in my stomach were getting stronger and I laid doubled up on the kitchen floor. I didn't know if I was going to be sick or not but I certainly felt very ill. Then Aunt Lucy came in and she was a nurse at Kings Lynn Hospital and I thought she must know what to do and she did. She made me drink a big glass of cold water into which she put what appeared to be a large spoon of Andrews Liver Salts, which bubbled like lemonade and was not very nice to swallow but I did and what happened next was an embarrassment which is best forgotten. However I went to bed and I know that grandfather had a few sharp words directed at him when he came home. The next morning he did ask me how I was and said that if I wanted any more carrots I could help myself but I can not remember eating any more after that

For all the tricks he played on us I feel that not only all his grandchildren but every one who had any contact with him for what ever reason liked and respected him. I did know that he was in great demand by people to build brick ovens, brick copper fires and sink wells. This of course brought in extra money which I am certain he needed but he and my uncles all had several allotments between them. At this point I must fit in a little detail of the house they all lived in at Back Lane, South Creake. This was a flint and brick building made into three houses and my grandparents lived in the end next to the river Burn with its ford and footbridge. There was a very quaint old lady lived by herself in the middle one and a young couple by the name of Deakin lived in the end one. They had a small baby which was sometimes out in the back yard in its pram. Now the windows both upstairs and downstairs were not very big at all. The front room door opened out directly onto the road but there was a small garden under the window. The inside of the house had one big room downstairs at the front with the stairs going up next to the big fireplace and an oven for cooking in the centre of the wall on the left as you came in from the front door. The most amazing thing about the inside of this house was that the kitchen was one step down and from the yard outside it was two steps down. Both of these being made of some sort of stone and it was on these steps that all the kitchen knives and anything else were sharpened. It was a bit awkward opening the back door from the inside, as small children had to stand on these steps and undo the latch then jump out of the way quick as the door opened inwards. From the outside this was easy but as this was not a very high door frame most tall people had to bend down to get in. Next to this end of the kitchen was a walk-in larder complete with shelves around the walls. At the opposite end of the kitchen was a cast iron fireplace with bars across the front and small hobs each side. As with all those old houses there was always a kettle simmering away on the hob. The only time the fire was let nearly out was when the fireplace got a clean with what most people in that part of Norfolk called black lead but was in fact Zebra grate polish. It was always nice to see a coal or log fire glowing in the grate. The only fire irons here were a poker and a small coal shovel. The ashes were cleaned underneath the grate by shovel and put in a pail and taken outside into an open sided shed. This small kitchen was really the whole hub of this building, around which life revolved. In the summer months the big room was used only in the evenings and for Sunday dinners. It was a bit eerie in there after dark in the evenings as it was lit by a small paraffin lamp with a single wick; this lamp was fixed to the wall to save space. There was no room on the table as every bit of space was used for something. Even the tea caddie and candle stick were kept on the mantle shelf. The cutlery, when not in use, was kept in the table drawer. As there was always someone calling in, the teapot and cups were in use a lot. One thing I did notice was that all the crockery that was used on the table was white china with a gold band complete with gold shamrock leaves around the top of the cups and around the edges of the plates and saucers. Some of the crockery had a few chips and cracks so how old it was I don't know. The teapot was quite a big thing holding nearly a kettle full of water. It was a brown enamel pot, again this had a chip or two on it. I wonder how many cups of tea had been made in it over the years. It also had a faded pink and blue tea cosy covering it keeping the contents as warm as possible for as long as possible.

The floor was made of pammets covered by coca matting for most of the area. I cannot remember any metal fenders at all around the fireplace only a raised brick hearth. The saucepans used were heavy black iron, and the frying pan was the same and this is where I slipped up one morning when my grandmother fried me some eggs and bacon for breakfast. I noticed that the bottom of the egg was rather brown and I brought this to her notice. I had never seen one done like that before. My grandmother was only a small woman but I found out that it was not the right thing to do to complain about anything. I suppose, with a big family like she had, she had found the way to solve any problems. There were a few harsh words and my breakfast disappeared into the bin that was used for feeding the pigs. One round of bread was not a good breakfast for a growing boy. As my grandfather and uncle kept pigs in sheds on their allotments any food that could be used in the house, (potato peelings, old bread and vegetable leaves) was used to feed the pigs.

This kitchen was a very busy place most of the time and the smells were always in competition with each other. There was the cooking, baking and frying and on top of all that was the smoke from Grandfather's pipe, which he always lit before he went out, besides my uncles' cigarette smoke. My grandmother was not happy with this and demanded that all smoking was done outside but no one took much notice if she was not around.

The main big room held a lot of furniture, mainly Victorian, big, heavy, mahogany stuff. In the centre was a massive table with circular, carved legs on big brass castors with what looked like marble wheels. This had a centre section that could be lifted up level with the top. There was also a big brass screw that could be worked by a handle to lengthen both end sections. This was only used when there were lots of people to sit and eat like at Christmas dinner and other family gatherings. It was also used for most Sunday dinners but in its closed position. Other pieces of furniture included a very big mahogany sideboard with two massive cupboard doors hung on heavy solid brass hinges. On each side of the doors were two half circle pillars and ornamental carvings. Over the top of the sideboard was a thick mahogany board like a table top with small shelves up against the wall. On this top stood some cases of stuffed birds and a red squirrel. Most of these cases had a big glass dome up from the base to cover the complete mount of birds, bush, grass and stones. Next to the sideboard was an upholstered Victorian sofa in black, buttoned leather. This had a sloping head rest that curled right round at one end and an upholstered arm rest about two thirds along one side, this was held up in position by a row of small turned spindles in a ornamental pattern. The whole thing was supported on short round turned legs on brass castors. I liked this because I would lay on it and count the brass studs where the leather was join onto the dark mahogany woodwork. It was on this sofa that I sat listening to the radio one night during the war and I heard Winston Churchill's, now famous, speech. The battle of France is over and the battle of Britain is about to begin and all the rest ending with we will never surrender. This speech has been quoted many times since. I often used this sofa for a rest as I could lay out full length in comfort but I always had to take my shoes off as did everyone else who laid on it. I came to the conclusion that this was my grandparents' most valuable piece of furniture. On the walls above the sofa was a clock with Roman numbers on its face with a mahogany case made by a person named Bone of Fakenham, clock maker, whose shop I went into once on a visit to the town to collect a watch that had been repaired. In the corner of the room near the bottom of the sofa stood a floor–to-ceiling corner cabinet, again in dark mahogany. I don't remember very clearly about the top doors but I think that there was glass in part of them. On the front wall next to the front door, that opened inwards, was another sofa-type piece of furniture but for some reason this was always called a couch. The difference from the other one was that the side was a solid upholstered section for about three quarters of the length and this was covered in a dark green fabric but still had the brass studs, only a little further apart. I didn't like this one much as it always seemed rough and prickly when I sat on it. This was also the one people in their working clothes used. So it was second best. The chairs in this room were a mixed bunch. One in particular that stood against the wall between the kitchen door and the door to the stairway was an early Victorian easy chair of about 1860. This had a button back and arms with a plain seat. The woodwork was mahogany with plenty of curves in the body and legs. This was not for anyone to use but was used only by a black whippet dog called Nell. She was my Uncle Ernie's dog and no one could go near him without being watched very carefully. A very faithful little dog but a bit of a terror if upset. Getting back to the chairs, the ones that were used the most were two Windsor chairs used my grandparents. Others were scroll Windsor and ballroom backed chairs. The carpets on the floor were hard wearing coconut matting with one or two mats made from old clothing cut into small strips about half an inch wide and about three inches long threaded double onto a hessian base by a tool like a sack needle with a wooden handle. Sometimes the base was an old sack. These mats were made by hand over a period of time and would last for years. There was also a black cooking range in this room. This had a large oven heated by a wood or coal fire but was not an open fire as a metal door had to be opened to get to it. I remember that baking and roasts were cooked in it. I was over there one Christmas when a goose was cooked in this oven. I must admit that I did not like the look of it and chose a piece of roast rabbit instead, I have never tasted goose since.

Upstairs in this house there were three bedrooms accessible by a winding stairway of plain boards. One bedroom, which was the main one with windows overlooking the road and the river, had a boarded floor with one grey goat skin rug at the end of the bed and two other rugs, one each side of the bed at the top end. The bed itself was a typical cast iron bed with a big brass knob on each corner post and thin steel strips fitted across both ways for springs across the main frame. Under both sides of the bed standing on the floor were two big white chamber pots. Also in this room was a very big light stained chest if drawers made of heavy pine. This had three big drawers. One of which, as I have said before, I once had as a cot. At the top were two small drawers the same depth but half the length. These all had very big wooden knobs on the front for opening and shutting. On top of the chest of drawers stood a dressing table swing mirror of the Victorian type; a very plain mahogany frame with two uprights from which the mirror was hung. Under the base were four round wood feet on which, the whole thing stood. I have a faint memory that there was also a light-coloured wash stand with a grey marble top with tiles in a wooden frame to make an upstanding back. It was complete with jug and bowl and soap dish. There was also a white enamel pail standing on a low shelf just off the bottom, above the floor. There was a round-faced clock on the wall. The other thing that stood out was a very big picture that hung on the wall above the chest of drawers. I don't know what the picture was about but it was in black and white and grey with lots of solders on horseback brandishing swords and spears. Some of them had high black fez-like hats. These were the horse riders. Some of the horses had been brought to the ground. It really must have been some battle. That is about all I can remember about the big room.

The next one was the middle bedroom and this was really where the stairway stopped and you had to go partly across the corner of this room to get to the main bedroom. There was not a window at all in this room and it was only the light from a small window in the side of the stairway wall that came in to stop it being totally dark. This small window was open nearly all the time. There were two single iron beds one at each end of the room both with a white chamber pot underneath. I don't really know what the actual bedclothes were except that on all the beds they always seemed very clean and white. I remember that there was a picture or two on the walls.

The third bedroom was a long narrow room over top of the kitchen. This room floor was not on the same level as the other two and you had to go down two wooden steps to the room floor below, which like the others had only a goat skin rug near the bed. The floor boards in this room had at sometime been dark stained. And in here again were two single metal beds, one at each end of the room and under each was a white chamber pot. Along the wall facing the back yard were two wooden windows which let in quite a lot of light and, because they were fitted with opening lights, which were used nearly every day, the room always felt clean. On the inside walls there was not a picture at all but only two colour samples in a rather nice wooden frame with each corner having the timber extending out about an inch each way. All the rooms had one thing in common and that was that they all had two or more straight backed chairs with thin, interwoven patterned, thin cane seats.

This particular long room was the one I slept in when I stayed for holidays and during the war I often heard German aircraft flying overhead and watched the searchlights trying to find them.

The yard at the back was shared by all three houses and each had a pail closet away from the house. Inside the closet belonging to my grandparents was a double wooden seat one of which was lower than the other which was for the children to use. There were also two galvanized pails used in this toilet. When one was full it was taken out from under the seat and replaced with the other one which was then used. When this one was full, which usually worked out each Sunday morning, my grandfather would take the yoke from off the shed wall. (The yoke was a piece of wood cut to fit on top of a person's shoulders with a piece of it sticking out both sides from which two chains were hung complete with a hook on each chain from which a pail was hung) He would hang the full pails on the hooks and with a full pipe of tobacco billowing out smoke would walk a quarter of a mile up to his allotment where the contents of the pails would be buried in a ready dug hole. He would give the pails a wash-out from a tank which held rainwater from the roof of a chicken or pig shed. He then carried them home by the yoke to repeat the whole process. There were no sewers or drains out in the country in those days and most people done the same thing in their gardens to get rid of the waste, using it as fertilizer. There was no toilet paper used by the ordinary people same as us at home. At that time we used just newspaper torn into squares, no complete story to sit and read.

17

Under the same roof as the closets was a long open fronted shed which was divided into three sections, one for each house. There was not much space for anyone in these sheds. My Uncle Ernie kept his motorbike in their section, a very shiny black and chrome Triumph Tiger 80 with a picture of a tiger on a maroon petrol tank. In the opposite end of the shed these people kept rabbits in wooden hutches.

Also in this backyard was a flint and brick wall joined onto the outside wall to form a square, about four feet high, topped with a curved tile. This area was used for storing the used cinders and ashes from the indoor fireplaces. I never saw this emptied but I was told that when it was, the contents were used for filling in holes on the rough farm tracks in the area. Some people used these cinders for garden paths but they did stick to your footwear when they got wet. There was always a very strong smell coming from the stored wet cinders.

Another thing in this backyard was a large wooden shed that was used for many different purposes. Stored in it were working cloths hung on nails on the walls. There were also tools, a bicycle or two, a big heavy mangle and it was also home to a big brindle greyhound. I think he was called Prince and at the time he could run very fast and some Sunday mornings he was taken out on to the big fields in the village to catch a hare. He would be let off the lead and would just disappear for quite a while but he would always come back with a hare in his mouth. His bed was in one corner which I kept well away from. Somehow I never did trust him. One other thing kept in this shed was what was used for washing clothes. Zinc baths of different sizes, linen pegs (home made like gypsy pegs) and on a shelf all the washing powders.

From the back wall of the house across the backyard to the shed was rope linen line held up by a prop cut from a hedge but the most used thing in the whole back yard was a great big heavy galvanised water tank with each corner held together by big rivets. There was a bar across from side to side to stop the sides bulging when full. I don't know how many gallons it held but it was quite a lot. It had a flat boarded top which was the work top for many jobs. All the male part of the family used it for washing and shaving as it was natural rain water all coming from the back roof of the house. No electric razors in those days, just the knife-like cut throat razor with a bone or wood handle which was held at 90o when in use and the blade folded into it when not in use. I don't think that I could have used one of those things but as I was too young to shave I didn't have too. The blades on these razors were sharpened by what was called honing. This was done on a leather strip about three inches wide by eighteen inches long, hung onto a hook on a door by a metal loop at the top and a leather handle held by the hand at the other. The cutting edge of the blade was moved up and down, turning over to each side as it went being held in the other hand.

There was another type of razor being used at that time called the safety razor and it is still in use today. This consisted of a short round handle with a small thread pin on top which was fitted into one of the three top sections which was the base and had three round holes across it. Onto that fitted the main cutting piece called the blade, which also had three holes in it and the third piece was the top which had three studs with the centre one being thread to screw the top of the handle to. The edges of this were made of a comb. The blades of this razor were used to the point when it was not sharp anymore and had to be thrown away. There was a razor blade factory in the main street of South Creake and my uncles always gave my father some when he went to visit. The outside wrapper had a Union Jack on the front but I can't remember what they were called.

The only time anyone was allowed to wash indoors was when it was raining hard or there had been a heavy snow storm. What amazed me about the water in the tank was it was full of little white larva which were hatched from the eggs of mosquitoes (what we call gnats). These little things were about half an inch long and had what looked like eyes in a small head which would just be out of the top of the water while the body hung down into the actual water. When the top was moved they'd squiggle down to the bottom of the water out of the way and no one ever caught one in the white enamel bowl or the wooden handled galvanized hand basin which was used for getting water out for any purpose. There was also a white enamel soap dish with Lifebuoy Soap in it kept on the boarded tank top. The only trouble I found with this was that in the summer, if the soap was left wet and the wind was blowing dust from the back yard would land on the soap and the next person to use it found it very rough to use.

Then there was the boot and shoe cleaning. This was always done outside also on the tank top, especially at weekends. I have never forgotten one weekend I was cleaning a pair of black shoes and my Grandfather who was very particular about things being clean said to me, "Make sure you clean the backs boy, because anyone walks behind you can see if they are dirty."

Now I liked going to South Creake for those summer holidays as everyone always made me, as they did all their grandchildren, very welcome when any of us stayed there. I learned a lot from my grandfather, Jimmy Mendham, because he had such a variety of interests and although I was very young he always wanted to show me how to do things. He was employed during the day as a builder for the Earl of Leicester at Holkham Hall near Wells. I always thought that he was a foreman or something like that as some of my uncles worked there as well and were always asking about certain jobs. I do know he was using tools and I often watched him go to work in the mornings with his bag of hammers, trowels, chisels and spirit levels tied to his crossbar of bicycle and with his pipe leaving a trail of smoke behind him. I know he was a clever perfectionist as far as work was concerned and someone was always asking his advice. The only time I ever saw him out of his bib and brace blue overalls with a wooden 2ft rule in the pocket halfway down the outside right leg was on a Sunday dinner time, when he would change into his best suit. I can remember him sitting on his chair reading, and for some reason which I could never understand this would not be a newspaper but some type of comic. It was said that he could not read newspaper printing but the amazing side of it was that he could (and I often saw him do this) read and draw up plans for buildings, getting all the details as was required.

One of the jobs he was asked to do in his spare time all those years ago was to make drinking water wells. Now I know that nearly every home had one or there was a shared one between houses. There was no mains water in the countryside in 1930-40's. Drinking water for my grandparents' house came from a well shared by four houses. Now the way it was done was like this, first the water had to be found and this was done with a Y shaped hazel twig or two thin metal rods which were held one in each hand straight out in front of the person trying to find water in the area where the well was wanted. Once over a source of underground water the twig would move up and down and the metal rods would cross over each other. This would rule where the well could be dug. Then the circle would be drawn on the soil by a two pegs and a piece of string. One peg would be put in the ground and this would be the centre of the well while the other peg would be tied to the string at half the width of the well. This would then be pulled around the centre peg with the string turning on the peg and this would mark out the circle. Next soil would by dug out to around two foot down and removed. The bottom of this hole would be made level and some timber about three inches by nine inches would be obtained, cut into short lengths by making an angled cut and laid out on the bottom of the hole to form a circle. Then the bricks were used, soft red bricks or any hard bricks could be used. In fact any easily obtainable material was used for this including, sometimes, old floor bricks. They were then laid on top of the timber and butted up together so the inside corner touched each other's and the brick corners were apart. This formed a V joint, the join on each course over the centre of the brick below exactly like building a wall but no cement or lime plaster was used. The circular wall was flexible. The next thing done was that a man climbed inside the well and started to dig out some more soil from the inside and at this point it could be thrown out of the well onto the level soil above to be cleared away. At the same time soil would be carefully removed from under the timbers around the base and the complete timber and brickwork that had been done gradually sank down to the solid and then another ten or more course would be build on top of the bricks already in there. This was repeated time after time and all bricks being laid from ground level. When a point was reached that the soil could not be thrown, out a block and tackle was erected and used. This was three poles out at a triangle around the well all meeting at a point over the centre where a block was fitted into the centre of the triangle and ropes put through it with a hook attached to a pail. The two ropes worked against each other, pull one and it dropped the pail down the well where it was filled with soil, pull the other one and the full pail was brought up to ground level. I never heard of a well caving in because the pressure of the bricks was against each other. When the right depth was found and by now water coming in could be a problem so each morning the first job was to pail the water out of the well this was also done during the day to keep it as clear as possible. As the well got deeper a ladder was used to get in and out for the man doing the digging. When it was finally as deep as required a square trench was dug out around the brick circle and filled with concrete to the level of the circle brickwork and then a brick square was built up to about eighteen inches high with the last course having bolts cemented into it to hold the wooden frame which was either flat across the top with a hinged wooden door fixed to it and with upright timber to hold the roller with the pail chain turned by a metal handle or a box-like cover shaped like a roof of a house with the roller and the chain hid up inside. There was no set design for these wooden tops and they were made to each person requirements.

Another thing that my grandfather did was a lot of flint walling for houses or around gardens and for built-in coppers for heating water for washing clothes, sheets and anything else that boiling water was used for. I also went with him when he was working on his many allotments which were used for growing all their own vegetables and also farm crops like cattle beet and mangolds, sugar beet and wheat. On one of these plots were several wooden sheds which were used for pigsties, where they kept some large, black sows and their litters, one of which was selected to be fattened up for the table. So there was never a shortage of meat and sausages. The pig from the litter which was kept for meat was weaned from its mother and put in a separate shed and was fed special food mix and any surplus bread from the local bakery.

One part of the sheds was used for straw and mangolds. Another plot had a big chicken run and sheds with nest boxes in. I think this took up more than half of one allotment and the chickens were of no particular breed. As long as they laid eggs that was all that mattered. I know that some were Rhode Island Reds, some were White Sussex and others were mixed to bring a total of about forty altogether, complete with two massive but very docile Rhode Island Reds cockerels. The eggs were collected mainly late afternoon in a small pail with straw in the bottom. All the arable allotments were not dug by hand as two of my uncles had land and one or the other would plough and cultivate with their tractors. The main trackways were wide enough to take machinery and from them, dividing each plot, were paths about one yard wide which were mainly rough grass although some plot holder did keep these cut. People took pride in their allotments and gardens in those bygone years, one of the main reasons being that, the more that could be grown the less that had to be bought. The one thing that I don't think that I will ever forget is the footpaths on some parts of these allotments that were used by everyone and this was because they were made of shells, cockle, mussel and winkle shells. It seemed as if all the people who had a plot took all their shells and dumped them there to walk on, and this could not be done quietly.

Another thing that stood out on all the grass verges and on any unused piece of grassland was the wide tall leaves of the wild horseradish it was everywhere, but I don't know if anyone ever dug up the roots up.

The last of the many memories that stand out about my grandfather was that he was always the first one up in the mornings and it was a regular thing for him to bring everyone a cup of tea in bed. As he got older I can say it was very difficult for him to remember which cup was for who and it was not unusual to hear him muttering people' names as he came up the stairs with a cup in each hand. He worked hard all his life. Even to the day before he had a stroke he was helping to lay a concrete floor, I can remember my mother going to see him when he was ill and I think that he died in this house.

I can remember his funeral as it was totally different from what is done today. I can't remember if we all went by train or hired a car and went just for the day but when we got there his body was in the coffin with the lid standing near the wall. This was the first time I had seen anything like this and to me this all seemed a bit frightening but this was the way thing were done in the 1950's. When it was time for the funeral the local undertakers came into the room and asked if there was anyone who wanted to say their last goodbyes and they left the room for a few minutes after which they came back and screwed the lid on the coffin. Then what happened next was that the coffin was lifted from the wooden trestles it was laying on and carried out of the front door and put on the bier. This was a high four-wheeled trolley with a handle across the back and a moveable handle in front to steer with. There was also a type of brake to keep it from moving when stopped. All the people who had any connection, family, friends, workmates, who wanted to walk behind the bier were all waiting to follow for the mile and a half to the church. This was the traditional North Norfolk funeral. No motor vehicles were used at all, not like our erea where they had been part of the funeral scene for many years. Although one thing was the same over both Norfolk and Suffolk and that was that most of the houses along the route would draw their living room curtains as a mark as respect but this did not stop them taking a look. Well with everything ready, wreaths and flowers on the bier as well we started off on Grandfather's last journey with everyone walking behind in twos and threes and Grandmother in front with support from two of my uncles, over the wooden footbridge with a handrail along one side where, on summer evenings with the River Burn bubbling along underneath, a group of old men (some with long white beards) would gather for a chat and pass the time away waiting for the Ostrich pub to open, down the road with the pub on the right and the bowling green on the left, (I had seen lots of these men on there, playing bowls on a Saturday evening, Grandfather included. I wonder how many woods he had bowled across that well kept grass in his lifetime), down past the razor blade factory on the left and the factory that made breakfast flakes on the right, built and owned by a man named G T Money, (I had some of these when I was staying there, quite a good breakfast cereal.). We carried on down the road to the school where we took a left branch up to the next right at Bluestone Farm and along the road to the church, which was near a corner that turned right and the road rejoined the B1355. It was in the meadow that there was a deep pond in the corner near the church and when the annual church fete took place an old telephone pole covered in cart grease would be put over the pond and anyone who crept across the pole the most times could win a pig from a local farm. I heard my mother say that Grandfather did win a few pigs this way. One thing I did notice as we were walking along was that several men who stood at the roadside all removed their hats as a mark of respect. At the church then were lots of people but I cannot remember much about the actual service but I was relieved it was all over and we walked back to the house with just memories of what Grandfather had taught me and to this day I feel much wiser for it.

Next in this family was my grandmother, a very short stout little woman who had very strict views on right and wrong and I suppose she had to be like that with such a big family. Even with a grown up family I never saw anyone attempt to cross her. What she said was done without any hesitation. She was always busy and it was only in her later years she would sit and rest in her Windsor chair and on certain times would let herself nod off for a quiet doze. I wonder what thoughts were passing through her mind. Sometimes she would talk about the neighbours and always finish a sentence with a determined shake of her head either in approval or disapproval. One thing I did admire her for was her determination to get things done. She was a very tidy person and believed in everything in its place. One thing I noticed was that when she was left on her own she was still in control. Sometimes I would go to Fakenham with her on a bus on Thursday which was market day and help her to do the shopping. For this trip she would wear her best clothes including a tall round black hat that most women had in those days. This was complete with ornamental hat pin.

As the family was mostly self supporting she only brought things that were not available in the village shops, one of which was on the opposite side of the lane to the house they lived in. This was owned by a Mrs Kay and I was often sent across to collect some sort of goods. This was mainly a grocer-type of shop but it did sell tobacco and cigarettes and thought nothing of serving anyone even if you were only a schoolboy and no questions asked and many times I was sent across there to get some cigarettes for my uncles and tobacco for Grandfather's pipe. I usually worked it out if I could get a bar of chocolate or a packet of crisps out of the change. Nobody ever said anything if I did. There were two other general store-type of shops in the village, one which was across the village green, Cartrights. Part of this shop was in use as the Post Office and the other part was a general store and sold all sorts of goods, such as groceries and vegetables, pots and pans, kitchen-ware, washing-powders and soap, in fact everything required by households. There always seemed to be a lot of people in this shop. The other shop which was nearly to the far end of Back Street was also a shop which stocked groceries and other household goods and was owned by people named Brown. I was often sent to either of these last two shops to collect goods but I was never given any money and I often wondered why this was. I did find out later as I got older and there were two reasons for this, one was because money was very short in those days and provided that everything was settled up on Saturday (pay day) you could have what you wanted during the week, the other thing was sometimes these shops got low on their stock of eggs and vegetables and they would have some off grandfather in exchange for goods. There were other shops in the village including two butchers. One was Barnes and Johnson on the side of the green and Hastings in the Back Street. I was sometimes asked to go to the one on the green to buy some bones for the dogs. I forgot how much these cost but I feel certain this was only a few pence.

One of the things I remember about my grandmother was how she would arrange a day out at Wells. Seats would be booked on Hawes' bus service from North Creake for a Sunday outing and she would pack up a bag of sandwiches, cakes and drink, which was very weak lemonade. Also in the bag was a tartan blanket which was laid out on the sand to sit on and eat the food. It was only when I tipped a glass of drink over on to the blanket, that I saw her real temper. I really got told off. All this was before the war and the beach was very different from what it is now. I know we sat just onto the sand a few yards away from the sloping path and the whole place was covered in shells of all sorts, and there were small pools of seawater full of wild life, small crabs and fish. Seaweed was everywhere along the tide line, large round stones, bits of fishing net, all that made a small boy very interested to collect. Despite the fact that there were beach huts along one side of shore line there was plenty of room to run about chasing a very colourful beach ball. Some of my cousins came on these trips as well.

We did, on the odd occasion, go to Hunstanton by bus as well but this was not like Wells. We would sit and have a picnic on the blanket but this time it was on the big sloping green, and watch the ships out at sea and also have a walk down the pier but for some reason the beach here was nowhere as exciting as Wells. Although there was plenty of seaweed the rocks that laid everywhere around seemed to spoil the pleasure we had unlike at Wells in the pools of sea water. Here the posts and girders that held the pier up were covered in mussels but I never saw any one take these to eat. This was the place from which I first went out to sea in a small boat and to be honest I wasn't very happy about it as I had to spend my pocket money but I could not complain really as my grandmother done her best to treat all the grandchildren as fair as possible. Both of them did in my opinion but sadly when she died the whole situation changed and I don't think we went over to visit anymore and by that time I was twenty four and had very little time for holidays away.

Well the next person in this family was Uncle Bob and one who I never saw. All I know is that he was in the army during World War One and my mother always said that he got killed in Palestine but I don't know when. She said that once he came home on leave and told her how they played football with big Jaffa oranges.

The next one of her brothers was named after Grandfather and was called Uncle Jimmy. He tried one or two businesses in this country without success, as I understood it. One was farming pigs and poultry and also selling wet fish, none of which were successful. So he made up his mind to work his passage on a ship to Canada and after he had been there a short while he met and married a girl from Great Yarmouth in Norfolk and had a family of nine children, including four sets of twins.

Then next came Uncle Fred married to Aunt Edith. They also had twins, both girls. I remember them well as I was over there once when they had a birthday and each had a big doll for a present. Sadly before their next birthday one of them died but there were two more in the family as their first child was a boy and I can remember him working on a local farm and during the war he was in the Royal Navy.

The last member of this family was another girl who I lost touch with for many years but by a very strange coincidence, by her talking to an old school friend who was also a friend of mine a phone call was made and we have been in touch ever since. I think that these cousins were the family I knew the best of all and I had many cousins around the country. This family lived in a flint walled cottage just a few yards from my grandparent's house, and I sometime went with Uncle Fred to milk two cows after tea in a big barn just down the Fakenham road. Whose cows they were I don't know but I think he done this to earn some extra cash.

Then there was Uncle George married to Aunt Violet. There was also a family of mostly boys and I think one girl. I did not know these very well, but I did visit their house once at Swanton Morley and I believe this was a house belonging to the farm where George worked.

The next one was Uncle Dick, as we all called him. It appeared to me that he was the odd one out of this family or at least the most unlucky one. I can only repeat what I have been told, that he was in the army in World War One and was sent to France and was fighting in one of the big battles that had a lot of hand to hand fighting. So when he returned home he was in a very bad state of mind as what he had seen and done had taken its toll of his self control. The story was that one morning early he had got up and, still thinking he was still at war, was in the kitchen shouting "Here the buggers come again", and was, in his mind, trying to blow up a German gun post. In reality he had a box of matches which he was striking and throwing into the fireplace, where the fire had been laid in preparation for lightening plus other things he had thrown onto the fireplace. It was very lucky that my grandfather came down to see what was going on and took the matches away from him and calmed him down. It took many years before he had complete control and settled down to as near a normal life as it was possible for him to live. He did like a pint of beer at the weekend and he worked on a farm to get a living and also done odd jobs for people for a bit of tobacco money. His only possession was an old, somewhat rusty bicycle. He never did make the steps for improvement like his other brothers.

I always got on well with him and he sometimes gave me a few coins spending money when he knew I was going out anywhere but his willingness to help people had a tragic end for him. As he was helping some man at Wells to stable his horse after taking it out of the shafts of a four wheeled cart the horse took fright at something and crushed him against a post and he never survived that. There was a story and a picture in the local paper. I think he was buried in South Creake churchyard. I don't remember what year it was or how old he was. I think he had been living in my grandparent's house on his own for some time.

The next one was Uncle Arthur who was married to a woman known to us all as Aunt Emily. She was a smart tidy person. She was very difficult to understand and bordered on being a snob, always giving the impression that she looked down on the Mendham family. She was fighting an endless task trying to bring Arthur up to her standards. She was a very religious person was this particular Aunt Emily not like Uncle Arthur. Whether she could not or would not have a family I don't know but they did adopt a boy which they brought up as their own family. I did have tea with them once or twice but I would avoid it if I could.

Now I spent a lot of time with Uncle Arthur as he rented a farm from North Norfolk County Council and known as County Farm. (The last time I saw it there was a housing estate there.) This had all new buildings, complete new farm house and dairy. I spent a lot of time with him on this farm which I suppose was about eighty acres of both arable and grassland. From the very early days of me having a holiday there I learned a lot from him. He had a herd of milking cows, some black pigs, a lot of hens, one Suffolk horse and a big tall red and green Oliver tractor and both tractor and horse implements. Now the horse was not used that much and spent a lot of time grazing in a big meadow near the farm and for that reason when it was used it was very fast. I was not allowed near it when it was in harness, but on the meadow it seemed very quiet. This meadow had a lot of ragwort growing on it and sometimes I would help to pull this weed up and carry it off the meadow and burn it. The herd of cows was a new thing to me as I had been brought up with horses. After the morning milking the whole herd would be turned out to graze on some meadows, which were quite a long way from the farm. There was a wide grass verge beside the lane where the cows walked and they had made their own footpath on this verge. The biggest cow always walked in front and the others walked in single file behind. So it was quite a long way from the first cow to the last but there was always some help at hand in the way of a crossbreed dog which was part collie and part retriever. He knew it was his job to keep the cows in order and he did it well besides protecting the farm itself and all of us who went there. Although he was never chained up he would not go on to the road unless he was told to do so.

The one thing about cows in those days was that they were hand-milked and I was not very old when my uncle learned me to milk. I must admit it was the most docile cow in the whole herd that I started to learn on. With my cap turned with peak to the back and sitting on a wooden stool I soon got the hang of it. As this was a small dairy herd all the milk was sold locally. From the milking parlour it was taken to the dairy in stainless steel pails and run through the cooler into large metal churns. There were some small hand carrying churns used where the milk was sold by pints and half pint measures direct into people's jugs.

There was quite a big milk delivery round from this dairy. As the village was very close the round was done mainly with bottles from crates pulled around by hand on a big four-wheeled flat-bottomed cart. This was done most days by one of my aunts who lived at home with my grandparents and it was not unusual to see the farm cat during the round with her. The other part of the round was done with a green Austin Seven van and this was to the surrounding villages.

One particular place was Sculthorpe common where we followed a rough track. I would go on this delivery with my Uncle and it was here, with the help of a cushion on the seat, that I was allowed to drive the van the short distance between the houses. As I was only seven or eight I had to stand up to put my foot on the clutch. On one of these deliveries I made one big mistake by asking if I could take some bottles of milk up to a house. It was agreed that I should do that at the next stop. What I did not know was the next stop was a big country house with a tree and shrub-lined, wide, stone drive. Well off I went with the bottles of milk in a small wire crate, up the hill towards the back door of the house. I was nearly there when to my horror, from across the lawn, came two of the biggest dogs I had ever seen. Now I did not know quite what to do. Should I run back to the van or carry on? I decided to do the latter and these two big brown dogs were by now walking beside me one each side. I went and put the full bottles of milk on the doorstep, collected the empty bottles and started to walk back down the drive. By this time I had decided that there was no danger as the dogs stopped, turned and went back

Four of the Mendham family women

Rose and May Mendham

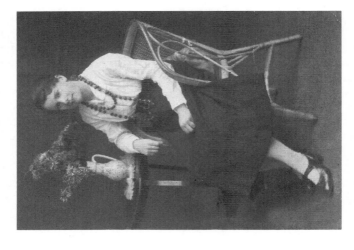

Eliza Mendham

Nellie Mendham
Who pulled the milk cart

across the lawn. When I told my Uncle about what happened he just laughed and said "You wanted to take some milk to a house", and told me that these dogs were bloodhounds and quite harmless. I got a Woodbine to smoke for doing that. I went on these delivery rounds several times but did not wear the traditional buff coloured smock with the dark brown hard buttons.

When we got back from the rounds there was the really busy time as every bottle had to be washed and sterilised and the same with all the churns, cans, and measures, in fact everything concerned with the dairy. The outside jobs that had to be done were cleaning out the cow house (milking parlour) and washing down with disinfectant all walls and floors, mixing the food for the cows to eat at the next milking time and feeding the calves in the loose boxes. Keeping everything clean was the most important job of all. This was totally different from when I first went over there as they only had a few cows then, which were milked in an old wooden boarded shed with a corrugated tin roof, no concrete floor or drains, just a straw covered floor.

I liked the harvest time holiday as I was allowed to help as much as I could to cut the ripe standing corn. My uncle had a red and green Oliver tractor and a binder but I can't remember what make it was. I was allowed to ride on the tractor but I had to stand on top of an oil drum to get onto it. How to drive this machine was explained to me as we worked around the fields, sometimes the part of the binder that tied the knots in the string would break and I learned how to repair this so it worked as it should. Then one day they let me drive the tractor when a field of barley was being cut. Now this pleased me, to think that I could drive a tractor, but to my amazement I had not been doing this long when my Uncle had to do what he told me was an unforeseen job leaving me on my own cutting corn. I was lucky nothing went wrong and he was not gone long and to be truthful I was glad to see him back. I done this job once or twice after then but they were in the field working most of the time so I was not alone. Most of the family helped after tea, carting the corn. I did not help to do much of this work as the horse was used in a cart and I was not allowed to get too near. I did have a ride on the trailer being pulled by the tractor but it was the case of getting the corn stacked as soon as possible. Sometimes men from the village came and helped as well. There was one particular part of meadow where the cows went out on at night so they were near the farm for milking the next morning. All around one side of this was a fence of stakes and wire interwoven with some blackberry bushes. At one point there was a most peculiar metal frame, which was made up of small tubes, square in shape but larger at one end and tapered off to a smaller end along its length. It also had tabs for supporting struts. The whole thing was about twenty five to thirty foot long. There were also some other sections of tube. I was told this was part of a crashed World War One aeroplane. I don't know what happened to it but I can't help thinking that it would cause a lot of interest if it was about now. One of the fields next to the road was made a bit smaller by a line of council houses being built on it. I can't remember how many there were or what year it was but as it was a Council owned farm I doubt if any compensation was given.

Several years later Uncle Arthur left that farm and bought a smallholding at Morley St Bololph near Attleborough in Norfolk. I would sometimes cycle from Wortham to there, early on a Saturday and help him with the farm work. He had a horse then but whether it was the same one he had on the other farm I don't know. I think both of them died in the 1980's.

The next brother that I remember was Ernie. He was the uncle with the motorbike, which I have mentioned before. He worked with my grandfather at Holkham Hall as a builder before he moved to London on new buildings and repairing bomb damage. After that he bought a small farm at Foulsham near Dereham, where he had mainly arable land, growing sugar beet and barley. His transport then was a Morris Minor pickup truck. He had a few animals on the farm but I don't know what they were other than some chickens for eggs. He did eventually sell the farm and buy a bungalow at West End Road, Costessey, near Norwich. I did make a new window and fit it in his lounge wall for him but after a while we lost touch. I have no record of when he died or where he is buried.

This now only leaves two more brothers. One of them was Uncle Johnny. He was, in my opinion, the most cheerful one of the family. If anything worried him I never saw it. He also had some fields around South and North Creake and grew crops of corn and sugar beet. I think he kept a few pigs but he never had a farm as such but a few rough buildings here and there. I know he helped Arthur on his farm at busy times but I don't know if he worked for any of the big farmers. I feel certain that he had at tractor and implements and also a lorry, with which he done contract carting, corn and sugar beet. I remember going to his wedding at North Creake Church to a local girl named Emily Francis. Our family hired a car from Bogy Weavers of Palgrave and Dad's Cousin, John Jolly drove us over a journey he done several times for various occasions. Now Johnny and Emily made their home in a small flint cottage beside the road in North Creake and they have three sons, one which joined the Navy and had the honour to be button boy on HMS Ganges the navy training school at Shotley near Ipswich. There again I lost touch but one of my cousins I know lives in South Creake at this time. I also have no records of this Aunt and Uncle from those early days.

Now this leaves just one more Uncle and this was Mother's brother, Percy. He always seemed to me to be a different type of person from all the other men. He also worked as a builder with my grandfather at Holkham Hall but was a very Christian man. I never heard him swear or talk about anyone in a bad way and he was always smartly dressed and took great care of his personal appearance. Whether he helped his farming brothers I don't know but I should think he did, as he was that type of person. He came and stayed

The Army side of the Mendham Family - Percy Mendham
My Mothers Brother

It seems strange that Percy should outlive all his sisters and brothers, it seems as if he is being compensated for all those years spent in a P.O.W camp

MENDHAM – On December 27th peacefully at Dorrington House, PERCY aged 97 years of Wells. Beloved husband of the late Audrey, dearly loved uncle of Geoff and Brenda, Terry and Sylvia, Mike and Rose (deceased), Marion and Phil. Much loved great-uncle to all his nieces and nephews. Faded away as old soldiers do. Rest in Peace.
Funeral service at Wells Methodist Church, on Friday, January 6th at 11.30 a.m. Family flowers only but if desired donations for Heritage House c/o S.T Sutton Funeral Directors, Wells next the Sea, NR23 1HL

From a news cutting 2011

with us at Wortham a lot. Our next door neighbour would collect him from Diss railway station in his car. I was over there on holiday in 1939 just before the war started and their was a lot of talk about him volunteering to drive fuel tankers for the RAF but for some reason this did not happen and he ended up joining the army, the Royal Norfolk Regiment. He never got above the rank of private as he had to go over to France in the early months of the war and he was one of the unfortunate soldiers who were unable to get to Dunkirk when France was taken by the Germans in May/June 1940. So from that time until the end of the war he was in a POW camp. I don't know if he was moved about but I have his metal tag which every POW had; this is a metal plate 4cm x 6cm divided down the middle to make two halves by perforations. On each of these halves were lots of identifications. One was the prison camp number – Stalag XXIB and the other was his British army number 6698. If by any chance a prisoner died while in any of the camps one half would be buried with the body and the other half would be sent back to England.

I know my grandmother was told by the War Department that he was missing and she let my mother know by telegram. This caused a lot of worry for nearly all the Mendham family but by chance our radio at that time, which was hand-made by our neighbour next door and was very temperamental, had a habit of loosing the station it was supposed to be on. It was one of these times of trying to get the station back we heard a foreign voice and it went like this, " Germany calling, - Germany calling - This is Lord Haw Haw speaking", and with that name after name of captured service men were read out in good clear English. Well we listened to that for several evenings and then at last we heard it, Private P Mendham, number 6689 of the Norfolk Regiment is a prisoner of war but we did not know where till my grandmother got a letter from him with an address on it. From then on letters were sent from him to us and from us to him. They had to be left open because everything had to be censored and the same with the parcels which were sent via the Red Cross and this went on for the whole time of the war.

In the end we did not hear from him for a long time until one morning early a Mr Hoskins put his bike near our gate and said that he had come home with Percy on the train and as he got off the train at Diss station Percy was still on going to Norwich and then to Fakenham. This man was in khaki uniform and had broken his journey home to tell my mother that her brother was on his way home. There was a lot of relief all round. I have a framed set of his medals and arm tags which he gave to my mother and had hung on her living room wall. He did not say much about his life as a POW but he did say that him and one or two others were made to work in the German Officers' cookhouse so he had a chance to get a little extra food for some of his mates. He also said that they would pee in the soup they had to make for the officers' meals. No one ever found out or there would have been trouble. He did manage to get a few eggs from time to time for the men in his hut.

There was a really bad time just before the end of the war when the Germans guards took them out of the camp and made them march for miles without food or water. During one of the small breaks they had for a rest him and some of the others managed to steal a few sticks of rhubarb from someone's garden and that was all he had to eat for six whole days of marching.

However when the Germans realized that they were losing the war, all the prisoners were put into another camp under armed guard but it was not long before someone found out that the advancing American army was only a few miles away. One morning the prisoners could hear and see this advance coming towards the camp. By that time they had all decided to break down the gates and fence to the camp, which they done, freeing themselves to run amok outside the camp, capturing the guards, taking their rifles and shooting their guards in revenge for the bad treatment they had received. The American army arrived and gave them food and drink and so started the journey home and back to civilian life.

All the time he was in a prison camp he had a young lady waiting for him at a place called Egmere and the house name was The Ruins because it was next to an old, derelict church. I can remember there was a crumbling flint tower in the middle of a park and also a very deep well, I often went out with her brother, David, for cycle rides around the countryside and to Wells' beach.

I can well remember cycling along the mile-long road beside the entrance to the harbour one Saturday evening when there was a big explosion on the marshes beside the road. As these marshes were mined nobody was allowed to go on them but a stray dog started to run across one part and it did not get very far. One particular day I went to that house for a visit and the whole park was full of soldiers and they were using water from the well. I had never seen the well used before.

It was just before Christmas 1945 that they decided to get married. Everything was very hard to get at that time as most things were still on ration, food, clothes etc. But somehow all the things needed had been obtained by family and friends. All gave a little each and I know that one of my aunts done a lot of baking. The reception was arranged to take place at her house at Egmere. The guests were all waiting in church to see Miss Audrey Williamson become Mrs Mendham after walking up the church aisle in her white wedding dress. They were waiting and waiting but the future bride did not appear and then someone told the vicar that the she could not come because of illness. I don't know what really happened as this was not one wedding we went to. All our family stopped home in Wortham. I think by what I heard the adults talking, that this particular lady was full of her own importance and rather looked down on the Mendham family. I do know that after the service was abandoned that my aunt who did the baking went to see her house to see how she was and there she was sitting on a chair eating sausage rolls as if nothing had happened.

Just a few days after Christmas the wedding did take place but not in her white wedding dress but in a bright red velvet dress much to the amazement of the family. Yet again we did not go. There appeared to be many rumours as to why the white dress was not worn, connected with some of the soldiers who were camping on the park around the house. At that time what people did not know they imagined adding a little more to it each time but that was a long time ago and in the past now.

I am not sure when but they had a little cottage in Wells next Sea. I know Aunt Audrey died just a few years ago but Uncle Percy, as far as I know, is still alive today, 6 August 2007. It seems strange that Percy should outlive all his sisters and brothers. It seems as if he is being compensated for all those years spent in a POW camp. I do know that he did get a new driving licence when he was eighty six.

Now about the girls of the family, my mother's sisters. Some I knew fairly well and some I did not see very often. It was mostly weddings and funerals when they all came home to South Creake. The one that I knew the best was Aunt Nellie as she lived at home with my grandparents and was really the odd job person for the family. It was her who pulled the four wheeled trolley around the village delivering the milk from the farm. She also fed the chickens and collected the eggs from the allotments. I think she had a very hard life. Being unable even to ride a bike she either walked or if she went into any of the local towns she would go by bus. I could never understand the reason for this as she always seemed very intelligent. I did find out later that, as a small girl, she had a very nasty accident which never really got better. It appeared that one day she went to get a saucepan of water off the stove but she got the wrong one and picked up the saucepan that Grandfather was melting some lead in, which of course was much heavier than she expected so she dropped it onto the hearth with the result the boiling hot lead splashed all over her body and legs, with the result that often in her life she was quite ill. But she did her best as well as she could. I know that she died before she was very old. I don't know the date only that she was buried in South Creake churchyard and the funeral procession took the same walk behind the coffin from the house to the church as Grandfather's.

The next sister that was really well known to me and often came to my grandparent's house, when I was there, was Aunt Lucy, mentioned before when writing about the allotment carrots. Most of the family looked up to her for answers to illness as she was a nurse but she was also a farmer's wife and her husband was a John Seaman and they owned a farm at Great Massingham. They always seemed to have plenty of money and besides being a farmer he was also a fireman and a member of the Great Massingham brigade. I can remember at one big fire he fell through a roof of the building and ended up with a broken leg. They had one son John, who I saw once or twice but I don't know much about him or for that matter the whole family.

Another Aunt was mother's sister, May, who married a man from the mining industry and lived somewhere near Derby. I only saw her about twice and never saw him at all. I have a vague idea they had a family but I never really knew them.

Then there was Aunt Rose, who was married to Uncle Albert. They both lived in Slough, London. They had a boy and girl whose name was Hazel, I don't know what the boys name was. I think Albert was a hairdresser. I saw him when there was a family get-together for whatever reason. Rose and Hazel came to South Creake quite often.

Well I think that is about all I know about my mother's family. I must admit I did like to go to South Creake for holidays. Some of my cousins I saw quite a lot. Others I hardly saw at all and at this present time I only know where two of them are, one of which I keep in touch with a phone call once each month, which is very nice.

South Creake adjoins North Creake with both having the B7355 Fakenham to Wells road running through them for several miles and the River Burn flowing clearly beside the road, where the ducks swim or rest on the bank. I rather liked South Creake with its flint and brick houses, its big farms again with flint and brick buildings and big farm houses with names like Blustone, Compton Hall, Hubbard's Farm, Leicester Square, Waterdon. When people talked about these places it was always – up at or down at, and it was always a bit of a puzzle which direction to go to get to these farms. One thing they had in common was they all had massive fields and you could walk for miles without seeing anyone at all. In the summer at harvest time some of these farms were the first ones in the country to have combines and at night they kept working until it was too damp to do. Some of the big barns on these farms had special, big, corn drying machines inside them and tons of corn was dried every year. During the war years this was not allowed because of the lights showing to German aircraft. During this time there was always plenty of aircraft about. I never actually saw one at night but I heard plenty. I saw plenty of English planes. Lockheed Hudson's of Coastal Command were always flying over and the smaller target towing planes which were always painted bright yellow. The target was like a big wind sock towed behind on a long cable quite a way from the plane. There was an army camp at Weybourne, right next to the sea complete with anti-aircraft guns and during the day they would practise by firing at the towed target. By night it was a very different story. There would be lots of noise as they fired at the German planes coming in across the coast. There was also lots of searchlights up. I think the nearest was one at Egmere.

There were lots of things I liked about South Creake, the empty shells of whelks, cockles, mussels etc. covering the footpaths across the football meadow and the allotments. All sorts of these fish were bought from a man who came round certain days with a pony and cart. He also sold green samphire, which was a plant that grows on the coast and can be boiled and eaten like a vegetable. By the sides of the roads there was always lots of wild horse radish, some of which got dug up and made into horse radish sauce. There always seemed time for people to have a chat on a nice bright spring morning with chickens cackling and the cockerels crowing over most of the village. If you stood on top of the hills in the village whichever way you looked there were meadows of grazing cattle, some being fattened up for meat and some milking cattle?

My uncle's cows would be kept near the farm at night. This made it much better for getting them ready for milking in the morning. The food had to be prepared and put in the mangers ready for them to eat. This was not done overnight as it could turn sour if any wet food was used (sugar beet pulp or mangolds) and of course there were rats on farms. Each cow had a name but I don't remember what they were. There was always a particular smell in the dairy at milking time, a mixture of fresh milk, wet concrete and disinfectant. I often helped to fill the milk bottles ready for going out on the rounds. In those days the top was sealed with a round piece of cardboard and in the centre a small circle was punched, which would push out leaving a small round hole, which a finger could be put in to pull the complete top from the bottle. In some cases people saved the tops and bound wool or cotton through the hole to the outside of the top. This was done in different colours and then they were all sown onto the outside of shopping bags, which made them look very nice.

Another thing I remember during the war was the large piles of granite-like rock which was full of holes like honeycombs and they gave off a nasty smell, theses were on the verge beside the road with the sole purpose to fill in bomb craters that could restrict the traffic as this was a coast road and was used by the army a lot.

The bowling green was surrounded by a high laurel hedge the opposite side of both the road and river and the Ostrich pub. On Saturday evenings could be heard the sound of wood on wood as the game was being played and the chatter of old men as they competed against each other. I should think the taking at the pub was up on those nights.

There was one part of the village I did not like and that was where Back Lane joined Back Street. At the fork in the road there was a slaughter house where the local animals were killed for the local butchers. Sometimes you could hear the noise of the animals and the shot as they were killed. There was always a smell as the bones were stacked outside to be made into glue. Thank goodness this placed was pulled down lots of years ago and houses are there now.

I have many fond memories of this area and the coast around it. I also learnt a lot from the people there, how to milk a cow, drive both a van and tractor, how to repair a binder in the harvest field and I also made some good friends but sadly I lost touch with them as that part of the family died over the years and we did not go out there anymore. I did go to South Creake a few years ago while on holiday at Kelling Caravan Park but a lot has changed since I was there. Maybe I will go back one day for the sake of old memories.

My Mother's Early Life, Continued

As I have said before, my mother moved with the family she worked for and, from what she has told me, I don't think life in London was a very happy time. She had to work much harder and had even less time to herself and her own family. The family she worked for were all strict about religion and church on Sundays was a must whatever the circumstances. It was at this time that the vicar of the church she attended noticed that she was not happy and asked if she would like to work for him. Which she did, finding out that there were people who had a less strict routine to work to. This was a Rev Moore and his wife. They in turn had two children, a girl named Eileen and a son named John and were about her age. This really changed mother's life, she told me. All the family had respect for each other. When the Rev Moore was offered a diocese in Suffolk, owned by Kings College, Cambridge, he accepted and they all moved into Wortham Rectory on 1 October 1925 and Rev Moore became the rector of St Mary's Church in this village near Diss. It was very different from the life in London but more about the rectory later.

However it was still church on Sundays and all the people who worked at the rectory had to go at to at least one of the services. It was tradition in those days to have your own family pew. The rector's family had the second one from the front on the left hand side of the main aisle. It was in this that the rector's family and all the people who worked at the rectory sang and prayed.

The Frost family had the second pew on the right, just inside the main entrance door and it was here that a young Robert Frost would sit with his family on Sunday mornings and listen to the Rev Moore's sermons, pray and sing hymns.

It was after the church service that the young girl from the front pew was walked home to the rectory by the young man from the back pew and a friendship was formed. Robert Victor Frost and Eliza Mendham were married at St Mary's the Virgin at South Creake on the 1 of August 1926.

They came back to Wortham and set up home in a rented cottage next to the rectory. It also belonging to Kings College Cambridge and the address was, Ivy Cottage, Rectory Road, Wortham. The rent for this one up and one down cottage was paid every month to the rector at the pricey sum of five shillings, a lot of money from a farm worker's wage in those days. I think that an average wage was around £1 per week. This included working Saturday afternoons. It was less if the weather was bad as in heavy rain or snow the people who did not look after the animals were sent home and pay was deducted from their wages.

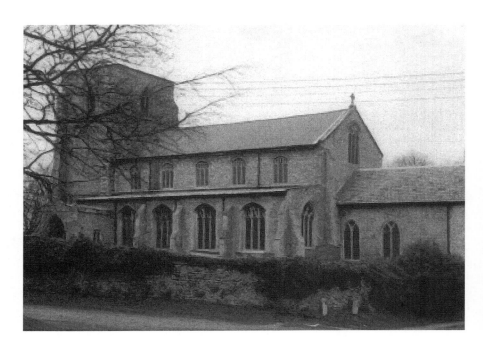

St. Mary the Virgin
South Creake

Mr and Mrs R Frost – Wedding Day
1st August 1926

The house where I was born (15 October 1928)

Ivy Cottage (Left), Rectory Road, Wortham as it was known then.
The front was covered in ivy and it was in a very bad state of repair.

BBC Radio Circle - Children's Programme - Uncle Mac
Cost a small amount, and your name would be read out on the wireless.
We would listen at the Rectory.
We had no wireless then, few parents could afford one.

I think that soon after 1926-27 the Saturday working time finished at 12 noon as I cannot remember my father working on those afternoons, only on special times of the year such as hay making and harvest and also sugar beet harvesting. The lorries carting the beet to the factory had to be loaded everyday, including Christmas Day and Boxing Day, which did bring in a few shillings extra for our family.

To get back to this little cottage, which was the south end of three. How old these cottages were I don't know and I have never heard anyone say but I do know that around 1860 these cottages were bought by the then vicar of Wortham, Rev Richard Cobbold who gave them to Kings College Cambridge to be used as a charity for the poor. That was to stop poor people being put into the union houses. They were at that time called Prymes Cottages. I have also mentioned before that Thomas Frost lived in one of these cottages sometime before 1905. When the name was changed to Ivy Cottage I don't know but there was ivy on the front walls shown on drawings and paintings done of these cottages during the 1800's and 1900's. The ivy was cut off the walls about 1950 and I remember helping with this very dusty and smelly job. Some of the actual branches of this big-leafed ivy were as big as a man's leg where it came out of the ground and took quite a long while to cut through with a bow saw. This stopped the annual job of cutting back with a pair of hand shears each autumn. All the clippings and the final removal were carted around to the rectory and burnt on an area of meadow kept solely for the purpose of burning rubbish, garden or otherwise.

The name was then changed to Rectory Cottage but was still rented out to tenants.

I cannot actually remember living in this particular end of those cottages but I do know that there was one bedroom, one big room downstairs with an open grate fire and a kitchen-come-wash room, which had a copper in the corner for heating several gallons of water for washing cloths and a long, galvanised bath which hung on the outside wall when not in use. There was a small strip of garden at the back and an oval shaped garden at the front surrounded by large flint stones. It was in the afore mentioned bedroom that I was born on 15 October 1928 just before midnight, so I have been told. I have also heard that in those days there were no trained midwifes. Women from the village helped with children being born as most women had their families at home but I can remember a Nurse Varnish from the Botesdale area coming to visit from time to time. I do not know the exact date but soon after I was born my parents had the chance which they took to move into the opposite end cottage with the rent being around about the same and still paid to the rector. The centre cottage was lived in by Will Percy, the gardener at the rectory, rent free. Now this was a more up to date house with one large room with kitchen-come-wash room and also a walk-in pantry with a cupboard under the stairs. It had two bedrooms upstairs. The smaller of the two had to be walked through to get to the main bedroom. This was a real luxury home compared to the very small home my parents moved from. In the main room downstairs was a black cast iron stove with an oven for cooking which was called 'The Little Hero cooking range'. This was part of an area under a big open chimney where there had been a different type of stove with a Dutch oven to the left hand side at one time. The oven had been taken out and the complete area made into a shelved cupboard for storage. This Little Hero was very hard to keep clean and it was a daily job with a coat of Zebra black lead stove polish. The hob on one side of the stove always had a kettle of water on it just keeping warm and could be brought to boil over the actual fire in minutes. The heat from the fire could be changed by the angle of a metal plate on the back being forced around the oven side of the stove for baking bread and cakes and also Sunday dinners. Saucepans for cooking were put on the other side hob. There was a wooden mantle piece over the fireplace with a piece of green, tasseled, velvet pinned so it hung down over the edge of the wood. On top of the mantle piece there were some ornaments with a clock in the centre. Between the top of the clock and ceiling, was hung quite a large oblong mirror. A black iron fender, with brass knobs and rails round, was the resting place for the poker and small coal shovel. The fender sat on top of the four inch by nine inch hard brick floor which was laid on a bed of sand which had sunk a bit near each doorway giving a slight dip in the red and green striped coco-matting covering the whole floor.

In the kitchen was also a copper which was a bigger one than in the other house. It had some planks of wood cut round to make a circle and a small strip across the top to form a handle for lifting on and off. This again was used for bath water and boiling Christmas puddings but at certain times, after a good scrub out, it was used for making home made wine. All sorts of things were turned into wine in this copper, wheat and barley (those two were nearly whisky when fully matured) cattle beet, carrots, potatoes, sugar beet, parsnips, beet root, blackberries, plums and greengages. Well wine could be made out of anything. When this copper was being used and as it was a grate built into brick-work with a metal door on the front to keep the fire in. The whole fire area was about 8 to 9 inches above the floor, allowing for the ash to drop and the draught to get in and keep the fire going. As there was no waste collection in those days anything that could be burnt was put on the copper fire, old leather and rubber boots, bark from the wood, old rags, paper and cardboard.

Inside the building there was a brick built chimney but outside above the roof were two four inch salt glazed drain pipes for the chimney and when rubber was being burnt the smelly, black smoke poured out like a steam engine. It was impossible to be in the line of this if the wind was beating the smoke downwards, which it did quite often.

Another thing that made life better at this house was that it had a drain, a square brick gully with pipes under ground to a ditch on the other side of our garden hedge. This was an open ditch and it did smell during the summer but no one took much notice of that. Pails of waste water did not have to thrown onto the garden any more except on the vegetables in hot weather. This drain had a special attraction. On dark nights the damp soil around the sides was covered in bright green lights of glow worms. These seemed like small stars moving over the soil but they were really small beetles.

The other thing that improved the way of life was that we had a well in our front garden and the buckets of drinking water had only to be carried up the garden path. Despite the odd toad or snail falling into the well the water always seemed to be clear and healthy and it did us no harm anyway. The only time we could not use the well was when the road was tarred as a dark brown stain use to settle through and make the water taste like creosote. We used to carry the buckets of water from the nearby rectory for a few days until the stain had settled. All three cottages and the two council houses down the road all used this well and I cannot ever remember it going dry. The water level would drop during a hot summer but not much. The other thing that used to cause an upset was when a pail hit the bottom it would fall off the sprung hook and the end of the chain and lay there and it could not be brought back up. We had what was called a set of creepers which was a three pronged hook which looked like an anchor; this was tied to a long thin strong rope. When dropped down into the water one of the prongs would catch onto the pail and it could be brought back up.

About ten yards from the back door down the garden path we had a luxury of a wooden privy with a galvanised tin roof also a clean pinewood seat with removable front section to remove or replace the handled galvanised pail, which had to be emptied in the garden when full. This was an early morning job. Another thing about the working class people's privies was that no one had toilet rolls (only the rich people could afford the Izal toilet rolls) and newspaper was used instead. This was torn into strips of about six inches by nine inches with a hole in one corner through which a piece of binder string was threaded to make a loop, which was hung on a nail in the wall. It always amazed me how you could read these pieces of paper and never find an ending to a particular story. Someone had always used the bit you wanted. You could never complete a crossword either.

In the front of the privy there was a rambler rose bush which covered the whole area to screen the complete building. This bush had small pink and white roses on from spring through to the start of winter. This blocked the door from view so in the warm weather you could sit on the seat with the door open and compete with the smell of roses. One part of the outside wall of this building was covered with a big ivy bush which was also over part of the roof therefore shading in hot summers. Underneath this ivy bush was the area that all unwanted and broken pots and bottles were thrown, well out of sight from the house. I can remember one particular flower pot which was a cream and gold with red roses on the outside centre. This had a wavy top edge which was covered with a thin gold strip. The whole pot had three brass chains joined to a brass ring at the top and was hung from the ceiling with an aspidistra plant in it. I wonder what it would have been worth now.

Every household had a piece of garden to be used as a dump and in the course of time these places got filled with soil or leveled over. What treasures lie under the soil in most of these old cottage gardens. Some of these old bottles and jars must now be collector's item if you could find them.

I can't remember too much of the really early years of my life at this cottage but I do know that my parents done everything possible to make all our lives as happy as possible. I remember the hot bath in front of a glowing wood fire on a Saturday night and also going to bed by candle light in the winter time with a hot water bottle put in a bed a few minutes before I was carried up the stairs and the way the hot water bottle was laid on the table and lent to let out the steam before the metal rubber-washered cork was screwed in.

Parts of the household items of that time were two galvanised baths, oval in shape with a handle at both ends. It was in those that the clothes were rinsed after coming out of the copper.

I can also remember the small two chimney stove with a long think wick which soaked up the paraffin from the container at the bottom. This was lit to heat the kettle and cook vegetables when the fire was not lit. Paraffin oil played a big part in the lives of country folk in those days. There were table lamps, wall lamps, hanging lamps, stoves of many makes, all using oil. We had a brass double wick table lamp with a tall glass chimney. The wicks had to be cut level or it would cause the lamp to smoke and cut out some of the light. When this happened the glass chimneys would have to be cleaned and sometimes they would break so a spare had to be kept. We used to get our oil from The Dick public house near The Ling, where they brought the oil in one big tank full and sold it out to customers at a gallon or two gallons as required. There were two other people who did deliver oil but more about them later.

Back to the cottage on cold winter nights with a warm fire in the grate and a lamp in the middle of the table also a big thick curtain over the front and stairway doors. To me at that age this was very cosy. This was home. At that time in the early thirties we did not have a radio so my parents would sit and read the paper, The Daily Herald and every Thursday we would have a magazine called John Bull with a man wearing a top hat, a long tail jacket and high boots with a bulldog beside him. Every Sunday it was the News of the World. These papers only cost a few pence and were delivered daily. This was the only entertainment they got as they were up early each morning to go to work.

I have completely forgotten what I done in those long winter evenings before I started school, when everything changed. I do remember the floor in the kitchen was about six inches higher than the living room floor and there was a stone step in the doorway. The pantry had shelves around all the walls and everything had a coat of white wash. The floor was bricks on sand and the same was done to the cupboard under the stairs. This is where most of the home made wine was kept. I was not allowed in there until I got older. We never had a stair carpet which meant that the wood stairs were stained with a dark brown substance. I never did find out what it was other than the name was Black Friars something, in a yellow tin. There was also a banister rail and post on the opposite side of the stairs from the wall and fixed to the wooden bedroom floor. Nearly all the doors had a double coat hook fixed to them where the coats, jackets and hats were hung. Inside the backdoor were two large straight bolts fitted to top and bottom and these were locked into the door frame each night. There was a Suffolk latch fitted as well but no lock that worked with a key. The front door also had two bolts that could be shut from the inside but this had a rim lock and key so that it could be locked from inside or outside. This door also had a brass letter box for the papers and any letters from other members of the family. With no electric, no mains water, no phones and therefore no bills (which I doubt could be paid anyway) there was very little correspondence to be delivered.

The opposite side of the good things are the bad things and our house was no exception and it had plenty of those. It was said at the time that Kings College had very little money so very little was done to the cottage or the rectory in the way of maintenance. If this was true or just an excuse not to spend anything on repairs was never found out. There were plenty of repairs that could have been done. The roof let in the fine driving snow in winter and pails and bowls had to be stood around the bedroom to catch the water dripping through the clay and reed ceilings when the snow melted but the worst thing that needed repairing was the windows, which had diamond shaped leaded lights with thin (2mm) picture glass in them. Most of the glass had moved from the joints in the lead and the wind whistled through and across the room. The bedrooms were the really bad ones and with the opening lights shut and the wind from the east the curtains would blow across the room. Condensation was never seen, or for that matter never heard of in those old houses. The opening lights were made of metal and fitted into a timber mullion frame. The hinges were just a metal eye fitting over a bent hook and could be lifted off very easily. There were two positions for these opening lights which was fully open or fully shut. When shut the whole thing was held in place with a metal hook that looked like a bird's head with a curly tail. As the pin holding these on had no head they were forever falling off when used. The opening stay was about twelve inches of twisted metal rod, held in place by two metal pins. I suspect that all metal windows were handmade at the local blacksmiths. The other outstanding feature of the front windows was that they had pelmet of lead over the head timber cut to half circle design across the whole length of the top. All sills and other timber were of oak, I would think grown locally and made whilst still green (as cut down timber, not seasoned timber). Owing to the bad fitting windows it was a regular occurrence, during the severe winters of that time, to find the chamber pot under the bed had a coating of ice after being used. Coats were put on top of bed clothes at night in an effort to keep warm. The one big fault with this cottage was that all the outside doors opened directly into rooms. There was no hall so that if anyone called the heat from the rooms went out through the doorway when the doors were opened but despite all its faults this old cottage was lived in and most of the time enjoyed by us all.

There are some things I can remember about the time before I started school. I had been bought some toys, that no doubt my parents had to go without something for. One was a teddy bear which I took to bed with me and the other was a Felix cat. After that someone bought me a golliwog. In the summer I spent a lot of time out in the garden, mainly in a hole dug for me to play in and with a few bits of wood and a lot of imagination this hole was a castle, a kitchen, a house and all sorts of things. Then I had a wooden horse on wheels which I pulled on long journeys around the garden. My mother used to remind me of my first attempt at gardening when I pulled up all the cabbage plants which had been set a few days before, saying they were weeds. I did not know that my father could run so fast as he came after me around the garden paths but sitting down was tricky after that and the horse did nothing to help. I can not remember ever having a high chair only a smaller version of a Windsor chair which I was tied into by a scarf. There was also a small haystack in the garden, which, before I was old enough to help my father, he would cut from the roadside verges and dry out in the sun and store for the winter feed for his rabbits. I would sit on this small haystack because the smell from this new hay was quite pleasant so it was a nice place to sit. I don't know how I got onto this haystack but I did. One day this all changed when I got stung by a wasp, so it was indoors and out came the Reckitts blue bag which was used for washing clothes and I had a blue hand. This was the answer to being stung in those days.

I can remember seeing a photograph of my mother in a long coat and a tall floppy hat standing at the end of Mere Street in Diss with me in a pram. This was beside the carved corner post which was in those days The Diss Publishing Company. This pram was a black straight forward run of the mill type of thing with small wheels and a white handle. I would not have thought this was new, considering the money situation in those days. This photo was about for years but what happened to it I don't know or the pram for that matter but I do know what the wheels were used for as I got older. They were put on the bottom of different wooden boxes and made into hand carts for me to pull around and cart all sort of things in.

Other things that happened during the early part of my life were my mother's shopping visits to Diss. She had what was known as a high stepper bicycle. This was a massive frame with two twenty eight inch wheels and also a basket on the front. When she rode this bike to Diss I was left with a dear old lady who lived in an end of three thatched cottages next to the pond near Beech Tree farm. This was quite an event as this lady always wore black clothes and black shawl around her shoulders she shuffled about in a pair of black plimsolls. Her silver hair and weathered, worn face I took for granted at that time. I realised later that she must have had a very hard life but I never heard her complain to anyone. What I liked about staying with her was her big tins of buttons and beads which she used to put on the floor for me to sort out. Some of these buttons were very pretty and even then very old and the same with the beads. She had some very black shiny ones of different sizes and also a lot of different sized pearls. What happened to them I don't know. Between her house and the pond she had a small strip of garden with flowers in front of the house and a very low box hedge about nine inches wide. At the back of the house were several small sheds made from faggots. Those had old boards nailed together for doors, held to a rustic post frame by well worn leather, and wood for the fire. One was used for a privy with a hole cut in a big wooden box for a seat and a proper pail inside. It was not unknown for a tramp to go in there if needed. Covering all these faggot sheds was a creeping plant with a pale green slender leaf and small pink flowers in the summer.

Between her garden edge and the pond was a drive leading from the road to the fields behind the house. This was part of a footpath from The Ling to the church. During the spring and summer this drive was completely covered in massive garden daises, white, pink and red. This dear old lady was known to everyone as Granny Baxter. I know she had one daughter who came and visited her sometimes and my mother used to visit her in a cottage, which was part of a row of houses that were pulled down to make way for the Roman Catholic church in Stanley Road in Diss.

The other person that I was left with lived in an end cottage at Roger's corner on Wortham Ling, which had a flint and brick wall that goes around the sharp corner on the road from the Dick across the Ling. This woman was totally different from Granny Baxter. She was about thirty five years old at that time and a wife of a farm worker. She used to try teach me to read as she had some family of her own and therefore took a much more active view of life. I usually went to hers on Friday mornings. By tradition this was the day most country women done their baking (My mother included). Now this woman would bake me gingerbread men. She also made shortcakes with currents or sultanas in. This was one of the most popular cakes of all country people. Both of these things were very nice. My mother made nearly all our baked food, bread, cakes and also puddings, apple, sausage and onion and lots of pies – apple, rhubarb, gooseberry, blackberry, black and red currents. Most of these fruits were grown in the garden but when the war started with its food rationing, things changed quite a lot. When I was growing up and getting to school age things were getting harder for country people but I did not realise that at the time. Workers in agriculture and other industries were on a very low wage and there were strikes for better pay and conditions. Many small farmers went bankrupt. I know of one in Wortham who lost his farm. It was a big turning point in the lives of farm workers in the early thirties when the weekly wage went up from one pound per week to one pound five shillings and a little later up again to one pound ten shillings per week (one pound fifty in modern money).

It was around this time that I was forced to wear boots due to a weak ankle bone but this caused no problem as I did plenty of walking. Sometimes walking was the only way to get about especially during the winter months. We thought nothing of snow falls of twelve inches and snow drifts up to seven to eight foot deep. As time went on my mother bought some new mud guards for her bicycle with holes in both sides all the way round into which was threaded a black and yellow cord all joining into a metal bracket on the wheel nut. This was to stop small feet getting into the moving spokes of the wheel. Also bought at the time was a metal seat which fitted over the mud guard complete with back and foot rests. This was a useful transport for young children in those days and still is today with some people. I remember that if looked down at the road it seemed to be flying past.

I was always trying to help one or the other of my parents. They let me have a small piece of garden in which I was given vegetables to set and look after, although at that time from setting to harvesting them always seemed a long time. I had my own small spade and hoe (the spade lasted years and was ideal for setting potatoes right up to the 1960s), but I could not understand why things took so long to grow and I can remember on two occasions getting a big fork and trying to dig up some potatoes and each time putting the fork through my foot. It was taller than me anyway. This always called for the iodine treatment which really hurt as this was the only antiseptic in those days, that everyone used. I always had the same treatment when I fell down the stairs into a wooden box with the nails sticking up. This box was used for keeping the sticks in for lighting the fire and was stored on one of the wide treads of the stairway. I still have the scars to show for it after all these years. As each bad winter passed followed by what seemed like a very hot summer I was growing up and starting school and that is another story.

Living in Houses

Most people lived in rented houses in those days except for the people who owned and lived in their own properties which had been handed down from previous generations. It was the traditional thing to do. No one would ever think of selling a house if the next member of the family wanted to live in it. In any case houses did not make any money when they were sold. One small thatched cottage in a village next to Wortham was sold in the early thirties for half a crown (two shillings and six pence or twelve and a half pence in modern money). It was sold just a few years ago with modernisation and extensions for around seventy thousand pound what a difference in sixty years.

Most farm workers lived near the farm and some, mostly stock men, pig men or horse men actually lived in tied cottages, that is, cottages owned by the farmer and as tenants they accepted things as they were and made the best of what they had. Some of these cottages were terrible places to live depending on whether the farmer had the money or thought enough of his workers to keep them in good repair. The trouble with this situation was that any quarrel with the boss and not only did they lose their job but also their home. Labour was cheap and many families moved for just a few shillings extra if they could get it or if a better house was offered. These people would never be able to afford a mortgage on what they earned and I doubt if many of them had ever heard of such a thing.

The late 1920's and early 30's were very hard times for the farm workers as far as money was concerned and most people took every opportunity to get a little extra by what ever means they could without changing jobs. There were some families where (despite it was considered that women's place was in the home) the women worked as well to earn a little extra money as well, to help out, thereby increasing the weekly income.

There was one tradition that was carried out on most big farms and this was done on the farm where my father worked. If there was a big hedge to be cut down or a tree top that had to be pollarded this was offered to the worker to cut down and have the wood for the fire provided that all the brambles, nettles and grass were cut as well and burned up. The farmer got a hedge or tree cut for nothing other than the time it took the worker who got the wood for nothing and everyone was satisfied. We used to cut our hedges and trees on Saturday afternoons or on a moonlit night. All wood had to be cut to short lengths for easy handling. We were allowed to have a horse and wagon to cart the wood home to store in the garden. Again this would be on a Saturday afternoon or even Boxing Day morning if the weather was good. As this job was during late autumn and early winter most fields were uncropped and therefore easy to get to. This was called a perk of the job in those days. Another perk was for the cow men who milked the cows. They were allowed all the milk they wanted for there own use, free from the dairy. After the wood was carted home it would be stored up against a tree and allowed to dry out until it was cut by a hand-saw on a sawing horse to lengths to fit the stove. We always had a wooden sawing horse but some people had those made from metal, mainly warn out beaters from a thrashing drum but those could damage the teeth of the saws. Sometimes a big crosscut saw was used and then father had to have some help as those were big, long saws and took two men to use. It was said that you got warm three times from this wood once to cut it down, once to cut it up and once sitting indoors watching it burn.

Before the Second World War the work done by women was mainly domestic. My mother worked at the rectory and also for a family in Diss who had a butcher shop in Mere Street. Details and memories of these places are still very clear and will fit in the story as we progress through the years.

Despite being poor we were much better off than a lot of people. We had our share of both good and bad, like most people at that time and whether the fact that both my parents were church-going people accounted for anything is hard to say. I was brought up in my younger years to go to church with them. Sometimes I objected to this but I had no choice as my father was very strict about his beliefs and he would not get into bed at night without kneeling down and saying a prayer as did his father before him. Religion was taken very seriously in those days and the churches always had a lot of people at each service Some people did go to all the services, communion, 8am morning service, 11am and evensong 6pm. Sundays were a very special day, a day of rest, of relaxation, when only the most important and necessary work was done by the men but the women still cooked the Sunday lunch. My memories of those days were wearing the best clothes smelling of moth balls, the two course meals after which we had a sleep in the chairs. When my parents were asleep we would sneak a look at the News of the World, a paper that had been delivered in the morning. I was not allowed to look at this and as I got older I could understand why. Several times I nearly got caught. I dread to think what would have happened if I had.

However despite the church on Sundays, working for a living during the week and cultivating the garden to produce as much home grown food as possible, my father still found time to enjoy shooting and fishing. This was another tradition that had been carried out by our family for years and as I grew older I also carried on with both of these till times changed and spare time became a thing of the past.

Getting back to the early thirties, even before I started school there were certain things that as a child I could not understand. Why, during the winter months on certain evenings, a man would come to our house dressed in a flat cap, a big heavy jacket and corduroy trousers and bull's eye rubber boots. He would always leave his big-wheeled, black bicycle at the black of the house. This must have been an important bicycle as it had two crossbars, made for a heavy person, also gas lamps on front and back. He would come in and have a chat with my parents and then he and my father would leave the house, he with the small gun and my father with his big gun, and disappear into the dark night. I was not interested by these comings and goings as I was in bed by the time they came back anyway. As this was happening on and off over the winter months I gave up trying to understand. However my mother did not seem concerned and would sit and repair clothes or knit socks while they were out. I did ask my mother why they took out guns at night and I was told they were shooting rats. I did know what a rat was as I had seen real live ones near our chickens in the garden but they did not shoot them. They were trapped in wire cages or steel gin traps and killed in other ways, nearly always shot with an air gun. One night I was indoors with my mother. A nice log fire was burning in the grate and the oil lamp stood in its place in the centre of the table. Outside the rain had started to hit the window panes and the wind was blowing hard and both men came in after being out only a short while. The guns were wiped dry and the pull through was used. This was a length of cord just longer than the gun barrel with about three inches of lead gripped to the cord on one end and a piece of soft cloth with oil on it at the other end. The lead went into the top of the barrel first and, when it came out the other end, it was pulled and the cloth came through cleaning the soot left in the barrel after a shot had been fired. These done, hats, jackets and boots came off and they sat chatting over a glass of homemade wine. I had been taught even at that age that adult conversation was to be heard and not repeated. I found out that if you were spoken to the best thing was to go shy. That night I saw something that took me quite a long time to work out before I could come up with an answer. During the talking that was going on I did hear my father say that one day he would teach the boy to shoot rabbits with the small gun (four- ten) but the real puzzle was not what I heard but what I saw. As the man's jacket hung on a hook in the kitchen, part of the inside was showing and there I saw the biggest pocket I had ever seen and sticking out of the top of this pocket were some long thin pointed black feathers. I was in bed before this man left and I don't think he came much more after the start of the New Year.

I can remember one year, before I had started school and the evenings were lighter, I saw a policeman opening our front gate. I did not like policeman, to put it truthfully I was scared of them. Anyone in uniform spelt no good in my eyes. I had seen another person in a dark blue uniform with red edging around the pockets and collar. He had a round peaked hat with red edging and a button on top in the centre. I saw him give my mother a piece of orange paper with some writing on and asked if there was an answer. She read the paper and I saw her face change and she wiped a tear from her eye and then said to this person that there was no answer. It was bad news from her family at South Creake. I was told this person was a telegram boy and I have often wondered what happened to him. Did he grow up to be a telegram man? I never found out. The police man was let in at the front door and I disappeared up the stairs shutting the stair door behind me. All the time I was thinking was he after me? What had I done wrong? Then it came back to me, a few days before I sat near the fire with our cat on my knee when it let out a terrific yell. The stupid thing had fallen asleep and caught it's whiskers in the fire guard It was not my fault but I got the blame. I crept down to the second stair from the bottom and listened to the talking. I heard the policeman say he wanted the four-ten. Mother said "can you manage it like that?" and he said no I will break it (and I was going to shoot that when I was older). Someone said, "You had better take some cartridges with you" and then he was leaving. I looked out of my bedroom window and saw him get ready to get on his bike and I could not believe what I was seeing. His bike was the same one as the man who used to come and shoot rats. Perhaps he had pinched it as it had two gas lamps, one at the front and one at the back but I could not see any gun. It did come back later but I did not see that happen.

Those old cycle gas lamps were a bit crude to say the least. They were made of two containers, one over the top of the other. The bottom one was filled with carbine, a white, chalky-grey colour and slightly hard substance and the top one was filled with water, which was allowed to drip in to the bottom container very slowly. In front of the containers was a big reflector with a glass front held in place by a metal ring all working on a hinge. So the whole front could be opened into this glass area. There was also a small circle of glass on the outsides of the reflector. The one on the left side was red and the one on the right side was green. These were small and dome-like and about half an inch across. Why they were there and what for I don't know. They looked like navigation lights when the light was being used but surely those people knew their left and right. The way these lights worked was very simple, water from the top container dripped very slowly, on to the carbine in the bottom container causing a gas to be made which came out by the way of a nozzle in the centre of the light. This could be lit by a match, which would show a good, shining light over an area both with the front and back light, which had a red glass instead of clear glass. One disadvantage of these lights was that if you were cycling downhill in a strong wind the flame would blow out, sometimes with a nasty result.

School

Well, as time went on life changed when it was time to start school, something that I had not been looking forward to. Against my wishes I was dressed in new clothes, a suit of brown, short trousers, brown jacket with silver-type buttons, socks that turned down just below the knee, a new shirt and a narrow woollen tie and clean black boots but I don't think these were new. I did not have a cap but as with other boys at that time I did have both belt and braces. There were no school uniforms in those days and children had to wear whatever their parents could afford and a motley lot we looked as well. So at the beginning of the autumn term, about mid September 1933 (I was five on the 15 October) I was put into the metal seat at the back of mother's bicycle and off we went. There were two problems with this seat, one was, if it rained you got soaking wet and secondly if the roads were covered in ice or snow it did not get used, and I had to walk to school in leather boots as I did not have any rubber boots at that time. Only the rich people's children had those. During the first winter the weather was very bad with lots of frost and snow and the boots were nearly always wet through by the time I reach school, a distance of about two and a half miles. This was not a good thing as most children ended up with chilblains on their feet during these winter months and I was no exception. Mine were bad and at some points nearly bursting open. In those days the old fashioned cure was to dip each foot in a used chamber pot, night and morning. Sometimes our hands had chilblains as well but I cannot remember doing that with my hands. The remedy for this was to cut a raw onion in half and lay it cut side down into some salt in a saucer. This was lifted out with the salt clinging to the damp cut side and then the whole thing was rubbed over the hands. If none of these things worked I was allowed to use my father's ointment. He like most farm workers had cracked and chilblained hands in winter. However I did eventually get a pair of rubber boots.

Anyhow after entering the school I saw some faces that I knew, which was a great relief. There were other mothers with children that were starting school on the same day. We were all taken into a classroom and told who the teachers were. At this point life became interesting in parts. Some of the children were crying as their mothers left them behind. I thought this is going to reduce my freedom and this is not for me but when I looked my mother and her bicycle had disappeared. Things were not looking too good. I also remember one boy peeing himself and leaving a pool on the floor. He was taken out into the corridor and was not seen anymore that day. I don't think he had been told about the school ritual that if you wanted anything you put your arm up in the air.

We saw all the teachers that morning. Mr Pursehouse was headmaster. He later moved to a school in Diss. Miss Cox taught the infants, Miss Kemp the next class up and Miss Bartrum the class before the headmasters class.

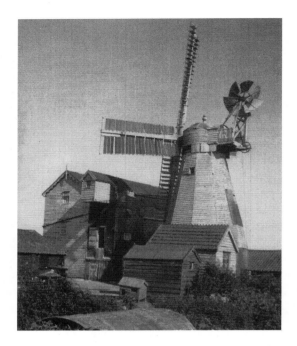

Rash's Mill was on south side of the A143 Rd
Just off Wortham Long Green

The school I went to
From September 1933 to December 1942

We did not seem to be inside for long when someone rang a bell and we all went outside into what was called a playground. This was a tarmac area with railings all round three sides and the school wall on the other. On the roadside were three arches with Faith, Hope and Charity carved in the stone above the arches. Being fenced in at that time I had lost faith, had no hope of escaping to go home and I did not know what charity was. I noticed that some of the older children had escaped and were playing on the grass on both sides of the road. They did not want to go home, well that's what it seemed like to me. Then someone rang that bell again and we all went back into school. This time things were a bit more interesting as we were all given flat trays with sand in them, a stick to level the sand and some small brown and white shells. We made shapes and letters with those. We also had coloured chalks and small slates with wood around the outside. We used a small sponge to clean the slates but were not allowed to clean them with water. I think someone did clean them, possibly the woman who was the school caretaker. We took turns to hand out and collect the slates and trays and some books with big writing under the pictures in them. This made us feel important to do these jobs but I did not like school much at first and I was glad when the first day was over. Also mixing with other people was something I had not been used too as I had no brothers or sisters. So to be amongst all those people did seem strange to me. However I soon learned to count shells on the sand and began to write on the slates.

We were all given a peg in the cloak room to hang our satchels and coats on. We used to take our dinners to school in these satchels which were made of leather, had a small pocket on the front to keep pencils and other things in. There was a thin strap that went over your shoulder. We all took our own lunch, some sort of fruit and sandwiches, cake and crisps for dinner, no school meals in those days. We also had a bottle of home made lemonade made from crystals or tablets. I can remember the hot days of spring and summer. Up to early autumn we were allowed to sit outside under the trees at the back of the school, in the shade. It was a time of very hot summers and very cold, wet winters. We had a five week holiday from late July to early September. Another thing about those dinner times was you had to wash yours hands in the wash basin in the cloak room with some carbolic soap, fancy having to wash before you could eat. The teacher knew if you had washed or not because of the smell of carbolic was very strong.

In time I progressed up to a dull brown pencil, an inkwell and a pen with a metal nib, also exercise books with East Suffolk Country Council on the front, different coloured covers for different lessons. In arithmetic tables were taught and we got told off by the teacher as the whole class made a song out of "once two is two, two two's are four' and so on. I was getting on well. We had books with big printed letters and I could join up my writing.

Then a nasty setback happened. I had been with the older boys many times,

57

watching them fishing for carp and roach in what was called The Home Meadow pit. I can remember the men on this farm all coming back in the evening with a big net and baths, pails and anything suitable and they took all the fish from a pit in the Barn Meadow because of the low water in the hot summer and put them in The Home Meadow pit. I watched my father help with this. Not having any fishing tackle of my own at that time there was nothing I could do but watch. I had caught newts in another shallow pond with a stick, a piece of string and a bent pin. Home Meadow pit had one shallow end and one very deep end. I had been warned by my mother not to go anywhere near this pit but warnings were sometimes ignored. As soon as my parents had gone to work I was off with the older boys fishing. Now this is where I made a big mistake. Not having a rod of my own, one of the other boys let me have a go with his rod. With hook baited I stood on a clump of rushes overhanging the water and trying to cast out I slipped and fell in. What an experience that was. I can still remember it to this day. I could feel the water covering my head as I sank down to the bottom. Being unable to swim, I could do nothing but wave my arms and legs about. I could feel myself rising to the surface and could see the pond weeds level with my eyes. I also saw my cap floating on the surface of the water. I saw some of the other boys running away down the meadow. I could taste the horrible water as I tried to keep my mouth closed but I went down for a second time. I began to feel weaker and stopped waving my arms and legs. The water felt heavy as if it was pulling me down deeper and deeper and then I was on the surface again and I could hear shouting. I looked towards the bank and there was part of a bough of a tree being held by two of the older boys and it was on top of the water beside me. I grabbed this with all the energy I could and hung onto this and was pulled up the bank. There is no doubt that these two boys saved my life that day and to them I shall be forever grateful. Unfortunately both of them are no longer with us, but if they had run away with the others there would be no story to tell. One lived in a house beside the Ling his name was Kenny Rice (Smirk we called him) and the other was Reg Collins. He was a near neighbour at that time, living in the council house just down the road from us and he did help me in this story by reminding me of some of the things I had forgotten. I worked with him on the on the same farm in the early fifties and if we ever had a difference of opinion he would always remind me of what happened and tell me to shut up, always with a sense of humour of course.

Getting back to where we were, after I was pulled out the pond I was taken to Reg's house and sat on a chair in front of the fire. I felt very ill. I was taken to the Jenny Lind hospital in Norwich. On one occasion I remember an orange coloured rubber sheet being laid over my face, and strong smell of something. I was breathing in chloroform. I don't know what happened after that but I was in and out hospital for the next six months, having caught nearly every illness there was, including having my tonsils out.

Nearly everyone I know had their tonsils out so I have often wondered why they were there in the first place.

I can still remember sitting out in the conservatory section of that hospital in the sun with wallflowers in the garden and the laburnum trees in full flower. There was also a girl had a birthday in there so we all had a piece of her birthday cake as the nurses gave her a little party. Also, one time I was allowed home and on the way from the station on the back of my mother's bike we stopped off to see my father working in a field near the Ling. When we got home and were having a drink, my mother let me sit on a chair in the garden. Our doctor called in to see how I was, which was not very well. He ordered me straight back to hospital and said I should not have been sent home in the first place. They were family doctors in these days. The cause was eventually found to be something I had swallowed while I was in the water. In one end of this pit was a wide and deep trench filled with water but separated from the main pit by some boards. The trench had, in the opposite end from the pit, a big wooden barrel let into the ground and the whole area was surrounded by wooden posts and rails. This was used for dipping sheep and it was discovered that I had swallowed some of the liquid used for this purpose. I cannot say if this was true or not but I was very ill. Looking back, surely if this was the case the fish would have suffered as well, but this was not so and as I got older I fished this pit many times but with extra care and better tackle.

One thing that stands out about the visits to the Jenny Lind Hospital was that most of the times I had to go I was put in the seat on the back of my mothers bicycle and taken to Diss railway station, then by train to Norwich, Thorpe Station and on to the hospital by tram or by walking up Prince of Wales road, St Stephens road past the old city railway station where steam engines could be seen moving trucks about. This station is not there now.

I did start back at school but I had lost a lot of time and the first few days were terrible. I had a lot to make up, but I was very lucky as the infants' teacher Miss Cox gave me lots of help. I soon began to catch up and I was allowed to take some work home so my parents helped as well.

Time passed and school terms came and went and with that everything began to become routine. Groups of friends were formed and school began to get to be a better place. Time came for all of us to stop going on our mothers' bicycles as we could now go by car. So we were picked up each morning and took home in the afternoons. This was a period between being taken by our parents until we were old enough to walk the whole distance from home to school. This car was a like a taxi with seven seats in the back, some of which folded up to make more room when not being used. I think it was an Austin Twelve. This car was supplied by a garage at Palgrave owned by a Mr Weavers (Bogey) but more about him and his cars later in this story.

We progressed from the infants' class into the next class, which was standard two. The teacher of this class was Miss Kemp, who lived in the Mill House just a short distance from the school, along the road in the Bury direction. Between two of the classrooms there was a wood and glass partition, which was opened every morning for assembly. During assembly we said prayers and with Miss Kemp at the piano we would sing hymns at the top of our voices. I remember "we plough the fields and scatter", because it was being done all around us on the farms in all the villages. "There is a Greenhill faraway", was another and of course all the Christmas and Easter hymns. This part of the day came easy to me because I was still going to church on Sunday morning with my parents.

The class work was getting harder as we progressed up the class numbers. I had, with all of the rest of Miss Kemps class, been let out at playtimes on the square of grass outside the railed-in playground. We were free and the noise we made playing football and cricket as well as getting in each others way was deafening. We also had something to eat and drink in the mid morning break, 10.45 to 11.0.clock. It was around this time that I had eaten an apple during the break and, as the teachers all stood together in a group at the corner of the playground talking, someone said that I dare not throw the apple core at them. I did and it hit one of them in the ear. Well the headmaster took me into his classroom and asked me to hold out my hands. I thought he wanted to see if I had washed but instead he got out what I thought was a short walking stick. He said it was a cane, not unlike the canes I had seen in the rectory garden holding up plants. He gave me one hit on my hands even after I told him someone had dared me to do it. I formed my own opinion of that situation. So with hands still stinging I returned outside to find the boy who had told me to do it. As I had no brothers or sisters to help I had to be a bit crafty about what I done. I had already been under pressure in one or two rows with some of the boys. I had also had a thick ear from one boy bigger than me and when I told my father about it I got another one from him for letting the boy hit me. I made up my mind that no one would hit me again or if they did I would not come off the worst. The boy who told me to throw the apple core one day brought a bag of peanuts to school and put them in his desk. I saw this and when the opportunity arose I went to his desk and took out the bag of peanuts put them on the floor and stood on them and then put the bag full of crushed nuts back in his deck. I don't know what happened after that as the shells were all mixed with the nuts. I doubt if he could eat them.

Anyhow lessons went on, reading to the class, which I hated, writing, music (quavers and semi-quavers), which I could not do very well. We did drawing which I really liked and arithmetic, six and seven times tables.

It was around about this time that Mr Pursehouse left Wortham and moved to Diss. I cannot remember the exact year. The school was left without a

Headmaster for short while but I can remember a new Headmaster coming. There was a school house that went with the job with a pond in the back garden.

There were several boys and girls all going to school from the Ling area and groups from all the main areas of Wortham, the Long Green, Magpie Green, the Marsh, the brook, besides a few from Burgate. We were all playing games at school and at home, football, cricket, bowling, hoops, spinning tops, hopscotch and in the right season there was conkers, popguns made from elder wood, which fired acorns. We also made small lengths of hazel wood into guns, to shoot the pips of hawthorn berries, by cutting a slot about one inch long in one end. Our own little gang from around the rectory area consisted of Tom Hughes, Derek and Leslie Hunn and me. We did go down onto the Ling and play football and cricket sometimes but we had a game that others didn't have. Tom's father was manager of the hardware department of the Diss Co-op on the market place and he had a car to go to work in. I think it was a Standard. In his garage he kept some used tyres. We were still small enough to roll ourselves inside these tyres and as Tom's house was on top of a hill. From the rectory to the church we would roll down this road as fast as we could. We would spend hours doing this to see who could go the furthest. We never thought that the further down we went the longer it took to get back up again.

At about this time we were told that we could no longer ride to school in the taxi from Palgrave and we all had to walk. Most of the time we would wait for the children from the Ling and all go in one big group together. By that time I was wearing shoes which made walking easy. We had the choice of three different ways to walk to school. From the top of Rectory Road, we could turn right and go down to the church and then turn left into Long Green Road and up to the Diss to Bury road which we crossed to the school. The second way was to turn left at the top of Rectory Road for about quarter of a mile then turn right into Marsh Lane. I can remember this being a stone track. We'd follow this up to the Diss to Bury road and turn right and the school was on the left. The third one was the way I liked best. It started along a cart track beside the Wigwam garden (Tom Hughes house) and went down to a big deep ditch crossed by a bridge into the next field. Beside this farm track was a hedge of bullace bushes, a wild small plum and in the autumn they would turn from green to yellow and were very nice to eat raw or made into pies. Once through this field the footpath went across two more fields, over a stile near a small wood with a hill in the middle, then besides a field of blackcurrant bushes and into a long narrow meadow. It came out of a gate between the end house of a row of red brick cottages and a long narrow pond. Then it went across a path on the Long Green and across the road to the school. Now this footpath across the fields was ploughed up each year so we had to make a fresh place to walk as straight as we could so as not to damage the growing crops. The best time was when the corn was in the ear and the wind was blowing. It looked like waves and we imagined we were walking through the sea.

Well time went on and I moved to the next class, which was Standard Three. The teacher was Miss Bartrum (otherwise known as Popsie) why I don't know. The lessons being taught were very different from the easy going that we had been doing. We were now doing arithmetic instead of sums, geography, history, art, composition, long word spellings, poetry, nature study, science with bunson burners and test tubes etc. This teacher was very good and very fair in my opinion as each and every one of us was given jobs to do. One job I remember was changing the weather cards each day to show what was happening during the four seasons. Someone else read the rain fall and made a record of it in a book. Our new headmaster a Mr Rodwell changed the whole attitude of how schoolwork should be done and gained the respect of everyone in the school, including most of the parents. He would visit every class during lesson time at some time of the day. He also changed the way the teachers worked, letting the class stay in the rooms and different teachers come in for different subjects. He was a great believer in letting people find out things for themselves. We done a lot of reading books, Toms Brown's School days and Pilgrim's Progress were a must. He also formed a library so we could take books home to read. My favourite was the Deerfoot of the Prairie series. This was about an Indian Chief and his black horse. Despite the fact that we were in Standard Three he did come and teach us a lot.

The class was divided up into four teams, red, blue, green and yellow and we all competed against each other. We had coloured bands to show which team we were in. Mine was red and all teams had a team leader who was made responsible for all the equipment that team used. I liked sport, football and cricket but not rounders or tennis and I was just useless at P.T (physical training). That was until one day when Mr Rodwell came out on the green to watch standard three doing all the exercise required. He saw that I could not do the forward roll so he took me to one side and folded me into a ball and pushed me forward. He was not angry but very firm in what he told me to do. I done this roll for him many times and from then on I would have a go at anything, high jump, long jump, hurdles and races. I enjoyed them all by the time we were playing on the green over the main road and this was where the sports days were held as was the cricket pitch. That was the reason for the teachers to stand at the west corner of the playground railing. The main football pitch was over the next road that went up to Speirs Hill and on to Redgrave.

There were several things that were part of the school year throughout the 1930's, things you never forget, like the school doctor coming and checking how fit you were, also the school dentist. It was always the policy of the school that you could go home if you had a tooth pulled out. My parents made me clean my teeth with Gibbs tooth paste, a solid round cake of pink toothpaste in a round aluminium container with the name pressed in the lid. As a result I can remember having one tooth out in all the school years. The other person who came round every so often was the nit nurse, in my option a funny, little, short woman, who no one seemed to like, in her blue nurses' uniform and black wide-brimmed hat. She had a sharp type of voice as if it was your fault if you caught these small vermin. She would go though your hair with a small tooth comb and would want to know how often you washed your hair but having clean hair did not stop these creatures from making your head their home. If she found any on anyone they would be made to take a note home to their parents, who had to buy and use the disinfectant to clean the hair. One of her tricks was to appear about a fortnight later and check up on you without any warning.

Then there was the teachers enemy the school inspector, a tall, thin man with a small moustache over his top lip, dark black hair and a rather sharp pointed chin. He always wore a buff-coloured rain coat over his tweed suit. He would nearly always come after the dinner break in a very small Fiat car of a dull red colour as if it never had a polish since new. This car was always left on the side of the road as there was not much traffic in those days it did not matter much. Why he did not park near the school gate always seemed a bit of a mystery. He did not seem to be very interested in the children that were always at school only the ones who did not go very often. I know the teachers always had a meeting after he had gone.

As we got older and further up in the classes they became more interesting and geography was one subject that all the class could take part in, by knowing about different countries and what they produced, by bringing to school wrappers from oranges, labels from date boxes, fruit tins and cheeses, empty match boxes and cigar, cigarette and tobacco labels and so on. These where all pinned to a board on one wall of the classroom with the names of the country they came from beside them. We also had in the room on the west side of the building in a tall glass-fronted cupboard an ostrich egg and a coconut complete with its fibrous shell. There were also certain types of sea shells but I cannot remember their names. Then there were the history lessons , how this country was invaded by the Danes and Saxons also the Romans, how they built forts and towns with massive stone walls and roads, one of which went past the school to Bury St Edmunds. How the roads were constructed using logs and stones. Then there was the different wars the Roundheads, the War of the Roses, the Kings and Queens of England, the Spanish armada and its downfall, King John signing the Magna Carter on Runnymede, a small island in the River Thames, Guy Fawkes who was going to blow up parliament. Then there was a war that was going on at that time between Japan and China. So the lessons went on, starting with sums then to arithmetic, which had now become maths, with all double figure tables, equations and percentages. Then there was nature study. I liked this because we would go on outside visits to ponds and streams to find out about fresh water life, weeds, fish, insects like water boatmen, dragon flies and then the visits to banks and hedgerows where we would be given a section of bank to make notes, recording all the grass and wild flowers, like willow herb, ragged robin, speedwell, deadly nightshade and bryony (both of which were poison if the berries were eaten), how to tell the age of a tree and also how to find out how to get out of a wood if you were lost by reading the trees as the foliage did not grow on the north side as well as the south side because of the lack of sunlight. There were mushrooms, toadstools and different fungi also mosses. We learnt how the weather affected plant life, what clouds brought thunder and rain, what caused fog and mist. I remember Mr Rodwell taking us outside to see an unusual sight. There was a strong wind blowing from east to west at a very fast speed and taking some white cloud along with it but above that there was a wind blowing from the opposite direction west to east and taking a layer of cloud with that as well. Clouds going in two directions and I must admit I have never seen that since. Other lessons carried out as normal but still certain things stand out that can never be forgotten.

We always had a Christmas party, with the children performing the nativity play. Lots of the parents came to help. On the roof of the middle room down on the east side of the school was an opening glass light where after the party Father Christmas came through with a bag of presents and down a ladder into the classroom. This man was Mr Needham from the post office on the edge of the green to the east of the school. He was a tall thin man with bushy hair and a thick moustache. He spoke with a squeaky voice but he made a good Father Christmas. I remember that all the children had a present each. I got a wooden pencil case with a sliding top one year. This was full of coloured pencils, rubber, pencil sharper and a six inch rule. I kept this for many years.

After one party my parents came to take me home and we walked down the road and past the church with only the lights of paraffin lamps shining behind drawn curtains in cottage windows on a very very dark night. I did not like that much especially with the hooting of an owl in the trees around the rectory. I don't really know how I got home from the parties other years neither did we know who brought the present, the food and drink also the balloons and crackers but I do know that it was all enjoyed by everyone. For some of the really poor families that must have been the only present that the children had. I can also remember that in most of the classes just before Christmas we made decorations, paper chains from coloured strips of paper and other things like Christmas trees from green paper with shaped coloured paper stuck on them as presents.

There was always one thing that happened a few weeks before Christmas every year and that was if you had special permission you were allowed, during the dinner hour, to go down the road to the post office and buy some of their seasonal goods. This was enjoyed because they stocked a large selection to choose from but you were always careful how you spent your hard earned pocket money. You were allowed to go across the green to Mr Clarke baker's shop, a little thatched cottage, part of which was used as a shop with some tiled buildings on one side which were used as a bakery. You could buy sweets, crisps and chewing gum from there. Although, like the post office, they did sell all sorts of groceries and bread and some quite nice cakes. A penny went a long way in those days but there was a limit to spending as I was made to save three pennies each week. The other place you could buy crisps and sweets was the Dolphin pub (landlord Mr Groom) but only if you went in the side door and waited in the passage way for someone to come. You were not allowed near the bar area.

Every spring as people walked across the footpaths on the Long Green all the ragwort plants were in bloom with their yellow flowers but the green foliage was being eaten off by some yellow and black striped caterpillars which would after a short while turn into a black-winged with red spots moth called the Cinnabar moth. These could be seen all over the green in daylight right into early summer.

Meanwhile with our lives outside school hours changing all the time, school itself carried on as normal with Mr Rodwell still looking for ways to improve his school. He still checked to see if yours hands had been washed and yours shoes cleaned. Ties were a must and had to be worn. My parents made sure I went to school in a new suit every September. There was no school uniform but whatever you were wearing had to be clean and tidy.

I had several friends, some who I still see now. I remember two brothers coming to school. I think they were living in a house on the Marsh at the time. I'm not sure now but I think their surname was Allam and they were made welcome because their father had been killed in the R101 airship crash.

There were other things that stood out during the 30s like when the whole school stopped lessons when the big steam plough engines of Sturgon Bros from Stanton passed by. These huge engines made by John Fowlers & Co, Leeds, worked in pairs and they moved from one farm to another one pulling the cultivator and the other pulling the living van, water rat and mole drainer. If these machines were required, they could be heard from quite a long way off with the rumbling noise getting louder until they actually went past the school. All conversation stopped and the windows and doors shook with the vibrations from these steam giants. The soil that collected inside the rim of the front wheels would go round so many times that it became very hard, sometimes about the size of a cricket ball. We would take these and use them for that very purpose, as we would often go and watch the steam engines at work. This I liked to see and watch the man with the horse and cart go to each engine supplying them with coal and water. Everything was done by a whistle on the engine, a special call for whatever was wanted and the same whistle communication from engine to engine as each implement was turned around after crossing the field. We sometimes paid a visit to the living van on the way to school and the odd rasher of bacon always seemed much better than what we got at home. The most common vehicles that passed the school at that time were the Foden steam wagons pulling a trailer. These were owned by the Blue Circle Cement Company, their yellow paint slightly covered in cement dust with both the wagon and trailer loaded with one hundredweight bags of cement, and then returning empty, it was a sight never to be forgotten. These machines had solid rubber tyres and they did not make as much noise as steam engines but travelled much faster.

Two other thing still stand out, like in the late 30s Mr Rodwell would take his class outside to watch the formation of biplanes that did quite a lot of flying around in this area nearly every day. Most of them were Gloucester Gladiators, D H Tiger Moths and others, most of them coming from Martlesham Heath or Mildenhall. The other thing was something that no one ever found out what it was and this was a bright silver object up in the sky to the north over Norwich and was there for several weeks. It seemed to sparkle on sunny days. Even now I don't know what it was.

Progress was still being made at school and by this time I had learned to ride a bicycle from a small wheeled one what was called a fairy cycle, (which spent nearly as much time in the ditch as it did on the road when I was learning to ride) to a much larger one altogether with the seat right down as far as possible and blocks on the pedals. I was told I would grow to it. I did not know what this was at the time but over the years the blocks came off and the pedals and the seat were put up. I had this until I left school. Through the summer and winters I went to school on it, even coming home for dinner in the later years.

Some of the winters were very bad with sharp frosts and ice on the road so we found a way to keep our hands warm by getting a cocoa tin and making holes in the lid and bottom with a nail. We then put a piece of wire around the middle of the tin and wired it to the centre of the handlebars. The tin was then filled with old rags and lit with a match. The rags would glow red as it burned and the tin got very hot as you cycled along and by putting your hands on the tin the cold soon disappeared but it had one disadvantage because your clothes smelt of burnt rag, and some of the teachers did not approve of that. Sometimes, if the roads were very icy, we would walk and some of the drivers of Bartrums sugar beet lorries would give us a ride in the lorry cab. Those old Bedford lorries carried about seven tons of sugar beet and would have to get into a low gear to get up the hill from the church to the Long Green with the metal of the bonnet shaking all the time. One very bad winter, after it had been snowing all night, we decided to walk to school. We had only just started to walk when we waited for the snowplough to pass. This was made with very heavy wood and was shaped like a V when in use but folded up for storage. Both the front and the bottom were reinforced with thick metal and it was pulled by two horses. There were two handles at the back to try and control it as it went through the snow. Best of all it had seats across from one side to the other and it was on these we sat and had a ride to school. One particular day we went into the classroom much to the teachers surprise as there were only about fifteen children at school that day. As we lived about three miles away, questions were asked how did we get there. Did you cycle? No, did you walk? No, did you come by lorry? No, we come by snowplough. They were pleased to see us and that was one of the best days at school I ever had as no lessons were given and we got sent home early in the afternoon.

If there was just sharp frost and no snow Mr Rodwell would throw pails of water across the playground to make massive slides for us the next day. I cannot remember anyone ever getting hurt but I did have a nasty fall by doing what some of the other boys did. Our bicycle shed was next to the road near the three arches and it had rails to put the front wheels of the bikes in, one high rail, and one low rail right across the length of the shed. I had seen some boys race up the playground lift the front wheels and fit it in between the rails. I thought I would try this so I peddled as fast as I could up the playground lifted the front wheel and missed the rails. I hit the boards, that were the walls of the shed, so hard that some were pushed back and I suffered a cut cheek (the scar can be seen to this day), bruised arms and legs. The front wheel did take a bit of straightening before I could ride it home. Someone put a plaster on my face but it was hard to understand why my parents made such a fuss when I got home. The wheel still turned although it did hit the forks as it turned, the handlebars could be pulled back into place and my jacket could be repaired by a few stitches. Who wants arms on a jacket anyway? I had to walk to school after that until my bike had been repaired. My pocket money was helping to pay for the repairs for quite a long while afterwards. Parents were mean in those days.

While I am talking about cycles, it was the school policy to supply, their own cycle to children who lived a long way from the school and could not afford to buy one. These cycles belonged to the education committee but had to be maintained by the person who was using them. Those bikes stood out in a crowd by their white mudguards and jet black frames and each had a number stamped on it.

It was around this time one of the oldest boys from a large family with no money, came to school in whatever clothes he could get and his boots were full of repaired patches. Now this boy was someone with very big muscles and as strong as an ox. He sat in the front desk of the headmaster's class and he always done his best to be clean and tidy. One Friday afternoon Mr Rodwell called him out to his desk which he stood in front of with a look of bewilderment, wondering what he had done wrong. The headmaster asked him if he could borrow his father's bicycle on Saturday morning and meet him at 9am outside the school house which he said he could. No one knew what was going to happen but when we got to school on Monday morning this boy turned up in a new, brown suit, shirt, tie and new shoes and socks, all bought for him by the headmaster. That was the sort of person Mr Rodwell was. From that weekend that boy never looked back and after leaving school he joined the Coldstream Guards and was very smart in his uniform. I don't know what his job was when he left the army but I do know he lived in Diss and made a scale model steam engine in his garage.

However back to school and events that were happening, outside on the road next to the school alterations were being made to make the corner safer by changing the angles of the surface. This was being done by a gang of men, a horse and cart and a steam roller. As there were no coloured cones in those days the directions of what part of the road was given by square red oil lights complete with red glass to be seen at night. These needed to be filled with oil every day and if they went out at night they had to be relit and this was the job of a man called the night-watch man. He was supplied with a small hut very much like a sentry box. He also had to keep an eye on the material and coal on site and make sure the fire was kept alight in the steam roller. All this equipment belonged to a Mr Arnold of Rickinghall, who was a road-making contractor, and supplied Suffolk County Council with the labour and machines for this kind of work. The steam roller was an Averling and Porter with a brass horse emblem on the front. We would watch this work going on during our playtimes.

Another thing that we saw going past the school was the bus chassis going to the Lowestoft Coach Works to have the actual body fitted. These were painted in silver primer paint. There was not much to them only a metal frame, back and front wheels, the engine and a steering wheel in front of a high metal seat on which the driver sat in all weathers. In the very cold weather they would be dressed in thick coats with a hood over their heads and goggles over their eyes. There would be three or four together and they seemed to be travelling very fast. I think they came from a factory in the Midlands and this was happening two to three times each week. I never did see any completed buses going back or know how the drivers got back

School work carried on and ancient history turned in to modern history. We learnt about the 1936 Olympic Games that were being held in Berlin and all the trouble that was going on at these games. The whole of Europe was changing. We learned about what was happening in Germany and Russia. We did not realise how serious things were getting. As far as we were concerned the situation carried on the same. We still cycled to school, played football and had matches against other schools in Palgrave, Redgrave, Eye and Botesdale. Our team colours were black socks, black shorts and white shirts with the letters WM on the back. These letters stood for Wortham Major, being the first team and not the reserves. Most of our opponents called us the Wortham Monkeys. The football boots at the time were made of real leather and had big round studs nailed to the soles and heels. The ball itself was made up of leather sections sewn together. Inside the leather case was a rubber bladder which had to be blown up with a pump and then the valve had to be turned over and tied with a piece of string. The case was then held together with a leather lace. When the ball got wet it was very heavy and, should you have been unlucky enough to get hit in the face by the ball lace first, it really took your breath away. We still played marbles on the footpath in front of the Potter Bros carpenters shop.

We had our sport day on July 4th nearly every year and some parents turned up to watch. I think that the Union Jack was flown from the flagpole in the playground on that day. Other days it was flown were on King George V and Queen Mary's Silver Jubilee 1935, the Coronation of Edward VIII in May 1937 and the Coronation of King George VI and Queen Elizabeth also in 1937. I can just remember the school parties for all of these when everyone was given a magazine.

Another thing that was happening at that time was the school had a small piece of land on the south side divided from the roadway by a deep ditch. This was used for gardening lessons. At the bottom near the school was a big lawn. At the top were two garden sheds side by side in which tools, wheelbarrows, seeds and stakes were kept. The lawn roller was kept outside. There were a few fruit trees in various positions around the gardens and these were used for learning pruning, control of pest, also use and storage of fruit. Now if this land was there when Mr Rodwell came I don't know but he did get another piece of land behind the carpenter's shop which was originally part of a farmer's field. This was ploughed up and left for the school to do what it liked with. I presume someone paid the farmer for it as it is still school property today only now laid down to grass. Then it used as a communal garden with nearly everyone helping to work on it. There was also a large rock garden at one end of the playground which was looked after by the boys while the girls were taught cookery and needlework. Most of the boys, myself included had to help on their parent's gardens at home so this was for most boys easy going.

Well time went on and more aircraft were seen flying around the skies above the school and we knew things were getting serious when the headmaster told us that it was now certain that there would be war in Europe and this country would be involved. There was also a big increase in army traffic movement along the county roads. Food was still plentiful in the shops and most people went about their daily business and I eventually went up to the headmaster's class. Here we were learning about Shakespeare and maths was even harder but the lesson that I really liked was art. We would go out onto the green and sit and paint pictures of the thatched cottages that were built around the edges. Sometimes we painted the willow trees blowing in the wind or the horse chestnut trees in bloom with their white and pink candle like flowers standing out against the green foliage. In the spring we were inside the classroom painting the sticky buds of these trees and in the autumn we painted the leaves, all onto A4 clean white paper. The other favourite leaf painted in its autumn colours was the red leaf of the virginia creeper.

Gardening was done but changes were being made as some land was divided up into plots, each one put in a four season rotation which included double digging one quarter of the plot each year. Then things began to happen quickly as gas masks were issued but I cannot remember if this was before the war or just after it started. Those little cardboard boxes which held the masks were carried by us most of the time. We had gas mask drill such as wearing them to do lessons in for short periods of time. This was alright when you sat at the desks and were watching the blackboard but to have your head down writing was a very different matter. I was always felt hot and shut in as adjustments to the straps made sure these things fitted tight. It was a great relief to get them off. I can remember when everyone was supplied with an extra green filter to fit on the end of the existing black filter on the front of the mask. This was an extra protection against another sort of gas but we never had to use them at any time and eventually they got left at home.

Then came the biggest change of all and this was the arrival of the evacuee children from London with their teachers. This changed our school life as they had to use our school and therefore doubled the amount of children for lessons. It was tried at first to have all us local children and the evacuees together but this did not work very well as most of the evacuees came from the East End of London. They seemed to us to be talking a different language, as no doubt we did to them. Their teachers did seem very tolerant as they understood what these children were going through, leaving home, not knowing what their parents were doing or where they were or worse still if they were alive.

There were three teachers with these children. One was lodging with a household in Magpie Green, Wortham and he cycled to school sometimes but most fine weather he would come by roller skating, a distance of about one and a quarter miles. He was a young man, I would have thought about 28-30 years old, and he seemed to have a way of dealing with any problem. I thought he was the best of the three. I think his name was Cornell. The other male teacher was a typical "Please Sir" character, an old gentleman always wearing a tweed suit and white shirt with stiff collar, brass stud and gold cuff links. His other features were a pair of horn rimmed glasses and every sentence he spoke was always followed with a turned up nose and a couple of long sniffles. He had grey receding hair with a very smooth bald patch on the back of his head. We said it was caused by his trilby hat which he would touch with his finger whenever he met any female teacher. His name was

Mr Wilson and his form of transport was an old upright gent's cycle with a wicker basket strapped to the front of the handlebars. I can't remember where he was lodging but I don't think it was far away from the school as he must have been well into his sixties then. He certainly had a very strict way of teaching and was very happy to use the cane for any opportunity on the London children. Most of the country children viewed him with some suspicion and did their best to keep out of his way or if the chance arose, to upset his immaculate routine. The third teacher was a dark haired good looking Jewish lady around her mid-twenties, very smoothly dressed with black high heeled shoes. Everyone thought she was the best. Her name was Miss Levine. I never knew her first name. I can't remember where she was lodging, but I think it must have been near the school as she always walked, mornings and afternoons.

Some of these children could not accept the quiet life of the country and some went back after a few months. School lessons were arranged so that us country children attended school in the morning one week and afternoon the next week, and alternate weeks thereafter with the evacuees attended the opposite part of the day and the teachers taking lessons with their own children. This did cause a lot of upset at midday which was change-over point. There were many fights near the school between us at first which would start from nothing really and would continue until one of the teachers intervened. Most of this was caused by misunderstanding.

We never had any billeted with us as our house was small. I can remember the first ones I saw. These were two girls staying at the Old Queen's Head on the Long Green and I saw Mrs Garnham, the owner, outside the front lawn combing their long hair. This brings me to another point about what was happening. I believe the nit nurse must have been a member of staff at that time as she seemed to be at the school nearly every day. The school doctor and the school dentist also appeared to be making a lot of visits, more than we had been used to before these people came. I cannot remember all the names of the children but some particular ones can still be brought to mind quite clearly. There were two large families, both of them staying on Burgate Great Green. One family whose name was Ellis, the oldest being a girl named Joan, who looked after the other like a mother hen, had a temper like a dragon and no one was going to upset her little brood. Even the teacher viewed her with caution. I knew some of the younger part of the family went back after a short while but Joan was still there when I left school in December 1942. The other family were the Ganges. These were much quieter people and the oldest again being a girl, Jean, looked after the rest of the family. But these ones mixed with the country children and were more independent and did not rely on their sister as much. This girl was also at school when I left. Why I remember the older ones of the family is because they were about the same age as me. The others I can remember were two brothers, Derek and Ronald Grabham, lodging with one of the Potter

Carpenter brothers who had the workshop next to the school. They stayed on and both left school to work for Savills of Mellis, Corn and Coal Merchants, who had a mill beside the railway line at Mellis Station. The other boy who I got to know was Willie Westgate, who was billeted with Mr and Mrs Hughes at the Wigwam, Wortham. He was a bit different from the others as he had his own bicycle which caused a great deal of interest as it was a cycle with a back pedal brake, something never seen around here before. The last we hear of him was a few years ago when a member of the present Hughes family found him doing a post round in Brentwood.

However most of them settled down, although a few did go back to London, so we could at last all intermingle and school became an all-day affair again, much to the disgust of both country and London children. We were taught by both lots of teachers. At that particular time we had school gardens and we were encouraged to grow vegetables for sale to parents for their kitchens. The local boys all had small plots which we had to crop in rotation every year, and during the winter we had to double dig one quarter section of the plot to grow root crops like carrots and parsnips. Lots of the vegetables grown on these plots were sold to the parents of children who did not grow their own crops. I kept a book on what was sold and the price it was sold for. This money was used to buy seeds and insects control powders like Derris Dust, there were no spray in those days. The evacuee boys all worked on the large section of land which was bought from a local farmer. As it had only been ploughed by horses at that time the section that they had to double dig was very hard and all credit was due to them for the efforts most of them put in, once they understood what we were doing. Most of them had no idea what a fork or a spade was for and some handles got broken and fork tines got sprung. I remember two brothers, one was John Lane, he was the older of the two, and the other was Dick Lane and they were always put together for gardening and one afternoon I found out why. We were all busy including our headmaster and Mr Cornell. I heard a shout and the younger of the two threw his fork in the air and started to jump around. I saw Mr Cornell rush to the boy and put a pencil in his mouth. With the help of John they both laid this boy on the ground and after a short while he stopped shaking and began to relax. I had no idea what had happened but was later told that he had an epileptic attack. This was the first time I had seen anything like this happen and it was quite frightening.

Most of us boys began to understand and respect the London boys and help them to understand what it was like to sow seeds and see things grow to fruition and good friendships were formed and I am sure that they learned a lot from us. They watched with amazement as we took a wheelbarrow in to the Long Green and collected manure from Mr Potter's pony which pulled their four wheeled works carts. This manure was put into five gallons cans with the tops cut off and covered with water and stirred with a stick about once a week. This fertilizer was ready for feeding the tomatoes after the first fruits had formed. The odour from this was a bit strong but it cost nothing to make.

I can also remember another little incident that happened this time with Miss Levine. This was during an arithmetic lesson and she sat on a chair in front of the open fire with her back to the fire guard. Tom Hughes and I sat in front of all the other desks on that row and the warmest part of the room. With our books standing on end on the front of the desk, we were quietly examining a live 2.2 bullet. Now one of us dropped this bullet on the floor and it rolled under Miss Levine's shoe and of course we dared not attempt to pick it up. As it had been snowing all morning and it was break time we disappeared outside for a snowball fight with the evacuees. It was during this we heard a very loud explosion come from inside the school. We went in to see what had happened and found Miss Levine surrounded by other teachers and she appeared to be shaking. There were small pieces of coal lying around the room near the fireplace. When asked what had happened she said that she found something on the floor and threw it on the fire. We never did say anything about that but we did not take live bullets to school again.

I think most of the evacuees went back much wiser to the ways of the country and I would not be surprised if some of the people moving to the London overspill towns, like Thetford, were some of the children who were evacuated during the war.

Out of school hours

At this point I think it would be worthwhile to mention some of the things we done out of school hours at weekends, holidays and nights after tea. In the spring we collected bird's eggs and put them in a flat box, lying on the soft husk of the flower of the beech trees. This was after making a hole in each end and blowing the yolk out. We all made it known to each other where the nests were and made sure that there was only one egg taken from each nest. The only nest where only one egg was left was moorhens. We collected these with a spoon tied to a long stick because most of the nests were over water, out of arms reach. We took the eggs home and had them fried with a piece of bacon and bread for breakfast next morning. We also fished with a bent pin on a piece of string tied to a garden cane or a strong stick, for newts and sticklebacks, a small fish with the male having a red area under its chin. What we caught was put into a 2 lb jam jar filled with water and returned to the pond when we had finished fishing.

We had our little woods all round the area that we played in and climbing trees and making dens was one of the things that everyone did, walnut trees in the autumn was a must as a shake would bring some nuts down and sometimes a tree of red apples in someone garden was worth a visit as long as nobody told your parents. We made high jump stands out of whatever material we could get and used a grass area that had been cut short for long jump, marking each person's landing spot with twigs from a nearby bush. We played football on three different places, using our coats or jackets as goal posts. We never had a crossbar or a net. One of the pitches was on the meadow next to the cottage where I lived and beside the meadow was a ditch which took water from the drains from the cottage. Now this was filled with a blue/grey sludge that could give off a horrible smell if disturbed. We all tried not to kick the ball into that ditch. The second pitch was on the top end of the Rectory Meadow near the footpath. We would play out here and as no one had a watch we played until we could not see the ball or if it was a full moon even longer. And the third pitch was on a piece of grass next to the Ling in front of the old Union building. This was our Saturday and Sunday pitch and games were arranged between us and the boys from Denmark Green. There were games with the whole purpose of winning, someone was always the ref but if they ever knew the rules it was hard to tell sometimes.

Then there was cricket, we made a cricket pitch on the Ling. This was beside the road on the north section just past Bartrums' cottage, and we dug out the turf after cutting the grass short and levelled all the soil and as it was sandy made it as solid as possible and re-laid the turf. After a short while and after a lot of watering we were able to play on it but we had one big disadvantage and that was if the ball was hit really hard it would get lost in the gorse bushes.

We held boxing matches in one of Mr Bartrums' sheds on Sunday morning after church. We also had some of the wheels joined to metal axles that had once been part of Mr Bartrum's carts for moving wood to his saw bench, to cut up into logs and carting the logs out to customers for burning on their fires. With these wheels we would run as fast as possible along the road and then turn off the road and jump on the axle and let the wheels take us down the hills and slopes across the Ling till they came to a stop. I sometimes helped Mr Bartrum and his son Don to deliver his chopped up wood around the village on a Saturday afternoon, this wood was sold in a wicker basket called a skep (bushel). Sweep Bartrum, as he was called, was a wise person and he knew how to sell wood and he would always put two big logs on the bottom of the skep and then fill the rest across the top of those two. Most people would have four or more of these skeps for which he charged half a crown each, 2/6 or 12 ½ pence of today's money. He had a big petrol engine that ran the big saw bench for cutting the trees into logs. This engine could be heard for quite a long way around when it was working. We got a few pence for helping if we were lucky.

We could go where we liked, nobody ever told us that we were trespassing. We went on the farms with the shepherds, the stockmen who looked after pigs and cattle and the horsemen whatever they were doing or wherever they were. In the harvest time we went into the fields where the corn was being cut with our sticks with a big knob on the end and we chased rabbits around the field till we caught them as long as we kept out of the way of the men with guns it was alright. The things we done was to walk around hedges and gather blackberries and hazel nuts. The blackberries would be put into Kilner jars with a rubber ring and a metal clip sealing the glass top and boiled in hot water for a time and put into storage in the pantry for the winter. Other soft fruits like plums, pears, gooseberries and raspberries were also treated like this but not the strawberries or blackberries and some plums which were made into jam. All these could be kept for nearly a year. The hazel nuts like some new potatoes were put into square biscuit tins and buried about eighteen inches deep in the garden, to be dug up again about two days before Christmas. Runner beans were also kept in Kilner jars but they were sliced up and stored in table salt.

The other thing that was kept in store was hens' eggs, as there was one part of the year when the hens did not lay any eggs and that was when they started to moult (lose their feathers). Until they had new feathers they did not even sit on their nests. The way people kept eggs was with a galvanised pail and some stuff very much like the white of an egg. It was clear and you could see through it. It was brought from the chemist and was called Waterglass. This was mixed with clean water and about three inches of this mixture was then put in the bottom of the pail and new laid eggs were put in until that level was full. This would be repeated until the pail was full and everyone had plenty of egg until the chickens started to lay again.

Peas were sometimes allowed to ripen in the pods on the plants and then picked and stored in glass sweet jars to be used in the winter for pea soup. These were always a round variety and not the wrinkled main crop.

Onions and shallots were pickled in vinegar and stored in glass jam jars with a piece of greaseproof paper cut to a circle and tied to the jar by a length of white string. I helped with most of these things and sometimes if there were a lot of blackberries they were sold for a few pence in Diss. Some mornings I would get up early and pick fresh mushrooms from the meadows around the Rectory.

Another thing that was done was to collect horse chestnuts in the autumn and have conker fights with them at school. The secret of this was to bake some big ones in the oven so they were really hard and would not break when hit. I preferred a leather boot lace to thread through the conker to hold it by.

Most of the toys that most of us had over the years were now being left in their storage cupboard. My train sets, Meccano sets, cars and lorries, the farm animals and carts, the lead soldiers and all the things of those early years, the teddy bear, the golliwog and the black and white Felix cat were all being surpassed by games like snakes and ladders, draughts and card games, table tennis and darts, dominoes and jigsaw puzzles.

Other things were getting more interesting as we all grew older. We were expected to work on weekends and holidays. No I have got that wrong, we were made to work. Once your twelfth birthday was over you had to earn money by some way or other. Some of the things done would be in other parts on different subjects, as everyone carried on getting older and learning from our parents also having more responsibility put on us. I had to keep helping with the gardening, cutting wood for the fire, cutting hay from beside the roads for our rabbits, and gathering hogweed, wild white clover, dandelions and vetch to feed them on. We carted the hay home on the wheelbarrow and dried and stacked it in the garden. Nearly everyone had tame rabbits and when the young rabbits were a month old they were put in the sale to be brought by dealers who reared them until they were big enough to be sold to the butcher for meat. This earned us a few extra shillings to help with household costs. In the winter the rabbits were kept in wooden hutches on beds of clean straw with heavy sacks covering the wire-netting on the doors at the front which was pulled up in the morning and put back down at night to keep out the cold. Their food in the winter was a bunch of new hay, cabbage leaves and carrots from the garden, although these had to be allowed to wilt for a day or two before being fed to them. Also fed to them in a little v shaped home made wooden trough, were boiled potato peelings mixed with bran and crushed oats. The hens also had this hot meal with some wheat and maize corn put on the ground for them to pick up. They also had ears of corn gleaning from the harvest field in summer. Both rabbits and hens had clean water daily, which would, on frosty nights turn to ice. For some reason which I never found out, if hot or warm water was put out, it always seemed to freeze over quicker than the cold.

The yard where the rabbits were sold belonged to Mr Gaze and the sale was held every Friday selling rabbits, chicken, eggs and anything of that nature. This yard was on the right-hand side of Shelfanger Road in Diss, a few hundred yards from Crown corner and is now a big car park. If we had any surplus eggs from our chickens we would sell them to a Mr Shave from Wyverstone near Stowmarket who came round on Friday morning with a little green lorry piled high with wooden egg boxes. He would collect from most households and small farms but Wednesday he would go to the big farms with a bigger lorry as they had lots of laying hens. He was well known for paying the best price for eggs whatever the time of the year.

By this time I had saved up enough money to buy myself a new bicycle, so one night I went to see Mr Madgett who had business in Victoria Road in Diss, repairing and selling new and second-hand cycles. I chose a brand new Hercules gent's cycle with an all-black frame with thin green lines on the frame and mudguard, chrome wheels, pedals and handlebars. This cost £14.00 but with trading the old cycle in I could just afford it. I used it for school for several years. I think that was one of the few new cycles being used for school. Most adults kept their bicycles for years. In those days only a few people had cars or motorbikes. Well time was going by and school was now more routine than important and I was looking forward to leaving.

The Cadet Period

I left school at fourteen years of age, just before Christmas 1942, to follow in the family footstep by getting a job at Hall Farm, Wortham, one of five farms owned by Mr Rash of Wortham Manor. I had been working there during the last summer holiday for a period of five weeks, helping with the harvest, so I had some insight as to what farm life was like, but what I had not allowed for was the fact that during the harvest in the summer the weather was mainly hot, sun beating down onto dry dusty soil, hardly any rain or cloudy days. What a different situation starting work in winter was, mud, ice, snow, cold, freezing winds, mainly from the north or east. Eating the midday meal under a hawthorn hedge in an otherwise open field was the usual thing. To eat inside a farm building was a real luxury, even if the cattle and pigs were the other side of the wall. There was a warm, sweet smell when sitting in a bale of straw or hay but I am writing more about this in a horse and farming side of the story.

Going back to the day I left school, I can clearly remember the headmaster calling us to his desk and giving us a really serious talk on the world of adult life that we were about to enter.

There were three of us leaving that day, one girl who was going to work at what is now the Co-op in Rickinghall, the other boy was going to work as an errand boy at Clarkes the bakers on Wortham Long Green, but was unable to leave for another six months because the Education Authority said that an errand boy was not a real job, and myself who as I said before, was to work on a farm. I must admit had I known then what I know now I would never have gone within miles of any farm. However, the headmaster's talk did impress on us that as it was wartime we should do something useful in our spare time.

Wortham at that time had an Army Cadet Force which used the school as their headquarters. This was made up of boys older than me, mostly from Wortham School and some from adjoining villages, Redgrave, Botesdale, Rickinghall and Mellis.

Most of the men working on the farm were in the Home Guard so in the course of working with them I let myself be persuaded to join the cadet force. After reporting at the school I was given a khaki uniform which fitted where it touched, complete with forage cap, hobnailed boots and khaki spats, which had to be blancoed every time they were worn. It was the same with the belt. The boots had to be polished and spooned and all brass buckles cleaned to a sparkling shine. I was taught to march in step with all the other boys and how to change step if required and how to march in line and all the other things required to be done in training.

Sometimes we did manoeuvres in the Long Green, crawling along ditches along bushes, covering our faces with grass and making ourselves blend in to the surroundings area as much as possible. It seemed to me that the sole purpose of the officer in charge was to get our uniforms as dirty as possible.

Another thing I learnt at that time was that when wearing uniform it did give everyone the right to swear as much as you liked, not always when you wanted to but at the ranks above you provided they did not hear. The other bad thing we were allowed to do was to smoke. I felt about ten feet tall when I bought my first packet of Greys cigarettes, but much worse after I had smoked two of them. I seemed to remember giving the rest away.

One weekend most of us were taken for a weekend course at the Old Convent at Woodbridge in a real army lorry with a real soldier driver. When we left Wortham that Saturday dinner time I reckon we could have won the war by ourselves that day. We were full of enthusiasm when going there. How disillusioned we were on the way back. When we got to this place there were army cadets from all over Suffolk there as well. I had never been shouted at nor had so many orders to obey in my life before. The whole thing was one big competition against each other. We were marched from one point to another, trying to get a better result for smartness and efficiency than anyone else. We did have a break for tea and then on to the assault course. Part of this was to climb over a twelve foot high wall with a Canadian rifle strapped to our backs. These things were about six foot long and seemed to weigh half a ton. This was done with some help from the other cadets. I soon found out it was better to be first than last on the course. The reason for this was that if you were first you did get help from the boys that were following. If you were last you got some help from someone laying on top of the wall and pulling you up. This gave your arm muscles a real stretching. This hurt for a few days after. However, everything was done in a fairly good humoured way. If I remember rightly we did have about an hour to go where we liked before lights out.

Now we had all been allocated one dormitory for so many boys to sleep in for one night. We were issued with two "biscuits" each. These were about three foot by three foot square, four inches deep canvas bags filled with straw. We also had one blanket each but no pillow. Your tunic jacket had to fulfil that purpose. With the "biscuit" laid on the floor to make a six foot by three foot bed, once you got under the blanket, which I am sure was made of porcupine fur, the chance of sleeping was about nil. About four of us had been allocated as fire pickets. One of this four was myself. Just after midnight smoke was detected in the building. The fire was found and put out without too much of a problem. Some twit could not tell the difference between a coat peg and an electric light bulb and they had hung their hat on the bulb and switched the light on.

After getting back to bed and the swear words had died down, you just had a chance to get some sleep before being woken up by shouting from the doorway. It was five o'clock in the morning and we all had to dress in just shorts and gym shoes and go down to the river for an early dip. Now knowing my past experience with water I had my doubts about going in the river but I soon found out that I had no choice in the matter because anyone not going in of their own accord was picked up and thrown in, whether you could swim or not did not matter. This was all part of the toughening up process. I must admit that we did feel warmer and fitter on the way back, totally different from the cold fresh air that made our teeth chatter on the march down to the river. After a very good breakfast, a wash and tidy up, back into uniform and drills and lectures, the morning was soon gone. We did have a meal at midday and afterwards an account was taken of all that had happened and points were given out. I can't remember where we came in this part of the proceedings but I do know it was not last. We had learned a lot about teamwork, the ability to help others, and enjoyed doing so. We left Woodbridge at about three o'clock and arrived back at Wortham around four o'clock in the afternoon. I was glad of my own bed that night and I have never been back to Woodbridge since.

Another outstanding incident happened on one Armistice Day in 1943. We had all been told to attend a remembrance service at Botesdale in the afternoon, so we had to meet near Rickinghall church. Most of us cycled over there ready to march through both of these villages to a service in the church hall in Botesdale. That particular Sunday morning dawned bright and sunny but with a cold wind from the west. The sun did not shine for long and the sky became very cloudy and by one o'clock a drizzly rain was starting to fall. By the time we started to march it was raining quite hard and the wind was getting stronger. As we passed Botesdale War Memorial the sky seemed to open and within a few minutes we were all soaked to the skin. Standing inside that hall during the service, wet and cold, we hoped that the weather would change before we had to march back to our meeting point. This was not so and if anything, it was raining harder. Trying to march with wet clothes was bad enough but the cycle home was even worse. Even our heavy boots were wet through but a good wash and a change to dry clothes soon made things seem better.

I was beginning to have doubts as to whether this was good thing to be in. As this was totally voluntary you could leave if you wanted to and after a few more evening attendances during which we were taught rifle cleaning and first aid I did just that. This went against the grain as far as the officers in charge were concerned but I was glad to hand back my uniform. My time was now my own and there was no more crawling around in the mud. If this was army life than I wanted no part of it but after a time of no commitment I began to look for something new to do. After a chat with some friends I decided to try something else and this was the start of a new era, totally different from the Army Cadets.

I told my friends about what life was like in the army cadets and why I could not see any advantage if I stayed in. So for a short while I carried on with other things until one day I was talking to some of my school pals who had chosen to join the Diss Air Training Corps (ATC) 1070, Squadron, and they suggested that I tried this out for myself by joining with them. They told me the advantages that could be gained by being part of this squadron. The uniform was much smarter, the buttons and badges were chrome and did not have to be cleaned like brass as they kept the same colour all the time. The bottom of the Air Force Blue uniform trousers were left loose over the top of the boots which were not the heavy type I had been wearing in the Army Cadets. These had to be kept clean and polished but as they did not get very dirty this was not a problem and I was told that a lot of the time a good sturdy pair of black shoes could be worn. I had never thought much about the ATC at that time but I was interested in the aircraft that were flying around. I had watched the air races in the mid thirties. Also I can remember going with my father on our cycles to watch an aeroplane giving pleasure flights (I think it was a Tiger Moth) from a meadow called Barley Birch, beside the 143 Bury St Edmunds road at Redgrave, opposite to Redgrave lake. This was the meadow on which the Rickinghall and Botesdale cricket club had their pitch, there were lots of people both watching and going for rides. The cost was 2/6 or 12 1/2p of today's money or 5/-, 25p, if you wanted to loop the loop, and that was as far as that point my knowledge of aircraft went. So after some very careful thought I decided that I would give it a try, and one Tuesday night I cycled to the ATC headquarters at Diss Grammar School.

I shall not ever forget that first evening but I cannot remember the exact date but that does not matter. I left my cycle near a wooden hut with some others and my pals told me to see the Commanding Officer, Ft Lt Fairs who day job was headmaster at that school. I walked in the main door and up the facing stairway to the big office and there sitting at a big desk was this rather thin faced man in uniform. I was told to sit down without him looking up as he seemed to be writing something in a book. I was beginning to have doubts if I should be here and what I had let myself in for. I did as he said and just then he finished writing, looked up and with a slight smile reached across the desk and with a hefty handshake told me who he was and asked me my name, where I lived and why I wanted to join the ATC. I told him that I had friends already in there and I was aware of what they done and was interested. What I did not know at the time was that you had a choice of what could be learnt. There were two sections of each squadron across the whole country, one was aircrew and the other was ground crew. I had no idea what the difference was at that time but I choose aircrew. Some of the boys had a quite a lot of flying I found out afterwards. I was measured for a uniform, complete with a forage cap. Footwear was black boots or stout shoes. This was on a Thursday night which was PT night. Tuesday was classroom night when the aircrew section learned about aircraft recognition, navigation, wind speed, types of cloud and everything to do with flying. The ground crew worked on aircraft

Diss ATC, 1070 Squadron

Disbanded 1946

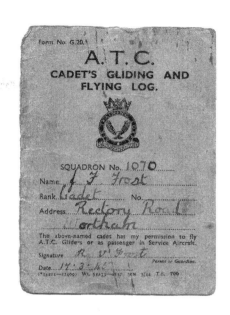

Form No. G.20.

A.T.C.
CADET'S GLIDING AND FLYING LOG.

SQUADRON No. **1070**

Name. *J. F. Frost*

Rank. *Cadet*   No.

Address. *Rectory Road*

Northall

The above-named cadet has my permission to fly A.T.C. Gliders or as passenger in Service Aircraft.

Signature *R. V. Frost*

Parent or Guardian.

Date. *17.3.46.*

(*14211—11409*) Wt. 52213—8147 50M 5/44 T.S. 700

FLYING LOG.

1948		AIRCRAFT		PILOT'S SIGNATURE Or Officer i/c.	DURATION	REMARKS
MONTH	DATE	TYPE	NUMBER			
Apr.	15	Mosquito VI	HR190	*R. Hughes F/o*	35 mins	V. good
Apr.	15	Anson	DJ-105	*R. Fowler P/o*	25 m	
May	20	Fortress	021	*J.L. Gallieh*	4hrs 45	over Germany
	28	Oxford	5276	*R. Gawler F/o*	15	
			5304	*R. Brown*	45	
	25	Stirling	7F-R	*F/o*	1.00	
			TG	*M. Hewitt c/o*		

1070 SQUADRON A.T.C.

The Welfare Committee, Officers and Cadets, request the pleasure of your company at a

Squadron Birthday Party

to be held on

Tuesday, March 19th, 1946, at 7 p.m.

in the Diss Church Hall

engines which were stored in the ground floor of Mr Hammond's garage in Mere Street where the Diss publisher company is now. Wednesday night was free unless there were extra things like rifle shooting in the drill hall in Sunnyside, now the headquarters of the modern ATC. Sunday mornings was a time of marching. Drill was the other thing that was concerned with discipline for all cadets. We always had a break halfway through the morning when the girls from the GTC (Girls Training Corps) made us cold drinks with something to eat in the summer and hot drinks and snacks in the winter.

Anyhow I done one Sunday morning marching in my own clothes and then my new uniform arrived which I took home and tried on straight away. I was pleased the way this uniform looked and it gave you the feeling of being one of the crowd and not the odd one out in civilian clothes. By this time I had met the other two officers who were there, one was a Mr Hodgerson who was the manager of Diss Co-op and the other was a Mr Hargreves who had a haulage contractor's business in Shelfanger and there was also a member of the Royal Observer Corps who was also a member of the ATC with the rank of Flying Officer, known to us all as Billy Cobb, who owned a cycle sales and repair shop on the left, halfway down St Nicholas Street in Diss. There were also two civilian men who helped at that time. One was a Mr Paterson' another schoolmaster at the Grammar School. He was the person who took us for sport and PT. We used the school gym on Thursday nights and school football field for matches on Saturday afternoons. The other man was Mr Wilfred Cattermole from Palgrave, I am not sure where he worked. It could have been at Mr Ford the wheelwright's or at Mr Howell the blacksmith's. Both businesses were on Palgrave Green. Wilf, as we called him, taught us model-engineering. We made model aeroplanes out of anything we could get our hands on, wood, metal, Perspex, wire and rubber. This was all done on Monday evening in the top floor of Hammond's garage, above the ground crew section. We also painted these aircraft in the proper finish, complete with all the required markings. Wilf was devoted to this job. He always gave a helping hand and good advice to anyone who wanted it. He also made models himself at home which he would bring in to show us and explain how it was done. I made a model Auster with real Perspex cockpit, wing struts and undercarriage from thin wire, painted silver with RAF markings.

My first Sunday morning parade in uniform was with the rest of the boys along Factory Lane, we turned left into Louies Lane then into Roydon Road and at Crown Corner, turned left into Shelfanger Road and back to our HQ at the grammar school. Most of the foot drill was done in Factory Lane. This came easy as I had been taught this in the army cadets, such as changing step while moving and all the other things like everyone's arms had to move in the same direction at the same time and how to space each person the same distance apart by putting your arm at full length and just touching the next person on the left of you with the tips of your fingers. I enjoyed all this and even more so with my well fitting air force uniform with chrome buttons and cap badge. The only thing I disliked was that every cadet had to take these Sunday morning parades and drill the whole squad under the watchful eye of an officer. I was not at all sure that someone new should do this but I soon found out that this was part of the training and there was nothing you could do about it. So I buckled down, gaining more confidence all the time.

I had my uniform about two weeks when we were told that the next Sunday, would be an airfield visit which meant that we would be away for the whole day. In the days coming up to this Sunday I was given a flying log for my father's signature to be put on the front, which enabled me to fly in any military aircraft. I had no idea what this was for but it appeared that if you were in the aircrew section you would be detailed to fly in certain planes. Some of the other boys told me what they had flown in and how high they had been. There was a lot of banter about the sick bag and how to use it. Well the Sunday morning came and with some apprehension I boarded the hired coach with all the other boys for the journey to Fersfield airbase which was a small airfield between Shelfanger and the Lophams. Now I did know that there had been aircraft of different sorts stationed there as they flew low over our house at Wortham as they took off and came into land but I must admit I had some doubt about actually flying as the highest I had ever been was on top of a hay stack on a thatching ladder. Well we arrived at the airfield by the back entrance over Shelfanger Common. As we arrived in front of the big hangar there were aircraft standing on dispersal points around the various parts of the airfield and some around and in the hangar. We all stood in line until we were told to break ranks. I noticed that most of the planes were Mosquitos with Anson and a Harvard. I was told that I would be flying with F/0 R A Nock in Mosquito HR 190, code name D-Dog. After going into the parachute store where I was fitted with a RAF harness for the parachute, which was given to me after it was explained how to fit it and how to get out of it by turning the centre fitting clockwise, if the need should arrive. To me, having never seen a folded parachute before, I was concerned about what would happen if I had to use it but at that time I would not admit it. The instruction given was very good and I felt a bit better until one of the WAAF's said that if I had to use it and if it did not open, to take it back and they would replace it. That sort of humour was not really encouraging to a sixteen year old boy about to take his first flight in a military aircraft.

All that over and we walked across to the Mosquito parked near the hangar. The aircraft was entered by a ladder and through the door near the nose and I think the small ladder was stored inside the cockpit and parachutes were stored in the positions as required in the cockpit. The pilot was a very talkative and helpful man, explaining everything that I should know very carefully. I was to do a visual navigation to get the aircraft to fly over the centre of Norwich. Well the Rolls Royce Merlin engines started with a burst of smoke and flame lasting only a few seconds. As this aeroplane was made of wood I had the awful feeling of whether I should be doing this but I had to quickly dismiss the thought that flame and wood don't mix. By this time we were steadily making our way around to the end of the runway. Standing on the grass just off the edge of the tarmac was the airfield controller's hut painted in black and white squares. With engines running nice and steady the throttle was pushed forward and both engines burst into full revs, rocking the plane gently and then a green flare was fired from the airfield controller's hut and I can remember the pilot looking at me with a thumbs up we were off. There certainly was no turning back now as we were gathering speed down the runway and we were airborne.

I watched as the pilot moved certain switches and the undercarriage came up, and then to my surprise the pilot's right arm came along the back of my neck and turned a valve beside me, which I was later told was the main fuel supply to the engines. There was a reason for this. It was 100 percent octane, which is pure petrol that these aircraft flew on, so when you were taking off there was only a small amount could be used and the main supply was turned on when airborne. A safety reason was why this was done. The engines were throttled back and were running, with a steady purr and the plane turned to starboard in level flight of 1,500 feet. I was supposed to tell the pilot the way to Norwich but for a short time it did take a little getting used too. I looked and the houses seemed to be the size of matchboxes. I felt certain that he knew the way and then I realise that we were over Thetford

ATC Cap Badge

forest and Honnington airfield could be seen down to the left. I found it hard to believe that that was what flying was like as such a vast area could be seen. Anyway we were heading over Bury St Edmunds out towards the east coast and over Stowmarket. I could see the London to Norwich railway line and we turned and followed the line into Norwich. As we were flying over the city the bomb damaged building could be seen quite clearly, also to the east the coastline of Great Yarmouth stood out. At that point I don't know what height we were flying at as I was completely amazed what it was like. There were a few bumps which were caused by the air conditions but I was pleased with this new experience.

As we came back the pilot who had been talking most of the flight asked me if I lived anywhere near here. We were over Diss where the Mere stood out very clearly. Over Wortham ling what surprised me was how clear the little pathways that were the cycle tracks were, weaving from one side to the other they looked like white ribbons. I could see the red tiles on top of our house which I pointed out and the pilot gave a nod and said we will go down and have a look. With that the aircraft started to climb to what height I don't know, but I was beginning to feel strange as the plane turned to the left and my knees seemed to go past my ears. This was my first experience of G-Force when the body pressure increases as turns get sharper and speed increases. However as we levelled out and dropped into a gentle dive, I could see the house roof getting closer and we passed over at about six hundred foot, I could see my father standing in the garden and with a wiggle of the wings we headed back for Fersfield and done a complete circuit of the airfield. The undercarriage was lowered and at 180 mph the runway seemed to be coming toward us until the tyres touched the concrete and the aircraft slowed right down and the propellers were just turning. We stopped at the same placed we left, and the engines stopped. Everything was quiet as I sat and relaxed in the navigator's seat. So this was flying and I really enjoyed it.

We both walked back to return our parachutes to the store with the pilots talking about the flights and way things were done. I was privileged to have had my first flying experience with such a understanding man and in one of the RAF's finest aircraft. The flying log was signed and we went our separate ways. I went into the mess hall for something to eat and drink and the rest of the day was spent with some of the other boys who had been flying. A few had been using their sick bags, having the mickey taking out of them. After which we all got on the bus and returned to the Grammar School where we all formed up on the tarmac roadway and were dismissed and went home.

There were many flights after the first one from this airfield, mainly in Mosquitos, and some rather low but exciting. It was normal to fly just above ground or sea level when the windscreen wipers had to be used to clean off the spray from the waves as we were sometimes as low as twenty feet above the water. Over land we often did what we called hedge hopping which was flying as low as possible to the ground. We even went under the telephone wires if they crossed open fields. The secret of this was to get as near the pole as possible as this was the highest point the lowest being the centre point between two poles. We also flew up rivers and across lakes, just above the water where possible. We flew on one engine sometimes to do experimental landings and although I did not know at the time but I have learned since that this was a dangerous thing to do but we were only young boys and I don't think fear was a word we understood at that age. The highest I flew in a Mosquito was ten thousand, feet just on or just below oxygen mask level and the view from that level was interesting. On one flight we could see dark clouds with rain pouring down from them, so we could easily avoid them and on another we were above the clouds which looked like a layer of cotton wool. There was always an adrenalin rise feeling about the flights in this particular aircraft but some flights had a move serious side to them and in my opinion the less said about those the better.

There were also several flights done from Shepherds Grove, an airfield beside the A143 Bury St Edmunds road, just before the village of Stanton. These were in Stirling bombers, one of which had the number TFR and another was TG. These very interesting flights and one particular flight will always stay in my memory. We had all met together after having a hot dinner in the mess and there were certain cadets picked out to fly in different aircraft and I was told to collect a parachute as I was flying in one that was doing engine testing out over the sea. I think there were four or five of us, including two young lads from Burston, who had never flown before. I think that they were a bit nervous by what they were saying. The pilot of the Stirling was a Canadian and this was his last flight as he was going back to Canada the next day. We took off and we were in the waist of the plane but when we got airborne we could go where we liked, within reason of course. The pilot let me and three others, including the new boys, go down into the bomb aimer position in the nose. We had a very good view of the ground under us as we flew across the countryside. I remember seeing two large, what looked like swimming pools, as we went over Southend and out over the sea. As the plane gained height we could see the wires on pulleys working the controls. We got to the top of the climb and one of the aircrew said that they were going to test the engines and with that the No 1 port engine stopped, then No 4 starboard, next was No 2 port and last of all No 3 starboard and we seemed to be drifting with just the wind whistling through the aerial. The two new boys faces began to change from a pinky colour to a very fearful look of pure white and then to grey. I am sure they felt a bit sick but they held on. Then after what seemed an eternity the nose was dropping down, No 3 engine started up and we levelled out and flew on one engine for a little while and then one by one they all started up. With what appeared to be the engine testing over the pilot said he would go wherever we wanted to go so we decided to fly down the Suffolk and Norfolk coastline and as we came over the sea at Southwold I could see a man sitting on the end of the pier fishing

I said to the pilot that I had done that many times myself. His reply was that we had better go down and take a look ourselves and with that he turned out to sea dropping down just over the waves and flying straight for the front end of the pier and with that the man threw his rod down and ran for the opposite end of the pier, much to our amusement, and so we continued around the coast up as far as the start of the Yorkshire border and then turned inland and flew across country back to Shepherds Grove and landed.

The next flight I had on a Stirling I was lucky because most of the boys had been chosen and were already on their way to the plane riding on a bomb trolley that was being pulled by an RAF David Brown tractor painted in air force blue. They were going round the perimeter track when I was told that I could go, I didn't stop for a parachute this time but I had to run across a lot of ploughed land to catch up with the tractor which I did .I climbed onto the bomb trolley and arrived at the Stirling and only then did we all realise that this flight was going to be different because behind the plane stood a troop-carrying Horsa glider. These were wooden aircraft with no engine at all but with very big wings. I had never seen one so close before and I did not realise how big they were. Well the Stirling started its engines and taxied around to the end of the runway with the glider behind it. I and the other boys were very interested to see something pulled by an aeroplane but we never did find out if the towing cable was a thick rope or made of wire. Anyhow the engines were revving at full throttle and we started to move forward down the runway. I was in the front as we left the ground but once we were airborne two of us moved to the waist and then down to the tail gun turret. To look out and see this big Horsa glider following us is something I will never forget. It was flying at the same level but it was not flying straight but swinging from to side to side and going out wider as it followed the aircraft on the turns. The pilot of the glider could be seen from the Stirling. We flew a long way over Thetford forest and out to the coastline over Cromer, turned and came back inland till we were over the airfield where we done a few circles before releasing the glider. To be above these gliders as they go down is an amazing sight to see. I had seen them land when we had been on the airfield before, sometimes quite close to them. They have a special way of landing. They circle around after being released getting lower all the time and then at a certain height they put their nose down in a vertical position and when they are about three hundred feet from the ground they level out and land with a roaring of wind caused by the aircraft going through the air. As soon as the wheels touch the ground they stop within a few yards.

Some ATC boys were killed when a glider crashed into the ground because someone didn't make sure the seats were bolted down securely and all the boys and the crew fell into the nose and the glider could not level out and land and for that reason no ATC boys were allowed to fly in any military glider. I never did know where this happened other than it was a London squadron on an airfield in that part of the country. Well our glider tow ended safely and so did the Stirling, stopping at the place we started from.

On another Stirling flight we were rather late taking off in the afternoon and this time we flew up towards the north of the country and were airborne for nearly three hours and when we came back a really nasty fog had formed and this did cause some concern when we landed, but we had a good pilot and he knew exactly what to do. I also had one short flight in a DC3 Dakota from the same airfield and this was one steady aeroplane to fly in. This was the workhorse of both the British and American air forces. One particular flight was from Downham Market in a Lancaster bomber, this plane was painted with a white fuselage under the body and wings and all the top half black. We went out over the North Sea on this trip but this was only a short time in the air but at least I had flown in a Lancaster. On this airfield we did a lot of link trainer practice. I was not to keen on these things. They were small, claustrophobic and very jerky, not a nice ride at all, but it had to be done. We had several visits back to Fersfield and flying in Mosquitos became normal routine. There were flights in other aircraft and I remember one flight in an Avro Anson or Faithful Annie, as the nick name for these planes was. When we flew over the Horsham Airfield, which was the base for American 95th Bomb Group which was flying B17 Flying Fortress from there, we flew very low along their main runway much to the amazement of the airmen there. Another flight I had was in an Airspeed Oxford this was Norfolk, Suffolk and Cambridge. Both these planes were slow flying and the engines did make quite a bit of noise but we were airborne and that to us was the most important thing.

One particular flight I shall never forget was a few days after the end of the war and a May Bank holiday Monday. A few of us boys agreed to meet at Eye Airfield. I saw this airfield being built in 1942 by American soldiers of an Engineer Battalion. We all cycled over to Eye and as we had put our ATC uniforms on it was the policy of the American Air force to let you onto the base and if there was a plane going up they would let you fly with them. We learned on that afternoon there were three B17s going up we were told when we went inside the control tower that one was going to Scotland, one was doing engine test and one was going over the continent. Three boys wanted to go to Scotland, two wanted to go on the engine test which left five of us to go on the trip over Europe, but we did not know where. That afternoon the sun, as we cycled to Eye, was beginning to get a bit clouded over and surround by what the country people called a burrow, which is a large or small circle of cloud with the sun in the centre. This was a very large circle and folklore saying was large burrow near rain small burrow far rain. The same thing applies to the moon at night. We had been taught about clouds, their names and formation in the classroom at the Grammar School, also working and living in the country we got to read the weather very well. I had a nasty feeling that the bright sunshine we had in the morning was not coming back that day. Anyhow the five of us left were Tom Emms,

Dennis Noble, Gordon Harbour, Tony Sealy and me. We were taken into the parachute room and fitted with the American harness, which was quite different from the RAF harness, which was easy to get out of but not the American. This fitted with hooks and buckles. I should think getting out of quickly was quite a job. I must admit I did not like wearing this harness. We got into a jeep near the control tower with the crew of the plane and started to drive along to the perimeter track to the dispersal point of our plane. One of the crew lost his hat and the jeep came to a very quick halt. The cap was picked up and we were off again. We arrived at the plane which was parked near the A140 road. This B17 number 084 was called Hunny Bunny and had a big pink rabbit painted on the nose. We got out of the jeep and I looked at the crew, thinking to myself that these airmen were not much older that I was. We found out later that the average age of these men was only twenty and yet they had been through so much. Well as we were getting into the aircraft the other two planes took off with the other boys on board and we took our places inside the plane. I was in the front and could see out very well. We taxied around to the end of the runway and awaited the signal to take off. The four Wright Cyclone engines started to gain full power and we were moving down the east to west main runway gaining speed all the time and then I saw something that I had not noticed before as straight in front of us was Eye church tower, but we were airborne and cleared the church tower and the town of Eye stretched out below us.

The railway station was clearly visible with the single track winding its way back under the A140 to join the mainline from Norwich to London at Mellis junction. It was this line that brought in lots of goods for the airfield and I can remember steam trains pulling a lot of wagons down this line and the driver had to get out and open the gates at the road crossing then close them again after driving through. The engine was not always used as it was downhill all the way from Mellis to Eye And if there was a single wagon to go down to Eye this would be given a gentle push by the engine at Mellis and a man would walk beside it to control the brake by a long metal handle fitted to the wagon, stopping when required, its own weight would start it off again and eventually it would arrive at Eye.

Anyhow we were now flying at about 1000 feet high and were going in a big circle with the airfield still visible as we were now coming from south to north over the A140 and looking down to the left I saw a big farm with a moated farmhouse at the bottom of a big park. I did not know at that time that in the future this was where I would work for nine years. I also saw the rectory at Wortham and the cottage which was my home. Several places that I had known all my life were clearly seen. I had told my parent where I was going to try and get a flight but where the destination was I didn't know at that time. It was about 3pm when we took off and we could now see the coastline and the English Channel in front of us. I had flown over the sea several times but not as high as we were now although I can not remember what that was.

I know we were doing just over 200 mph much slower than the Mosquito. We had a good chance to look at the surface of the waves being broken by a continual line of white foam. We were now getting out of the thin layer of cloud that was over us when we took off and the sun was beginning to shine making the sea sparkle. This was very interesting as the pilot had turned in his seat and was reading what looked like a book. He said that George was flying the plane. This was the name given to the automatic pilot. It was not long before the coast of Holland came into view and with that the view started to change. Large parts of the countryside were under water and all the houses, trees and farm building were flooded and practically out of sight, only the tops of the church spires and the tops of the windmills could be seen clearly. This had been done by the Germans as they retreated under pressure from the invading allied army. They breached the banks of the canals to cause as much disruption as possible. But not all Holland was flooded. There were parts where the green meadows, trees, houses and even grazing animals could be seen. On one big green meadow we were looking down and could see a bright silver Stirling which appear to have done a wheels up landing as the body and the wings didn't appear to be damaged at all.

As we carried on the steady drone of the engines and what we could see made this a very interesting flight and it was not long before we were crossing from Holland to Germany and then the view on the ground began to change. We were flying over an autobahn, which is a long straight wide road which seemed to go on for miles. One thing that was a bit frightening looked like little flashing lights but one of the crew members said this was caused by the sun shining on broken glass. The crew told us what certain things were that we flew over. There was a rail marshalling yard and the whole area was full of bomb craters and no complete railway lines at all, lots of damaged rolling stock lying all around and no building left standing at all. There were some of the fields in parts of the country that had a concentration of large bombs craters in one corner or along one side. We were told that had been a searchlight or anti-aircraft gun emplacement. There was nothing left of those at all either. We were by now flying up the river Rhine and the damage along here was sheer devastation. The roads came up to each side of the river to parts of bombed bridges and with some there was a bit of bridge left in the middle of the river but not one complete bridge anywhere. At one place a flare factory was on fire with it flares exploding everywhere, reds, greens and yellows coming up into the air. I could not see anything trying put the fire out. We came to the city of Cologne and there was devastation as far as you could see and it was at this part of the river Rhine where every bridge was destroyed, even worse than we seen before. The railway yards were nothing but massive bomb craters. The roads had disappeared under rubble and it was at this point that we dropped down from 2000ft to 300ft and flew low over this city. We done two or three circles around the cathedral with it pointed towers just below us. What the crew could not understand, we could see very little damage on this building itself but the most amazing thing was amongst all this rubble stood one house without a tile off at all. We found out later that this was the bishop's house and it was the policy of the German people that the bishop should always have a roof over his head, so any damage done was quickly repaired.

We changed course and set off towards the Belgian border, but while we were still over Germany we had gained height and were flying at around two and half thousand feet but there was still plenty to see. At one big town we saw two massive gas storage tanks with the tops looking like two big spiders webs the only difference being that both these had a big hole in each top where a bomb had gone through these we saw on a photo taken by a Mosquito pilot at a later date, shown at one of our evening classes at the Grammar School. We were asked how we saw these tanks and it did cause a bit of a stir as according to this officer we should not have been over there. We also flew over Essen where the devastation was again very bad for miles around but despite all this one tall factory chimney stood up amongst all the large destroyed buildings and painted from top to bottom in very large letters was the word KRUPPS. I believe this was a firm that made ball bearings. Another part of the flight while we were still over Germany we saw in two different places large fenced-in areas. There were a lot of large brick buildings with lines of small huts also a lot of military vehicles around. One member of the crew pointed out that a lot of the small huts were on fire and the smoke could be seen drifting across the countryside. He told us that this was Belsen, one of the concentration camps, and the other was intact with no burning buildings but still with a lot of military vehicles about the camps and the same sort of building inside a large fence. Both of these had some wooded area around them.

Well while we carried on flying the weather was getting bad, bright sunshine had been replaced by gathering dark clouds. We were now over Belgium and all we could see was countryside with damaged buildings, roads and railways, and it started to rain, very light at first and it was at the point the pilot told us that they had received a bad weather warning. We knew that something was wrong because the flying was getting a bit bumpy. We were told to wear our parachutes and were given crash instructions. Three blasts on a hooter, if this changed to one long blast bale out. Three green lights, if this changed to red bale out. We had been told that we could look over the plane if we wanted too. The rain was now beating down very heavily. Gordon Harbour and I had a look in the bomb bay and then made our way along to the waist gun positions. It was at this point that we became a bit scared because not only was it raining it also seemed to us to be hailing as well. Then there was a terrific flash of lightening and a crash of thunder. We looked out of the windows and it looked like each time there was a flash of lightening sparks seemed to shoot off the tips of the wings and it was very bumpy by this time. At times it seemed the plane stood on the tail. Then we heard a noise in the fuselage and saw what appeared to be a massive rugby ball being inflated, we learnt later that this was a float to keep to aircraft from sinking if it crashed into the sea. We heard the three blasts on the hooter and just looked at each other and nothing was said. It was at this point with the plane doing all sorts of bumps and turns, and still very heavy rain, that there was a very bright flash of lightening followed immediately by the loudest clap of thunder I have ever heard and then everything went black and we both knew we were dropping straight down towards the sea. There had not been any order to bale out but this was not funny. I had my eyes shut when I was thrown across the plane and my legs seemed very heavy and the reason for this was that I had what appeared to be two electric motors across both legs. I pushed them off and looked for Gordon and he was on the floor covered nearly all over by 50 calibre machine gun bullets. I pulled him up and moved the bullets. There were other things that had been thrown around the plane all lying on the floor. We could hear the engines pulling hard and we looked out of the window. The rain had nearly stopped but much to our surprise we appeared to be just over the top of the waves. We both remarked how low we were. It was decided to go back to the cockpit to find out what had happened but we could feel the plane climbing to gain height. There was a lot of talking going on amongst everyone and we found out that we had hit an air pocket and dropped 2000 feet in one go. Everyone seemed shocked at what had happened but we were now flying a level course for home.

By now the rain had stopped and the sun had started to shine again and the English Channel was clearly in view and just off the coast was a convoy of ships sailing in line from south to north. That was the best sight I have ever seen in my life. It made you feel much safer knowing that there were other people around. We came in over the Suffolk coastline. I think it was over or very near Dunwich and Laxfield could be seen down to our right, and then very quickly Eye airfield was below us. We circled over the surrounding area and got permission to land. We were now dropping down nice and slowly and the runway was in sight, the wheels touched the tarmac with two puffs of smoke and the engines were throttled back and we moved along to our dispersal point near the A140. We had stopped and each engine propeller idled to stop. Hunny Bunny 084 had got us back safely. I think the crew and all us boys were glad to be on the ground and the time from take off to landing was four hours and twenty five minutes, a much longer flight than I had ever done before. We all stood on the tarmac and waited for a jeep to come and collect us. The crew all said that it was the worst storm they had ever been in and they were scared themselves but they would not tell us because they were afraid one of us might panic. However with our log books signed and a jeep ride back to the control tower we left our parachutes in the Jeep and went our separate ways.

I have always felt that the pilot Ft Lt Goldish saved our lives that day. We had a few worrying moments but what an experience. We learned that our aircraft was the only one to complete its mission that day. The one on engine tests had an engine catch fire and had return to base and the one going to Scotland also hit bad weather and decided to turn back to base. My parents were worried when I did not turn up for tea and my father was walking up the garden path when he saw a B17 circling round over the Eye direction and was pleased when I turned up back home. They also had a thunder storm.

I don't know what he would have said if he had been told about some of our Mosquito flights. I had a few more flights in various aircraft from Fersfield after that but the purpose was not as urgent as far the ATC to RAF was concerned and the Diss 1070 Squadron was disbanded a short while after 1946. We had to take our uniforms to an empty shop on the left hand side of Market Hill but I kept a flying log and a cap badge which I still have. This was not the end of flying as a friend and I did a trip in a four seater Auster along the Norfolk coast one Sunday afternoon. I never did know if he enjoyed it or not as I sat in the front with the pilot and every time I looked back at him his eyes were shut. The take off and landing was on a grass strip and very bumpy. A lot of years passed and on the 31 August 2003 I had my first flight in a helicopter. The next year on 20 June 2004 I had great pleasure in taking our youngest grandson, Matty, on his first flight, also in a helicopter. We liked it so much we did this again last year. Well so much for all the time spent and friends made, a most enjoyable time, which I hope I shall never forget and I will continue to fly whenever the chance comes along.

Wartime ATC members made trips to Holland

Mystery pictures from previous Memory Lanes continue to provide debate across the world. The latest letter winged its way all the way from New Zealand and concerns the Diss Express of August 24, which had a picture of Diss Air Training Corps.

Sqd Ldr Tom Hughes, a retired member of the RAF, wrote to say he could not identify any of the people in the picture but did send details of his service with 1070 (Diss and District) ATC Squadron during the Second World War.

He wrote; "I was a member from 1942 to 1945, an exciting period for a young man of 14. During this time the squadron was attached to many local RAF stations and we had regular visits for flying activities to both RAF and USAAF stations such as Fersfield, Shepherds Grove and Tuddenham as well as American stations at Eye, Thorpe Abbotts and Mendlesham where we had trips aboard aircraft of all types such as B25 Mitchell, Mosquito, B17 Fortress, B24 Liberator and Stirling bombers with Horsa gliders in tow."

"These were great times for us aspiring air cadets, a few were even taken on operational trips over Holland to drop food to the beleaguered Dutch people. "Our ground school evenings were taken up with lessons on airmanship, navigation, and principles of flight given by RAF officers and foot drill and PT. We particularly enjoyed the annual summer camps at local RAF stations and we were very proud to be a part of the local RAF."

"Drill was practiced regularly for parades and visits and we loved it all. A few NCO cadets were selected for flying training on gliders, (I was one of the fortunate cadets) which we carried out every Sunday at Bury St Edmunds for six months. That was really great fun."

"I eventually left to do my National Service in the RAF as a pilot, being granted a commission from the Queen in 1952, one of the first to be commissioned by Queen Elizabeth II in February of that year."

"I made a full career in the RAF until 1985, having served for 34 years, retiring as a squadron leader in the service I grew to love and be very proud of."

Mr Hughes is now a resident of Papakura, New Zealand, but used to live at The Wigwam, Wortham.

The Shooting, Poaching and Fishing Story

Although I had at odd times been out with my father when he went shooting, I had always been kept in the background but even so, by careful watching and listening I had started to learn the art of catching rabbits and pheasants. I was about seven when my grandfather explained to me what a catapult was and how to use it. Now there was a very dangerous weapon if used incorrectly, as it was almost silent when used. A lot of men working on farms always carried a catapult in their pockets as this was their tickets to an easy meal and was as important to them as belt and braces. Now you could buy a ready made catapult from almost any ironmonger's shop but these were frowned upon by the experts and by experts I mean the men like my grandfather who always said that he could shoot an eye out of a gnat from a hundred yards away.

The shop catapults were all made the same and was only good for knocking tin cans off gates. They had a flat metal with a crotch on top with a hole in each upright. The inside of this crotch was shaped like a half circle and was not very wide across from inside to inside and for this reason any big stone used as ammunition would sometimes hit the upright and be the cause of a very sore thumb or rebound and hit you in the face creating some rather strong words not taught at school. The elastic used on these was about a quarter of an inch wide and eleven to twelve inches long. Two pieces of this were used, one end of each fitted to the two holes in the crotch, folded to the uprights and tied with a thin string. The other end was done the same but tied to a small piece of soft leather. As people's arms are not all the same length these manufactured catapults were not easy to use and had to be adapted for personal use but the catapults used by the farm workers were a very different story.

These were made to each individual's own requirements as following the elastic used in these were brought from the ironmonger's who stocked this in rolls and you could buy as much as you required as this was sold by the foot (12 inches) minimum length. This was also very different from the browny/ grey sold with the manufactured catapults. This was a dark black rubber which gave off a smell like a new car tyre. The crotch was special piece of hazel wood cut from the hedge and shaped like a Y. The top of the uprights were split with a pocket knife and the elastic was put into each split and folded around and then tied with a length of waxed thread used for repairing boots. The leather at the other end was made from a tongue cut out of an old boot. It was soft to hold and very flexible. This gave a very firm grip with the first finger and the thumb of the left hand. The crotch was made by two branches growing out of one piece of wood. This did give a much better opening for a stone to go through, and the stones were picked up off fields or gardens and were as round as possible and about the size of a large hazelnut. The most prized ammunition was found on a visit to the local garage when we collected used, steel, shiny ball bearings about half an inch across. These were used for pheasants and partridges only and were deadly accurate.

It was not long before I had made a catapult of my own with a little help from my grandfather. With each shot I was gaining more confidence and a few dented cans and one very sore thumb due to an over big stone. My lust trying this thing got the better of me and anything that moved ran the risk of being shot at. I was about ten at this time and trips around the meadows and gardens belonging to the Rectory, catapult in hand, were an almost daily routine. Although a trip onto other people's property was not ruled out if the opportunity arose.

Our family had permission to shoot on all the rectory land, the lawns, the gardens, the tennis court meadow and some of the fields adjoining the meadows. There were also two medium sized woods. One was full of tall fir trees and the other was all mixed trees, ash, oak, elm and a lot of hazelnut bushes also plenty of brambles, wild roses, blackthorn and elder. This particular wood had a thick hawthorn hedge around its outside boundary and the shape of the wood was like a long triangle with two very big oaks and two high Scots firs at the pointed end. A lot of these trees had ivy growing on them, as had the boundary hedge. Now this was ideal pigeon and rabbit country. In the centre of this wood was a big, deep hole but it was not a pond, at no time was there any water in it. Ivy and nettles grew amongst the ground elder. On one side of this hole stood a massive gnarled oak tree. It must have been hundreds of years old as some of the top branches never had any leaves on and were favourite perches for pigeons, and sometimes an owl. Rabbits had burrows in the sides of the banks and sometimes if you were careful you could see them out during daytime but they were a cautious lot and disappeared at the slightest noise. The other wood was a very different situation as this was a spare piece of land at the bottom of the rectory kitchen garden and was therefore enclosed by a mixed hedge enclosing a metal fence consisting of round half inch rods fitted through half by two inch uprights. This fence and hedge was all round the garden of about an acre of land. The trees here were nearly all tall pine trees with a few odd elder bushes and stumps from old trees covered in ivy. The ground cover was mostly tall nettles and ground elder and because this area was at the bottom of the kitchen garden this was the dumping ground for rubbish, cabbage stalks, potato tops and hedge cuttings, this became a ready larder for the rabbits and there was quite a lot of burrows in this area. Now in all this time I was getting better at using my catapult and it was in this wood that I shot my first rabbit.

I was walking very careful and watching for any movement in the undergrowth when I saw a rabbit sitting under a tuft of grass. With a nice round stone in my catapult I stood still and very slowly pulled back the elastic taking aim by shutting my left eye, why I did this I don't know as a catapult has not got a sight like a gun. I let go of the leather releasing the stone and with a dull thud it hit the rabbit. It was totally amazed and shocked at what had happened. I picked this rabbit up and went straight home and was given three pence for it by my father. It was put with some he had caught and later sold to a butcher. But this did not happen again when I found out that the butcher was paying two shillings for each rabbit. Also about that time the other boys and I were shooting with our parents' air guns.

They were all different makes and ours was a Diana air gun No 1 which fired a small Black Boy lead slug. Our targets were match boxes, old tins or posts. We sometimes made targets from an opened cigarette box drawing circles with a small dot in the centre and we would see who could hit the middle. These guns were not very powerful and if you shot at a pigeon the slug would roll off its feathers. There were two other airguns being used by people at that time they were No 2 and No 3, each firing a slightly larger lead pellet than the No 1. Our family did not own any of these larger guns.

Confidence was increasing all the time and by the time I was ten I was at last allowed to use the small four-ten single barrel gun. This fired two different cartridges, a short cartridge for vermin (rats) and a long cartridge for rabbits and pigeons, and it could get a pheasant if it was close enough. The big advantage of this gun was that it could be folded up and hidden inside a big jacket, it was light to carry and there was not too much kick when fired, but if fired in woodland there were a sharp crack echoing throughout the trees. Many hours were spent walking around farm land with the gun under my jacket as we had not permission to shoot on this land. The gun was only brought out from under my jacket when I knew that what ever was shot could be picked up and put in the big pocket inside the jacket and an escape made onto somewhere safe very quickly.

By this time I had grown older and very much wiser and was now using my father's double barrel twelve bore shotgun. This gun had quite a kick when fired and each barrel had its own use. The right hand barrel would spread the shot at short distances but the left barrel was called the choke barrel and was designed to hold the shot together for at least one hundred yards before letting it spread out, this was independent of whatever cartridge was being used or whatever the shot size was. This was a hammer gun so it could be set ready to fire at any time but this was something dangerous to do if you were not careful. It was also one of a pair purpose made in Scotland for my father and his brother, but as his brother was slightly taller the barrels on his gun were a quarter of an inch longer.

As I learned more about poaching and earning extra cash from selling rabbits and game, this then became a running battle with the local gamekeeper who was a naturally crafty person due to his job, and it was very satisfying to know how to pull a fast one over him. I must say at this point what I had learned from my father and grandfather had helped me in keeping out of his way but I must have to admit he did get too close for comfort sometimes. Like the morning I shot a cock pheasant and had just picked it up when I saw him through a gap in the hedge across a neighbouring field coming straight for me. I was next to a pond full of thick bulrushes, and I had no choice but to jump into the edge of the water and keep out of sight in the rushes and wait for him to go past. It was a bit painful as one finger on my right hand caught between one of the triggers and the trigger guard and the whole weight of the gun twisted on that one finger. I had a large lump come up on the inside of that finger and it stayed there for years. I heard his footsteps pass within a few yards and then fade away into the distance. He was wearing Wellington boots and these made a slumping noise on the grass of the meadow around the pond. I was lucky he did not have his dogs with him, one was a black retriever and the other was a brown and white spaniel either of which would have found me I have no doubt about that. I had one disadvantage that day as I was also wearing Wellington boots (Dunlop Bullseye) and the freezing cold water filled them when I jumped into the pond. When I thought it was safe to move I very steadily made my way out of the pond with the pheasant in one hand and my gun in the other, my boots making a noise like the tide coming in with every step I took. It was not wise to stop and empty any water out until I was on safe property. To be caught with a boot off would have been disastrous.

I really enjoyed a walk around the fields and woods with this particular gun at this age as there was a purpose and responsibility attached to it, like earning some extra money and also some extra food on the table. I did get a gun licence but never a game licence, this was an unnecessary cost as far as our family was concerned. There were always plenty of rabbits about in those days. Some would sit under the shelter of an overhanging bush on the side of a ditch, or under a big tuft of grass on a bank or in a meadow. These places were called seats and were used on regular basics by the same rabbits. If you saw an empty seat anywhere it paid to keep an eye on it as sooner or later it would be occupied.

Some rabbits would dig a short burrow in a ploughed field and these were easy to catch. What we did was to guess where the rabbit would be by the amount of soil dug out at the entrance to the hole. We then sealed the hole by stamping a foot over the top soil and squashing it flat, and then with a stick from the hedge we poked into the ground. You could trace the rabbit's position if the stick was hard to push it was going through the soil, when it went in easily it had gone into the rabbit's hole. The rabbit could be found when the stick appeared to spring back in your hand. There would nearly always be fur from the rabbit's coat on the end of the stick. It was then you could take out the soil from above the rabbit, put your hand in and lift the rabbit out, and then holding it by its back legs and giving a sharp quick blow with the side of your hand behind its ears you made sure its running days were over.

Rabbits caught this way were the ones most favoured for the cooking pot at home as there was no lead shot in them. One had to be careful with these holes as in the spring lots of rabbits dug out these short burrows and made nests in the ends of them. You could always tell if there was a nest by cutting a small barbed bramble or a rough edge of a stick, if it came out of the ground with a lot of soft white fur on the end then it was a nest and the hole was left. There was no useful purpose from our point of view to destroy a nest. Also one had to be careful if you put your hand near it because the rabbits would smell that something was wrong and abandon the nest. We did keep a watch on these nests and it was always a pleasure to see the small fluffy rabbits appear outside these small burrows.

There appeared to be two types of rabbits in the countryside in those days. There were the ones that, as I have just written, lived on top or just under the surface of the soil and those that lived in a colony within a warren. This is a big collection of deep burrows mainly in sandy soil on a steep bank or around the edge of a dry pond; some were even in old meadowland or woodland. The surface rabbits were mostly individual living their life mainly on their own, but the warren rabbits were of a totally different character. They were like one big family and made themselves very visible by appearing in twos and threes at the mouth of their burrows. Sometimes in the early morning I have seen five or six sitting around eating everything in their sights except nettles and for some reason they did not seem to like them.

The farms crops around these areas were always eaten short and quite a lot of damage was done whatever crop was planted, whether it was corn, sugar beet or grass and it was for this reason that the farm where my father worked always had the gamekeeper and an assistant doing what was called rabbiting. For at least three months over the winter period, this was an intense search and catch operation, with the use of loose ferrets, line ferrets, a long narrow half round spade for digging on one end, with a strong ash handle about seven foot long complete with a metal hook on the other end, for hooking the line on the ferret in the ground on the other, string nets, 12-bore guns, and dogs. The ferrets were transported in a wooden box with a leather strap that went over a person's shoulder. The whole idea was to catch and kill as many rabbits as possible, sometimes up to one hundred on a good day. The way the rabbiting was done was an age old idea which had been done for years.

At the start of rabbiting season which was mostly the first or second week in November, rabbits traps (gin traps) were set in the mouth of the burrows, to catch rabbits leaving to feed, by digging out some soil, setting the plate on the trap and holding it up with a stick. Soil was gently placed over it to cover up both the plate and jaws of the trap, which was held in place by a short length of chain or wire attached to a stake in the ground. Many rabbits were caught like this but it was a cruel way as most times they were caught by one leg only and the only thing they could do was to crawl around in a circle allowed only by the length of chain or wire tied to the stake. You could always see where this had happened as the soil around the stake was pressed down hard and smooth. Sometimes there was not even a rabbits left but just a foot in a trap where a fox had made use of an easy meal.

I would like to say at this point that our family had these gin traps and the smaller plate traps used for rats which were used inside our own sheds where the rats would come in after the stored potatoes and chicken food. Any rats caught would be shot with the air gun. The big rabbit traps always hung on a nail in the shed. We had other ways of catching the rabbits we wanted.

Getting back to the gamekeeper, the morning after trapping all the rabbits and traps were removed and some of the surface holes of the burrows were filled in with soil, a few were left open and a net was placed over them. This was a string net of about one inch square mesh, covering an area of about a yard across. It also had a cord threaded through the outside of the mesh with both end tied to a wooden stake in the ground. When a rabbit ran out of the hole it hit the net which folded up pulling the cord tight and the rabbit was trapped. There was a labyrinth of holes under the ground at these warrens and there were always bolt holes which were escape routes in the most unlikely places. Some were in the middle of a clump of brambles or several yards away from the main burrows on high banks but always hard to find.

The next thing was the ferrets. Possibly two or more were taken out of the box and put down the holes, they were loose ferrets not line ones. The gamekeeper and the other man loaded their 12-bore guns and stood on opposite sides of the warren waiting for the ferrets to search the burrows underground and either bolt the rabbits into the nets or out through the bolt holes. The net ones were caught by hand and any using the bolt holes were shot on the run. The dogs were trained to sit and wait until told to go and pick the shot ones up. The ferrets would stop down underground most of the time, only coming up to the surface when all the rabbits have been cleared or they took a wrong turn. If this happened they would be put back down the hole. One warren might take hours, depending on the amount of burrows.

The holes that had been sealed with soil had to be checked to see if any rabbits had come up any of them, much the same as the surface holes explained earlier. Sometimes there would be two or three rabbits in these places and nearly always with a ferret behind them.

At the end of each day all the catch would be gutted and a slit cut in one of their back legs and the other leg was threaded through to make a loop. All rabbits would then be put on poles cut from the hedge and carried with heads hanging downwards on the shoulders of each man walking in single file with the keeper carrying the guns and the other man carrying the box of ferrets to the nearest farm to await collection by the local butcher. The only time this system was broken was on Christmas Eve, when every married man could go pick out two rabbits and every single man could have one rabbit as a present from the farmers for a whole years work so in our house we had a total of three because by now I had left school and was working on the same farm as my father. Our combined present came to five shillings or 25p in today's money. Some families were very grateful because not everyone did poaching. As to us, three rabbits and more were caught on a regular basis.

Many changes were taking place at this time and new ways of living were slowly developing. One was that I had as I have said before started work on the same farm as my father and I was now earning 14 shillings a week (about 70p of today's money), less National Insurance stamp, so my take home pay was 12 shillings, of that I had to give my mother about 8 shillings for what she called house keeping money, helping to buy things for the house, food, coal, paraffin oil and other goods. But we all got a slight increase in wages each year, which all employers, not just farmers, were very reluctant to pay.

I had gained confidence with the twelve bore gun and was now earning extra money by shooting rabbits, pheasants, partridge and pigeons. As the war was on anything that helped with the money or food situation was a big help. I enjoyed doing my bit towards helping and was happy to have a gun under my arm and some cartridge in my pocket, until one day the farm foreman said to me that I would have to help the keeper to do the rabbiting for that winter. I was horrified I hated ferrets, the smell of these animals was bad enough but to handle these creatures well was out of the question. It was not the only reason why I had to get out of this one and not work with this man. I had for quite a while been guided into the secret world of poaching by my elders and any smells of ferret could cause a problem.

I saw this keeper one day working in a ditch with a hedge along the top on one side using a line ferret on its own. The ferret had done one of two things, as the line was joined to a collar around its neck it had got the line caught on a root from the hedge above or it had killed a rabbit underground and was having a meal of its own. Either way it would not come to the surface, so the only way to get it out was to dig it out by digging where it was thought to be, finding it and lifting it out. There were no modern tracking devices in those days and digging could take many hours, so those days not much was caught. This was not for me and I did manage to work my way out of it.

However we were catching several rabbits by snares which were set in the evenings and checked early next morning. A snare was a length of brass wire with a round eyelet on one end with the other end pushed through this eyelet and tied to a piece of strong cord which was in turn tied to a wooden stake. The snare was set as follows, first you found what we called a rabbit run, this was a path used regularly to go from one point to another. There were parts that were flat and parts that were slightly higher. It was these parts that the rabbit was jumping over and where the snare was set. The stake was knocked into the ground with the heel of your boot and the brass wire was formed into a circle and held upright across the run by a thin stick with a cut in the top into which the wire was lightly pushed. The bottom of the circle was a few inches from the ground or the distance of a hand placed on edge on the soil with the thumb on top. As the rabbit jumped forward its head would go through the circle and the wire would pull tight and kill the rabbit. The next morning it would be as stiff as a board and it was hard to hide if you had many to carry. So we made a bag from an old sack with a leather strap from old harness which went over one's shoulder to put our catch in.

This bag soon had other things in it as the prices for rabbits and game increased and they could not be put on ration. Up till now all our poaching was done for a few extra shillings or a meal on the table. Then by a twist of fate one of my mother's brothers, my uncle, who was a builder was sent to London to help with repairs to damaged buildings and of course he had to find somewhere to live and it was just by chance that he found lodging with a family at No 6 Alder Grove, Cricklewood, (Tel Gladstone 4969) where the man was a manager of a big butchers shop in Kilburn. This man came and stayed with us one weekend and in the course of conversation we all realized that here was an opportunity to help each other and poaching was done on a more regular basis and really one could say to order, in return for cash and goods not obtainable in the country. One of the conditions being that all rabbits were to be gutted through a four inch cut and no more, this took some getting used too, as our butchers did not worry too much about that. As eggs and fresh chickens were hard to get in London, with the help from small farmers arrangements were made to supply a few of those goods as well.

Another thing that happened was not only rabbits and game was supplied but also moorhens as these were prepared by this butcher and sold to restaurants as wild partridge. The only problem with moorhens was that these birds cannot be plucked like chicken or game and have to be skinned. Although I've never eaten one myself, they can be with herbs and spices made to taste quite good.

The way this system worked was as follows, at six o clock on a Friday night I would go down to the telephone kiosk on Denmark Green and wait for the phone to ring (very few people had phones in those days). I would then go in and answer it to find out what Mr. Davis the London butcher wanted for the next week and let him know if there was anything to be picked up at that time. If there was this is how it was done. Someone in London had converted an ordinary Ford eight car to carry all these illegal goods back out of sight.

One particular incident I remember very well. The car stood in the farmyard and under the back seat was an empty space when it arrived but was now packed full of plucked poultry ready for the table. Between the back of the front seats and on top of the back seat itself were trays and trays of fresh eggs which had not been covered up. At that point into the farmyard came a car with a Ministry of Agriculture inspector driving it. These people were employed by the government to make spot checks anywhere at anytime, just to make sure that everyone was keeping to the rules, one of which was that everything sold was done through a licensed dealer and records kept. Well the man driving the car and the farmer knew what to do as the inspector got out of his car. Tray by tray the eggs were unloaded and gently put into empty incubators. One of the things you were allowed to do was to hatch eggs for future stock. It did not take long for the inspector to take a look round, check the books and with a cup of tea and a homemade cake also six eggs straight from the nest he went on his way happy.

Visits from these people did not happen very often and I never did see one of them again. After a little while the eggs were reloaded and the car left the farm. This car came down to Wortham many times but not always empty sometimes it had meat, sausage and bacon which were shared out between people in the know. Nobody ever asked how they obtained the petrol. This went on for quite along time until one weekend the driver was taken ill driving back through Epping Forest and help had to come and collect the car from London. Everyone was hoping that no one found out what the car was loaded with. Sometimes it was game and rabbits, and sometimes poultry and eggs. I don't think the car came any more but a lot of money and goods had changed hands.

To complete the poaching orders kept us on our toes and some nights we had very little sleep. One way we caught pheasants was to peg down a short length of fishing line with a small hook on the end covered with a dried currents or sultanas. These were put down on the ground near a hedge or wood and the peg was covered with a bunch of dead grass. This was hard to see by anyone who did not know what to look for. The pheasants would pick up the dried fruit and swallow the hook, and were then caught by hand and killed.

Another way was to watch which trees the pheasants went up to roost in the evenings. This was quite easy as they made a noise when they flew up and a kind of chuckle as they settled down for the night. The following was done mostly on moonlit nights. We had a cocoa tin lid, painted black to cut out any reflection from the moonlight, nailed to the top of a very long garden cane. On the lid would be placed two lumps of carbine (same as used in gas lamps) into which a drop of water would be added by human means. This gave off a strong smelling gas. It was pushed up very carefully under the sitting pheasant which would then breath in the gas and after a few minutes would lose its balance and fall to the ground where it could then could be picked up and killed and put in the shoulder bag.

Both these ways were used as much as possible because they were quiet and did not harm the bird (No lead shot). Sometimes the pheasants would roost up higher in the trees and that became a job for the gun. I was out one moonlit night at the corner of the triangle wood. I know there was a pheasant in the ivy on this tree, but looking up into the moonlight I still could not see anything that even looked like a bird. But then something happened that made a cold chill go down my spine. I had seen and heard different things at all times of the night and at different places and had never been scared but this was different. There was a most particular noise very hard to explain, something that I had never heard before. It was like a birch broom being rattled but in short spells and it seemed to echo through the trees. I had learned when I was out with my father how to walk on twigs and leaves without making a noise, so off I went very quietly to see what this was. As I got closer it seemed to come from different places in the undergrowth on the ground until at last I saw what it was. I was surprised that was such a small thing could make this terrifying noise. All it was, a small hedgehog would walk a little way then lay on its side and scratch its bristle with its back feet. I watched this happen two or three times, but as I walked away this noise could be heard for a quite along way off. By now clouds had covered the moon, so that finished any hopes of shooting pheasant for that night.

There were several times during the poaching period when strange things happened. Sometimes there was a reason and other times it was hard to find an answer.

Getting back to the fish hook, there was one occasion when I nearly got found out. The farm foreman and I were walking towards the big barn to feed the chickens that were kept there when he spotted one of the big cockerels flapping its wings and going around in short circles. I knew what had happened so I suggested to him that I take a look while he fed the rest of the chickens. He agreed to this and off I went. By this time the cockerel was getting very upset and I had quite a job to catch it but I did and managed to get the hook out from its mouth with my pocket knife. I them let it go and it ran back to the hens and to my relief it started feeding none the worse for its ordeal. I removed the fishing line and put it in my pocket and carried on with the work to be done. When asked what the problem was I had to say that it was caught in some fence wire. This was accepted and was never talked about again, but this was a bit too close for comfort and from then on all hooks were checked very early in the mornings when we checked the snares.

I also remember one evening, just as dusk was started to fall. I put a cartridge into each barrel of twelve bore and went to see if there were any rabbits in the kitchen garden of the rectory. After walking down the centre path of this vegetable garden with the fir tree wood at the bottom there was nothing except the odd pigeon coming into the tops of the trees to roost for the night. However when I got to the bottom of then path I looked over the clipped hawthorn hedge and there about eighty yards away near the hedge on the opposite side of the meadow sat a rabbit which appeared to be washing its ears with it front paws. I watched for a time and then pulled the hammer back on the left hand barrel. By this time it was getting darker by the minute. I waited for this rabbit to move out onto the grass and start feeding but it was getting darker by the minute so I took aim and gently squeezed the trigger. There was a loud bang echo amongst the trees but my rabbit was still busy washing itself in the same position. I put the gun down and got through a gap in the hedge and walked across the meadow to the spot where I had shot. In the fading light and the gentle puffs of wind I had shot a tuft of dead grass. Bits of grass lay around so I had hit the target but there was no profit in that and I never told anyone.

At the other end of the scale, one morning very early I thought I would take a look down the road from the rectory to the church. I knew there were some rabbits' burrows in the high banks on each side of the road. I had just got past the Wigwam when I saw a rabbit sitting on the grass verge next to the road. I quietly stepped on to the grass and moved a little closer. Raising the gun I squeezed the trigger of the left barrel and the rabbit fell down. I went to pick it up and put it into my bag and to my surprise there laid three rabbits two of which I did not know were there, so that made up for the cartridges I had wasted on the tuft of grass.

Another such incident happened one Sunday morning as I was walking around the back of the shrubbery in the rectory garden. Glancing through the bushes I saw a big cock pheasant walking across the front lawn. Well I could not let that one go so with careful aim I shot it, then rushed out of the bushes and picked it up and put it in a bag. As I was a server at Wortham church at that time and I had to attend the eight o clock service that morning I jumped onto my bicycle and went to church. When I arrived inside the church the Rev Hiller was walking down the centre aisle and the first thing he said to me was did I see anyone shoot a gun in the rectory grounds as he said that he had heard a shot while he was shaving in the bathroom, which looked out over the north lawn the opposite side of the house to where I had been. What I could say as you don't see yourself when you shoot a gun. The only thing you see is what you are aiming at, so I had to say no and with that he walked away and no more was said.

It was and still is the law that nobody shoots any sort of game birds on a Sunday. But our family always took the view that if you could sell it or eat it then get it whatever the day of the week it was, but that was a nice pheasant.

In those days Wortham Ling was covered nearly all over with gorse (what we called furze) bushes. Some were very tall and some were new growth and in the spring all these different levels were coved in yellow flowers which looked a real picture, but there were places that had short grass patches kept down by the rabbits and also there were wide and narrow grass paths also where the rabbits fed. Now the Ling at that time had many ups and downs making it a very uneven terrain which was ideal for rabbits' burrows and there were many of them all over the whole area of about three hundred acres. I used to love walking over this area along the footpaths in the early morning carrying my gun looking for something to shoot. I was sometimes there before four o clock in the morning and the rabbits could be seen feeding on the short grass patches.

This was the place where if you were careful you could get more than one with one shot. But there was one big disadvantage if you were walking east to west as the sun was rising. It cast a long shadow which the rabbits saw before you saw them. However there were also pheasants and partridges about as well which made an extra bonus if you could get these, and sometimes the odd duck on the river Waveney.

I can remember one particular morning I was walking around the back of the mould (What we called the battery) and I saw in the ashes, where someone had had a bonfire, there was a covey of partridges having a dust bath, so with careful aim and left barrel I shot into the centre of the bunch. Then with a cloud of dust and feathers one bird only was trying to get away. I put the gun down and caught this one and went to collect the others. I had shot a total of fourteen partridges with one shot. I had already two rabbits in my bag, but it took twelve of the partridge to fill it. Changing the rabbits to the top of the bag over the partridge, (bearing in mind none of us ever had a game license) I was at a loss what to do with the other two as I had to walk on the road to get home. Then I thought of a bright idea. I put the other two birds inside my Wellington boots and started to make my way home. As I went around a corner, who should I see riding a bicycle but the village policeman.

He stopped and we had a chat but as he was a friend I was not worried too much, that was until I felt one of the birds starting to move inside my boot. I had to do a bit of quick thinking so I offered him a rabbit which he accepted and we both went our separate ways. He was pleased he had a meal and I was glad to get on my way. I think he knew what I had but as he sometimes went out with my father at night on a poaching trip, it was in his best interest to turn a blind eye.

At this point I would like to explain what the battery was. In the 1914-1918 War troops were stationed at Roydon Green, also other villages around Wortham. They built this huge hill packed tight with faggots and covered it with tons of sandy soil. At the bottom on the east side a trench was dug with concrete walls all around, deep enough to hide a man. What the soldiers done was to use this big hill as a shooting range with targets put up to shoot at. The men in the concrete trench had a disc on a long handle to show the target had been hit. From the bottom of this mound towards the east, across the Ling and over the road up to the back of Mill House at about one thousand yards apart were what was known as the butts. These were mounds of soil about six yards long by four yards wide and about four foot high with a flat top where the soldiers laid on to shoot. I can not ever remember anyone saying that the road was closed or that there was any warning.

I once shot from the first butt with a 303 rifle when I was in the army cadets. Us boys, when we were young, would take spades and dig out the lead bullets and melt them into lead blocks over a fire. Some can still be found even today if you know where to look. During the last war this shooting range was still used by some soldiers and the Home Guard. I can remember some Americans coming there to practice shooting but I don't think they were allowed to come anymore after they were shooting wildly all over the place.

One man, a Mr. Noble, lived in a cottage on a part of Roydon known as Freezen Hill on Upper Roydon Fen when one day a bullet from an American gun went through one wall of his bedroom and into the wall on the opposite side of the room.

Another interesting point about this area is the part of the Ling also on the east side, if you look very carefully on the ground, you can find very small flint chippings about the size of a thumbnail giving an indication that people had made flint tools here in the stone age.

Getting back to the poaching, there are two more things that I would like to record, both of which concern my grandfather. The first one took place on a small field near Beehive cottages, where the gamekeeper lived. Now this field went by the name of Minter's field and did at one time belong to a Minter, one of Grandfather's relations, before coming into his possession. I think that some of it was used as a garden, and chicken were kept on part of it as well. Now as this field was also next to an osier bed (Willows grown for making baskets) and there was always lots of pheasants coming out to feed, Grandfather devised what he called an oven trap. This was a wooden frame with two doors with wooden frames made of tile batten timber about one inch by one inch, coved with half inch mesh wire netting. Each door was fitted with a small set of tee hinges which were screwed to the two inch by two inch frame from underneath. These were fitted with a mild spring, something from an old cycle pump and were from each door to the top of the frame. The whole thing complete was about twenty four inches square. A deep hole was dug in the ground and the frame was fitted over the top, held in place by a piece of thick wire, shaped like an L, with the longest section put in the ground and the shortest section stapled to the frame so everything was secure and held in place. Then grass was put over the netting doors and some grains of corn scattered around and over the doors so that when a bird was feeding and it stood on the doors they dropped down into the hole and the bird was trapped in the hole and easy to catch.

The other thing concerning my grandfather was that after each harvest the stubble on the cornfields was what we called bushed so that nobody could drag a net across at night to catch resting partridge. Well as my grandfather had retired and only worked a few days each week on odd jobs, it was his job to cut branches of hawthorns and put over the fields at irregular intervals so there were no straight lines. Well there could not have been a better person for this job, as he had a lot of experience over the years both on where to put them and how avoid them. The way he did it was very misleading because to look across the field it looked impossible to get a net anywhere between the bushes. But because partridge would creep across the ground and not fly at night they were easy prey and the way it was done was in a shape of a Z. The net would be put down, with a man at each side, and very quietly and slowly would be dragged from North to South and then at an angle from South to East and then from East to West. This would be done several times on a big field and the catch would be mainly English birds and sometimes there would be a pair of French partridges as well, what we called Red Legs.

Netting fields took a long time so we did not do it very often. We did once or twice catch a hare and the odd rabbit. The weather also ruled this as a bright moonlight was a big risk because it cast a shadow also the gamekeeper and his dogs would see you as well. I can't say I enjoyed that sort of poaching but it was extra cash in the pocket. When out during the day with the gun, we did have the chance to shoot the odd woodcock or snipe, which we sold.

What I did like was pigeon shooting and the farmers would want you to do this so they gave you permission to go anywhere on the farm to do it. If there was a field of peas or clover just coming through the soil we would watch to see what part of the field the most birds were feedings and which tree they were sitting in, then we would find a deep ditch and made a pigeon hut as near the trees as possible. This was made from branches cut from the hedge we put the thick end in the ground and the twiggy part upwards to form a circle across the ditch, then we scattered long grass all over the top of the branches we left one end over the ditch so we could get through. We would then set out in the field some wooden decoy pigeons or set up one or two that we had shot earlier. These had small pieces of twigs put under each wing to make it look as if they were just landing. Then with pockets full of cartridges (Special size shot for pigeons) and a sack to sit on and take the birds home in, we would settle down and wait for whatever flew into the trees or onto the ground to feed. They would see the decoys and drop down to join them. It was possible to see through the top of the hut to see what landed in the boughs.

I liked doing this type of shooting as the farmers did not want their crops spoilt and it could be done anytime of day, early morning till late at night. Now pigeons were peculiar birds because if you took a look from inside the hut there would be nothing to see or hear and a few seconds later there would be some sitting on the trees appearing to come from nowhere. This was not the time to shoot as one by one they would drop on the ground to feed and it wasn't long before there were twenty or more on the ground. Then you could aim at the centre of the bunch with the right barrel and you could get five or six, and as they flew up into the air you aimed with the left barrel and you could get four or five more. You had to take this opportunity to go out and pick up the shot birds as these pigeons flew off to some other trees at the opposite end of the field. Why I have been saying "we", is because someone else would be doing exactly the same thing in a hut which had been built over there. It could be part of the family, our workmates or even the gamekeeper.

Now these huts were over ditches, on grass verges near high hedges, in fact anywhere on the farm where the birds could feed and do some damage. After you had shot and got back into the hut the whole scene would be quiet. Perhaps a passing rook would give a call or you could hear lapwings on adjoining fields. Also there would be a pair of Blue Rock pigeons land in the trees. These were a much smaller bird than the big wood pigeons that we were after. These did not go in flocks like old woody but mainly in pairs and were a smaller bird and not worth much money so it paid to let them go, although some did get shot if they were feeding with the wood pigeon on the ground.

After a short while you could hear shots being fired from the other person and it would not be long before they were up in the trees and returning to where you were. All this shooting took place in late winter and early spring as the crops were just coming through the soil. The second Saturday and the fourth Sunday in February were declared pigeon shooting days all over Norfolk and Suffolk and anyone who could fire a gun would go in to hiding anywhere they could to shoot these birds and hundreds were shot. A lot of them were pigeons from the continent in big flocks to winter in this country. People had bags of well over one hundred after a few hours shooting. Most of these were sold to game dealers for a few pence, just enough to pay for the cartridges and a few pennies for themselves.

In the heart of winter and the very bad weather it was better to go in the woods where the birds would go to roost in the trees. Only a slight bit of hide would do as the birds would sit in the high branches and one shot could bring down several birds and as it was getting darker all the time they only took a short flight and came back to the same tree. Then it got too dark so it was time to go home, bagging an odd rabbit on the way if we could.

We often had roast pigeon for a meal as they were very good to eat with your own grown vegetables and Bisto gravy. I can well remember when my father plucked these birds he would sit in his chair with a small tin bath to let the feathers fall in. We liked to keep all the feathers for the copper fire, but at that time we had a black and white cat which would sit and watch the plucking being done and when the bath was full of feathers it would jump in and send feathers everywhere, much to the annoyance of my parents.

When we were school boys we sometimes went to these pigeon huts and collected all the spent cartridges cases, one to see who could get the most and second to see who could get the most colours. Sometimes a farmer would want these types of huts made near freshly sown cornfields and get his men to shoot rooks which were eating the corn. A lot of rooks could eat a lot of seed especially if shoots were just coming through the soil. Now these old rooks were crafty birds and if they saw one person walk to a hut they would find another field to cause damage in but if two people walked to a hut and one walked away they would come. I don't think they could count very well.

I once was in a ditch between two fields near the River Waveney with the farmer's own gun that he had lent me. Both fields had been sown with oats. This ditch was very deep and I could just see over the grass verge and there were lots of rooks walking around so I waited till there were quite a lot together and as this gun was very heavy I laid it on the top of the grass, pulled the trigger and whether I was not holding it tight enough I don't know, but there was a terrible bang and the gun seemed to jumped back at me. It hit me in the cheek and ear and the butt hit my shoulder with such a force that the next thing I knew I was laying in the bottom of the ditch. I never even hit a rook as they all flew off. I said a few words in Broad Norfolk and picked myself up with what I thought was a broken jaw and a very sore shoulder. I was lucky it was only a bruise but I did have a black and blue side to my face and ear. I took that gun back to the farmer. I did use it again but with care.

But we stopped the rooks from eating the oats and this is how we did it. Some people would shoot a rook and hang it up between two sticks with its wings outstretched but we did not do that. We got three rabbit traps and dug a hole in the soil to sit the trap in and with a stick would hold up the plate and gently cover the whole trap with soil and then ease the stick out. We would fit the stake which was joined to the trap by a chain into the ground. Then a few oats were scattered around over the trap. We would leave to let the rooks come down to feed. Eventually one would step into the plate of the trap which would spring and the bird was caught. Now when this happened the one caught would flap around in a panic and all the others would fly round and round in circles getting higher and higher a making a terrific noise above the field and could be seen from a long way off . This would be the time to shoot the trapped rook with an airgun.

In those days (1940s) these birds were classed as vermin and could be destroyed by whatever means were available. In fact at Rookery Farm and St Johns Farm at Wortham, where the parks had lots of tall trees in them and hundreds of rooks, there was always two or three times in the spring, after the young rooks had hatched in the stick nest, there were organized shoots

112

by the farmers to get rid of the young rooks. But despite all this the farmers liked to see the odd rook walking down a row of young sugar beet picking out the wireworm. Some of the older people at that time used to say the meat from the breast of the rook was good to eat but I never knew of anyone who did.

To conclude about guns and poaching, I must admit that we did not catch something every time. There were times when someone had been round before and scared everything away or sometimes a cat or fox would eat a rabbit caught in a snare. Also it was no good going out in gale force wind because animals and birds would if possible keep under cover. But it was not all shooting and poaching as the other pastime our family had was fishing, both freshwater and sea water but mainly freshwater from rivers and lakes.

Church was given a miss if fishing had been arranged for a Sunday. I fished in various ponds around this area for small fish like carp, roach, and rudd ever since I got over falling in when I was five. I also fished for newts in the pit near our house using a bent pin on a piece of string tied to a garden cane. As I got older I was given a short two piece rod and an old wooden reel and some line and hooks. This was ideal for pond fishing and my parent's fishing tackle was not much better as a lot of it was homemade as they could not afford to buy the really top class equipment. The floats were made from big corks and quills from goose feathers. The gaff was an old broom handle with a grove cut in the top about one foot down, half inch deep and a quarter wide. Into this was put a piece of thick heavy wire turned at the top to make a loop with the end filed to a sharp point. The other end was turned at right angles to fit into a hole drilled in the bottom of the grove and all held in place by sharp staples. A lot of the pike tackle was a pair of treble hooks fitted to a rabbit snare wire. The spinners used as moving bait were cut from an old aluminium teapot or kettle and fitted with a swivel. How they worked with the rods they used I don't really know. My grandfather's creel was made with wood boards, complete with leather hinges and clasp and carried by a thin leather strap which went over the shoulder. The whole box painted green. I still have this box today. The other thing homemade was a piece of thin wood about six inches by two inches with a cut made in each end leaving two prongs sticking out. Several yards of fishing line was wrapped around from end to end until the area between the prongs was full. The floats were painted with either red or green top half and white on the bottom half with a thin black line between the two colours. On the pike tackle line between the end of the rod and the top of the float was another small coloured float, that we called the runner. This was a round piece of cork painted a different colour to the float. This also was allowed to move anywhere on the line and the purpose of this was to let the person know which way the caught fish was going because once the bait was taken the float was pulled under the water no one could see the end of the line, and a hooked pike nearly always made for a bed of water weeds to hide in and it was sometimes very hard to get the fish ashore. But with the runner the line could be pulled to keep the fish in clear water.

As time moved on and the family began to get a little more money together the fishing took a turn for the better and more modern tackle was brought and used. We sent away for catalogues of all sorts of fishing tackle but mainly Allcocks. I cannot remember where they came from but I think it was Reading but I may not be right on that. In the early years all fishing was done locally in the river at Hoxne and Redgrave Lake, which was at that time owned by Squire Wilson who also had a lot of land and farms let out to tenant farmers.

The actual big house which was known as Redgrave Hall was set in many acres of parkland with some very big trees all over it. I never did go any nearer to this house other than on the road which went past the front of it and one thing that stood out during the autumn was the orangery with all oranges standing out against the greenery. At the entrance to this park from the road from Redgrave to Botesdale was a set of very heavy ornamental gates which were nearly always open and a small bungalow in which lived the water bailiff. The lake itself covered several acres but was longer than it was wide and at the opposite end to the road it came to nearly a point where there was built what we called the round house. This is where the gamekeeper lived. In the lake in front of the hall was a boat house, a wooden structure with a galvanized roof. Kept inside here was a small black painted rowing boat called POP-POP, which could be hired for fishing. I think the whole place was designed by Capability Brown.

I went fishing there a lot with my grandfather before the war and before I left school. I liked lake fishing better than river fishing. We would go to the river each side of the bridge between Oakley and Hoxne. This was the River Dove which flowed from Eye and joined the Waveney behind Hoxne church. Depending on how high and how fast the river was flowing was sometimes a problem but we did have some good catches of pike and eels from deeper parts. It was always best to fish where there was a bend in the river. When the water was clear you could see the shoals of roach and rudd but getting them to bite was a different matter.

Back to Redgrave Lake everyone had to have a permit to fish which could be bought for a year or a day. We all had yearly permits which allowed for one pike rod and one rod for other fish, but there was a way around that which I will explain later. In those days anyone who caught a fish could, if they wanted, take it home to eat. We often did and a nice pike, roach or trench with mashed potatoes made many a meal, all after scaling and cleaning, sometimes left with the bones in, or cooked as a fillet. Eels were different they had to be skinned, cut into small pieces and left in salt water overnight before frying. Carp and perch we did not eat as they took much more preparation to get ready so most of these were put back in the water.

There were certain areas around the sides of the lake where Grandfather liked to fish best. One side being next to the road as the water was deeper at this end. There were also some big high trees and tall hawthorn bushes, ideal to sit in the shade waiting for a bite but not very nice if the line get caught in them when casting out. There was one particular space where a big tall chestnut tree had fallen into the water. This was an excellent spot to fish for trench as long as you did not get caught on some of the under water branches.

Another place where the water was very deep was opposite the bridge. Under the road going out into the lake was what we called the running board. This was a long flat wooden surface held up on thick posts knocked into the water. This was about thirty six inches wide and about ten yards long with all the top surface boards covered in coconut matting. This is where the people swimming would run along and dive into the water. We would sit on the end or side and fish when it was not being used which was most of the year.

People were allowed to swim in the lake free of charge but at their own risk. There was a wooden diving board anchored down at about thirty yards out, in front of which was a building called the changing room. A few sheets of galvanized iron painted green nailed to posts and set at an angle so no one could see in, this also doubled up as a GENTS toilets for the anglers fishing there.

There was another thing that I remember about that end of the lake, which like the other end came to a point and this is where the water overflowed across a weir and into a narrow stream running down beside the road and turned to go under the road bridge. It was here that a square brick building was built into the stream. The walls were one brick thick and the inside held water and some small fish. Part of the stream went around the outside and part went through the bricks. But the most amazing thing was inside the walls was a rusty pump which was working all day and night but how, I never did know. There was no engine, no electric, just the steady thump, thump, which could be heard quite a long way off. The only thing there was water, which somehow kept it going, as the stream ran through the fields down to the River Ouse.

Sometimes as a family, my grandfather, father, uncle and myself would all go together for a Sunday fishing in the lake and by that time we all had better tackle, split cane rods, short rod for pike and long rods for other fish and some course fish lines with stronger breaking strains, which were made to float on top of the water and were self drying. They no longer had to be hung out to dry after fishing and covered with Vaseline to stop them sinking.

Usually on the Saturday we would take a big net that fitted from side to side of the river Waveney on the Ling and put this across where the river turns, called Sandy Bottoms and then we would go up to the Doit Bridge and walk in the river up towards the net, driving the fish into the net so that we could all have some live bait. We had fishing kettles to put some of the fish into for moving around. We all had tanks in our gardens where we put these fish into over night and give them some food. We took as many as we thought we wanted and let the rest go back into the river.

This was one of the baits used for pike, bread was made back to dough by wetting and rolling into balls, usually when we got to the lake. Sometimes this was mixed with bran to make ground bait, which was thrown into the water in front of where we were going to fish to encourage them to the bait. The other baits used were Birds custard powder, slightly wetted with water to make a paste. This was used for catching tench. We bought maggots in different colours, pink, yellow and white and used whichever colour that attracted the fish most. But the most common bait of all was freshly dug earthworms out of the garden or these could be picked up off the lawn at night. If you jumped up and down on the lawn the worms would come out on top of the grass. I don't know why they should do this but it did work.

We would arrive at the lake early in the morning. I liked this best in the autumn when there was very little wind and the surface of the water was calm with perhaps a covering of thin mist. It was nice to hear the moorhens and coots splashing in the reed beds along the side of the lake. Down at the far end near the keeper's cottage were several Canadian and English geese making their honking call. They always seemed to keep that end. It was very rare to see them much past the boat house. Sometimes a pair of swans would drift past looking as if they were towing four or five grey cygnets behind them. It was not unusual to see a pair of kingfishers dashing about and with pigeons cooing in the trees this was a relaxing time of day.

Sometimes the silence was broken by a fish jumping out of the water and causing ripples. At the edge of the water and on the bank would be the shells of fresh water mussels in all different sizes, from about four inches to the large ones, sometimes as big as nine inches long by four inches wide. I don't think anyone ever ate them, other than otters and I never saw any of those there.

We would put all our tackle together and bait the hooks. We each had one coarse rod and one pike rod, perhaps worms on the long rods and live fish on the pike rod. These would swim around so you had to keep an eye on the float. By now we had metal rod rests and both landing and keep nets. Now as the license only covered two rods we got around this by using the line on the piece of wood with the prongs on as mentioned earlier. This would be unwound to make a circle on the ground then we would add the small loose runner float and then the big float fixed to the line, then the trace and hooks to which the live bait was attached, complete with lead weights. The line was then whirled around above the person's head like a lasso and when you thought that you were going fast enough you let go of the line. This sent the whole lot out into the lake uncoiling the line as it went. This method of fishing had been done in the past for years. No one ever gave a thought for the fish that were being used as live bait in those days. With all the lines now out it was wait and see. A cup of hot tea from the flasks and a cheese sandwich and we were now ready for what ever took the bait.

Fish are peculiar creatures. Tench would slowly suck the custard powder bait without moving the float and unless you pulled the line in quite often you could have an empty hook and not know it. Eels were the same. They would gently eat the worm off the hook and the float did not move. However most of the other course fish would snap at the bait, move the float, which would soon go under the water and you could reel the catch in. The pike would make a dash for the live bait and have it in seconds, then swim off to have a meal in the nearest weed. What the fish did not know of course was that the person on the bank could see that something was going for the bait or what we called "got a run" and with the big float under the water was watching the runner float to see where the pike was going. When this stopped moving it was the time to strike (pull the rod upwards) and this would check the line forcing the hooks into the pike's mouth.

Then began the struggle to land the fish. It would do everything it could to avoid coming to the bank and sometimes, if it was a really big one, it would break the line and get away. When you got it near enough the gaff was used by putting the hook part of it in its gills and lifting it out of the water. All coarse fish caught were put in the keep net placed in the water but pike, if not big enough to eat, were put back straight into the lake. At the end of the day the same was done with the fish in the net. One of the biggest pike I ever saw caught was one that weighed twenty four pounds.

Another thing about fishing from the bank was that there were two men from Cambridge would hire the boat for a day and if they were not catching much and they saw you were, they would row Pop-Pop in front of where you were fishing and try and catch some for their own use. This did annoy the bank angler's. One of the men was a big fat man (unusual in those days) who had a very squeaky voice and dressed in very peculiar clothes. We called him Mr Punch.

Along the south side of this lake the water was very shallow except for one place near a tall elm tree where there was a very deep area which was ideal for perch fishing but here it was better if you had a feeder on the line between float and hook. This was a round container with holes in the side. It was cast into the water with a baited hook of worms or maggots. Inside was filled with bread crumbs mixed with custard powder which would filter out of the holes to make a cloud in water which would attract perch. There was some big fish caught in this spot using this method.

One man who you could be sure of seeing, when fishing, was the water bailiff, Mr Willmott. It was his job to make sure everyone had a permit. He knew all the people who were regulars but he had to check with anyone who he did not know. Being deaf he did talk a bit loud and could be heard coming quite a long way off. Everyone knew what he was going to say when he got to where you were fishing, "Huya had na luckk?", which if you had, was his way of asking if you had a spare pike. I should think that over the course of time he had more pike than anyone and never even used a rod and line.

We did not always catch fish. Sometimes you could be there all day and not even have a bite, especially if someone had thrown all their spare bait into the lake the day before which the fish had eaten during the night. The other times would be in the winter when there was frost and fog. I would use spinning tackle in those conditions because you could walk along the bank and keep warm and if you were lucky catch the odd pike.

The whole situation changed during the war. The hall itself was taken over as an American hospital and the large piece of grassland between the south bank and the A143 road and known as The Warren, was built on to make a POW camp. The peace of a day's fishing was shattered with vehicles going to the hall and German and Italian voices chatting away in the camp. This was not a relaxing place to be any more.

Eventually the fishing rights were bought by a consortium from somewhere in Suffolk and local anglers were not allowed to go any more. I can however remember a very hot summer but I am not sure which year it was other than in the late forties or early fifties, when the lake nearly dried up. I can remember going there and walking across from near the boat house to the bank on the Warren as there is a stone roadway across the lake. I don't think this had been seen before or since. There was some water up at the road end and near the keeper's cottage. The weir and the overflow stream were dry and the pump had stopped working. Around the edges of the lake laid many dead fish. Some of the pike must have been at least thirty pounds if not more and some coarse fish, roach, perch and tench, which must have been four or five pounds, besides lots of smaller fish but no eels as they seemed to stay in what water was left. The smell was terrible as a lot of fish had been partly eaten by birds and any rodent that wanted any easy meal. The lake did fill up again and has been restocked.

There was one other place I used to catch pike and that was in the River Waveney near the back of the battery (shooting range). There were two very sharp turns in the river here also it was quite deep and some roots from trees could be seen down by the side of the bank. It was here the pike could be seen resting in the water. Now this was a different way to catch them, no hooks, lines or rods were used just a rabbit snare and strong garden cane. The snare was opened to make a circle and with great care it was dropped into the water behind the fish and very very slowly it went over the tail and along the body till it was level with the gills then with a very quick jerk the fish would be out of the water on to the bank. This was done many times as these were big enough to eat. Some people caught eels in traps made from wire netting. I have seen them in the river but never used one.

We did go sea fishing from Lowestoft and Southwold piers and Yarmouth harbour walls, also Southwold and Dunwich beaches. The tackle cost more to buy. The bait (rag worm or dead herring cut up) cost quite a lot to buy as well. On the piers the hooks got entangled in all sorts of debris on the sea bed. Sometimes you could catch small cod, flounders and plaice but I did not like it like freshwater fishing but life was changing and soon the fishing and poaching stopped.

Wortham Rectory as I knew it

As I have said before my mother came to the rectory with the Rev Moore, his wife, son John and daughter Eileen on the first of October 1925 complete with a brown Airdale dog named Taffy, who had the run of the house and gardens. I did not know too much about this building when I was very young but I can say that it was very much a second home to me as I was taken there before I could walk, I have been told. But as I became older the memory of what it was like is still very clear. I liked being in this big house it had a warm welcoming feel about it, the smell of toast at breakfast time, and fresh mint in the potatoes at dinner time, the fresh brewed coffee mid morning and on certain days of the week the smell of silver polish from the butler's pantry came out into the passage from the kitchen to the dining room.

The kitchen was divided from the passage by a big green baize door with brass studs around it. I think most of the big houses had one of these doors in those days it was the dividing line between the gentry and the servants. The cellar was on the left entered by the first door into the passage and it had a peculiar damp smell that came into the kitchen when it was opened. This was the wine store beside lots of other things kept down there. Next to the green door was a wide winding stairway which turned at the top into a passage way to the bathroom and bedrooms. This was the stairs which the kitchen maid had to carry the brass and copper jugs of hot water up every morning for washing and shaving. It did take a lot when people wanted a bath.

There was no hot water taps upstairs in those days, just cold water to the bathroom and to flush the toilet from a tank in the attic through black iron pipes and lead fittings sweated to the taps and ball valve. All waste pipes from, bath and wash basin were lead also sweated onto the actual waste fittings and to complete the fitting were the lead traps with a brass screw on the bottom for cleaning. The pipes from the toilet were made of cast iron with a big flange for fitting the toilet pan to and each section of pipe was joined. This iron pipe was fitted to the outside wall facing the north lawn and joined into 4 x 24 inch salt glazed pipes to a brick inspection chamber with a cast iron lid. Where it went from there I don't know but there must have been a septic tank somewhere. There were two drain surrounds for the smaller lead pipes. The one from the bathroom was near the cast iron pipe at ground level near the north wall and the other was on the bottom of the outside wall of the scullery which faced west.

The east front of Wortham Rectory as is now.
During the 1930s and 40s I spent a lot of my early life here

The south side of the rectory showing the blocked up window to avoid window
tax. The conservatory next to the brick wall was where the massive black grapes
were grown. I helped to prune out the small bunches and unwanted wood.

Inside the scullery was a very big York stone sink about six inches deep and on one end was a hand pump which pumped water from an outside well. I can remember that the floor of the toilet and bathroom were black and white square tiles and small ones on the walls to about four foot high with a two inch ornamental tile all round just below the top tile. There was no showers in those days and the bath was not used that much. A strip wash in a bowl was what most people done, especially the farm workers whose only source of water was from a well or a tank.

Getting back to the rectory and the people who lived and worked there, the kitchen maid's name was Maisie or a word very much like that. She did actually live in the servants' quarters at the rectory but went home some weekends. The cook was Gladys Sharman, a woman who lived in a cottage on Wortham Long Green with her husband and son, who I went to school with. I think that she biked to work every morning. She was an excellent cook and I remember all the lovely smells coming from the kitchen every dinner time also when baking bread and cakes was being done. This was the main meal of the day but breakfast was also a big meal with pleasant smells, bacon, eggs, fried bread sometimes kidneys if the butcher could supply them and of course toast and marmalade.

It was tradition that the family had their food first and the staff (I won't say servants because being employed by the Moores was not too bad) had their food afterwards. It was an unwritten law that the same food was cooked with enough for everyone. All this cooking and baking was done on a massive cast iron range with hot plates on top to heat the hot water in big black heavy cast iron kettles. Other things were done in a lot of different size saucepans with metal lids. The baking was done in the oven part of the range.

Now my mother was a sort of Jack of all trades person she could do any of the jobs done by the other people and she was also a very good cook but when the kitchen maid was away it was her job to go to the rectory very early and clean out this big cooking range and light the fire so it was ready for the breakfast preparations. The next fireplace to have the same done was the dining room and then the sitting room and so on throughout the whole house. This was the winter time procedure, but during the summer it was only the cooking range which was lit.

I did go with her on some of the cold winter mornings this would be about four o clock and it was a very weird feeling to unlock the side door and go into the kitchen. It was cold and dark and except for the big clocks ticking, very quiet. One great big grandfather clock would strike every quarter of an hour and at that time in the morning it always seemed very loud. Work on the fireplaces and range was done by candle light which did not help. The heavy metal fender of the range stood on the red pammets complete with metal fire irons, poker, shovel, brush and tongs. These all had to be moved before any cleaning out could be done. On the fireplaces in the rooms there was much more luxury, marble hearths topped by brass fenders and fire dogs (Brass brackets) with all brass fire irons resting on them both sides of the hearth.

The coal and wood for these fires was in wooden scuttles with brass handles. All these were highly polished and stood on the floor beside the hearths but the kitchen range had just a big galvanized scuttle very much like a pail to look at. These were filled every day by the gardener/handyman, a Mr Will Percy, who also chopped the sticks and took ashes out which were used to make paths in the gardens.

I always thought that the rectory was made up of two buildings, the older part being on the west side with a newer hard greyish brick Georgian building put on at a later date but this was not the case. I have found out since that this was built in 1827 by the Rev Richard Cobbold, who was rector of Wortham for forty six years. There is a plaque on one of the walls confirming this date.

The chimneys were all swept once every year by a chimney sweep from Diss by the name of Marjoram. He came in a pony and trap with all his brushes and chimney cloths. He was a most interesting person as could throw his voice to make out that there was someone up the chimney. I could not understand how he done that but it was fascinating to hear him having a conversation with this person up the chimney. I also heard him doing this at another cottage in the village. I never did find out what his first name was as to everybody he was known as just Marjoram. It was a big day when the sweep was coming. All the furniture was moved as far away from the fireplace as possible and covered up with all sheets and anything else that was available. The carpets were rolled back and any other surfaces were covered with old newspaper. The sweeps pony was taken out of the cart and tied to a stake on the small piece of grass in front of the coach house where it grazed until it was time to move to another house after it had been given a pail of water to drink.

From the very early days, when I was allowed to play on the kitchen floor in one corner, I spent many hours with some of John Moore's toys which were mainly a big wooden horse and cart with metal wheels and also a wooden four-wheeled truck full of square wooden bricks. Another thing was a cardboard box full of shapes of all different coloured pieces of wood which I built into houses with pillars and arches and with a little imagination all sorts of interesting things. As I grew older I was allowed to go outside by myself and it was then that one thing that I had never been able to understand was found out.

During those dark winter mornings when were inside lighting the fires there always seemed to be a lot of noise outside on the road which turned out to be two Foden steam engines pulling a big heavy trailer each. These belonged to a Mr. Bedwell of Hall Farm Redgrave who had several sets of these engines.

They were all painted a dark grey and were used for carting all sorts of goods. What these particular ones were doing was carting sugar beet from farms to Bury St Edmunds' sugar beet factory. I think they carried about seven tons altogether. They did not seem to go very fast so what amount they carted a day I don't know.

Back inside the house, which was quite big, there was always some work going on as it did take a lot to keep clean but there was an everyday routine, which was kept to most of the time. All the time that I was in or around the place I can't remember any decorating done either inside or out but there must have been some, because everywhere always looked clean and tidy. I think I must put that down to not knowing too much about that sort of thing at my age but I can remember all the fuss cleaning up after the sweep had gone.

There was a linen line across the north lawn and this was where the carpets were hung and beaten clean with willow carpet beaters. Some of the other carpets from the other rooms were cleaned by the same method. (No vacuum cleaners in those days.) Upstairs carpet and mats were swept with a stiff broom, also the stair carpets but the stairs near the kitchen did not have anything on them at all, just plain Oregon pine boards with mahogany rails.

The scullery was quite a big room with a large window and a stable type door, both facing west. Adjoining the scullery on the north side was a walk-in larder and cold store, which was kept mainly dark. Although there was a small window looking out over the north lawn but I never did see it opened. Next to that was a passage along inside the south wall which joined the scullery with the kitchen and halfway along was a big solid door with a letter box in the centre, this was made of brass and had to be polished regularly this door was known as the tradesmen's entrance and all the people coming to the rectory used it unless they were special guests. There was a very heavy brass knob bell-pull beside the door frame, which when used rang a bell in the kitchen. On certain days this was going quite a lot as each tradesman delivered goods. Some rang the bell and walked straight in. Others waited for the door to be answered.

To the left of the passage was the door to the stairs, which went up to the maids' bedrooms and also a door to the broom cupboard, which was the home to all sorts of goods. Besides brooms there were steps and stools, galvanized baths and pails, the box irons with their solid blocks of metal, which had to be in the fire until it was red hot and then transferred into the actual box with a pair of strong tongs, which was quite a dangerous thing to do. It was no wonder that these irons had wooden handles. Another thing stored in the scullery was the big heavy wooden roller mangle in its green and red paint. It was worked by turning a big wheel, connected to the rollers by several cog wheels and on top of the whole thing was a metal handle that could be turned to adjust the pressure on the rollers by a big iron spring. The tighter the rollers were the less water was left in the washing.

The washing itself was done in a big copper built like the one in the cottage that I have mentioned earlier but on a much bigger scale.

Carrying on into the kitchen from the passage was another heavy pine door which I can remember for a special reason as I had at that time a loose tooth which was on the point of coming out but would only move loosely around, so Gladys the cook said that I could have a bar of chocolate if I let her take it out. So I was sat on one of the kitchen chairs by a lift from her strong arms and without saying anything she tied a piece of strong thread to my tooth and then on to the knob of the heavy door which was open. Then with a shout of hold tight she slammed the door shut. Well it is hard to explain what I felt like but the tooth was on the end of the bit of thread and I got my bar of chocolate but I vowed never again. As the rest of my first teeth came loose I kept quiet till I got them out myself.

Getting back to the kitchen, which had several cupboards from floor to about four foot up the wall, the tops were used for standing all sorts of things on and one thing that I can still see quite plainly was a dish of fruit which, in the summer through to winter was always filled with own grown apples, pears, plums and some walnuts and hazel nuts. Now it was my job when there was no one around to just test these things but of course I had to dispose of the shells, cores and pips which I done with great ease by putting them in some of the ornaments that stood on window sills and shelves. The other thing that had to be tasted was the black and green grapes grown in the green house. But I made two big mistakes.

Someone must have found the bits put in the ornaments and had the cheek to say I had not asked if I could have them as the grapes had to be checked at every chance I had. I was able to have enough time in the privy to read a book if I had been able to. My parents said I would get no sympathy from them. I didn't know what that was so thought that I was best without it anyway as I had a big problem of my own as it was. There was one fruit that I could not get to and that was the peaches that grew on the south wall of the house. When they were on the tree I was not tall enough to pick them but someone must have done because there was always a big dish of them in the sitting room on top of the sideboard and I did see some being bottled in Kilner jars for eating in the winter. Gooseberries and plums were also done the same.

Back in the kitchen there was a massive Welsh dresser stood against the wall opposite the cooker. This had two big drawers above two large cupboard doors with shelves inside on which was all the crockery used for meals with the exception of the plates which were kept on small shelves fitted to the back of the dresser. The top over the drawers was used for storing the silver meat dishes, gravy boats and all the other silver used at dinner times, also inside the drawers themselves were kept all the table cloths and place mats and salt and pepper pots. Some were silver with blue glass interiors. There were also two wooden handled copper bed warmers hanging on the wall besides a few copper pans and kettles. Although I never saw them used they all had to be cleaned and polished.

Two other things stand out about the kitchen one was the big copper dinner gong on a wooden stand with its leather ended stick to beat it with so that everyone knew when dinner was being served as this could be heard all over the house. The other thing was the line of small bells at the top of the room wall which had written underneath which room it was so that when it was rung the staff knew which room to go too. Even the bell-pulls on the outside doors rang a bell here as well. All of them worked on wires from different directions.

In the centre of the kitchen stood a big heavy pine table surround by three chairs each side and a carver at each end. As I have said before, the butler's pantry was on the left hand side of the passage going down to the dining room. It was in this pantry that Will Percy would put on a leather apron and clean all the silver, copper and brass using Silvo for the forks and spoons and all the dishes, tureens, salt and pepper pots, sauce boats and any other silver, including trays. The brass and copper was cleaned with Brasso. Both these two cleaners were in round silver tins with blue strips around them.

There were other things used for cleaning as well one was methylated spirit, also lemon slices. Wood was polished with bees wax and pure turpentine. This included the green baize lined cutlery boxes used at meal time and the handles made of wood on the bread knives and the wooden trays. Other things kept in the pantry were, the knife sharpener which was a steel tapered rod over which the knife was drawn, also real feather dusters, yellow cloth dusters and polishing cloths, in fact most things connected with keeping the place clean.

Near the door but in the passage stood a very big grandfather clock which chimed each quarter, half and hour with the chime as loud as Big Ben. Late at night when place was quiet this always seemed louder. At the east end of the passage it opened out into three rooms. On the left was a toilet with black and white tiled floor and walls. There was also a heavy, white wash basin here. The toilet itself had a long pipe up to a cast iron cistern, with a chain to pull to flush it. This gave off a heavy rattle when used. This place had a soap dish and Lifebuoy soup and was complete with IZAL toilet paper hung in a roll on a holder, no torn newspaper for these people.

The next door on the right opened into the study, which had a pair of French doors in the outside wall. This room had a homely feel about it as the Rev Moore spent a lot of time in here at his desk, writing the Sunday sermons. There were some armchairs covered by piped upholstery, really old material.

One particular chair seemed to be Taffy's as this was the only one he was allowed to lay on but he did lay on the carpet in front of the log fire in winter. There was also a glass fronted bookcase in this room full of all sorts of books but I was too young to understand them in those days.

But the real treasure of the study was the black telephone made out of Bakelite, a new material and the forerunner of modern day plastic. This was used at the time when you had to ring the operator and tell them which number you wanted and they would get it for you. How times have changed. There were not many people had telephones either, only the people who lived in big houses, farmers, the rector, policeman, schoolmasters, some pubs landlords and of course the village post office but thankfully for us not the gamekeeper.

Back to the study, the other things about this room were the very old wall to wall carpet over a wooden floor and the wall clock with a wooden case inside which a pendulum swung endlessly day and night. This had a chime on the hour only and as it had Roman numerals on its face, when I was very young I could not tell the time by it. This room was a very private sanctuary of the Rev Moore and I was not allowed in there on my own.

The passage carried on to another doorway, which opened out into a very large hall with a double door opening into a south facing conservatory, in which black grapes were grown. In this hall was a very wide stairway. Against the inside west wall at the top of the stairs was an equally wide balcony against the north and east wall. I remember the heavy hardwood hand rails and spindles with curled rails on the corners I think this was one of the very dark mahoganies but I don't know which one, the whole thing was very well polished.

Leading off the hall were two heavy pine doors opening out into two large rooms. One was the dining room. The other was the sitting/drawing room. Both had two large windows facing east complete with wooden shutters inside the rooms and also very heavy curtains, tied back with a tasselled silk cord.

The first room was the dining room which had wall to wall carpet over a wooden floor. I don't think this had any sort of pattern on it. The main feature of this room was the marble fireplace, complete with clock on mantelpiece and the other was the very heavy mahogany table that stood in the middle of the room. This was surrounded by upholstered dining room chairs. The advantage of this big table was that it could be extended to nearly double its size. There were more chairs to match the ones around the table, positioned all in spaces between the sideboard and other furniture around the walls.

I can remember this table at Christmas when it was used to its full extent. Other than eating and food areas all the rest of the table was covered in what looked like snow. I'm not sure but I think it was cotton wool but it was not level. There were parts made to look like mountains and some parts were level. At the centre of it all, on one of the high places was a stable with a crib, three wise men and the animals. Around the rest of the table were all the other things that go with Christmas, robins, holly, ivy, pieces of twigs painted silver, bells and of course candles in silver candlesticks.

Up one corner of the room was a Christmas tree in a wooden tub. This was decorated with trimming of all sorts, packets of sweets and chocolates and on the end of some boughs were some coloured candles in little metal clips to hold them on and right at the top was the fairy holding a wand. Around the room were paper chains and all sorts of trimmings. I did sometimes get some chocolate from the tree if I was lucky. The big long sideboard was at this time of the year filled with all sorts of fruit, sweets, wines and all the things that went with Christmas in those days.

The gentry lived very well in the twenties and early thirties, all the year round and not just at Christmas. The vicar was always given a brace of pheasants in season beside as much well rotted farm manure for the gardens as he required.

Getting back inside the house and the dining room, I must mention the side table where all the hot food was served from big dishes, gravy boats and tureens. The plates had been warmed beforehand in the kitchen. Also in this room coal was always burnt on the fire. There is also something which I think should be written at this point about the entrance hall at Christmas.

This in itself was a sight to be enjoyed as there was no middle floor in this room just ground floor to ceiling and in the centre of the ceiling was a big glass chandelier, from where trimmings were hung to the walls of the room. Holly, ivy, laurel and mistletoe was woven between the rails of the stairs and coloured balloons hung everywhere. Sometimes I was given these balloons to take home when the Christmas period was over. One thing I liked to watch but not touch was when the tree trimmings were taken down as all these baubles, birds, stars and half moons were all thin coloured glass and would break very easy they had to be packed in boxes of cotton wool. The same was done with the table ornaments. All paper trimmings were folded and stored for another year.

The next door opening out from this large hall was into the sitting/drawing room and in my mind the most comfortable room in the house. It had a wooden floor covered by a very colourful Persian carpet but not wall to wall. There was a space of about three foot between the edge of the carpet and the wall where there were stained boards. There were armchairs of different sorts, some were winged chairs, some big floppy types, but all very snug to sit in, with the soft cushions. I liked this room with it round table in the centre, green baize card table and leather pouffes for resting your feet on. I think there was one soft settee to match the two chairs. The fireplace was the same as in the dining room except wood logs were used in this room and it was the room where smoking was allowed. The aroma of pipe tobacco, which seemed quite pleasant at the time, would seem to hang around in there most days.

The Rev Moore liked to have big parties quite a lot and the drawing room was filled with the sound of wine being poured into glasses. This also meant that the staff had extra work to do, preparing extra food, tea and coffee, but the worst part of this was the extra washing up. They got no increase in their pay for the work they done but some of the guest would give them a tip in the way of money, which they put together and shared out equally. This of course was greatly appreciated in those hard days.

I was too young to be very interested in these parties and had the idea that it was best to keep out of the way as much as possible. I did get to know some of the guests as they came more often. One was a man called Ronnie Gladden he was John Moore's pal and came on a motorbike. He lived at Bressingham Hall with his family who farmed there. Another family were the Ogles from Park House in Diss (Now the Park Hotel).

In those days beside the roads was a high flint wall with broken glass on top. These people used to bring their dog over and it would run around the gardens with Taffy. I don't know what breed it was but always seemed bad tempered, best to keep out of the way of that one. I was glad to see them go home. Nobody every told me how they travelled. To me they just appeared.

The best one of all was a man, who they called Father Hepworth. The Rev Moore's services in church were very much like the Roman Catholic services, so it was said at the time, and Father Hepworth was a priest of that religion, so he got on well with the Moore family. I liked him as he would sit and talk to me in the kitchen but as he was Irish I didn't understand much what he said but he would give a few coppers for sweets. When I was older I was told by a member of the bowls club of one incident that he was involved in. It appeared that he was invited to one of the club meetings. When he turned up he took a large bottle of whisky from his pocket and put it on one of the tables and everyone thought that he was going to give them a drink. They were all very friendly to him and he made a speech and thanked them for their hospitality and then turned round picked up the bottle of whisky and walked away, much to the amazement of the bowls club.

Well the upstairs of the rectory was very private place and the only room I remember was what they called the box room. This was in fact a store room where all sorts of things were kept including the Christmas trimmings. There were a lot of cardboard boxes but what was in them I never found out, also some furniture that was not used in the house. I would have liked to look in those boxes now, what treasure did they hold?

I can remember some of the things in the bathroom, like real sponges, the loafer for scratching one's back when in the bath, the glass jars with glass lids with a round knob on top, filled with what was called bath salts, but were in fact nothing but small pieces of coloured soda, the wooden bath bridge for keeping soaps and things in, also the Gibbs toothpaste in their round aluminium tins and the other toothpaste in the red and white tins which was called Zucarel or a similar name. Both these were not like today's toothpaste in squeeze tubes but solid cakes like soap.

Then there were shaving mugs and both cut throat and safety razors, not forgetting the nice smelling Erasmic shaving sticks, also the small stick that was put on a cut to stop it bleeding. It used to sting when used but a small piece of toilet paper would do the same job.

This is about all that I can remember about the Rev Moore's rectory, with the exception of the lights. Some were candles with one or two table lamps that used paraffin oil but the main ones in every room on the walls and hanging from the ceilings were gas lamps. This was gas made from carbine and produced in a shed about twelve yards from the scullery door at the west side of the house. This had an apex tiled roof and was built of brick. It was also divided into two sections and had a door to each section. One section held the gas making equipment, consisting of a big boiler-type container and water tanks, and carbine containers which were about three feet high and one and a half foot across. They were circular in shape and corrugated like a sheet of galvanized steel. We used to cut these open and flatten them out and use them for the roofs of rabbit hutches or build sheds with them.

Inside the building everything was covered in a white slimy substance, even the brass dials and pipes. The smell inside was terrible and because of the gas no one smoked near this shed. There were warning notices on the door. How the gas got from the shed to the house I never really found out but it must be presumed it was by small pipes and I can't ever remember it going wrong. Inside the house the lights were lit by matches and this was used until electric lights came in the late forties.

The other half of the shed was a very different story. This was the boot shed where all the boots and shoes were cleaned. There were benches with polish and brushes, different sorts of polishing rags, an area where the dirty boots were put that needed cleaning, and those that had been cleaned, mainly brown and black, but in the summer white tennis shoes and in the winter the odd pair of Bullseye rubber boots.

Parts of the outside grounds and buildings I can remember quite well. From the scullery door there was a narrow path down the middle of a cobbled area to an archway through a ivy covered wall. There was a shed on the left hand side before the arch, in which the coal and logs were kept. This was also where the sticks were chopped for lighting the fires. The gardener would do this if there was a wet day or snow in the winter.

Once under the arch there was a large, wide, cobbled roadway from the front gate through to the tennis court meadow gate. Directly across the roadway stood a big brick building, known as the coach house. This had a double storey, red brick, outside wall with a few inside walls covered by plaster. It was divided up into various sections, the coach area which could hold up to four horse drawn coaches and the stable area which was again divided up into stalls by heavy wood and metal curved sections. In each was a manger for each horse to eat from. Also in this section were the pegs on the walls where the harnesses were kept. On the opposite side to the pair of big solid doors was a large room that was used for storing the garden tools and lots of other things including the lawn mowers, one of which was a very big Acto with a very large grass box. The other mower was a small push one with no engine at all made by Qualacast. This was used for very narrow grass paths.

Some of the tools were very old well used but done the job well. One thing that was in everyone's garden shed in those days was a besom broom. This was made by putting a bunch of birch twigs together, winding wire around them to keep them tight together and a piece of rough wood was pushed into the top for a handle. They always seemed to be having new ones because they were used for getting dead grass from the lawns and sweeping leaves off paths and all that type of work so they were worn down very quickly.

Another thing kept in this building was the metal-wheeled, wooden wheelbarrow. This was very heavy especially when it had the sloped wood extension on top to carry a bigger load. You always knew when this was being used as the metal wheel made a lot of noise over the cobbles. Combined with the gardener's hob nailed boots there was quite a din. A pair of lawn edgers hung on pegs on the wall and different sorts of shears, some with angled blades with short and long handles were also hung up. There were different sized sieves for using to get the soil fine for potting. All these had wood bent into a circle to hold the mesh. As this was quite a big room there were a lot of shelves around the walls, some of which were high up and on these were the sprays that were used on the plants to stop bugs and disease doing any damage.

There was, on one wall, an old pine cupboard with locked doors and this could only be unlocked by the gardener because kept inside was a lot of poison in bottles and also some white lumps like sugar cubes. This I found out later to be cyanide which was used for killing wasp's nests by dropping about two pieces down into the nest after dark. Another one of the poisons was a powder called Blue Viteral, which was used to cover seeds, peas and beans to stop mice eating them when planted in the ground. This was also used by farmers on seed corn to stop it being eaten when planted. All these things could be obtained from chemist shops in those days.

There were lots of other things kept in this room. Big bunches of raffia (Bass to us) hung from pegs. There were several sizes of wooden steps for hedge cutting, also mole traps and a lot of terracotta flower pots of all different sizes, plus the watering cans with each for its own use.

As there was no door into the coach house from this room, entrance was by a door on the north facing wall and just inside the door were several sets of lawn bowls that belonged to the club. I did sometimes watch these being cleaned by the gardener. At this point I would like to say I spent a lot of my time with him as I was growing up and he always had time to tell me what things were used for but he did catch me once trying to drill a hole in a stone path with his brace and bit, which he then took away with the words, " Don't meddle with that boy".

Next to that door was another door which opened outwards. The reason for this was that just inside was a stairway which went up to a big room over the top of the coach house. As there was not any place in the village at that time other than the school this room was known to everyone as the Sunday school room. It was where all the village meetings were held. The Bowls Club, The Tennis Club and The Church Committee all held their meetings in this room. Whist Drives and Beetle Drives for their many causes were held in there but we must not forget its main reason and as the name implies its main function was the Sunday school services held there every Sunday afternoon for the young children before they were old enough to go to the children's services in the church on a Sunday morning from ten to eleven.

Inside this room was one big solid pine table and lots of fold up green baize topped tables used for whist drives and a lot of fold up wooden chairs. I did go to a few of those whist drives when I got older and one of the things that were done at these was to hold a raffle for prizes. Everyone brought tickets which were torn into two halves. One half was kept by the purchaser and the other half was put into a tall top hat. When it was time for the draw the person who done that would look the other way shuffle the tickets about and then draw out one half and call out the number. Whoever had the opposite matching number won a prize this was done until all the prizes had gone. Not everyone won a prize.

When I was about fourteen I went to some of these whilst drives. A lot of us young people did. Not because we liked whist but to confuse those dedicated old ladies who played every game as if their life depended on it. I did win two raffle ticket prizes. One was a brown paper bag full of green cooking apples. The bottom came off the bag as I was just about to come down the stairs. The apples arrived at the bottom before me and my empty bag. They were very bruised and totally useless for anything other than the compost heap. The second thing I won was a duck. As none of us liked duck I sold it to a butcher in Diss.

132

What I and some other people knew about this room was that this was the only way to get into the wood and glass observatory, which was on top of the roof of this building. Inside were some wooden seats and it was inside here that the then vicar of Wortham, Reverend Richard Cobbold, wrote "Margaret Catchpole" and in 1860 "A Victorian Village", all about the people who lived in Wortham at that time. Now we were very lucky because if we asked Will Percy, the gardener, if we could go into the observatory to make drawings of the wonderful views over the Waveney valley, including two churches, Wortham and Roydon, he would fit the ladder to the trap door for us to get in and out. Sometimes we would take books to read.

The old coach house at the rectory Wortham showing the observatory where Richard Cobbold wrote his books. This coach house is now a dwelling.

Inside Wortham church porch - names of rectors 25 July 1903 - Rev Fanning was vicar during my father's young years. He retired to live in the Wigwam just a few hundred yards down the road to the church.

The other part of the top floor over the stable area could be got into by the way of a stairway next to the inside of the south facing wall. This started next to a single opening door, which was used by the horses for entering and leaving the stables. There was an open area over the doorway, where the hay and straw was forked up onto the floor and stored for use in the stables below. This open space had posts and removable rails fitted to the floor as a safety measure. But the best thing as far as us children was concerned was that under the sloping stairway was kept a pony-sized rocking horse where we spent many hours being cowboys and Indians. We must have ridden hundreds of miles without even going outside.

Most of the floor of the whole building was made of a hard yellow brick laid on sand except for the stable floor which was black/grey brick made with two high sections per brick to look like cobbles and to stop the horses slipping. Quite a large area outside the doors on this side of the building was also cobbled with round flints.

There were two other parts to this building on the west side. One was the old pail toilet and the other was the rough stick shed where the sticks for peas and beans and also garden canes were stored.

There were two more sheds at the back of the rectory and north of the coach house. One of these had an open end, which was where the little pony cart had been kept. This had been used for different jobs in the garden so I was told but was not there in my time. This shed was used for storing leaf mould and compost also broken pots and the machine that marked the white lines on the tennis courts.

The other shed was near the pond on what we called the tennis court meadow. This had a stable type door of two halves and a metal hayrack on the wall and I can only guess that this was built for a pony stable. When the Rev Moore was there chickens were kept inside as his son John kept lots of laying hens in huts on metal wheels all over the meadows as there was a lot of what was called Glebe land that went with the rectory. Some was arable land some was meadow land and John had a lot of that for his chickens. I did sometimes go with him to take water for the hens to drink. This was carted in a galvanized, oval shaped, tank on high metal wheels supporting a metal frame with a V shaped joint on both sides where round pins on the tank dropped into two handles that were used for moving this tank about. When full of water the tank would swing on the pins and keep upright. A small plank of wood floating on the surfaces of the water stopped any from spilling out.

Now all this Glebe land had heavy square gate posts and ornamental gates, all painted in white gloss. What we called the rectory meadow had a public footpath going through it but at each end of the path was a kissing gate, this was a half circle made of fencing and posts and the actual gate was hung from a centre post so it opened each way inside the half circle. This was to stop sheep and cattle getting out.

Beside the conservatory, joined to the house, there was also a big greenhouse near the open end shed. This was also used for growing grapes. Beside other things there were metal pipes in here joined to a boiler in a fireplace which burnt coke to heat the place up in the winter. I never did see this in use.

Now all the main lawns and gardens had a metal fence made from strips of flat iron with half inch round rods going through them. With three rods going into each three foot upright there must have been miles of rod used. A hedge was planted near the fence in my time and I think still is grown up and over to cover most of the metal work. This hedge was cut every year to look neat and tidy, including the acre of kitchen gardens which was allowed to grow to about five foot to keep out the wind, I liked the big lawn, gardens and shrubbery that were in front of the house, the big red poppies with their silver/green leaves in the half circle gardens at intervals beside the lawn, also bright and dark red peonies and blue, purple and yellow Iris all sets against a background of yew and laurel shrubs. There were circle beds in the side sections of lawn next to the road going down to the church. These were set with flowers of the seasons, daffs, tulips, begonias and dahlias and always looking very pretty.

On the north side of the house was another big lawn surrounded by very neat laurel bushes and still northwards, behind the bushes, was what we called the square garden. This was also surrounded by laurel bushes. It was called the square garden because this was a massive area of land with a grass path all round the outside and grass paths from each side crossing in the middle to form four separate square gardens. These two paths had pergolas over them and were covered in all different varieties of rambler roses and the fragrance in the summer was breathtaking. In one corner of this garden was a very big clump of pampas grass which looked really nice when blowing in the wind but the best of all, which was the favourite of all us young boys, was a giant of a walnut tree. Every autumn we were given the privilege of scaring the rooks away from the tree and stealing the walnuts. We would not even think about doing this ourselves, well not until they had dropped to the ground first but you had to be a bit careful because the green outer case always left a stain on your finger. There were other rose beds about at certain places in the gardens besides lilac bushes, laburnum trees and many ornamental bushes and trees.

Two other places I think should be mentioned also. One was the area that was surrounding by well cut hedges where the lawn clippings and material being made into compost was stored. The lawn clippings were in two big heaps. One was fresh clippings and the other was year old clippings which every autumn were carted away and dug into the vegetable garden, which was not all used in the Rev Moore's time. Now the smell from this rotting grass was very strong and as the new cut grass was put on this heap some soil was laid on top of it and marrow and cucumber plants were set in the soil. As the grass heated up this was ideal for these plants and large amounts of lovely marrow were cut and used in the kitchen. Everything that would make compost was put on this heap. I clearly remember the lemon peel and half grapefruit skins that were there beside cabbage leaves, carrot tops, potato peels and hedge cuttings and in the autumn all the leaves that had been swept up. Number two was the mint and herb garden. There were several different types of mint grown in rows beside parsley, sage and thyme. This area gave off a very pleasing smell all the year round.

In those days nearly every house had its own dump, as there was no refuse collection then, and the rectory was no exception. As this was a big house where lots of entertaining was done, there were wine bottles of all sorts, broken or unwanted crockery and kitchen utensils, broken ornaments and everything that had its contents emptied was thrown away but all cardboard and paper was burnt on a bonfire.

In 1933/34 there were things happening that I was too young to understand. First was that the daughter, Eileen, never seem to come home, only on very rare occasions but when she did there were always paintings in oils in the house. She did give me one once of a horse's head on a dark yellow background and this hung in my bedroom for years but where it went too I don't know. I learned when I got older that she never really left London.

Also about that time John Moore was getting over a gate with a loaded gun and what caused the gun to off I don't know but somehow it did and he got shot in the arm. Gladys the cook found him lying on the ground near the gate. I think everyone including my mother and father helped with his chickens at that time. I know he ended up with just his right arm but he was a strong man and it was not long before he was back and working as best he could. I did my best to help by getting the eggs from the huts in the meadow always keeping an eye on the big Rhode Island Red cockerels that shared the meadows with the hens.

The most unexpected thing of all was that the Rev Moore decided to change to a smaller rectory so he and his wife moved to Ringstead near Hunstanton in North Norfolk. I remember our family going to see them once and it was certainly a smaller house in a proper little coastal village with flint stone houses and within the smell of the sea. It had a much more open garden with hardly any shrubs and trees.

Meanwhile Wortham rectory was left with only John Moore living in it but my mother made sure the place was kept clean and tidy and every morning John came to our house where my mother made him a good cooked breakfast. He supplied the eggs with some for us as well. He always had bacon, sausages, kidneys, fried bread with tomatoes and mushrooms from one of the glebe meadows. Now this was the first time that I had ever seen a person with one arm eat a meal and this was done in a very clever way. He had a combination of fork and knife together. This had two prongs of a fork on one side and the other side was solid to form a knife with the sharp cutting edge along one side.

John was a very determined person and for this reason he soon made the best of his misfortune, even to feed his chickens and pulling the tank of water for filling the drinkers. Will Percy helped with the bags of feed corn. Now this went on for a few months but then everything disappeared. I don't know if it was sold in Diss markets or at a private sale. I can remember walking across one meadow and all that was left was chicken manure, a few feathers and bare soil in certain places, no grass at all.

The whole place seemed quiet but the house itself was not empty. A lot of the furniture and other goods had been left behind. I don't know if these things went with the house or not but the same happened to the outbuildings and the goods inside them. I know the rocking horse was left. Also at that time Will Percy was still looking after the gardens. Some of the church services were taken by another parish priest but it was not long before we learned that another rector was taking over the church duties of Wortham and would live at the rectory.

At that time the church council was run by a lot of the whist drive women with an attitude problem. They were hoping for an elderly vicar who was like the Rev Moore (but more about them later) but what they got was a go ahead young family man who could change the whole parish and, on 12 September, 1935, the Rev Hubert Hiller, his wife and son George moved in, complete with their own cook, Miss Walton, who had been with them for quite a long time. She appeared to be a very good at her job type of person. I am not sure but I think that they came from somewhere near Manchester. To complete the family they had a grey/black spaniel called Whoopie. As it was such a big house, all the furniture they brought with them added to that what was left behind by the Rev Moore still left plenty of room for changing things around.

After a few days of them being there, a message was sent to my mother to go and see them with the idea of her working for them. But this was a different situation to what she had been use to. These were more of a country type of parson people. The strict church on Sunday law was done away with which was the first sign and it was up to you if you wanted to go. Mother was offered a job to help on certain days at her own convenience or if anything special was taking place.

All the big parties stopped and the grand Christmas table disappeared. There was a certain amount of decorating at that time of year but nothing like the Moores done. This was a time of big change. The Rev Hiller made his study in the bedroom above the former study downstairs. Mrs Hiller helped with all the housework and the meals that had to be prepared. She didn't mind peeling potatoes or getting the cabbage ready for cooking. She and Miss Walton made a good team but it was obvious that there was far more to do than what they had been used too. What we did find out was that Rev Hiller was deaf in one ear so it was always best to talk to him in his best ear. Some people at first thought he was ignoring them but soon found out this was not so.

There is no doubt that after he settled in that he would change the village as well as the church and rectory. One of the first things he done was to meet as many people as possible by going to visit them and people soon got use to this fairly tall, plumpish chap dressed black or grey tweed suit and a wide rimmed black trilby type hat. Although he brought a big heavy bicycle with him he chose to walk around the village on his own but at the later end of his time here he did have to rely on a walking stick to help him along.

One of the first things he had done was to have all the rectory and outbuildings repainted in white gloss on door frames and windows with Brunswick green on doors and windows frames. This was the time when painted surfaces were primed with red lead as a sealer. All outside walls that were not brick were painted in yellow, buff or red ochre, which was a pigment which had to be mixed up by the decorator, as did the paints in the nineteen thirties. The person who did this was a Mr Berty Hales, who employed several men in a painter and decorator's business in a building down an alleyway between what was then Easto's wet fish and a fish and chip shop and John Aldridge ironmongers at the bottom of Pump Hill. I cannot ever remember the inside of the rectory being decorated although I think it must have been at one time because the kitchen was changed from magnolia to pale yellow.

Mrs Hiller also went for walks around the village wearing what looked like quite expensive clothes, complete with large brimmed felt hats but what stood out most was her hand knitted stockings. I am not quite sure if she actually started the Wortham branch of the Mothers Union but she did play a very active part in it for many years. Like her husband, she would always be ready for a chat. It was not long before they both became really well known and respected by the villagers with the exception of the odd one or two people.

The church was beginning to get fuller each week for the eleven o clock service as more and more people liked the way the Rev Hiller preached. No one went to sleep during his sermons. I, with a lot of my friends, was asked to join the choir, which we did.

Lots of other changes were being made. The front lawn of the Rectory was being cut every few days so the bowls club could enjoy a really competitive game. The tennis court was given the same treatment and was used most of the summer. The kitchen garden was extended, and more vegetables were grown. A large area was made into a fruit growing section complete with posts holding wood frames, to which small mesh wire netting was stapled. This was a permanent fixing but the top was fitted with two or three rails from side to side and a small mesh net was hung over during fruiting time. The fruit grown inside was strawberries, raspberries, black, red, white currents and gooseberries. Trained along wires, held in place by wooden posts, peaches were done the same. In all this was quite a large area of garden. Another area of garden fenced off was where the cabbages, Brussels sprouts, cauliflowers and all other brassicas were grown. This was done by stakes and wire netting let into the ground a little way to stop the rabbits. This was not a permanent fixture and was moved each year to follow the rotation of the garden.

Also a new plant was introduced to the kitchen garden. Several rows of which were grown each year and this was the tobacco plant, which looked pretty when in flower but it was the big broad leaves that were picked and hung on wires across the ceiling of part of the hay loft over the stables. Up there they dried for a long time, after which they were treated with some form of sweetener then pressed and put into a hand operated machine to be cut into fine strips for smoking in a pipe. The Rev liked his pipe and home grown tobacco which he was never without.

He was also a very keen gardener and could be seen most days working in the flower beds or vegetables gardens with Will Percy. The whole place began to take on a more tidy appearance. The roadside hedges were kept cut, the tall shrubs each side of the path, between the tradesmen's door and the road, had their tops cut so they looked level across at about six foot high. The trees in the orchard were given a good prune and the apples, pears and plums all increased in size, especially the Victoria plums. They were very big and, if you could get one ripe, excellent to eat.

I was now old enough to help with some of the small jobs, like watering the young plants, hoeing and lawn edging and, as I had helped on the garden at home, I knew what to do. It was not long before I was shown how to use the small lawn mower and from that onto the big Acto. I enjoyed this, a machine that I could control, but I must admit that making a mistake with the throttle sometimes found me trying to cut a gravel path.

It was during one summer holiday that I worked there for five of the six weeks and learned how to prune and dehead roses, how to pot up plants after making compost for the job. I did have a problem with the big heavy lawn roller. It was alright when started and would run on its own but starting to pull it was as much as I could do. However the old wooden wheel barrow was replaced with a light metal one with a solid metal rubber tyre wheel. This was easy to push.

There was also a change as far as leaves were concerned in the autumn. As the metal barrow did not have any extra fittings on top to take a bigger load, Rev Hiller had a very useful cart made of boards with a wood handle and metal brackets each side, into which were fixed bicycle wheels with pumped up tyres. This held, when filled, about six to eight barrow loads of leaves besides being used for grass cutting and other things.

One of the job I had to do was to take the wheel barrow and pick the onions off the tops of the tree onions, which were planted each side of the path down the kitchen garden. I must admit that being allowed to use a new barrow with a red painted wheel and frame was something that made my day and I made that job last as long as possible. The onions I collected were taken indoors and pickled.

Our new vicar certainly brought some new life to the place as out in the orchard were five hives of bees and it became a familiar sight to see him with his hat on, complete with a fine mesh net over his face, also using his hand bellows puffing smoke into the hive when extracting the honeycombs, which were then put into stainless steel containers with a handle on top connected to a spindle which, when turned, spun the combs around fast enough to throw the honey out into the container, where it was then drained out at the bottom. Most of the honey was put into jars and stored till it was used in the house. We did have some of it at home and very nice it was too. In those days bees had plenty of flowers to get honey from. There were fields of red clover, beans, peas, and all the fruit trees, beside the meadows full of wild flowers. Neither Will Percy nor I would go near the bee hives. I never saw the vicar wear gloves but I cannot remember him getting stung.

The other life he brought to the place was eight chickens and one cockerel. These were totally different from the breeds that we were used to, like the Rhode Island Red and the White Sussex. They were Grey Wyandotte, which was a chicken with grey feathers with white dots all over them. Their home was the old pony stable.

Some things that had been done any time were now made to a routine, like cutting the front lawn on Saturday mornings ready for the bowls meetings in the evenings.

Just into the shrubbery, near the scullery door, fitted to a concrete base was a fairly big black Hornsby Ruston petrol engine, which had a big orange flywheel each side. This was completely covered by a grey wooden shed with a sloping, galvanized roof, which was all fitted to rails for moving along when the engine was in use. This was every Saturday just before dinner time, when a belt was fitted from the engine to a big wheel that drove a pump that carried water from the well near the outside corner of the scullery wall into the attic tank. The steady thump of the balance weight and the cogs on the wheel could be heard a long way off. Adjoining this mechanical pump was a tall, lead covered hand pump with a big metal spout, topped with a hook where a pail could be hung.

While we are in this area, up in the gable of the roof, fitted onto the outside wall, was a little belfry complete with one brass bell which was rung for one of three reasons, 1 if Will Percy was wanted in the house for something, 2 if any of the family were in the grounds and were wanted for something, and 3 if it was twelve thirty and lunch time. This bell could be heard for nearly a mile away. The bell was never rung in Rev Moore's time.

Getting back to the engine, on the opposite side to the pump was the saw bench and the driving belt would be fitted to that to saw up logs for the fires. All cut down timber was stored near the saw.

Now between the Reverend and Mrs Hiller they were looking for ways to raise money for the church and they started what a lot of villages were doing then and that was organizing a church fete and flower show. This was held about the last Tuesday in June and all the school children were allowed the afternoon off to attend. I would like to point out here that this was the only day the chickens were shut up in their shed. The rector had a lot of trestles made to take boards made into sections like table tops for the flower show, which was held in the coach house. Most people were keen gardeners in those days, more a necessity than pleasure, and the competition was intense with the prizes being a few shillings. When beer was three pence a pint this was well worth winning.

There was an entry charge of six pence to be paid at the front gate and members of the church or the council would sit on chairs to collect the money as people went in. I was lucky as I could get in the back way from our garden. As long as I kept away from the gate I was sixpence in pocket. Some of the flowers and vegetables shown were very good, also the home grown fruit. The allotment holders and gardeners would walk around after the judging to see who had won prizes. There was always a friendly banter amongst these hard working men. The judges were mainly from some parish a long way off so they did not know the competitors. There was also a section for the women of the villages for home made cakes, bread, sponges, pickles and jam and here the competition was even stronger than the men's section and a few more snide remarks I can recall.

There was always music from a wind-up gramophone and someone made the announcements on a type of loud hailer. The children had races on the front lawn and there were several sideshows jotted around the grounds. Some were the regular ones like coconut shies and bowling for the pig, this was getting wooden balls through a board with holes cut in. Each hole had a number painted over it and at the end of the day the person who had the highest score won the pig. This was a small pig given by a local farmer but of course whoever won it had to have somewhere to keep it. Other things were hoop-la stall, where a small wood circle had to be thrown over a prize on a table, of which there were many, all donated by the parishioners and for the very small children there was the Lucky Dip, little wrapped up presents in a wooden barrel. Who supplied those I don't know.

There were many other games and competitions to have a go at. There were also soft drinks and ice creams supplied by Bumshi's of Diss, who would bring two big red painted barrels, one full of white and pink ice cream, complete with the tools for filling wafers and cornets, which he supplied as well. These barrels stood on the ground in front of the east windows in a shaded area. Two people volunteered to serve these ice creams and the barrels would be collected when empty. Several pounds were made at these annual events.

I never knew of any beer or spirits being sold at these gardens fetes but with three pubs in the village at that time it was not needed. The pubs were - The Dick (Wortham Ling), The Magpie (Magpie Green) and The Dolphin (Long Green). Now there is only one left The Dolphin.

Well, after the flags and bunting were put back in their wooden tea chest until another year and table tops and trestles stored away, the lawn edges repaired and footprints raked from rose beds and gardens, life got back to normal at the rectory.

As autumn arrived the floors of the stable stalls were covered in straw. The apple crop was laid out on it for winter storage. The main potato crop was lifted and was also stored in the stables under a covering of straw. The onions were tied together by string in big bunches and hung from the ceiling in another part of the stables. The walnuts and hazel nuts had been gathered, dried and put in tins and stored on the top shelf of the pantry. The grass clippings and compost were carted to the kitchen garden and dug in.

Both the Rev Hiller and his wife carried on with their every day life. He was visiting people and one local farmer told me that he would appear just as his family sat down to have their dinner. Not wishing to be rude and tell him to go away, the farmer said to the vicar, "Would you like a hot boiled potato sir?. Much to his surprise, the vicar said, " Yes please" and pulled a chair up to the table and sat down with the words, "I'll have some gravy too if you have some to spare". The vicar must have taken a hint because he never appeared at dinner time again.

Mrs Hiller had meetings to attend all the over the place and became firm friends with lots of people, always ready to listen to other problems. Also there was quite a lot of visitors coming to the rectory to see her. One particular couple who came a lot were Mr and Mrs Tooth from the Grove, a big, grey brick, Georgian house with lots of outbuildings, trees and land just past the Magpie on the Redgrave road. This house had a lemonary, a great big glass building next to the wall of the house. Anyone going past on the road could see the lemons getting yellow as they ripened. They both rode high bicycles and Mr Tooth, a well known magistrate, would, other than on very hot days, always wear a waterproof cape. I saw him once cycling very fast down the hill from Magpie Green past Wortham church with his cape blowing in the wind. As he was a man of few words he held up his hand as he passed me. In the early hours of that morning there had been a terrific thunder storm, flooding the road past the church. The water had drained away but it had left a sheet of mud across the road. As the cycle hit the mud, the front wheel slid across the road and Mr Tooth was laid on his back inside a muddy cape. His trilby hat had gone a few yards further up the road. He picked himself up, banged his hat on his head and, with mud dripping from both his hat and cape, jumped on his bicycle and went up the hill to the Wigwam as fast as he could. In all that time he never said a word, only a few grunts, but that was him.

There were changes going on inside the house. One major change was from the old gas lamps to paraffin oil table and wall lamps. These took more looking after than the gas. The wicks top had to be cut to stop smoking and making the glass black. If it was it had to be cleaned off. They also had to be filled every day during the winter and of course someone had to light them and turn them out. Most of them had brass mounts (oil containers) but a few were glass and ceramic and it changed the smell of some of the rooms. This was where the candle and candlesticks came into their own as they were used for going upstairs at bedtime.

Some new furniture had arrived with the Hillers by the way of very comfortable willow armchairs. I had never seen anything like these before. They were very heavy to move and woven like a basket from top to bottom but with big soft cushions on them could be ideal for a snooze, something the Rev done if he had a chance and so did Whoopie if he got the opportunity although he sometimes got taken off and put on the floor which did not suit him at all. He had complete run of the house and gardens, which he used to his advantages. If the weather was bad, no matter how much he was called he always found somewhere to hide.

One of the things that Whoopie really liked was walking with the vicar around the village, always about two yards behind but sadly this was to be his downfall. One particular day in late March, I'm not sure if it was 1943 or 1944, but a strong wind was blowing from the west. Most of the day there had been clouds of dust coming down from the Brecklands, spreading over Diss and the villages both sides. What reason the vicar had to be walking out in it I don't know but he was and took Whoopie with him. Beside the garden of our house stood two tall fir trees. As the vicar continued walking up the road from the Dick towards the rectory, the gale really peaked and the clouds of dust were darker than ever, as great gust of winds were blowing trees down all over the place. One particular extra strong gust blew the fir tree near the road down right across the road and into the meadow opposite. Just by chance, within a few minutes of that tree falling, from around the corner came two men who were local tree fellers, who lived in the village. Knowing the vicar quite well they offered to clear the road by cutting the tree into moveable lengths. As this tree was, or rather had been, on Glebe Land the vicar thought it was his duty to see this done and to reward these men for their trouble. It was quickly done and the men were duly rewarded from the vicar's wallet and everyone proceeded on their way. I was told that Whoopie had gone home by himself as he was nowhere to be seen, but he had not and no matter how much people called and hunted for him he could not be found. However I went to see if I could claim a length of tree trunk for our wood pile and looking at the soil covered roots of the tree I saw to my dismay a small piece of black hair under all the weight. What had happened was that he must have been having a look inside the hole from where the roots of the tree had been pulled when the men cut the trunk. All the soil and roots dropped back to the place they came from and he never stood a chance. We dug him out and buried him in the shrubbery in his favourite hunting ground. The rectory was a sad place for many weeks, and they never had another dog.

Meanwhile more work was being done in the butler's pantry as all the brass oil lamps had to be kept polished. Miss Walton kept things more organized than they had been so the place was run well to an almost daily routine. My mother helped on certain days with the cleaning and cooking when she was required. New things were being brought like a new Hoover instead of beating the carpets. This was hand pushed machine which had to be cleaned quite often. I think this was called a Ewbank cleaner. There was also an apple crusher for making juice or cider. Nothing was wasted. The fires were not lit so early in the mornings and life went along at a leisurely pace until the war came and things changed (see the war section).

The one person who did not appear very often was the son George because he was away at college but I don't know which one. He had a very interesting hobby. Up on the top floor beside the drying tobacco leaves he had put up the trestles and table tops used for the flower show around the outside and across the middle of the room and on top of these he had a railway layout. I don't remember what gauge it was but it was much bigger than the ones we had with just a few lines to make a circle, a clockwork engine, tender and two coaches. This had a double track on top of the boards with sidings, buffers, points, signals, signal box and two stations. There were more things like telephone posts, notices, level crossings, arches, bridges, station trolleys everything to make up a model railway. The wagons and trucks were about eight inches long. The coaches were about double that length and the engines and tenders about twenty inches long. Now I never knew what propelled these things along as not once did I see them working. We would go up the stairs sometimes and make up a train load of wagons or coaches and push them by hand but I am sure that was not the right way to do it. In the end, when the Hillers left the rectory, all the complete set was dumped in the deep dry pit in the triangle wood. I can clearly remember seeing all the lines lying on top of the wagons and coaches. What can one say now (if only). They would have been worth a small fortune now in a sale. I expect that George had not used them for many years.

He chose a life in the army and trained as an officer. What his rank was I don't know but he did go to some foreign countries during the war, where he was in charge of a gun crew, who lost control of their gun being towed along and it went in to some deep hole or ditch. In the process of getting the gun back on to the road he accidentally got jammed by the gun and something else, which crushed his chest. After a time he was allowed to come home and I did see him but he looked very ill and it was not long before he died. I'm not sure but I think he was buried in Wortham Church yard.

So once again the rectory was a sad place for a long while. Rev Hiller still went for his walks and visits around the village but now he was slower and had a walking stick to help him on his way, but his interests for the garden and the rectory in general never faded. I would sometimes go up to his study and have a chat with both him and Mrs Hiller. Then one evening he was sitting in an armchair which had about seven or eight inches of wood legs showing below the upholstery and he asked me if I would cut off three inches from the back legs to make the chair comfortable to sit in. I did this for him and he rewarded me with the biggest bunch of black grapes I had ever seen. I had helped Will Percy to prune the grape vine in the conservatory but I did not know they got as big as this.

Another change that came to the rectory was that Will Percy bought himself an old Austin Popular car with what he called a dicky seat in the back. The reason for this was that the back cover could be lifted up and two people could sit on a seat in what would be the boot of the car. But this car had its problems and broke down many times. He sometimes took someone to Diss railway station on certain Sunday afternoon and he would take either my mother or father with him for the ride or so he said but I think it was to help push it home, which they had to do many times. Eventually he got another old car. This time it was a bullnose Morris. In part exchange he got rid of the Austin and he was much more mobile.

The Morris had seats in the back for passengers and a canvas roof over the top and around the back with a celluloid window in the centre. It also had metal doors along each side but the top of the doors were open, no glass, no canvas just an open space. This car engine was also started when the handle was cranked. But, other than that the dashboard had to be pushed back into place when a red light came on and the gear stick would come out when changing gear, it was in good order. It always got home safely. Both these

146

cars were coloured blue. Part of the coach house was used as his garage. I think petrol at that time was a few pence a gallon.

The Rev Hiller also had a car at that time but his was a much more modern one. This was a black Morris Eight, which was also kept in the coach house and I think that Will Percy sold his bullnose Morris and used the rector's car when he wanted to. During the war when only certain people could get petrol this car's allocation was used on the lawn mowers and after draining the radiator it was put on bricks to keep the tyres off the floor and a tilt put over the top and was left like that till after the war, when it was put back to working condition and used for its rightful purpose.

Unfortunately one day the vicar was going to Diss driving with his pipe in his mouth when, at the junction of the Redgrave road and the road from the Dick on the Ling, he met another car coming from Diss and there was a collision between the two cars and the pipe he was smoking was forced up into the top of his mouth causing him a great deal of pain and he was in hospital for a long time. What happened to the cars or the other driver I don't know but I don't think the vicar had any more cars. ,

Miss Walton seemed to be getting on quite well with a few occasional days' help from my mother, who by now had nearly had a full time job working in the fruit section of Hall Farm. I had other jobs to do but I do know the Reverend Hiller retired in 1959 and moved to one part of the manor house in Roydon, where I did some work for him. Both he and Mrs Hiller were getting quite old by this time.

In 1970 a new vicar had arrived and I was not having any contact with the rectory at all. Later a new rectory was built, which was about one third of the size of the original one, in one corner of the orchard near the road. The old rectory came up for sale and the house and gardens were divided into two separate units and two different families lived in the house. The coach house was also converted into living accommodation.

The Rev Hiller died on 2 January 1970 and Mrs Hiller died on the 26 July 1975 and both are buried in one grave in Wortham churchyard. Both these people had been very good to me and my family and what I have written under this heading is not quite all the story about them but the rest is added in other chapters.

The Farming Part of the Story

From the time before I started school there was always a connection with farming, which was very different from what it is today. Horses and manual labour was how the work was done. Only the really big farms had a tractor. I can well remember the hot days of harvest time and all the hard work done by the men's wives to make sure that they had a hot meal at midday and plenty of drink (mainly cold tea) to last them through the long hours of a working day, from seven in the morning till eight o'clock at night, five days a week and Saturdays seven to five if you were lucky or till a certain job was finished.

But I cannot remember in my time the men doing what was then called taking a harvest. This was a meeting attended by all the workers, the foreman and the farmer, and they all agreed on a certain price to get all the corn off the fields and under cover, either into stacks or barns and also allowing for wet weather by fitting in a clause in the contract to clear a cattle yard of muck and to cart it into a field ready for spreading. After all this was done a certain day was chosen for what was known as the harvest hawky. This was a feast of bread, beef, cheese, homemade cakes and anything that was available at the time, all washed down with plenty of strong beer and cider. In all a good time was had by all as the workers wives were invited as well but most people had problems getting home after one of these meals as the beer and cider took hold. Depending on whose farm these meals were held, the main building they were held in was either a barn or a cart shed complete with a few decorations of some kind.

The farmers were very good at keeping their hands in their pockets as far as money was concerned, so to pay for all the food and drink on these occasions they would go around to all the people who had supplied goods to them over the years – blacksmiths, iron-monger, millers, harness makers, agricultural engineers and so on, and ask for a donation. Most people would give a little cash which was all totalled up and paid out as required. It was the one time of the year when the farmer was a "Good Old Boy".

I never actually saw or went to one of these meals myself but my parents did and one of the traditions in those days was that the last load of corn carted from the field had a twig of oak leaves on top. I did see this happen one particular harvest but this was quite a long time ago and what the purpose of this was I can't remember.

There were many older people when I started work who still believed in being superstitious about some things in their lives. Some of these at that time came right and others were just plain imagination. I know some of these things could have happened, like the weather lore that these people worked by. They could read the sky like a book, use the way the birds and animals were acting to predict future happenings of nature, was it going to good or bad harvest and so on. One of these things I remember them doing, and even my own parents did when I was very young was to open the front or back door when there was a thunder storm. The theory being that if a thunder bolt came down the chimney it would go out of the house by the open door. This does not happen now of course because lots of houses have central heating so there is no need for a chimney. I will fit some other things in as the story unfolds.

My first time of having anything to do with the farm that I can remember is going to the Royal Norfolk Show, which was on the meadows where Diss High School now stands. I cannot remember which year it was but I was in one of the two brand new single horse light harvest wagons from Hall Farm, Wortham. I know my father took a young horse in this one but who brought the other I don't know.

I was growing up and I had no idea what the future had in store at that time. I was a young boy mixing with some very old men but I listened and learnt a lot, I mixed with the farm animals but mostly the horses. No one took any notice of where you went or what you done. All the young boys whose families worked on the farm were regarded with respect provided that you took an interest. I later found out why this was. You were given little jobs and errands to do and it was only when you got older did you realise that you were working for nothing. I very often went with my father to feed the horses at weekends as most people had certain horses they used and these were ones that made up the plough teams, which they all took pride in.

I think I was about eight when I first lead a horse out on my own. I was so pleased to do this, although this was only from the stable to the meadow, I had control. Little did I know at the time that there were two or three elderly horses that were used for odd jobs around the yards, carting straw, hay and food for the cows. If they were left on their own they would have gone down to the meadows on their own anyway.

But horses were not the only animals that I had contact with when I was young. I can remember the sheep being sheared as two farms had quite large flocks, one at Hall Farm and one at Beechtree Farm. I did not have much to do with the Beechtree flock, which were all Suffolk sheep. I did sometimes help the shepherd to set out the folds in the fields of mustard or turnips in the summer. This was hard work as some of the folds had sheep netting around them which meant that big stakes had to be knocked into the ground for the netting to be tied too. But a tool was used to a make a hole which was called a fold-drift. This was a round metal bar with a big tapered point on one end and pointed like the sharp end of a stake. The other things used to make up the fold were iron hurdles, which looked very much like a gate but had a pair of small metal wheels fitted to the upright with a metal bar made into a axle at right angles. These were about two foot from each end with a small chain about halfway up the ends this was so they could all be chained together to make a long line or a square whichever was required. I liked helping to carry some of the stakes into the fields of mustard which were at that time much taller than me.

The shepherd for the Beechtree flock was a Mr Reggie Potter, Dodger as he was known who lived in a council house on the edge of the Marsh at Wortham next to the A143 Bury road, no tied cottage for him. He would let me ride in the tumbrel when the sheep were moved to another field even if it was loaded up with stakes, netting and feeding troughs. Sometimes other boys came to help but I never knew if we were a help or a nuisance as he never said anything. Nobody did in those days. I know he had a very friendly collie dog, which he relied on quite a lot as it really knew what to do when moving sheep. With the shepherd in front and the dog behind large flocks of sheep were moved for miles without any bother.

Now the Hall Farm flock, were still black faced Suffolk sheep it was a very big flock and very well looked after by a dedicated old fashioned shepherd by the name of Saddler Musk. He also had a collie dog, very much the same as most shepherds had around this part of the country. Now I did not have much to do with these sheep except at shearing and lambing time, which was carried out totally different than it is today. There were no big buildings built of solid walls and sheet roofs but they had to make do with what materials they had which was wooden stakes, sheep netting and straw. It was worked out as to where it was going to be and this was mainly on a gentle slope near the farm and as sheltered from the weather as possible. Then the stakes with the netting was erected side by side with a space of about a yard between them this space was then filled with loose straw and pressed down tightly. No bales in those days. The roof was made by stack tilts, held up by long timbers cut from a hedge or wood and covered over with a straw to make it warm and weather proof. The whole floor was kept warm by clean straw but part of it was left open. The covered area was where the sheep went to have their lambs.

The shepherd hut, which was on cast iron wheels, could be moved about near the lambing pen, mainly near the entrance. As the shepherds had to be about at any time of the day or night, they did have another farm worker to help so they could get some sleep. Inside the hut was a bunk bed with warm blankets, a tortoise stove which burned coke or wood, kettle for hot water and most of the utensils required to make life as comfortable as possible. The sheep dog would sleep either inside the hut or outside in the straw.

One night it was in the lambing pen with the shepherd and it laid down on its stomach and its hair on its neck stood up straight and the lambs parted to each side of the pen. Then through the straw wall came a white apparition which appeared to walk across the pen and out through the straw wall the other side. This was not seen again to my knowledge.

This shepherd did live in a tied cottage or part of one as a farm labourer lived in the other half and this was a thatched cottage at Willow Corner, Wortham Long Green. This man had a very large family, boys who were older than me. One with the name of Sub Musk a very rough character indeed, helped him on the farm. All the girls came to Wortham School but only one, Carol, was in the same class as me. I must admit they were all very tidy with smart clothes for such a big family. I think the mother was a smart type of person but I did not know her personally.

Getting back to the shepherd, as I said, some of his ways according to hearsay were a bit odd. It was said that he would not burn the tails off new born lambs but instead bit them off with his teeth and the same thing was done with the lambs that had to be castrated but I did not see this done so whether this was true or not I would not like to say.

Both these flocks had a time when they had to be dipped. I had a good reason to keep well away when this was being done but I liked shearing time as this was done in the big barn at Hall Farm for their flock. My father helped with this job, which took quite a long time and several men. I liked the whole atmosphere inside the barn at this time. The smell of sheep's wool after it had been cut and the oily feel of the fleece as it was rolled up combined with the strong smell of lime which was used for putting on any cuts made during the shearing. The old way of shearing was with a pair of hand clippers which was two sharp blades on a U shaped handle.

When I saw it done it was a more updated, by a machine, which was a set of cog gears with a flexible arm to a cutter, very much like a barber uses today. This was turned by hand to make it work. Usually there were two or three of these machines on one operation, all operated by two men each.

One thing I liked about this time of year was that on that particular farm at the west side of the farm buildings they had started to dig out a sand and gravel pit, solely for their own purpose and some sides of the sand was being used by sand martins for nesting, which they done by digging out holes in the actual steep sides. This bird was a smaller version of the swallow and I liked to sit and watch them flying around. There was quite a lot of these birds. Whether they are there now I don't know because during the war this pit was taken over by the government to dig out gravel for the local airfields.

I remember there were three very big draglines digging out the gravel and loading it into a fleet of small tipper lorries to cart to where it was required. I do know that Mendlesham was all built with this material, the runways, the roads and perimeter track, also the floors to the buildings. I think these little light green lorries belonged to a firm called Cubitt and Gotts and how many there was I don't know but there always seemed to be some moving about somewhere and the weight they carried was about seven tons each.

Another thing about this sand pit was that it once was the bottom of the river Waveney, which stretched across from Roydon to Palgrave, about three miles across. I know that part of a Viking or Saxon boat was found in the sand when it was first started to be dug out, which at that time was done and carted by horse and cart.

While I am writing about sandpits, there was another one quite close at Roydon on the opposite side of the river, just off the 1066 road. The materials from this pit was used on several airfields locally, Eye, Thorpe Abbotts, Fersfield and there were a lot of lorries about most of the time but the big difference here was they were digging up some very large stones mixed with a lot of other sizes so they made a decision to grade these for other usage. So there was a big machine built in the pit and the stones were put in the top and allowed to fall down and come out in heaps of different sizes. We always knew when this machine was being used as the noise of the stones falling could be heard at least 2 to 3 miles away. This pit is now a very nice small lake. As time passed by and as it was wartime the farmers were glad of any extra help they could get so it was not uncommon to be offered work on the farm during school holidays or at weekends. I would be joined by two other boys who lived nearby. We would all work together, pulling fat hen, a tall weed that grew in the sugar beet. This was alright when it was dry but when it was wet we were sometimes soaked to the skin as this weed had to be carried to the edge of the field so the seeds could not drop off and grow again.

There were lots of jobs we were given but not always together as sometimes we had to go and help the men. I was nearly always put with my father and therefore learnt a lot quicker than the other two. I soon learned how to harness a horse and use it on different jobs, although I had done this when we had borrowed a horse and wagon for carting wood. Some of this harness was quite heavy for us young boys. The collar was always put on the horse's head upside down but some of the older horses were a bit crafty and would lift their heads up as high as possible. Once the collar was over the head it had to be turned to a working position, then the bridle and saddle were put on.

What I did learn was that each horse was an individual and had its own little ways, which of course we had to find. The ones that were born and reared on the farm were quite easy to understand but the ones brought in from the marshes were totally different. They were almost wild as they had not seen many people or been handled and some were a real challenge and had to be handled with care. We usually helped with these ones to get them to know what we wanted them to do. This sometimes causes a smile nowadays when the modern TV shows a film called, "The Horse Whisperer". I was doing this when I was twelve years old. This saved the farm money as a boy was doing a man's job but I must admit I loved every minute of it.

One job that I disliked did not involve horses at all and this was done during the winter and early spring. In the autumn when the fields of potatoes were harvested they were not stored in big buildings, like they are today, but in what we called clamps, which were always near the road or farm track. When the potatoes were lifted in October they were taken out of the ground by a machine drawn by a pair of horses with a seat for the driver to sit on. This machine was called a potato spinner, which was two metal circles joined together with each circle having two sets of metal rods at alternate distances apart and opposite spaced on each circle. These rods were about six or seven inches long and dug into the ground when turned and levelled the soil while at the same time bringing the potatoes to the top of the soil. The whole machine was geared to work from both wheels and the spinner could be stopped from working by a hand operated lever.

Local women were hired to pick up the potatoes into wicker baskets and each person was allocated a certain length of the field to pick, marked out by sticks cut from the hedge. But some of these women were a little crafty and if they saw an opportunity they would move these markers closer together so they did not have so many potatoes to pick as this was hard back breaking work.

What happened after the baskets were full was this, three men with a horse and cart each emptied the full baskets into the cart. This was done in such a way that after the start in the morning there would always be two carts out in the field picking up potatoes and one at the clamp unloading. Now starting of a clamp was fairly easy, as all these carts had, at the centre of the front, a rather crude tipping gear. This was an upright bar with holes the same distance apart all the way up. The back of the shafts had a spring loaded handle with a round metal pin that fitted the holes on the uprights. This allowed the cart to be tipped a small amount at a time or a full tip. After the first load came to start a clamp the ground had been levelled so it was easy to just tip the cart up. The second load was tipped on top of that one and so on and the potatoes began to pile up to a base of about eight foot wide by six foot high, pointed at the top. This carried on along the ground load by load with some of the potatoes being unloaded by hand using a special fork to reach the top of the clamp. This fork was very much like a sugar beet fork but with a lot more tines and a small round ball of metal on the end of each tine. After a time the whole field was stored in one long clamp. How many clamps were made depended on how many fields had been set.

Sometimes if it was a long field they would want an extra horse and cart and this is where the boys would come in. This would always be the most stubborn horse and the heaviest cart. It did make it a hard job to do but for some reason I liked every minute of it. Autumn was just beginning, the mornings had freshness in the air and the smell of fresh moved soil, even the potatoes had a smell of their own.

The next thing that was done was all the clamps were covered in wheat straw, laid on like thatch, and then a single horse pulled a plough around the bottom of the clamp several times to loosen up the soil and then about four men from the farm would dig out the soil laying it on top of the straw until the whole thing was covered with pressed down soil and this was the way the potatoes were kept safe from the winter frost and snow.

Meanwhile, back on the field two horses were a light gang of harrows bringing all the missed and damaged potatoes to the surface and they were picked up and carted away for the pigs to eat.

I did say before that the job I disliked did not include horses at all just labour. This was a late winter job, which involved three men and a boy, which always seemed to be me. This was a complete reversal of what was done with the potatoes in the autumn. Shop keepers, chip shops and restaurants would order what amount of potatoes they required to use over a period of time and then reorder as each amount was used up. This job was called riddling the potatoes where a hand driven machine was used. This all started by getting the soil off the clamp, which was quite a hard job as sometimes this was frozen solid and a pick axe had to be used. Then the straw was taken off and heaped up ready for covering the front of the clamp at the end of the day.

Now this machine was a metal and wood construction consisting of an open front, two sets of circular mesh which let the potatoes through with the small ones dropping out at the front into containers for pig feed, and as the potatoes moved along and around this machine all fell into an elevator which conveyed them up into a box at the top, which had a movable flap to turn them left to right through the box into Hessian sacks hanging on hooks. When full each sack was put onto a set of Avery scales to weigh one hundredweight (112 lbs). This machine was worked by a set of geared cog wheels turned by a big metal wheel with a wooden handle at right angles. As the clamp was used so the whole thing was moved forward. Now the job of the men was as following.

Everyone helped with the opening up and covering up. One man forked the potatoes into the front of the riddle, another man stood at the side of the elevator picking off the stones and damaged potatoes and anything else that shouldn't have been there. The third man took the full sacks off the machine and done the weighing and last of all came the boy who turned the wheel all day, usually me (muggins). The only advantage of that job was that you could keep warm. Depending on how hard we worked but anything from three tons to seven tons per day could be done by this way. After a while a lot of farmers fitted a Lister or Petter petrol engine to the machine therefore doing away with the boy.

Well to get back to the horses, every chance I had to use them while I was working I took, even the small things like harnessing up. Bearing in mind this was only a part time job, I enjoyed every minute of it. I was by now handling all the horses on the farm both young and old, which I could do with confidence. October 15 1942 came and went and I was now fourteen, old enough to leave school but not till the end of term, which was 22 December 1942.

Hall Farm Wortham, where I started work in 1942.
Ransom's YL Plough, which was used on all Mr Rash's farms.

Depper, from Hall Farm pulling one of Young's of Diss
rubber tyred tumbrels. Bob Davis on board.

Frank Stevens, with his Burrell threshing engine 'Brittania'

Clem, who was at Hall Farm when I started work there. A real son of the soil.

Me with one of the horses near the stables at Hall Farm.

My father with a cart and trace horse at the top of the farmyard.

On 27 December 1942 I started as an employee of R H Rash at Hall Farm Wortham. No more odd days and holiday working to earn some cash for pocket money, from now on this was the real thing. I did know most of the people who worked there so this was a big help. I started off with my father to walk from home to the farm in my hobnail boots, heavy coat, cap and wide, leather, brass buckled belt around my waist. There was also a frail to get use to. This was a square type of straw braid, flexible basket with a fitted top to stop anything getting in and carried on the back by two leather straps. Most farm workers had one of these. Inside was a tin of sandwiches, made from homemade bread, and cakes. This was considered to be a bit childish to take sandwiches as all the men took a large bit of bread with a round section cut out to make a hole which was filled with hard cheese or drippings, a fat that had melted from roasted meat, and all cut with a sharp pocket knife. Sometimes the homemade bread would not keep very long and the crust was coated with blue mould. The flavour of this was covered by eating with a pickled onion. To complete the basket was a bottle of hot tea with no sugar or milk, kept warm by putting in an old sock but in winter this soon cooled down and this winter was a very hard one, sharp frosts and lots of snow. No wonder my father was wearing his Dunlop Bullseye rubber boots as were most of the other workers.

This particular winter, 1942-43, was one of the worst for many years, roads blocked by snowdrifts and freezing winds. I soon realised that I made a big mistake to wear leather boots, even if they were treated with Dubbin, which was a kind of a grease put on the outside of the boot to make it waterproof. My feet were frozen all day, even as I was walking about. By dinner time the tea in the bottle had ice on it.

It was dark when we left our house but this was soon changed by spots of light across the sky. As it was wartime the B17 and B24s were taking off from the local airfields and getting in formations for raids on Germany. As we approached the farm, other workers were coming from different directions and all heading for a square shaped clay lump building that was used for a cart shed but with the exception of a broken tumbrel and a few bags of fertiliser it was empty. This was used for storing the workers' bicycles during the time they were out working and where the foreman at 7:15am everyday gave out the orders for what work had to be done that day.

There is one thing that I would like to say at this point about the inside clay lump walls of this building was that a lot of them were covered in fork art. This was something that was done with the tines of a pitchfork and was circles, leaves and flower petals beside other shapes. Lots of clay lump walls on other farms had this kind of art done on them.

To get back to orders given for the day, a lot of the workers were cutting down hedges and digging out ditches. There was no frost in the bottom of a deep ditch. There were two horses and carts used entirely for feeding and littering down the yards where the animals spent both day and night in this cold wet weather, with two men to each cart. I was told to help out on one of them. I was told to get a two tined fork for moving the straw and hay. I did not know at that time that the farm did not supply the tools to use. I saw one in a shed which I picked up to work with and I was told in no uncertain terms to buy one for myself. So that is what I did and I made sure no one else used it by branding my initials into the handle with a red hot poker. I learnt later that there were two kinds of fork. One was a short loading fork and the other was a long handled pitch fork. The short one was used on most jobs.

On another farm was a dairy herd of one hundred milking cows plus a bull and all the follow on of calves etc.. This is what we had to do day after day, cart straw for bedding, hay in racks for eating. All the cows were fed milled corn, cotton and linseed cake, which had been crushed in a machine by hand and the main food, which was wet sugar beet pulp, all mixed together and put in concrete troughs at milking time twice a day.

My first day was very tiring and at the end of the day I had learnt a lot but I was glad to get home.

Now these two horses we used for the work during the winter were not the oldest but two with a calm personality to be amongst other animals and another thing that was special about them was that blacksmiths had fitted them with special shoes. As the roads were covered in ice and snow, their shoes had holes drilled in them which had a screwed thread for which a metal stud (like a football boot stud) could be fitted to stop the horse slipping. We always carried some of these in our pockets to be used as required. Well after the first day I did not go to work in boots but in a pair of rubber boots and very thick wool socks and we kept on doing the same old job except Fridays and Saturday mornings, when we had to work twice as hard to prepare for the weekends.

But as time moved on and winter changed to spring so did the work on the farm and all this time I was learning more and more. The cows at Low Farm were put out on the meadows around the farm, which cut down by half the work we had to do inside the cattle yards. We always worked it out so that we could have our dinner inside one of the buildings but now that was changing and there was a longer distance to travel as we had to go out into the fields to cut kale and lay it out in long lines on the meadows. Now this kale was four foot or more high and the stems were three inches thick at the bottom near the ground, where it had to be cut. Sometimes the hook being used would not cut but slide up the stalk and cut into your finger or hand. I still have some of the scars to this day.

Now we had some change to where we could have our dinner, no more sitting inside but standing out in an open field in the cold wind but what we did find out was, if we were in a kale field, we could cut ourselves a space between the plants.

By this time I did not have a man to help as they were on more important jobs so I had a friend one year younger than me. His father was manager of the hardware department of the Co-Op on the market place in Diss. In those days they sold small tins of solidified methylated spirit which we took to work, also a small tin of baked beans and in amongst the kale we had a hot dinner.

But some changes were being made elsewhere. As the arable land became more workable the cows could come out on the meadows to feed during the day but still had to be fed with other things. As the kale was finish we had to start on the cattle beet (mangolds), which, like the potatoes, had been in a clamp all winter. These had to be loaded into our cart one by one with a two tined fork. These were big, heavy beet, orange skins on the outside and white juicy flesh on the inside. All the cattle loved them. Some were used for the fat cattle after being put through a grinder which cut them up into slices like chips.

The horses we were now using, our ones we used during the winter being used on more important work, were the two oldest ones on the farm. Mine was an old half Suffolk, half Shire and he was called Short. I could understand that because he had a short black tail and also a mind of his own. Walking speed was very slow with his head down and nose nearly on the ground; it was not uncommon for his nose to hit a molehill for which he would stop dead having anyone off the cart, if not on guard for it. He was crafty old so and so. By that time it was just me carting straw and mangolds and what I did was to take the horse and cart into the meadow several yards, hang the reigns on the cart and start throwing out the mangolds by fork. Now a cartful of beet had to go a long way for so many cows but old Short had his own mind about that and after five or six yards he would turn round and head back for the gateway. I thought that I would get the better of him so I made him pull the loaded cart up to the other end of meadow and faced him towards the gate. I no sooner started to throw out the beet than his head went up and he nearly broke into a gallop towards the other end of the meadow.

Another thing he did not like was the watercart, which was just a cast iron tank on wheels, two at the back and one at the front joined to the shafts for steering also on top were two wooden doors to stop the water splashing out. Now old Short would back this cart into a pond to be filled up but would not pull it out when full, so what we had to do was to take him out of the shafts and put him back in the shafts facing the cart and he would back it out with no bother. This did not happen every time just when he had one of his awkward modes on.

The other horses all made up plough teams of two horses each. The main team used by the head horseman at that time was two grey Percherons named Doddy and Duke, a good team working together, but in a cart one had to watch them carefully as these were only young horses, freshly broken in by the head horseman, Mr Harry Hawes, who lived in a thatched cottage next to the Dick Inn on the edge of Wortham Ling. He was a very quiet spoken man and a very good man to work with and had a lot of time for us boys on the farm, always telling us what to do if any of the horses was being any trouble. I liked working with him when I could.

I learned a lot during those times. By this time I was working with horses every day but there is just one comment I would like to make about ploughing at this point and that was that nobody was allowed to use a furrow wheel on any plough. These had all been taken off when new. All the ploughs were single furrow and if the horses pulled well together they could be set to be controlled by one finger without the furrow wheel. Most of the farms had Ransoms of Ipswich YL blue painted ploughs, but some had Swotman ploughs made by Youngs foundries at Diss near the railway bridge. They made lots of other horse drawn implements and also repaired steam engines. I don't think they actually made any complete steam, self moving engines but could have made portable engines which had to be moved by a horse but I never saw one so I am not sure on that one. Now there was another plough on the farm but this was discarded in the nettles because it was a two furrow plough requiring three horses to pull it and it was a bit of a problem to turn on the ends.

Most of the other implements used were also horse drawn. The horses used when I worked at Hall Farm, Wortham, were eight altogether, a mixed lot as following. Boxer a brown horse with black tail and mane aged about ten years old always walked with his head up as if he had stiff neck usually a hard working, and part of a plough team whose other part of a pair was Depper, a slightly smaller horse but a true bred Suffolk with a chestnut brown coat and a lighter mane and tail. He was very hard working in any gear and very reliable, one who could be taken anywhere.

This plough team was used by a dear old gentleman named Fred Howard, who lived in a house at the bottom of Union Lane, right next to where Wortham Ling begins. Next to his house was a very tall popular tree, which could be seen for miles around. Now Fred was a very interesting man who had his own opinions about most things, a very interesting person. I liked working with him. I remember he did not agree with time change and would never change his watch to British Summer Time, so after the end of March you had to allow an hour in front of what he told you if you asked him the time. I never saw him ever wear rubber boots and I doubt if he ever did, always thick leather boots with both heel and toe irons complete with hob nails covering the soles. One thing that I could never understand about him was every autumn he would say that he had started to wear his, what he called autumn gandies. I never did find out what autumn gandies were. But I do know that he, like so many old people of that time, always wore very thick clothes, like very thick tweed or corduroy trousers and jackets with a white, black striped calico shirt complete with a red white spotted neckerchief and flat cap. These clothes kept the heat in during the winter and the heat out during the summer.

Another thing which he did was to wear a pair of corduroy buskins strapped to his legs just below the knees, whereas most people always had black or brown leather ones shaped to fit around the calf of one's legs, between the knee and the ankle, held in place by straps top and bottom. I myself had a pair of these, which kept the legs warm and trousers clean when ploughing.

To get back to Fred and his views on these times, he always said that he was as nature intended things to be. He said that his bedtime was the same as the birds and he got up in the mornings the same time as the birds started to wake up and I see no reason to doubt that. Also he was a very religious man. Like our family, he had a pew just inside the door of Wortham church. Of all the years I knew him I never once heard him swear and only once did I see him annoyed.

Whenever he had to use a single horse he always took Boxer. One day I was leading the horse for him while doing the final hoeing of sugar beet on what was called Oxer, a field of about thirty acres, during the July of one year. Now part of this field was adjoining the farm buildings. It was also next to the road that goes from Wortham church up to Magpie Green, which had a gateway about half way between the two places. This particular day the weather was cloudy with thunder storms around all sides of us. Then one storm started to come our way with rain becoming heavy and as we were in the middle of the field with no shelter, it was decided to leave the hoe in the middle of the field and let Boxer go to the gate and come home by road while we took a short cut across the beet field. By this time it was really raining hard. When Boxer went out of the gate on to the road, instead of turning left to come home he turned right up towards Magpie Green. So Fred said a few choice words and hurried across the field and up the road and caught Boxer before he got too far. By the time they got to the farm they were both very wet.

Fred's position on the farm was second horseman, which he was very good at, taking pride in all the work he done especially his ploughing and drilling, a real son of the soil, I am pleased I had the privilege to work with him.

Also in this stable were two more horses which were totally different from the plough team I have just mentioned. One was a twenty two year old Suffolk mare, light honey coloured coat with very light tail and mane. Her name was Lady I have mentioned her carting cattle food and she was used for light work, only pulling the smallest wagon or cart and the same with field work. It would be flat rolling or light harrowing. However she did get used for yard work, straw for pig yards, cattle food in the yard and on the meadows. This was quite easy for her really as even at her age she still could be relied on to do whatever was asked of her, with the exception of one thing. If anyone stopped for dinner and left her standing in the shafts of a cart she would fall down asleep if someone did not shout at her to wake up. We found it safer to take her out of the shafts and tie her to a fence during meal times.

Her stable companion was another Suffolk mare named Blossom. This one was very dark, almost black coat, tail and mane, which seemed rather strange as she was the daughter of Lady, but I was given to understand that true breed Suffolks came in a range of colours from very dark to very light, depending on the stallion used. Now Blossom was the anchor horse out of all the eight horses at Hall Farm.

Harry and Fred came to work from different directions but one thing they both had in common was the fact that they both walked to work on a footpath across the fields and meadows twice a day to get to work and home again, morning and night. Lots of people walked in those days as there was no other means of affordable transport.

Now Blossom was Harry's horse but other people did use her when he didn't. She was the one used to break in the young horses for farm work as a plough team and then cart work. If I got a chance to use her I would. This was the most reliable horse on the whole farm at that time. This was helped a lot by the fact that she had a very quiet nature and no matter what any young horse done beside her she was in full control and most of this was the result of the way Harry had treated her when she was young. Now his job was totally different from Fred's. It was not only feeding and grooming but it was traditional on most farms at that time for the head horseman to stack the corn at harvest time and this was an art in itself as each stack was different depending what type of corn was being stacked.

Oats were the longest sheaves and barley was the shortest which meant there was far more sheaves to each round of the stack. Most stack sizes depended on the size of the field but the average size was about nine yards by four yards or twelve yards by four yards and much depended on the man helping to stack. If the sheaves were forked to you the right way round all the man stacking had to do was lay them in place. It was easy but if they had to be turned around it was very hard work. Now wheat was a little easier as in those days it was grown for its straw as much as its corn. The sheaves had been cut by the binder and tied very tight and were about 3 to 4 foot long. They held together much better. The other thing that was cut long was beans but they were like sticks and had to be handled with care to stop dropping out.

One other crop was also harvested at this time of the year and this was peas.

163

They were different to the other crops because they could not be cut with a binder but by a special curved hook called a pea maker. They were cut when the stems were starting to turn from green to brown and the peas were just starting to ripen but not dropping out. When cutting this took most of the men on the farm to do as they were all hand cut by this long handled hook and made into round heaps which had to be turned, before carting, at least once sometimes twice or they would go mouldy and rot. These were terrible to load on a wagon and stacking them even worse. No one envied the head horseman that job. Now other work had to be done on three other crops grown on the farm but these will fit in later.

The head horseman had lots of other work that was classed as his job. Breaking in the young horses to work was another of them. Now this was quite easy with the ones born on the farm because they would have a halter put on them after they were a few days old and most days were walked around and slowly over a period of time other things were added to their life, so by the time they were old enough to work they were familiar with what was going on.

When I left school to work in December 1942 new arrivals in the stable next door were a pair of Percheron colts straight in from off the marshes near the coast. They had not been near people much at all. It was Harry's job to turn these two into ploughing and cart horses. My father helped with this as this was a two man job. Now to make a team out of these two was going to be a bit of a job because they were not of equal size. One, named Duke, had a light coat and small hooves and little feather on the legs but the other one was slightly taller, a darker coat and hooves as big as frying pans but there again very little feather. The main thing to make these two into a plough team was to put the big one in the furrow to make them look a level team over the top of their backs. This meant that the big footed one had to learn to put one foot in front of the other. This was against the unwritten law of a plough team but Doddy, as he was called, surprised everyone by doing this job really well, once he had been broken in.

Breaking any horse in is a challenge that any head horseman has to do, and there was two ways of doing this. One was what some farms did, which was in our opinion was a very cruel way, by using a stick to beat the animals and another trick was to chisel the bit to make points which would eat into the horses mouth, another was to wind a piece of rag around the bit so big that the horse was trying to champ the bit all the time and there again making the mouth sore. Another thing done, to stop a horse going backwards when it should not do so, was to put a thistle under its tail and press hard on its tail. There was also a method that was the opposite of that. If a horse would not go backwards two heavy nuts taken off bolts were tied to a piece of string joined to a short length of wood and tied over the top of its bridle (The Norfolk name for a bridle used on the farms where I worked was a Dutfin.)

and hung down in front of its face, so if it moved forward the metal nuts would hit it on the face.

There were many other things done that no one would talk about including if a horse reared up when in shafts a person would stand on the shafts with a glass bottle full of cold water and, when the horse reared, the bottle would be broken on the brass buckle on top of the bridle and the water would run down its face to make it think it had hurt itself. There was many other things done which were never spoken about and the farmer turned a blind eye. The farmer who I worked for at that time had well over one thousand acres made up into three different farms with six and ten horses on each farm and another farm with about one hundred milking cows, two bulls and several calves, which of course made lots of work. Details of these and what I done on the cow farm to follow later.

To keep with horses at the moment, there are two things that I think have to mention at this point. It's the stable mates of the two young Percheron colts. One was a young Suffolk, born on the farm and, being too young to work, was being tied up and fed with the older horses to get it accustomed to what it would have to do in the future. Not only that, the horseman would lift each foot in turn to get it ready for the time it would go to the blacksmith's to have its shoes fitted. This was done with all young horses if possible.

I would like to tell of what happened when I was very young and before farmers started to breed their own horses. This would be in the late 1920's, early 1930's. Horses were brought untamed and unbroken from dealers, who made a living from buying and selling from other people. It was my father's and another man's job to get on the train at Diss station and go to Stowmarket station to collect two unknown horses and that was not all. They also had to collect about thirty head of Hereford long horned cattle for fattening up for beef over the winter, which had been bought by the farmer from a cattle dealer in another part of the country. Why they could not be brought to Diss station by train I never did find out. However from Stowmarket to Wortham is a distance of about fourteen miles. To fit a rope halter into two strange horses and then ride them home bareback and keeping control over thirty cattle wandering all over the place took some doing as these horses had not been broken in at all. All I can say is that these two men knew something about horses that others did not and I think I must have inherited some of this besides what I was told as will be shown later.

Meanwhile it was my job, with help from others, to cart food, hay and straw for the livestock on the farm and as I was getting older I was being trusted with more important jobs, some of which were longer journeys away from the farm with younger horses. At that time tractors were beginning to come on the scene and at Hall Farm there was a Case imported from America. The model at that time was a grey L design, with metal wheels front and back with the back ones fitted what was called spuds, a V shaped piece of metal about four inches long by three inches wide with the ends bent at right angles to bolt onto the metal rim of the wheel in two rows with alternative spacing. Now it was illegal to travel on the road with the spuds on the wheels, so what they had to do when crossing the road was to lay some wide boards down and run across the boards to stop the road surface from getting damaged. This also meant that the tractors had to be left out in the fields at night. In the winter the radiator had to be drained to stop any water freezing in the engine. There was no anti-freeze in those days. These early tractors ran on tractor vapouring oil (TVO) but had to use petrol to start to warm up the engine. Also there were no press button battery starters. This was done by a cranked handle at the front of the tractor which caused a spark on a magnet which ignited the petrol and caused the engine to turn over and start running. All this created a job which I liked.

The TVO and petrol was kept in an open shed and every morning I had to fill about six five gallon drums with TVO and a two gallon can of petrol and a container full of clean water, take whichever horse and cart was available and transport all of this to the tractor out in the field. Sometimes the tractor would be ploughing a field a long way from the farm so it took a long while to get there and back as you had to wait for the cans to be emptied for use again the next day. The tractor driver would grease up both the tractor and plough while he was waiting for the fuel to arrive. The plough being used was a two furrow Ransomes trip plough which was lifted in and out of the ground by a rope from the plough and tied to the tractor seat and was given a sharp pull to operate both up and down positions. The driver of this tractor was a man by the name of Vic Frost (No relation) who lived with his brother, John, in a thatched cottage on the right hand side of the Long Green going up from the school towards Speirs Hill. Vic always wore a rather large trilby hat; I never did see him in a cap. Both came to work on bicycles whatever the weather. Vic was a man of few words, knew his own mind and stuck to it and was an excellent tradesman at everything he did.

Now this particular model of tractor was made in America for one special purpose and this was belt work as it had a pulley fitted on the right hand side looking from back to front. Whether this one was bought with this in mind I don't know. Hall Farm, like many others in those day, had its very own threshing set of Burrell steam engine, Marshal drum, straw elevator, chaff cutter and seed huller. But lots of steam engines at that time were getting into a state of disrepair and were costing a lot to repair so tractors were beginning to take their place during threshing and it was no different at Hall Farm.

The Burrell was left standing out of the way in the corner of the stack yard and the Case took over but with this arrangement there was one big snag. The threshing drum had to be moved from farm to farm and with no tractors strong enough to pull this wide, wooden wheeled, six ton machine this had to be done by horses. The best and strongest four horses were used for this job. They all came from Hall Farm but there was another problem which had to be dealt with. As the Hall, as it was known, is at the bottom of a hill from whichever direction you go to it horses could not hold the drum when going down hill. The worst hill of all was the one from Wortham Rectory to the church. But there was a way of controlling this, the horses were stopped and a block of wood with a thick metal plate bolted onto the bottom of this twenty inch by three inch piece of hardwood. Strong chains had also been fitted. This was put in front of the near side, back wheel and the wheel was gently moved on the block. The chains were then hooked between the spokes of the wheel and the axle. This stopped the wheel from turning but it did leave a mark on the road. At the bottom of the hill the slade, as it was called, was taken off and everything was working normal again. Sometimes to get this drum back up this hill another horse in trace gear was added to the front of the other four horses to help pull this heavy machine.

There was another Case tractor at the Hall at this time. I don't know which one came first but this was a model C.C. row crop, built the same and coloured grey the same and starting with a handle but there was one big difference, the wheels. Hence the model being called the row crop for a special purpose of working between crops of sugar beet and that type of root. The back wheels were much bigger and taller but about half as wide as the other tractor but still fitted with spud grids and the axle was adjustable to suit the width of the rows of the crops. The main feature of this tractor was the front wheels. Although there were two of them they were made to be together to form one wheel at the centre of the front on a very short axle. Now this worked alright and was easy to steer on level fields and average soil, but given sandy soil on a slopping surface and the whole thing changed into a very hard machine to drive straight. It seemed to have a mind of its own.

Now there was one thing all the grey Case tractors had at that time and that was the logo which was adopted from an army regiment in the American civil war in 1894 and this was an eagle standing on top of a globe and was used on all tractors made for the next 75 years. The driver of this tractor was a man named Stanley Ruddock, who lived in half of Hall Farm house, which was divided into two houses for different families. Stan, as he was known, lived with his parents, his father Jim Ruddock being the farm foreman, a real chapel man, which he cycled to on Wortham Long Green every Sunday afternoon. He always wore a trilby hat winter and summer. Two other things he was known for, one was the size of his boots which were very large. At a rough guess I would say about size twelve and the other thing was, when it was raining or better still a thunder storm, he was always found to be walking about the farm with a fork in his hand, unblocking the surface drains so the water could not flood. I never did see him shelter so with an old thick corn sack over his shoulders, tied with a length of binder string he was keeping dry. The only trouble was he expected every one else to work out in the rain as well.

There was another tractor used on this farm beside the two Cases at this time and this was a model N, green, Standard Ford with rubber tyres on the back wheels and metal wheels on the front. Now rubber tyres were something before their time in 1942 as most farmers thought that they compacted the soil down too tight so these wheels were taken off and stood up beside the shed wall and they were replaced with a set of spade lug back wheels. These all-metal wheels consisted of a round strip of iron connected to metal spokes which had on each side a four inch by one inch metal square which was welded onto each side of the iron circle, cutting into the soil to get a grip. This tractor was not as powerful an engine as the two Cases but worked the same, petrol start by turning the crank handle changing to TVO once running warm and all of them having sliding drawbar for pulling implements. The big difference was this tractor was driven by anyone at anytime, no permanent driver. I myself did use it to do some light harrowing. The foreman found out that I had used my Uncle's tractor on his farm.

At that time in, this part of the country, not many implements were purpose made for tractors and horses were the main pulling power. There was a lot of interest shown when all the three farms that had horses were each having two new rubber tyred tumbrels made at Young's Foundry, near the railway bridge beside Victoria road in Diss. There was quite a change when these arrived on the farms. First of all they were much bigger than the old wooden wheeled carts, quieter when moving, new tipping design that did not rattle and the axles were not metal on metal but roller bearings, which made it easy to pull for the horse. In their new buff and red paint complete with bright red harvest ladders for a bigger load of sheaves they really looked smart. But for some jobs there was a big disadvantage, like loading sugar beet, which was all done by hand and these carts were much higher to throw the beet when loading. More about sugar beet later.

New things were beginning to happen on the farms at that time and the new carts were the thin edge of the wedge. With the war on, farms all over the country were getting out of the depression of the early 1930's and were being asked to supply more cereals, milk, corn and meat. So this in turn made farmers richer and stopped them going bankrupt. The workers just got on with what was asked of them and were not made to join the forces because of what they were doing, but some were taken from the farms where there was a lot of labour employed. These were replaced with Land Army girls and new machines being brought in from America on what was known as Lease Lend agreement.

We always had to keep an eye on what was going on both around and above us, especially if you were using horses. It was not unusual for low flying German aircraft to machine gun people out in the field or both British and

American to fly very low but it did not seem to frighten any of the animals, neither horses nor cows.

By this time I was learning more about farm work and never refused to do anything I was asked. There were many, various loads to be taken out from the farm. During my first year I had a horse and cart and had to take bags of corn to Kemps Mill just off the Bury road at the Dolphin end of Wortham Long Green. Most people called this mill Rashes mill because I believe it belonged to that family at one time. Who owned it when I was taking corn there I don't know but Mr Kemp was the miller and his daughter was one of my school teachers.

Another place we had to go with loads of various goods was Diss. I liked some of the places like the Cuthbert Stores brewery stables (they still used horses to deliver beer) on Denmark Green. Everyone liked going there because the men working there had their own casks of different beers and you was always offered a choice of drink. What we delivered there was big bales of stuvver (clover hay) cut from the stack by a big heavy bladed knife and tied up with binder string. As there was no balers in those days this was a two man job to cut and load and a boy's job to unload. The other thing we took there was mangolds which they sliced up for their horses to eat.

Now these loads could be a problem, as most loads were piled high on the cart and had to be tipped up but with care as the building they were put in was on top of a slight paved hill. It had been known for a lot of beet to roll a good fifty yards downhill, which was where they should not have been.

The other place that used hay at that time was the Council yard. Diss Council still had horses for different jobs about the town. It was later called Willis Yard after a certain second hand furniture dealer who had the old stables and hay loft as a shop. This was and still is used for different shops and businesses today. Then came the cafes and fish and chip shops, which had new and old potatoes throughout the year.

Also there were the forty gallon drums of tractor oil which had to be collected from the goods sheds at the railway station. I had to collect one of these barrels once and I took Depper in one of the new rubber tyred tumbrels. Loading up was easy as the floor of the good shed was built up to be level with carts so this was just a roll on job. A block of wood was put behind the barrel to stop it rolling backwards. We started off for home past the station entrance and were level with the first signal when a steam train drew in and stopped beside us and, at the same time, let off steam which frightened the horse, which then jumped into the air causing the barrel of oil to roll over the block of wood and hit the tailboard of the cart. This in turn rattled the chains on the harness and cart and also made the front of the shafts stick up in the air therefore making the bellygat strap tight against the horse's stomach. With the horse running down the road as fast as it could while I sat on the cart holding the reins we went onto Victoria Road and I turned her under the railway bridge. When I thought we were away from any train noise, I pulled her to a stop, got off the cart and quietened her down and after a short rest started to level the cart by pushing the drum of oil up the front. So off we went nice and steady down Victoria Road and I thought to myself that we were doing really well when, as we were approaching the Co-op store, what was coming up the road from the opposite direction was a very large flock of sheep, with one man in front and one man behind, controlled with collie dogs on both sides. I stopped the horse and let the sheep go by with no bother. Thankfully Depper was not afraid of them as she had mixed with them on the farm. When I got back and unloaded the foreman said, "You got on alright then?". I just nodded and carried on working. The less he knew the better.

Now at this point there were two things that really interested me and I made it my job to get some answers. First of all I think that Hall Farm house had been completely surrounded with water but now there is what is known as The Moat all along the east side of the house and farm buildings. There is a stone roadway going down from the stables to the water's edge and down this roadway all the horses from the stables were let out to run down to the moat to drink. This was done twice each day and they would come back up the roadway and into their places in the stables to feed. Now at the top of this roadway near one of the stable doors and level with the stones was a short length of cast iron pipe, one end disappearing under the soil and the other broken end could be clearly seen. Also in the grass at the bottom of the thick hawthorn hedge there was what looked like heaps of rusty metal but this was not just any old metal but lengths of broken chain and broken pipes with the chain having, at about every nine inches, a metal disc about three inches across and about quarter of an inch thick. I tried the disc to see if it fitted the pipe and it did exactly. What these heaps of rusty metal turned out to be was something I had never heard of before or seen before which was a chain pump. This was a chain inside the pipe with the discs picking up the water from the moat and carrying it to a tank up near the stables. I could not find anyone who had seen it working and there was a difference of opinion from some people who knew how it worked. Some said it was done by hand with a wheel like a domestic mangle and others said it was done by a horse walking round and round in a circle while being connected to cog wheels by a wooden pole. If it is taken into consideration that there are two lengths of chain, one going down empty and one coming up full, both forming a continuous chain circle I would have thought the horse theory was correct. It would be nice to find out if these things were used much anywhere else.

The other thing was something very different and I did not take much interest at first but it was seen everyday and had stood in that place for a very long time. That was beside of the roadway that went down to Hall Farm and people called it the bullock cart. It was in fact a cart but not the normal everyday cart. This was a very heavy, strong built, wooden, cumbersome thing with a slightly curved roof and a space at the sides and front, to let the air in, with a cranked axle and it was low to the ground. The complete back dropped down to form a ramp for the cattle to walk up when loading. The wheels were very heavy indeed, at least four inches across each spoke with very big hubs. It had shafts about twice the thickness of an ordinary cart. All metal work was very heavy and when loaded with two fat bullocks weighed from three to three and a half tons. This required two strong horses working in tandem together to pull a full load. Now I never actually saw this cart being used but some of the older men told me they had and I could make out this was a job that no one liked.

All this happened before the farmers reared cattle for beef in big numbers as they did during the war. They just fattened up a few for the local butchers. The ones from Hall Farm were taken by the bullock cart to a slaughter house just into Chapel Street, Diss owned by a family of local butchers with shops in the town. This is now a furniture shop but the rails and hooks where the carcasses of animals were hung are still there. The men who took this cart to Diss with the animals inside did have a very big problem, I was told. As they went by Park Road and up Mere Street the horses could smell the blood from the slaughter house and they refused to go any further than the Dolphin public house. So what they had to do was to turn the whole thing around and put the cart before the horse, so to speak, and the shaft horse had to back the load down Church Street and Chapel Street where it was unloaded.

After it finished its life on the road as a cattle carter, it got hauled up the fields by a tractor to a new home over the top of a shallow ditch in the middle of the strawberry and blackcurrant fields and it was inside here that the fruit was weighed and packed in two pound punnets ready for sale. It was only strawberries put into theses thin wooden baskets with metal handles across the top joined on each side by a rivet so as to fold over for packing.

Now this was one job I really liked, taking a horse and one of the new carts filled with punnets of fresh picked strawberries to Mellis station goods yard and loading them into railway wagons for the journey to London. Not only was this a nice ride there and back but was also paid overtime as picking did not finish till after six thirty in the evening.

In the late 1940's, early 1950's there were people who had lorries doing livestock haulage but most farmers could not afford to have stock carted by them so they chose to either cart or walk the animals by their own workforce. There were several agricultural sale yards in Diss during that period. There were two main ones at different places in the town and only one remains today. Thomas Gaze owned the one beside Roydon Road and sold all types of heavy cattle, horses and sheep. The cattle pens are still there. The meadow, which is now covered by tarmac roads, and shingled selling area also doubled up as Diss Town Football grounds and other big events of the day. Every year during June or July this was covered in pens and the sheep and lamb sales took place here.

There were two more sale grounds in that area, one beside Roydon Road next to their old offices. This was where the calves were. We often had to take one or two calves from the Low Farm down a drive from Magpie Road to this sale in a tumbrel with a net over to keep the calves in, on certain Fridays. They were usually easy animals to cart so this was a nice little trip and most of the horses knew the way so they seemed to enjoy it and were no problem. The pig sale was in the same place but the pens for this were nearer Denmark Street and the entrance was just past the Beehive pub. This was quite a large yard to turn anything around in. Most of the animals sold were pigs for slaughter, old sows and very small piglets for rearing.

I once had the job one Friday, which I have never forgotten. It was a cloudy day and the rain was pelting down in buckets. I had Lady pulling an iron wheeled tumbrel and with three men to help we loaded up one of the oldest and biggest large white sows into the tumbrel for its trip to the sale, covered over with an old rope net which was tied to the hooks on the cart. It was custom with farm workers at that time to keep their clothes dry by covering over with some sort of sack, either corn or pulp sack. I found a very heavy corn sack and folded one corner inside the opposite corner to make a hood with the rest of the sack hanging down my back. Sitting on the front of the cart with my feet on the shafts we sat off with the rain still pelting down. I was comfortable as we were going at a steady pace. The chains on the cart and the metal tyres on the wheels were rattling in time with the motion as the horse walked. I turned to look at the old sow as we turned Dick corner on to the Ling and it had laid down on the floor of the cart. I don't know what made me do it but, halfway between leaving the Ling and Denmark bridge, I turned and looked again and to my horror I was sitting on the front of an empty cart. What had happened was the tailboard of the cart had somehow come out one side and dropped down breaking the net and leaving nothing to keep the pig in. Then of course there was another problem. Where was the big sow. I turned the horse and cart round and retraced my journey back the way I had come, knowing that somewhere between the Dick and where I had turned round was a very heavy sow running loose. As we approached the edge of the Ling I saw her digging holes in the grass beside the road. We got level and heard her grunting with contentment and making no attempt to run away. Now here was a problem, how to get this big pig back into the cart. Looking around I saw a gully that drains the water off the road, so I backed Lady until the wheels were in the gully at right angles to the road and therefore lower to the ground and by this time the rain had eased a little but everything was still dripping wet including the sow. By that time I was beginning to wonder how I could lift such a weight back into the cart when two men from Redgrave, who were cycling to Diss, stopped and lent me a hand by holding hands under the sow and lifting it back into the cart, tying the back board in with a piece of binder string and securing the net tight. Thanking the men for their help, back to Diss we went, arriving at the sale ground just before eleven o'clock, which was the time for all sale goods to be there or I would have to bring the pig home and done the journey all over again.

There was another market in this area and this was near the car park beside Shelfanger Road. Whether this was owned by the same people or someone else I can't remember but this one was used for selling poultry, rabbits, goats and eggs. We did put some of our tame rabbits in this sale at various times. This was one of two poultry sale in Diss at that time. The other one was at the side of the Saracens Head in Mount Street but actually a little further down the yard near a haulage contractor by the name of Jack Pipe, who had a fleet of green painted lorries for carting livestock, sugar beet and corn. This sales ground was owned by a firm of auctioneers by the name of Witton. These people also owned several farms in the surrounding villages, including Speirs Hill farm at Wortham. This sale had a good reputation for giving value for money and lots of full grown rabbits were sold for £1 each, a lot of money in those days, considering that if they had been sold to a butcher he would have paid about five shillings, 5/- or 25p in today's money.

One point I would like to mention about this area at that time was that even further down past the sale ground was a small meadow with a hard oval roadway running around it and all the way round next to the hedge was a grass area and inside the track was another grass area all of which was piled high with timber, stairs, cupboards, tables, nearly all in lovely pine and oak. There must have been tons of this stuff everywhere. I can't remember who the person was who all this belonged to, but I do know that it all came from bomb damaged buildings in London. You were allowed to pick out what you wanted at will and I can clearly remember going down there one Friday morning and picking out a lorry load of wood to make into things at home. I had by that time brought myself a sixteen by twelve foot wooden workshop. Now this load of wood I had bought cost me eight shillings or 40p in today's money and, as I asked a friend of mine who had a fleet of lorries to cart it home for me, it cost me ten shillings to cart home, 50p in today's money.

The last of the markets was between what was Park House and the Park. This area is now a housing estate. This market dealt in live stock and dead stock and was owned by a firm of auctioneers named Apthorpe, whose office was just on the right going down St Nicholas Street from the Crown.

Most farmers did business with both sale grounds. In March/April when the cattle had been in the yards and fattened up for beef, both Hall Farm and Beech Tree Farm picked out four of the best bullocks and walked them to the sale on alternate weeks so each auction had a share of selling the cattle. It was a job for three men to walk theses animals to Diss and I must admit I liked helping on this job, especially if it was to Gaze's sale as this took more time. When we got to the crossroads of Denmark Street, Croft Lane and Park Road we had a choice of going up Denmark Street or Croft Lane. We always choose Croft Lane as this was the easy route and at one time some men took some up Denmark Street and when they got nearly to Crown corner and going past Wallace Kings' shop, which was there at that time, one of the animals saw its own reflection in the big plate glass window and went right through the glass and into the shop.

Apthorpes was a lot easier to get too and did not take so long. Even putting the cattle in the sale pens was a quite straight forward job. But the best part of all these journeys was the way home because when we got to Denmark Green we would call into Sonny Youngman's fish and chip shop, which was next to the Cock pub, and get a fish and chip dinner and take it into the bar at the pub and have a pint of beer before walking home to Hall farm. By taking the longest way round we would get back about 2 o'clock and then sit down to have our own packed up dinner. Needless to say we did not eat much but we still had our half hour stop anyway. Now all that got stopped when the foreman realised what we were doing and the farmer came down to whichever sale ground we was at and brought us back to the farm in his car.

Meanwhile I still had to cart food for the cows out onto the meadows and all the yards still had to be covered with clean straw every other day. One other person had moved from another farm so I had some help on lots of the work. The cows by this time were out on the meadows during the day and the grass had not really started to grow and for that reason we had to cart them a load of mangolds (cattle beet) everyday. When we started to throw the beet from the cart onto the meadow we noticed that the big Red Poll bull was always getting in front of the cows to start eating the first beet off the cart. So we thought that we would play a trick on him and what we done was to cut a deep groove around the middle of the beet and then we tied a long rope into the grove. With the horse still walking forward we threw the beet onto the grass and as usual along came the bull with his head down ready to eat the beet and just as he was about to bite we would give the rope a pull and the beet would move away. After this had happened two or three times he began to get really angry so we thought it would be safer to start unloading so all the cattle could feed.

I was also doing a lot more different jobs and I took every opportunity to learn as much as I could about as much as I could. The first year was passing and spring with all its various jobs was a very busy time because there was plenty of horse hoeing to do and weeds had to be killed with the hoe as sprays were only just being invented. The one that appeared on Hall Farm first was in orange, five gallon drums and called Cornox. It was used on all narrow leafed crops.

Now beside the Case tractors they also had the dark green Standard Fordson, which had what was called Power Drive Gearing and it was to this one that a suitable spray tank was fitted and using this was quicker and easier than the horse hoe to kill all broad leafed weeds like speedwell, garlic, dandelions and many others. The horse hoe was quite easy to use and I did not mind leading the horse on this job. As it was another of those horseman's jobs so I was nearly always working with Harry Hawes with Blossom in the shafts. Once the hoes were fitted across the bar in the right position it was easy to work, as this was a very simple but efficient implement. The shafts were joined to the axle supported by a thin metal wheel each side. At the back was a pair of wooden handles fitted to two bars, one in front of the other to which different types of hoes were fitted for whichever crop was being hoed. All that had to be done was to lead the horse in a straight line at the front and move the handles at the back to either right or left to keep the hoes in between the rows of the crop.

The hoes which in my opinion were the hardest to set up and use were the discs used for sugar beet. These were shaped like saucers and made to run together in pairs with adjustment so they would cut a ridge of soil as wide or as narrow as was needed, leaving a row of small sugar beet plants down the centre ready for the men with hand hoes to chop out unwanted beet, and leaving the best plants to grow on at about eight inches apart. The other hoes were all what was known as A hoes. These were all different sizes for various crops.

One of the jobs I liked was using two horses pulling a set of chain harrows over all the meadow land to take out all the dead grass and level the mole hills. This started the new grass to grow. All this was then top dressed with what we called Basic Slag by a one horse artificial fertiliser drill. Now this slag was made from soot out of the big industrial chimneys which made this a very dirty job both emptying the sacks into the drill and walking behind if the wind was in the wrong direction.

Preparing the land for drilling was the main job at this time of the year and some of the traditions of what the head horseman's job was taken very seriously indeed. By that time the two young Percheron colts had been broken in to work as a team with the help of Blossom helping each one separately until they could work together. Each of them had learned to work alone on shaft work but we had to watch them with care. They had also been taught to back a cart but as with all young horses it would not be wise to trust them too much. But the best result of all was when they were working as a plough team. Doddy, the biggest one with big feet, took to walking in the furrow without any problems and with Duke walking on the land they made a good level team and also they pulled very well together. But I must admit I always thought a team of Suffolks looked better.

175

There were three sorts of harrows used on the farms being pulled by horses and the ones being used first on ploughed land were what were known as ducksfoot harrows. These two massive harrows had great big pieces of metal on the end of each tooth, which was shaped like the web foot of a duck, hence the name. The teeth or tine were made of one inch by one inch metal with a curve about the centre of the nine inch tine made so it would really dig into the soil. The two were joined together by a four link chain to allow them to move about when being used. Each one had a handle as part of the framework at the back and if the land was really solid a half hundredweight measure was hung on each handle. This was a really heavy load to pull and had to be done by three horses coupled to the harrows by thick iron whipple-trees, and for most of the time this job was done by the head horseman, who used this opportunity to put a young horse in the middle of the three when being broken in. The next gang of harrows was the medium size consisting of four heavy sized metal frame made in a zigzag pattern with eight inch slightly curved tine and sharp points. Each harrow had a hook on the front to which the chains from the wooden pole were bolted through. This pole was about three inches by four inches with the edges planed off to make a rounded corner and was what we called a hos tree to which the two wooden whipple-trees were hooked into two metal rings. These harrows were pulled by a pair of horses coupled about eight feet apart. The harrows broke the clods left from the ducksfoot into even smaller pieces, getting the soil ready for drilling.

The next set of harrows consisted of six zigzag patterned all chained together the same as the others with about six/seven inch slightly curved pointed tines facing forward but there was a difference. Each one of these harrows had a hook on both front and back and so with a pair of horses and with the same sort of hos tree and whipple-trees these could be pulled both front and backwards. I liked using this gang of harrows to finish breaking the soil down for drilling and it was easy for the horses to pull. These were also used on growing crops, mainly wheat and beans, for what was known as waking up after a hard winter by drawing them backwards to let the air in and to break off any dead leaves from the plants.

Now this time of the year was one of the times I really enjoyed, especially working on the beans as these plants were about four or five inches high and it was not usual to find one or two leverets hidden in the crop. These young hares, just a day or two old, would not move away when the harrows went over them but would just roll along like a stone from the front to the back of the harrows and then sit there absolutely still till they were found again by their mother. Spring was in full swing by this time and the grass was growing, the trees and hedges were coming into leaf, the birds' song was everywhere and some of the pheasants and partridges were hatching out eggs. Now the English partridge was a crafty old bird and if by chance anyone walked onto a pair of partridges with newly hatched chicks the hen bird would flap along as if it had a broken wing and try and lead you away from her brood of chicks.

There was other work going on at this time of the year, the main one of course being the drilling of corn, sugar beet and other seeds. Some wheat, barley and beans had been drilled in the autumn and were growing well. Now the drilling of all these spring crops was the head horseman's job and this is where the use of one of the colts with mainly Blossom as the main horse made up the drill team. The drills used on most of the farms around this area were made by a firm by the name of Smyth of Peasenhall near Saxmundham, Suffolk. They made several designs for different jobs but the main one was made so it could drill all sorts of seeds and this was known as the fore steerage drill, which was operated by two people, one to look after and put the seed in the drill box and one to guide the horses and steer the front wheels of the fore carriage to keep the rows of seeds being drilled straight. When new, these drills looked a picture against the brown soil and green hedges as they were painted as following, main seed box dark blue, wheels of drill itself bright red. These were quite big narrow wheels with one on one side fitted with a cog driving wheel on the inside to turn the black painted seed barrels as were the small metal wheels of the fore carriage steering. All metal chain work was black as well. The flexible funnels which the seeds went from drill box to the coulter that put the seed in the ground was also bright red. There were different sized cups on metal discs which adjusted to suit what seed was to be drilled. Most drills were wide enough to drill ten or twelve rows each time and by using a marker to which the steerage wheel ran in when doing the next round most joints came the same as the width of each row. There was one metal ring on the very centre of the fore carriage to which the hos tree was fitted, always with the hook pointing downwards to stop it dropping off at every turn, and now with the whippletrees fitted and the horses in ploughing gear, several acres could be drilled in one day.

To get the coulters out of the ground a simple handle was moved to control the drill when not drilling.

Also during the drilling season there were two more jobs I really liked doing and that was another ground preparation, both of them could be done with rolls. There were always a few crops to be sown later such as swedes, turnips, and maize and all wanted a good seedbed. There were two types of rolls. Neither could be used when the soil was wet so it was always a nice dry day for this job. One type of roll was the Cambridge rib roll, pulled by two horses. This was a very heavy implement with a horse in cart harness inside a set of shafts on one side and a whipple-tree with a horse in plough harness on the other. This was also a good thing to work a colt on. Now the roll itself consisted of a heavy wood frame about six or seven foot wide with metal side fitted by bolts to the frame. At the bottom of the frame was a steel axle and the roll itself was made up of metal-spoked wheels with a narrow rib on the outside centre. This left behind rows of ribbed soil and broke up any clods. The noise these rolls made as they turned could be heard from quite a long way off.

The other roll was the one I really enjoyed using. This had the same sort of wooden frame but this was a one horse implement and therefore had the shafts in the centre of the frame. The rolls of which there were two or three, depending on the width of the frame, were completely smooth and left the soil flat over the whole field. Unlike the rib roll which you had to walk behind this one you could sit on the front of the frame as the horse was driven along. On a nice warm sunny spring day and with a steady horse this was one of the best and easiest jobs on the farm.

As spring progressed the sugar beet was showing its first four leaves and the men on the farm were taken off all other jobs to bring their own hand hoes and chop out the small plants to an age old custom of leaving the strongest plant at about seven inches apart or as near as possible. This job like the old harvests was what was called piece work. This was the farmer wanting to get the work done as cheap as possible and the men wanting to work for as much as possible. A meeting was held between both men and farm foreman and, as there were three different farms owned by this farmer, they all had to agree on the same price per acre (Half a hectare in today's measurements). This meeting took place on or around May eighth, at Hall Farm, in a cart shed where everyone gathered first thing in the morning as the meeting usually took some time because, like the harvest used to be, men were working for themselves only now it was not a joint effort but every man working to his own individual skill. The harder one worked the more could be earned.

I had been leading the horse with the horseman doing the control of the horse hoe using the discs and 'L' hoes on the beet fields, leaving the actual small beet plants on narrow ridges to be singled out with the hand hoes. The unofficial law that governed the width of these ridges was a normal size match box, just enough soil left to keep the plants alive but not too much too make the hand hoeing hard work. Wage per hour was very low and I am sure the price to chop out an acre of beet was not that much more than double the hour price. The whole secret of this job was in the first two days and this was to bend down as much as possible and keep down. This gave the backache a chance to wear off. A lot of men could not do this so had back problems for several days.

The fields had all been measured out into acres ready. This was done with a special chain consisting of many lengths of thin metal rods about eight inches long all joined together by small circular eyes making it easy to fold up and very flexible to use. Every so many yards were solid brass symbols to make measuring easy. The whole length of the chain was twenty two yards (The length of a cricket pitch). It was very rare to get two acres of land exactly the same because the soil could be different across parts of the field, and not every field was the same shape and size or the same level for that matter. Even a pond in a field could make a difference to the rows in an acre. If it was a long field there might only be fourteen rows to an acre or if it was a short field there could be as many as forty rows to an acre.

Then some fields were odd shapes and to work on these was known as short work and an acre was worked different and this is how it was done. Most could be based on a rough triangle or something with three straight lines although these were not always equal on all sides. First of all the longest row was chained out and then the shortest and from those two the centre row was counted and that was also measured by chain and then by adding one short row together with the next long row to the centre row a square acre could be obtained to take in all the uneven rows.

The beet chopping out season lasted through May and June and all the available men from all the three farms were called in to do this work on each of the farms. I was lucky as I was not asked to do this job because I was leading the horse on the horse hoe for the horseman to steer and keep the hoes in between the rows.

Because this was wartime all people involved got extra food rations for the following jobs, chopping out beet, all work being done to get in the hay, the corn harvest and the sugar beet harvest. There was certain amount of food allocated to each worker by the government. I don't know who supplied the extra food but, on the farms I worked, everyone had to go to the farmhouse where each foreman lived and collect this food.

Because of this change in labouring work the work I done was also changed. When not leading the horse in the hoe I had other jobs to do as this was the time we set the potato crop so the fields had to be prepared for them and I had two horses on harrowing and rib rolling. The early crop was already growing well and the main crop set later was just showing through the soil. I did not have anything to do with setting the potatoes as this only required two people from the farm. One was the horseman with his plough team and a Ransoms plough made solely for this purpose. This had a wedge shaped share in the centre at the front with a breast each side. This plough didn't make a one side furrow but instead made a deep 'V' shaped furrow with the width of a ridge between each furrow. The other person was anyone who was around for a few hours with a horse and cart, to cart the bags of seed potatoes from farm to field.

The actual planting was done by the same gang of local women who picked the fruit and potatoes when they were fit to be harvested. Setting the seed potatoes was very hard work as you were bending over all the time and walking on uneven land besides carrying a full basket of seed. Each potato was set at the same distance apart and that was the length of one's foot as you moved one foot at a time along the furrow. As each row was finished the horses would walk the distance of two furrows apart and the plough would split the ridge covering up two rows of potatoes.

Next was where I came with one horse and the flat roll with some weights tied to the frame to make it heavier and rolled all the ridges to the firm soil around the new potatoes. No more to do to this crop until the ridge plough moulded up the growing plants. I was pleased to do this flat roll job as it was suggested that the new Percheron colts could do more shaft work at every opportunity so I had to take the smaller one which was Duke. It had been found out during breaking in that this was the most nervous one of the two but he done this job without any bother and I felt I could take him anywhere.

Most of the men were still chopping out the beet, so all the regular jobs done by some of them had to be done by the horseman, the stockman and myself. I found out that someone had told the foreman that I could drive a tractor and I was asked to drive the Standard Fordson, which was the green 'N' model which had the spade lug wheels from the back removed and replaced with rubber tyred wheels so it could be used on the road. I did not say that I had not driven one of these before as my uncle's tractor I used on his farm was a larger Oliver and a bit more heavier machine altogether. As this was wartime testing for driving was not done but everyone had to have a licence to drive a car, lorry and motorcycle but no one seemed to mind about farm tractors or who took them on the road. There are still some people about today still driving and have never taken a driving test.

This was the thin edge of the wedge of a big change that was coming to agriculture and the horse disappearing from the farms but nobody could foresee how quick this would happen. I done a lot of work on small pieces of ploughed land to set maize for cattle feed in the middle of summer. I enjoyed driving this tractor. It's hard to imagine that these machines cost only three hundred pounds when new.

There were two other jobs that had to be done all year round and one of these was the work in the mill. At Hall Farm there was a big brick building where all the grinding of corn for animal feed was done for the other farms. So it was a two, sometimes three day a week job. Although the stockman fitted this in with his feeding this was not always possible. I often helped with this job as there was quite a lot of work to be done as quickly as possible once the engine got started, which in itself was a experience never to be forgotten. This was quite a big Hornby Ruston orange and black painted, water cooled, hot bulb engine with a six foot flywheel and a massive piston. There was a big round galvanized water tank, which could hold several gallons of rainwater, outside the building, used to cool this engine and if the engine had been running for a long time steam could be seen coming out of the top of the tank. The whole engine was bolted on top of a thick concrete block about twelve inches high resting on the building floor.

It was not an easy job to get this things started and if there was someone around to lend a hand with turning the flywheel then it was a two man job otherwise it was a one man struggle and to a fourteen year old boy there was only one way to do this. The flywheel was so big and it went into a hole in the concrete floor when turning. So the procedure was as following, there was a big blow lamp that was lit with a match and pressure was pumped into it with a handle and the flame was put onto the bulb on the end of the engine until it was glowing white hot. Then the tap for the paraffin which the engine ran on was turned on and it vaporized. At this point the flywheel was turned to get the single cylinder working and the engine would run and providing there was enough paraffin in the tank the engine would run forever. However I solved the starting problem by pulling hard on the top of the wheel and as it started to turn I would jump on one of the spokes until it got to the level of the floor and then jump off. This would normally start it but if by chance you jumped off the wheel too soon the whole thing would go backwards and smoke would come out everywhere instead of through the wall in the exhaust pipe as it should do. No Health and Safety in those days.

I don't remember what horse power this engine was or the model number. All I knew was it had a job to do and I had to make it do that job. The opposite side to the flywheel was a pulley wheel to drive a belt which in turn drove another pulley wheel on an axle which was the whole length of the building. Also along this axle was several different size pulleys depending what machines they had to drive with a few odd ones for more machines if needed. The machines were as following, mill for grinding corn, a mixer for mixing corn, an oat crusher and a winch to chain lift bags of corn or meal up through a trap door into the top floor above.

Now this milling job was not as simple as it looked. Different animals had different mixes at different times of the year. Horse feed was barley meal, bean flour, crushed oats, some kositos (crushed maize) and a little bran all mixed together in the mixer, and one of the things that you had to take great care with was the bean meal which had to be adjusted as to how hard the horses were working. There were times when the horses were not doing much only standing in the stable and then too much of the bean meal would make their feet hot which was not good for their health and this would make them kick their feet hard on the stable floor which would loosen their shoes and then cost money to have them reshod. When it was time to turn them out onto the meadows to stay out all night the bean meal was stopped altogether. There again May eighth was the main date for turning the horses out on all three farms.

Now the food for the cattle and milking cows was two different mixes. The main meal for both mixes was barley meal but then the mix changed. The milking cows had two different types of cake. One was cotton cake which came in flat slabs about eighteen inches wide by about three foot long and one inch thick. The other was linseed cake of the same size slabs. This was a dark brown and the cotton cake was a buff light colour.

Before going into the mixer these cakes had to be crushed by a hand turned machine consisting of two metal rollers with some thick metal pointed spikes which, when turned, interlocked into each other when the rollers were turned. One of the rollers had an adjustment so the lumps of cake could be made large or small. This was quite hard work on the linseed but the cotton was a softer, woolly texture. There was also some kositos in both mixes but not much. The cows also had few crushed oats but not the fat cattle. Both had sugar beet pulp hand mixed into the meal but this had to be soaked with water to make it swell before being used. The fat cattle also had mangolds which had been through a cutter, again turned by hand, to cut each root into chips mixed with the meal and beet pulp.

There was an extra special item that was added to the fat cattle menu and that was locust which was imported from Africa. This was not an insect but looked like a big beetle. It was a hard black nut which had a soft brown centre and was full of vitamins and when eaten it tasted like liquorice. We often ate these nuts ourselves but it would not do to eat many as this could have some very nasty after effects. These came to the farms in Hessian bags of about one hundredweight each. Some of the local millers would grind these up and mix them with pig meal for farmers who had not got their own mill. We never done that as they were for fat cattle only here.

We had pigs of all sizes from breeding sows right up to fatteners that were sold to the bacon factories at about two hundred and twenty pounds in weight. Each farm had cattle and pigs besides their own horses, and each farm had their own pig man/ stockman who looked after these animals. When I was working in the mill the mix for the pig meal was barley meal bran and kositos and in the winter time some bean meal was added, but no oats of any sort was used. When mixed this meal was put into bags and then put into tubs or tanks with water added and stirred into a wet paste and let to stand for a few hours to allow the bran to swell. There were two feeds per day seven days a week. But this was not all of the food given, as this was still wartime and the second job I done which was quite a good job on a cold winter's day and this was steaming potatoes.

There was a government policy to take control of some of the things done on the farm. This was called the Ministry of Agriculture and Fisheries and an offshoot of this was the Potato Board. People from this would come onto the farm and inspect the clamps of potatoes and if they thought they were not good enough for human consumption they would condemn them for animals feed. But if a clamp on this farm was condemned you were not allowed to use them yourself but they had you take off the soil and straw and some men from the Ministry would come and spray all the potatoes in the clamp with a purple dye, and they would then be bagged up and carted to another farm sometimes miles away and in return we would get a lorry load of purple potatoes from some other farm. No one ever knew where they came from as the lorry drivers were not allowed to say. For all we knew they could have been our own potatoes that had been carted away from the farm a few days before. I could never understand the logic of this procedure but it was done and a lot of farmers earned money from this as the purple dye was not poisonous and quite easy to wash off and so lots of the potatoes were sold to people in the village with no questions asked.

Here at Hall Farm was a clay lump shed joined onto one end of the mill shed and this is where the steaming took place. There was a boiler standing between big galvanized tanks each side with a removable lid on both of them. First of all the boiler fire had to be lit and we had to make sure there was water in the boiler to the required amount shown on the glass gauge fitted on the front beside the steam pressure gauge which measure pounds per square inch.

Now, with plenty of coal on the fire and both tanks filled with potatoes and turned upside down with the lids on the bottom and the steam was at the right pressure, taps were turned on to let the steam into the tanks and left like that for about thirty minutes by which time all the potatoes had been steamed. The tanks were then turned over bringing the lids back on top and by moving to an angle they could then be emptied.

During the winter some of us had hot steamed potatoes or it could be done another way. Some of the best potatoes were wrapped in silver paper and put inside the firebox of the boiler and we had jacket potatoes for dinner. I am sure the pigs enjoyed a hot meal as well but this was not all they enjoyed, as there was a mixture that was supplied to the farmers and poultry farmers to feed their stock with and this was called Tottingham pudding. This particular stuff was brought by the lorry load of so many sacks full per ton. This was a mixture of all the waste food collected from hotels and restaurants in London and taken somewhere (I don't know where this was) and cooked and sterilised to make a brown type of pudding which was then put into Hessian sacks for carting. This finish product was a bit awkward to move as it was a bit floppy to lift up so the answer was to cut each bag into smaller pieces by a spade and put it into a pail and then into the troughs.

The pigs loved it and would fight to get to it. After they had finished we would look in all the feeding troughs to see what we could find and there was plenty of knives, forks, spoons, some of which were silver, coins, pennies, half crowns and sixpences but there was a few bad points as well as we also found broken and lots of whole glasses and broken crockery but for some reason the pigs never seem to cut themselves. We could keep most of our lorry load of this food away from the birds but most of the poultry farmers kept theirs outside and it was not long before the starlings had pecked holes in the bags and were eating lots of this stuff. There were virtually hundreds of them and with their fighting and screeching they became a real pest and for that reason a lot of them got shot.

At certain times of year other government surplus food came onto the farms. There were bags of broken chocolate and wooden boxes of dates. We were told these had been soaked in sea water. Whether this was to stop these being eaten by people I don't know but they didn't seem to taste of salt and the pigs never complained as there was always clean troughs after each feed.

There was one more food that was mixed with the pig swill and this came in wooden barrels and was known as whey which was a sticky peculiar watery liquid left after the separation of curds from milk. The barrels were never really got clean and always had a sticky feel left in them and could not be reused for water storage. I sometimes fed the pigs and cattle if the stockman was away.

I can remember very clearly one Sunday morning carrying a pail of swill in each hand through the boiler shed and the air was filled with the roar of B17s and B24s engines as the planes were circling all around getting into formation for a raid on Germany. No one took much notice of this as it was by now an everyday occurrence. I heard two B17s above the farm buildings when suddenly there was a terrific bang and a bright flash as one plane hit the other and the sound of an aircraft out of control as one of them crashed into a field beside the Shelfanger road about a mile out of Diss. The engines from this plane landed next to the walls of the council houses along factory lane nearly onto Roydon green, I don't think any of the crew got out alive. The other plane crashed somewhere near Brome Airfield where it was based.

These crashes of all sorts of aircraft happened quite often and the farm workers were sometimes the first on the scene and done what they could to save the crew. Most of us knew that just behind the cockpit there was a small door where an axe was kept and this was the first place aimed for to cut people out of the damaged plane, but with most crashes they were either deep in the ground or they were on fire. Some of these things were not very good to see but usually rescue teams from nearby airfields appeared within minutes. They always appreciated what was being done but we was warned to keep well away if there was any fire as live bullets would be flying all over the place and they have no telling if there was any unexploded bombs on board.

Out in the fields there was sometimes all sorts of things being found, live bullets, empty shells cases, a lot of windows (long narrow strips of silver foil) also German propaganda leaflets written in English but the thing that one had to very careful about was cardboard boxes. These had been used as a toilet and thrown out of the planes.

Meanwhile as all this was going on the men singling out sugar beet had nearly finished and were moving on to other jobs like hand hoeing mangolds, planting new strawberry plants and cutting some hedges and heaping the cuttings to dry out ready for putting on the bottom of the hay and corn stacks.

Another job I done was to take the horses to the blacksmiths for new shoes, mainly taking two at once or a single one if it was very bad. There were three blacksmiths used by these farms, one was at Palgrave Green and the furthest away from Hall Farm. This was owned by a man named Howell who had some of his family working for him and also employed two or three other men. This was by far the biggest blacksmiths and outgrew the forge and at a later date moved to a big new building just off Rose Lane at Palgrave so the horses had to go further to be shod.

The second one was on the Long Green at Wortham, just up the road to Speir Hill on the left hand side of the road and this one was owned by an elderly gentleman by the name of Harry Rice. With the help of another man he was happy to jog along day by day. This really was the smithy under the spreading chestnut tree as there was four massive chestnut trees growing next to the forge. It was from his anvil that the sound of the hammer could be heard when I was at school. I cannot ever remember him raising his voice at a horse or using a twitch on one either.

A twitch was a short piece of wood sometimes cut from a fork handle with a hole drilled in one end and a loop formed by a length of thin rope running through the hole. If there was a horse being a trouble when being shod, like not standing still or leaning on the blacksmith when he lift its foot up (Some horses did this on purpose if they took a dislike to the blacksmith) the answer to this was to put the loop of the twitch over the horse's top lip and turn the handle until it was tight, and then the person taking the horse to be shod would be told to hold this thing tight. I cannot remember being told to do this as I did not agree with this at all. I preferred to hold the horse myself and not tie them to the rings in the walls of traverse (the building next to the forge where the horses were shod). I think that because Harry was such a quiet man lots of the local farmers would take their colts to him for the first shoeing. He was also classed as the best man to repoint any sort of harrow and for this reason he was always busy.

Now the other blacksmith was a man known as Pip and this blacksmith shop was next to the Redgrave to Wortham road at the Magpie Green part of Wortham and this was all part of the Magpie pub property of which Pip was also the landlord. I think this was a Lacons pub at that time. Lacons being brewers in either Norwich or Yarmouth. I am not quite sure which came first with him the pub or the blacksmiths which was a main business. The only help he got was from the people who took the horses there. This was of course free labour for him. Some farmers would not have anything done there as there was always an unknown waiting time. This man was very quiet, (a man of few words one might say) but I got on very well with him. His main fault was that he would not come out very early in the mornings but working in the pub at night that was understandable. My own personal view was that he was not a very fit man and sometimes the horses would have to wait quite a long time and it was not a rare sight to see the foreman come cycling up there to see where you were.

He gave me the chance to learn how to shoe a horse and how to put a metal tyre on a wooden wheel. This was a two man job to do anyway and he was pleased with the help, but this was one of the things I enjoyed doing. Sometimes I would give him a shout when I took a horse to be shod and as the smithy was locked he would drop the keys out of the bedroom window and say you know what to do. With this I would unlock and tie the horse up in the traverse, rake the clinkers out of the fire and lay on some fresh kindling over a piece of paper with some small coal on top. Then I would light the fire and get the bellows working and it was not long before the fire had a lovely red glow to it. A little more coal and use of the bellows and it was ready for use.

The horseshoes came in all shapes and sizes and were hung on the wall over metal rods, one pair for the front and one pair for the back. Once these had been selected there was always some adjustment to be made by heating the shoes up and working them on the anvil. The next job was to cut the turned part of the nail from the hoof and remove the old shoe with a big pair of pincers. After the hoof had been cleaned and cut into shape the shoe was heated really red hot along with an old file that had been pointed so that the end fitted into the nail hole on the hot shoe. This operation caused the hoof to give off some nasty smelling smoke but it also burnt a brown mark on the bottom of the hoof and both the hoof and the shoe could be made to fit comfortable and this is about as far as I got before Pip appeared after which he took over and made sure the shoes fitted. He would then dip the hot shoe into the water tank to cool it down and with four nails on the outside of the shoe and three nails on the inside it was then fitted to whichever foot it was made for.

Bit by bit I was shown what to do and by the time this blacksmith shop was closed down I could completely hot shoe a horse which is something I never forgot. After then it was always up to Harry Rice's forge to have the shoeing done, and just holding the horse while someone else done the shoeing.

In the meantime all the sugar beet had been singled out and most of the other root crops had been hand hoed and also most of the horse hoeing was finished except the last, a hoeing of the sugar beet and this could not be done until what we called the seconding had been completed. This like the singling was done by piecework as the men and foreman had agreed a price per acre which was about half the price of the first time. Now this was the easiest job of the lot as each man had the same acres as he had singled out and if he had made a good clean job the first time round there was nothing to do except, take out the odd double beet that had been missed and any big weeds that had grown. The rows of potatoes had been moulded up by the second horseman and his team.

The next big job I helped with was hay making as it was very labour intensive and involved most of the people on the farms. There were many different types of hay which was harvested in different ways. First of all there was the meadow hay which in those days was full of wild flowers; oxeye daisies, buttercups, sorrel, purple clover (wild), white clover, bee and other orchids and several types of grass. This was cut as low to the ground as possible to get the low growing white clover and this was done by two horses pulling a Bamlett finger grass cutter which had a long pole fitted to the cutter held up by two big leather straps fitted to the bottom of the horses' collars. This red and yellow machine had a four foot cutter bar with the knife moving back and forth between the sharp pointed fingers. This bar could be flat to the ground for cutting or folded into a moving from place to place position by putting it up on end beside the machine and taking it out of working gear. The whole thing was driven by the two main wheels which had cog wheels fitted to the inside and was controlled by levers by the person sitting on the seat which was at the very back. This made everything in front easy to see. The horses could be controlled from this seat by using the very same plough line (thin rope) used for other jobs.

Now my job while all this was going on was to sharpen the cutter knives. As they were cutting so near the ground and hitting soil and stones they became blunt very quickly and we had to always have a sharp one ready for use. It was the usual to have at least three knives on the go at one time because sometimes the actual blades would break or come loose and had to be replaced. It was an unwritten law that no one ever stood in front of the cutter bar when the horses were on the pole so all knife changing was done from the side.

It was with the knife sharpening where a small change to farming started to take place. Up till about 1941 all cutter and binder knives had been done with a file with the knife clamped to a metal trestle with the legs splayed out. Now we had something that was much easier to use which looked very much like a hand drill. It had a handle that was turned but at the other end where the chuck was on a drill it had a barrel shaped carborundum sharpening stone it also had a clamp that could be fitted to any level surface like the top of a gate or stile. When the handle was turned the barrel fitted over the blades of the knife and sharpened it like a hand file did, a much easier job altogether and quicker.

Another thing about control from the seat was that you could see in front of the cutter bar which was a good thing as far as pheasants were concerned as they had a habit of nesting in a meadow of hay and they would not move for the cutter instead they would get down as low as they could with the result many of them got cut and did not survive. There were two alternatives to this. One was to make the bird move out of the way and lift the cutter bar over the nest of eggs but here was a problem as magpies, rooks, stoats and rats all liked eggs and could find the nest very easily. The thing which I was very much in favour of was to get the hen pheasant to leave the nest then take all the eggs and give them to the gamekeeper who always had a few broody hens which he could put the eggs under. He would then rear them till they were big enough to let out into the wild. This did boast our poaching during the winter and put a few pounds in our pockets. I always thought that the sound of the grass cutter was the sound of spring's arrival especially if there was the sound of a thunderstorm in the distance.

Once the hay was dry by turning it with a fork and then making it into round heaps we called haycocks the smell of real meadow hay was very pleasant and could carry quite a long way. For some reason the partridge did not nest in the meadows but preferred a bank or a corn field. The other meadow hay which came from the low water meadows was full of course grass, thistles, rushes and buttercups and was not of much value at all, and was only given to the fat cattle when they first came into the yards in the autumn. The other two types of hay was a totally different proposition altogether as they were both drilled as a crop into the barley stubble in the autumn. One was red clover which had a big pink flower head and the other was trefoil which had a dark red raspberry shaped flower head. Both grew to eighteen inches or more high but there was one big difference and that was that after it was cut, turned and carted away, the clover was left to grow again and when it was about six inches high, usually mid September, it was ploughed in as green manure followed by being drilled with wheat in the autumn. The trefoil stubble was cultivated and left quite a while before being ploughed in as it did not regrow like the clover.

I helped to get both these crops ready for carting and stacking, but I did not think very much of using a special fork made purposely for loading loose hay of all sorts onto the wagons which had a longer thicker handle and wide thick metal tines twice as long as an ordinary pitchfork. To use this thing all day was very hard work and was to be avoided if possible as far as I was concerned. Both these latter crops grew very thick so the nesting pheasants could not be seen and it was not unusual to find up to four nests in one field with lots of feathers and broken eggs where the hen bird had refused to move.

I liked the work that we had to do about three weeks before the carting started when all the wagons had to be checked for any faults. All damaged woodwork had to be replaced (mainly floorboards) and wheels had to be checked for shrinkage and if any was found then they would be taken off and thrown in the moat to soak and swell out. All axles would be greased up at the same time. There were three wagons at Hall Farm, two light buff and red ones, and these were taken to the Royal Norfolk show when it was at Walcot Hall. They were brand new then. The other was a great big blue heavy road wagon used for carting sacks of corn out to stations for journeys by rail. This one was always pulled by Blossom.

The best part of all this as far as I was concerned was taking the empty wagons from the stack yard out to the field to be loaded and bringing the full wagons from the field back to the stack yard to be unloaded. The loads were held on the wagons by thick, long ropes both front and back fitted to metal hooks on one side and tied by a knot on the other side. This was also the way to get on and off the load by climbing up or down the rope.

I was told that before I started at Hall Farm there was an incident with the heavy road wagon. This wagon had two shafts that could be put on the front of it and allowed two horses to walk side by side to pull it. When this was done, at the centre front there was a wooden seat on chains that could be pulled down allowing the driver to sit and drive the horses. I did find out who the driver was on this particular day but he had to go to the goods yard at Mellis station and collect two tons of cotton cake meal for animal feed. Everything went to plan and on the way home through Burgate he filled his pipe, lit it and started to smoke sitting on the wooden seat but unknown to him a spark from his pipe set fire to the two hundredweight bags which he did not notice until till he got home to the farm and by that time all the bags had the top half burnt off. It was quite a job to get all this meal out of the wagon which did not go down very well with the foreman.

Meanwhile everything was changing as spring was turning into summer. Also the two Percherons had been broken into most of the jobs they would have to do. They had been in iron tyred wheeled tumbrels also the newer rubber tyred type which was a lot bigger than the iron tyred and therefore could carry a bigger heavier load. I helped to learn them to pull a load forward and to go backwards with a load, but one of the main things was to learn them to stand still both with a load and an empty cart. As all my family had been with horses much of what they knew was being handed down to me, so I took a keen interest in all this and was often told to use these two colts on my own. Using young horses never worried me but as I was only fifteen there were times when it paid to be firm.

I still remember taking Doddy with a load of muck into a field where the gateway was set at an angle to the road also it was up a hill. Now it was always the proper way to lead a horse was on the left hand side holding its bridle near the bit which was in its mouth. I think he must have sensed that he had got to pull a load up a hill because just before he started to increase his speed he was lifting his front feet higher than normal to get a good grip on ground and as his front feet came down it jammed my foot between a hard tarmac road and nearly a ton of horse. I was lucky really because I was wearing a good strong leather boot on that day so all I had was a very black sore foot. It was a good job that I was not wearing rubber boots or I could have had a broken foot. So it was carry on as normal but with a limp and after that when turning a left hand corner I always held him at arms length.

Then as harvest was approaching it was decided to use the two young horses to pull a wagon each, so we thought the best thing to do was to use the two light wagons. Now this was a totally different thing to pulling a cart. A saddle was still used but there was no weight on it like a loaded cart would have. There was also the fact that a wagon made much more noise when moving and got heavier as it was loaded. But the most important was the fact the horse had to move and stop when told because of the men working to load it, and another point was it had to stand still while the load was taken off at the stack. Years ago a boy used to ride on the horse to do this job and always shouted hold tight before moving the horse and wagon forward. The way this problem was solved was to tie a piece of rope to the ring on the bridle and let it hang down onto the ground so if the horse moved forward it would stand on the rope and so pull hard on the bit and stop. The man who was working next to the left hand side of the wagon was the person lifting the rope and leading the horse forward and it was not long before the young horses knew what to do. This was the time of the year between the end of the hay season and the beginning of harvest.

As things slowed down a bit the horses were out on the meadows both day and night except for one of them being brought in for odd jobs and once a week one of the plough teams were brought in to use on the potato digger. The new potatoes were now ready to take up as required, which was usually one ton per week taken by cart after being bagged up at one hundredweight each bag to Diss for one of the cafes or fish and chip shops. I liked this chance to have a ride to Diss and most places were easy to unload at and I made sure that I took one of the older horses that knew the places we went to.

Most of the men had finished work on the sugar beet and were hand hoeing the cattle beet to take out the big weeds and a few of the beet themselves if they were growing too thick. By this time all the haystacks had been thatched which was done by the gamekeeper on this particular farm. Another job the men done around this time was to lay straw along the rows of strawberries to keep them clean for picking in June.

This was the time of the year for repairs and maintenance. All broken harnesses

I had taken down to the harness maker in his workshop in Chapel Street in Diss, which was the flint and brick building, now a ladies hairdresser's, about one hundred yards from the turning into Mere Street. This man by the name of Mortimer who was I think the last harness maker in Diss, always done an excellent job on both new and repair work. But like a lot of things of those days this trade disappeared from Diss.

There was one other harness maker in the town at that time and he was a man with the surname of Cory. I never knew his first name and did not ever take any harness there. His was one of the little shops opposite the White Horse beside the road from the market place to Mount Street. I don't believe he repaired any of the big heavy horse harnesses, just the light weight pony harnesses. He was a great big man. I think he made a good living because he sold other things which were the mainstay of his business. I went into his shop a lot to buy real leather hob nailed boots and Bulls Eye rubber boots. He was always glad to see anyone who went in there. He would sit in a chair at one side of the shop with his flat cap on repairing something and let his mother, a short pleasant woman, serve you what you wanted. This was one of the few places in Diss from where you could buy tins of dubbin, a grease-like substance that would waterproof leather boots. But what he was known for was the fact that he would not let you leave the shop without having something even if he had to give you a pair of hand cut leather boot laces.

Another thing done was checking over the two binders on the farm. One was a six foot cut red and buff Albion and a red and green four foot cut Massy Harris, both of which could be pulled by tractors but at that time were not power driven (driven straight from the tractor) but by a big wide wheel fitted in the centre of the machine with special square linked chains which clipped together to make an endless revolving on different cog wheels. When being moved this big wheel was cranked up by a handle and a small wheel was put in both back and front and the pole was put in under the platform and by cranking up the end of platform small wheel the whole machine was pulled long ways from field to field by a tractor.

The Massy Harris still had its long pole as well as a short one and could still be pulled by horses if the situation arose. This was done by a team of three horses in plough trace harness, working from morning to dinner time when they were changed for three fresh horses to work in the afternoon and evening. They all got extra oats in their meals on that job. All the knives used for the binders were sharpened the same as those used on the grass cutters.

There was another job done at this time of the year as both Hall farm and Beech Tree Farm grew about twenty acres of peas of which two thirds would be picked when green and the other third would be left to ripen for seed. After being cut by a special hook on a long handle and turned once or twice they were carted and stacked and threshed out by drum during the winter. There was a certain way these peas were cut as I said by a hook purpose made for the job. These could be bought new from blacksmiths or ironmongers but for what a short period they were used it was not worth spending money on, so most farm workers made their own by cutting the front off an old reap hook fitted to a smooth length of hazel cut from the hedge and if kept sharp would last a lifetime.

It was a bit of an art in itself to use these things as when you cut the haulms they had to be cut in small circles so they were left in little clumps so they could be turned to dry if needed and they could be picked up quickly when carting. When threshed the straw was only good enough for pig litter. The green peas only took two men to look after as this usually lasted a week including Sundays. People came to pick the peas from all walks of life, local and travellers because it was easy to do and depending how hard you worked easy money to be earned. This was the reason two men were required. I can remember the bags supplied always smelt of tar and had been dipped in a dark brown substance. When full, a bag weighed fifty six pounds or half a hundredweight. If it was a good crop it was possible to stop in the same place all day. The price paid was half a crown a bag or in today's money 12 ½ p which was good money in the 1930/40s. Each bag picked was brought to the scales to be weighed and if they were over full the surplus was taken out and put in the pickers next bag to be filled.

Now this was where the two men came into their own as some of the pickers were not always honest and it had to be spotted what was done. But what we knew and the pickers didn't was the fact that when the bags had been weighed and were tied at the top with binder string saved from the sheaves when threshing (nothing wasted in those days). On the front of the sacks there was some printed lettering and the string had to be just above that. If it was on the lettering there was something wrong. When we changed the contents into another bag we found stones, clods and anything heavy they could find to make the bag weigh more. However we found a simple answer to that problem and that was to put the contents of each bag brought up for weighing into an empty bag before we done anything else and gave the same bag to the picker for a refill.

All picking stopped at 6pm. Any part filled bags were paid for by the amount in the bag and we made them up to full with these odd bits. We had a little bonus here because any left over we kept to take home. No one ever spotted that we always ended the day with a full bag. At about seven in the evening a lorry would come and pick up all that had been picked that day and take them to London, Covent Garden for selling in the shops the next day. Vegetables were not on ration during the war.

All the green haulms were horse raked into rows for easy carting and then unloaded next to the pig yards where they could be thrown over the wall a few forkfuls each day for the pigs to eat as an extra food. The land would be ploughed up once perhaps twice before being drilled with an early variety of autumn wheat. Little did we know what changes would happening in a few years from now to the way peas were grown and harvested.

This was a little quieter time on the farm. I liked this relaxed atmosphere, the calm before the storm was the way some of the men thought of it. The hedges each side of the gateways to the cornfields had been cut back so they could not get caught on any loads passing through. If it had not been for the vapour trails and the aircraft noise most of the time these days the stillness would only be broken by a turtle dove or a wood pigeon calling from the hedgerow where it had a nest. There was of course the odd military vehicle driving from an airfield to somewhere out in the countryside but most private cars had been put on blocks in garages due to only special trades could buy petrol and even then it was rationed except for farmers and for lawn mowers for certain people. Most people had dug up their lawns to grow food and the lawns that were left had to be cut by a hand pushed mower. I did find out how this petrol was obtained but more about that later.

There was one particular lorry that was seen on the road every day and that was the lorry collecting the milk churns from the dairy farmers. Most farms had at least ten to fifteen cows and it was a common sight to see timber platforms beside the entrance to the farms with the top platform level with floor of the lorry. The full churns were put onto this platform and the lorry driver would load these up and leave empty churns in their place. Some small dairy farmers sold milk direct to the public by carrying two five gallon churns complete with half and one pint measures held by brass hooks on the top of the churn and they would then come to the house door and put how much milk the person wanted into your own jug. Some farmers even made butter to sell but to get this you had to go up to the dairy door and collect this as it was impossible to carry this around the countryside especially in hot weather.

Some farms had quite big herds so besides selling to the Milk Marketing Board they also had big milk rounds in different villages, but this was done by a pony and a cart purpose made for the job which was about the same size as a pony trap. The name of the dairy was painted on curved boards above the big wheels and entrance was made by a metal step and door at the back. The two churns carried in the cart were about the same size as the ones used for collecting milk but far more ornate as they had brass bands around them. The churn itself was actually bigger on the bottom tapering up to the top which had a lid fitted into the churn complete with a brass cap circle in the centre. This was then completed with a brass tap fitted into the side at the bottom from which the milk was taken into a measure and put into the customer's jug. All the brass was kept polished and shining.

Most of the milkmen on these carts always wore a light brown smock coat but as this was an all weather job they often got soaked to the skin in wet weather. They also had a brown leather bag with a strap over their shoulder for the money as most people paid weekly or on delivery each day.

All this stopped when glass bottles capped with cardboard inserted lids were introduced. Also gone were the pony and carts and special vans were being brought into use. There were other things happening to small dairy farmers in this part of the country at that time but the farmer who started it all had no milking cows at all but reared calves to beef cattle. One day the Ministry Vet declared that some of his cattle had Foot and Mouth disease and would have to be killed. This sent shock waves amongst all farmers in the district.

I can well remember in the late thirties when I was still at school a big dairy herd, on a farm along the Wortham to Redgrave Low Road, caught this disease and had to have all its livestock with cloven hoofs killed and burned. This horrible smelling smoke hung in the air for many days. But this time it was a different situation as it was wartime and a very new set of rules were used as no burning was aloud as all fires had to be out by nightfall. So the method used was that there were big deep holes dug in a field as before but this time tons of quick lime was put in and all carcasses were put into this and after all this was completed the soil was put back on top of it all.

Strict precautions were taken on farms around the affected area. Straw was laid on all roads leading to these farms. The straw was soaked in strong disinfectant to get on the wheels of anything passing over it. Beside that there were containers filled with disinfectant as well, as everyone had to dip their boots in to stop any spreading. The actual farm where this disease was no unauthorized person was allowed to enter. There were red warning notices on the gates and police keeping people away. But one of the worst things to come out of all this was the fact that neighbouring farms, small dairy farmers with milking cows, which were perfectly healthy cows had to have them all killed as well, and most of them never restocked making this the start of the end of milk production as we knew it then. The cows on the farm that we were carting food to during the winter were not affected, neither was a big herd just over the river Waveney at Roydon, also a big herd on a farm beside the A143 road at Wortham.

All this was the start of another change in farming as meadows now not used for grazing were ploughed up to grow arable crops. For hundreds of years these hedges, about eight to ten foot high, had a special purpose around the meadows as they kept the cold winds out during the winter and made shade during the hot summer days.

Not all summers were hot but I seem to remember the hot ones more than the wet ones, but one particular wet summer I think the year was 1943 when it rained for weeks in July and August the land was so wet the tractor could not pull the binder. Even the small four foot cut would not run as the main wheel just skidded along on the wet land. We also had some severe thunder storms complete with big hailstones but some of the old farmers always said that a thunder storm helped to ripen the corn. I could never understood how that could happen but what it did do was a lot of damage to the standing corn especially oats as these would be blown down flat to the ground and had to be cut by mowing with a scythe.

The time I remember, this was only done as a last resort and not day after day and field after field like the days before the binder when there was twenty to thirty men working one behind the other each with their earthenware gallon bottle fitted to their leather belts. This was before my time of course but they told me how hard this work was and how they would drink at least three gallons each of beer a day, usually the first one before ten in the morning. It was said that they could hold a whole bottle full of beer between their thumb and first finger and tilt upwards as the beer ran down into their mouths and it was really strong beer not like the coloured water of the modern day.

However there's one very old horse drawn machine that came into use between the scythe and the binder period which could cut corn on wet land or very short corn and I only saw this used once and that was on barley which had not grown no more than ten inches high on sandy soil. This machine was called a sailor and it was pulled by two horses in plough trace on a long pole. This also had a big driving wheel but had round metal rods driving cog wheels to make the knives and sails work, no chains, no knotter, no string involved. In fact it was less than half the weight of the binder. There was a big difference however as it had a metal, quarter shaped platform into which the cut corn fell only to be swept off at the back by four wooden sails which flopped round instead of just turning, leaving rows of small loose heaps, which then got carted away and put into a stack. The machine was put into a shed after that and I never saw it used again.

Getting back to the quiet time before the start of the harvest with the pink and white of the hawthorn blossom gone from the high hedges they were now nearly all a darker green with shades of lighter green interwoven by other things like hazel, elder, oak, blackthorn, crab apple and many other plants. There were some bright spots among these hedges like flowers of spindle wood which turned to bright red berries in the autumn. My favourite was the delicate pink of the wild rose also the smell of the wild honey suckle. The blackberries and the elderberry had done flowering and were changing into green fruit.

Writing about these big colourful hedges I remember them well. Most people walked to work in those days on the footpaths which crisscrossed the countryside. It is not possible to repeat those walks these days for a number of reasons which are not for the better I might add. Back then Sundays was really a day of rest except for the people who had good reason to work, like the people who fed the animals and even then their work was made as easy as it could be. For most families a Sunday afternoon walk was a complete break from the hard graft of a working week. These footpaths were used as a relaxing place to walk, meet other people and have a chat. Some old horsemen would just be nosey and look to see if your ploughing or drilling was better than theirs. If it was good no one said anything. If it was bad the customers in every pub in the village would know by the end of Sunday evening.

There was another good reason for those walks along the footpaths which was a personal one amongst the male members of our family myself included and that was that we had to know these places well as we had to sometimes use them as escape routes on dark nights when poaching and very often used the hedges to hide in to avoid being caught. This particular part of Wortham was and still is very special to me, so many memories, some happy and some sad of those years of long ago never to be repeated.

There is one small part of the churchyard where my parents and my grandparents lie buried all together under a flat piece of grass, as most of the churchyard is today, but was once a well kept area of clipped, well looked after graves. I did go down there during spring and summer to keep everything tidy and put flowers in the vases to the background of the jackdaws disagreeing in the church tower and the chatter of the magpies in the high hedges around the meadows.

The piece of long grass at the back, north side of the church, where there were no graves and grass snakes could be seen if you knew where to look, was untouched because this, like in most churches in the villages, was the last resting place of the people who had died from the Black Death or the plague as it was called, which was caused by black rats which escaped from ships. This disease swept across the whole country from 1348 to 1350 and killed thousands of people. In most churchyards this was sacred land to be left untouched forever, so you understand why I was absolutely shocked to find out that someone had allowed the graves of our ancient ancestors to be concreted over to make a car park. Was this the same person who had, a few years before, decided that no one was allowed to rebuild sunken graves but to let the whole place turn into a flat area. I personally disapprove of both these things being done as bit by bit the countryside as I knew is disappearing.

Lots of things were changing and old ways were made to be done by machines therefore were much more easy to do. So with the war still on and the demand for food increasing the start of modernisation was beginning in earnest.

But going back a few years, the footpaths were still there but not used as much. The one that I remember and used several times was started from near Wortham school and from the A143, Diss to Bury St Edmunds road down to the church and through the centre of Hall Farm into the meadows, where it became a cart track, still going northwards towards the Ling. Where it passed near a gateway into a field was a gamekeeper's gibbet, where, hanging on wires, were many skeletons of vermin also some fresh bodies of shot magpies, rooks, hawks and any other birds of prey besides the stoats, weasels and anything else that would attack the game birds, which were all hatched out in the wild as it was several years later that game birds were reared and let loose for shooting. There were other gibbets on different parts of the farm but in all the time they were there I only saw one fox.

At certain times of the year these meadows had young cattle grazing on them, often complete with a bull, but no warning notices then and it was up to you to get out of his way if he got upset. When the farm workers were out for a walk on a Sunday afternoon it would not run away but could tell if you were afraid or not, which most of them were not so the bull did not cause any bother. But I would not be taking a full grown bull for granted especially if he was with a herd of cows, if it was a footpath or not.

But to continue with this farm track through the last meadows and a field gate onto Wortham Ling and then still on a cart track to the road down to the road bridge over the river Waveney and up the hill to the A1066 Diss to Thetford road, this walk from one road to another was one of many that went for several miles. The main hub of these footpaths, which I used many times, was centred on the church and Hall Farm.

These footpaths which must have been used by many people brought to mind a rather big family that lived in a house beside the Ling to Redgrave road and walked to Wortham School around about the same time that I started 1933. Always came both boys and girls without any shoes on their feet at all. They came whatever the weather absolutely bare footed. I don't think this was allowed for long.

There is one more footpath/cart track I think there is a good reason to record as this starts from Hall Farm as a cart track and goes through the meadows behind the church then bears to the left, continuing through the horse grazing meadows, as a cart track, northwards with one of the high hedges on it east side, passing some of the meadows that had to be ploughed up by orders from the ministry. This soil was nearly black like the soil on the fens. It grew some very good crops also plenty of weeds so was labour intensive to keep clean. Now this cart track was running parallel to the cart track which was from A143 to A1066 and the reason for this will follow, but the cart track stops abruptly at a gateway into a field and then turns into a footpath making its way to come to a style out onto Wortham Ling from behind the cart shed belonging to the Dick pub.

This field was called The Marlepit field because just inside the entrance was a big deep marlepit, which even then had some tall fir trees growing in it. I don't know when it was last used but it was well before me or my parent's time, but my grandfather could just remember some of the marle being carted out from it many years ago. Marle was a very hard substance, slightly greyer than chalk but was very hard wearing and this was the reason the old time farmers used it to make a floor surface to their open cattle and pig yards. This was laid at three or four inches thick and rammed down hard. The floors of open horse yards were made from flint stones because the iron shoes on the horses would dig into a marle surface. I only knew of one other marle pit in the district and this was on the opposite side of the road to Redgrave church.

During the summer someone had to go down to this field everyday and collect a small load of Lucerne, some of which was laid out on the meadow at a rate of one heap per horse, and some was taken into the field and stack yard for the horses working in the harvest. Lucerne was a blue flowering plant very much like clover with a pleasant smell when moved. There was always an old grass cutter and a horse rake left on this field as cutting was done every two days and this plant would soon regrow after cutting so there was always plenty to go at.

The moat at one time surrounded the Hall farm house had been partly filled in but was still a very big piece of water and like all moats it had to have an inlet and outlet. The inlet for this one started a long way from where it entered the moat at least two miles away on land that belonged to White House farm on the edge of Wortham Long Green. It was here that it began as a small ditch and came between several fields and meadows with high hedges on one side or the other. The further it got from its source the wider and deeper it got, collecting water from over ditches running into it from both directions each side, until it came to a right angle turn under the high hedges, around the cow meadows of the Low Farm where the milking herd grazed. Up to this point all the bridges over this ditch had been old tree trunks filled with turf and soil and stones. But just past this corner was a gateway into one of the meadows and this was the first brick archway along its route, which made one think how old these bricks could be. Next gateway was from the meadow into the road and another brick arch but with a bench mark on it which was the sign made when that particular point was measured above sea level. Then it ran down beside the road and across the meadows and under yet more brick arches until it entered the moat near the stables and the horses went down to drink.

This end of the watercourse hold some good memories for me when myself and other school friends would race what we called ships on this very full, fast flowing water. Starting at the bridge with the bench mark we would see whose ship could reach the moat first. It was done mostly on Saturday mornings but the ships we made were a bit crude being made from an old piece of board using a wooden meat skewer for a mast and a Players or

Woodbine cigarette packet for a mast, but it kept us happy anyway. We did have little bets but not with money. Our prize was marbles.

It was also tradition in those days for every boy to have a shut knife, a piece of string and a catapult in his pocket. The knife was used for making pop guns out of hazel and elder and would shoot acorns. The bit of string was for boot laces, and the catapult, well it had many uses. One was hitting a matchbox which had been stood up edgeways on a gate post. But if you had a Swiss army knife, well you were really someone as it had a big and small blade, a corkscrew, a small screwdriver, which was made with a curved pointed part for opening bottle tops, and a sharp round piece of steel rod about two inches long what was used for getting stones out of horses hooves. I still have mine from all those years ago and I also have another one which was brought before the war from a shop soiled sale on the small area at the bottom of Market Hill now mostly used as a car park.

The shop it came from was an ironmongers and hardware store belonging to the Aldrich family until, one Friday afternoon in the summer but I can not remember which year, one of the staff went into the cellar to get some paraffin for a customer from their storage tanks and as he was smoking a cigarette, some hot ash fell into the paraffin that had dropped on the floor. Within minutes the whole area was well alight and it soon spread to the shop itself. Being Friday, a market day, there were lots of people about and to the best of my knowledge everyone got out of the shop safely, but the place was completely destroyed. I was in Diss later that day and saw several fire engines everywhere. Some I heard had come right from Norwich. I also saw hoses lying around with a lot going down to the Mere. During the war this area was made into air raid shelters for public use. Now there is a very good ironmongers/hardware shop which has been built on the same site after the shelters were pulled down.

But to get back to where I was before I was sidetracked about those early years, the moat outlet was a much wider watercourse than the inlet and much deeper. The meadows ran down from the footpaths either side on a gentle slope to the edge of this watercourse, with the flowering buttercups, scotch thistle and the odd ragwort standing out amongst the clumps of rushes and all of this was an area that the horses would not graze in. The watercourse itself was rather slow flowing with sedge and reed growing on the edge of the water and as it progressed through the meadows there were patches of meadow sweet and pink willow herb with a few big water butter cups growing from the centre of the stream. As the waterway was making its way northwards it began to get wider and deeper as some land drains poured their water into it. Then it took a turn eastwards along the side of a wood of willow trees which were part of an old osier bed which had been allowed to grow on after they were too big to use.

There was still a part of this that was still used, as osiers were willow rods that were cut, tied into bundles and sold to basket and fencing panel makers. The men of Hall Farm had nothing to do with cutting these willows as this was done by the men of Ling Farm and the bundles of willow were stored for a short time in an open sided cart shed in the stackyard of the next farm past the manor called Alger's Farm next to Slade Lane. It was here there was, on a piece of spare land, a flint and brick cattle pound, which had been built many years ago.

The next turn it changed to a much wider and deeper also clearer watercourse as it ran down the side of Minters Field, which was once owned by my grandfather. There was a lot of waterweed growing in it here with water snails and small fish and I once saw a small pike about ten inches long swimming in it. How it got there is a mystery as this stream, as it had now become, continued through the meadows under another brick arch, which the cart track went over, and out beside Wortham Ling.

This was a very interesting stretch of this stream as there was a lot of wildlife, dragon flies, water beetles, water boatmen and many others. The sedge and reeds had gone and in their place were yellow flag iris, water plantain and arrow head water weed, but most of all which was very important to all our family was the watercress as this was the best around for several miles, even better than growing in the main river. We went to cut bunches for Sunday tea during the summer and my grandfather cut bunches and sold them to people in Diss for a few extra shillings. This stream turned and flowed under the road and down to the River Waveney and so down to the sea at Great Yarmouth.

The work on the farm had been going on towards harvest and some days the weather was hot and sultry and the midges covered everything including ones face and arms making a persistent nuisance of themselves, a sure sign that harvest was here. Then in the third week in July four men would go to the first field of ripe oats, two would mow an area about six feet wide around the field, and the other two would tie the cut oats but they did not use string. Instead they used a handful of oat straw in each hand and made a knot of the ears of corn leaving the long straw to tie around a bundle of loose corn and make a sheaf. This was done with all types. But they did change jobs with each other so the hard work of mowing and the back bending job of tying was shared out with each other.

When the cutting was completed all the way around the field, a small square area was cut near the gateway to allow the tractor and binder the space to change from pulling on the road to working on the field. The small road wheels had to be taken off and the big wheel on the binder lowered to working position. Also the pole by which the binder was pulled along had to be changed from under the metal platform, that the cut corn fell on, to the front of the binder itself. The next thing that happened was that the tractor ran along the area that had been cut by the scythe, with the binder, making its first cut of the harvest after everything had been checked, that all the chains, wheels and pulleys had been oiled and greased and two new balls of string in the string box which had two holes cut in the front so it could be seen when it was getting empty, and so harvest had started.

After about six rounds men were sent into what we called shocking, which was gathering a sheaf under each arm and standing them up with the bottoms spread out and the tops close together to form room for the air to pass through. I often helped with this job, but it did get tiring after eight or ten hours each day. I liked the smell of the fresh cut corn and all the undergrowth that went with it, wild mint, mayweed, coltsfoot, and in every corn crop there was always clumps of green thistles. These were very sharp and you had to be very careful when picking up the sheaves with these in.

Another point worth making about shocking, and it did not matter what type of corn was being worked on, the problem was the size of the fields. From thirty acres up to well over fifty acres it was a long way round for the first and second rows of shocks, which took up to three hours to do and all this time without a drink and when you did get round to having a drink it was mostly cold tea without any sugar or milk and a bottle of this had to last half a day until dinner time when a second bottle could be started. How things have changed as nowadays some people cannot walk anywhere without a bottle of water and taking a drink every ten yards.

As harvest progressed the oats were cut and next was the barley, then the wheat and last of all the beans, which were by far the worst of the lot to shock. They were tall, heavy and very rough, especially if you was working with your shirt sleeves rolled up. I tried to avoid this job if I could and by being the boy on the farm I had other jobs to do, like cutting and carting the green maize and laying it out on the meadows for the milking herd of cows, also carting water to fill their tanks. There was also the lucerne to be carted out for the horses.

As the war continued some extra jobs had to be done and one of these was horse raking between the rows of shocks on certain fields which were not near a pond. The rakings were carted and made into a small stack which was added to as all the raking was done.

Then I had a job I really liked. With the rubber tyred orange Fordson tractor and a Martin nine tined cultivator I had to cultivate all the strips of the cornfield between the shocked corn and do away with all the stubble and to make this a bare soil area, all because the German bombers had a nasty habit of dropping incendiary bombs on the field and burning the whole area of dry corn and these cultivated parts acted as a firebreaks. We were very lucky as this did not happen on any of the farms that this farmer owned, but in the next village of Palgrave one enemy plane did drop what was known as a bread basket bomb. This was a big bomb full of incendiary bombs. This thing broke its casing on the way down and the incendiaries scattered over a wide area setting fire to everything, when they hit the ground.

But whatever happened harvest carried on. I had the job of taking the empty wagons to the fields and bringing the loaded ones back to the stackyard, each wagon being pulled by a different horse. The two Percheron colts took to this job very well but it still paid to treat them with caution. The other horses had done it all before which made the job much easier. If the field was a long way from the farm then an extra wagon and driver was used and we changed wagons halfway, both keeping our respective ends. We did change ends some days as the person at the field end had to be very careful to cross the field with a load because all the old plough furrows had to be crossed at a 90 degree angle to stop the load moving about under the ropes on the wagon, but the worst problem was the gateways from field to road, as these only got used at certain times of the year. On corners and at very difficult angles, turn too sharp and a loaded wagon would turn over, breaking the shafts and scaring the horse but thankfully this did not happen very often. Good co-operation between driver and horse was a must. After carting had been going on for a few days as many odd grains of corn would drop onto the tarmac road the metal tyres of the wheels would crush it and there was two lines of white substance like milled flour.

In the first few years Hall farm never had any sort of elevator to build the stacks with and all lifting had to be done by a long handled pitch fork. As the stack got higher and the roof was started one of the men who had been helping the horseman to build the stack took up a position on the edge of the wall in what was called the chair hole and his job was to lift the sheaves up even higher as the roof was built. When it reached its very top, a ladder was laid on the roof and, with a few loose sheaves packed into the chair hole to fill it in, it made the roof sloop complete.

There was a unwritten law about corn stacks that was used on most farms and it worked like this, no stack was made of mixed corn, for all stacks to be in pairs, that is two wheat or two barley, two oats and two beans. Each pair were wide enough apart to allow for the threshing drum to stand between and also because two corn stacks equalled one straw stack and this was because different straws were used for different jobs. Wheat straw was always used for thatching. One particular variety of long straw wheat was grown for this purpose alone. The remainder was used over the winter for the heavy animals, horses and fatting cattle. Some barley straw was used with hay as food for the cows and litter for the pigs but nothing was wasted.

As the harvest was drawing to its end more changes were taking place. Most of the farm workers had by this time brought bicycles, which were mainly second hand, but got them from A to B, leaving just a few walking to work but bringing enough food and drink to last a long day. Also the war was still on and the men had to work till dark on all fine days and with this came the change of having one whole hour for dinner during the middle of the day. This also made a big difference to the women as they had to stay at home and serve up a cooked meal instead of carrying it round to the men in the fields and sitting on the side of a ditch to eat it. The horses had a heap of fresh cut lucerne each during this lunch hour.

Each field was horse raked in turn and carted to the stack and all corns were mixed together, including the beans, but even after all this there were always a lot of beans, that had broken off, left on the ground. We had to pick up all these loose beans and put them in a cart with one of the old horses pulling it. This was a slow and back breaking job and I really hated doing this as it took ages to get a load of these things, which were then unloaded near a pig yard and thrown into the yard for the pigs to eat. But one good thing did come out of it all. Most farm workers, myself included, kept a few chickens in the back garden, so on a Sunday afternoon many people could be seen gleaning wheat ears from the fields. These sacks full of wheat ears would be stored in a dry shed and used as an extra feed for the chickens. No one minded that this was being done and always turned a blind eye however much was being taken.

It was the same when fields were being cut with the binder. As the amount to be cut got smaller, there was always rabbits that kept in the corn. This was the time when boys came into the fields with a stick cut out of the hedge, mostly with a big knob on one end and notches cut into the wood to let people know how many rabbits that stick had killed. The gamekeeper was nearly always there with his gun as well, so no one was allowed in the area that was in the range of his gun. As the piece of uncut corn got smaller one end normally came to a point and the boys who were old hands at chasing rabbits across the freshly cut stubble knew a thing about all this as they would stand around this point and watch the top of the standing corn for any movement as the rabbits ran down the space between the drills and this is where they usually came out. When the cutting of the field was completed the rabbits were laid out in rows and counted. Then all the men who were working in that field had a choice of a pair (brace) of rabbits for themselves and then the boys would be given one each for their trouble and the remainder the keeper would take to feed his ferrets on.

Work was now changing again and some stubble was being cultivated by tractor, others were being ploughed by one of the Case tractors and a Ransomes two furrow drag plough, which was lifted up by a piece of rope tied to the tractor seat. This was pulled again to trip it into a working position. Height and depth was also controlled from the tractor seat by long handles that turned and worked by a worm thread. One of the first stubbles to be ploughed was the bean field ready for a very early drilling of wheat in the autumn.

The next big job which I had to help with was the muck carting. This involved all the carts and rubber tyred tumbrels and nearly all the horses. This included the two colts which had to be held while the load was put on and as the load got higher on the cart some would fall of onto their backs which they didn't like, but after careful handling they soon got use to this. All this was being done for two reasons one was to clean out all the animals' yards, loose boxes and sheds ready for the next winter's bedding to keep all the animals dry and warm. The second reason was for the manure to be spread on the land and ploughed in to feed the soil. It was my job to take the full loads from the yards out to the fields. Two men loaded the carts with special, sharp, thin tined muck forks and this was not easy. I had to keep them supplied with empty carts, at the same time keeping the horsemen with full carts to empty and the way this was done was very precise. The muck was pulled off the carts by what was known as a muck crome, of which there were two sorts, one being made by the local blacksmiths, which was two prongs of flat pointed metal, about ten inches long, turned and joined like a U shape at the top making a hollow stem into a long piece of hazel wood cut from a hedge. It wasn't perfect but it done the job. The other was like a sharp pointed muck fork bent at right angles to the same type of handles used on pitch forks. These could be bought from the ironmongers for a few shillings. All heaps were pulled from the cart to be about the same size, all at seven yards apart and seven yards from row to row so when the field was finished all heaps were in a straight line whichever way it was looked at. And there was trouble if one heap was out of line as a great deal of pride was shown in all the field work done by those men.

And there was another reason for this precision as all muck was spread by men with a muck fork, throwing this stuff around to form an equal covering all over the field. This job always heralded the start of autumn. The hedges were changing their colour as the wild fruits were ripening, such as blackberries, hips, haws, sloes and hazel nuts. These were all there for the taking, which many people did of course, and there again no one minded people walking around the fields. The only thing that was left alone were crab apples, but some people did get some of these to make crab apple jelly but I must admit that I have never tasted any of this. My parents never made any to my knowledge. A lot of these apples looked as if they were ripe in their red and yellow skins and they would fall from the trees into the ditches and they would lie there all winter and even then if anyone tried to take a bite they would still be very sour, even the mice would not eat them.

During the war the haws, which was the fruits of the wild dog rose, would be collected by the school children and taken to a central collection point, which I think was the village post office. They were then taken away and I don't know where they went but they came back in bottles of orange liquid and called Rose Hip Syrup, which was given to very young children as it was supposed to contain lots of vitamins.

The other things collected were acorns which were given to farmers for their pigs, and also sweet chestnuts which were stored in a cool dry place until Christmas. Some Octobers were really lovely to be outside in, as the weather was cool in the mornings and the clover stubble was covered all over by gossamer, which was tiny spider webs, which seemed to cover the whole field, and the days were bright warm sunshine. This weather was known amongst country people as an Indian summer.

This was also a busy time on the fruit farm. I helped to cart off several acres of old blackcurrants bushes which had been pulled up by tractor and chains. These bushes were suffering from big bud which is a gall mite which infests the buds on the bushes and makes them swell and die, so we had to tip them into a dry pit and they were burned to stop this thing spreading to the young, new bushes which would be taking their place. Blackcurrants gave off a very pleasant smell when moved so it was quite nice to do this job.

Another job which I had to do with the current carting was horse raking the old straw off the rows of strawberry plants as this was used to help to burn the bushes. This was also the start of the apple picking season which was done by the regular group of women who picked the soft fruit and potatoes. Where they all went to after they were picked and stored in the old coach house and stables over the winter I never did know as I never done much at Wortham Manor at all.

The next job that was done and started in mid-September was the sugar beet harvesting and, depending on the winter weather, could last until the first weeks in March the next year. This was a horseman's job to lift the beet with a special plough which cut the soil down the side of each row and on the front at the bottom was a small plough share which lifted the beet up out of the soil a few inches. This loosened them so they could be pulled up by hand, knocked together to remove the soil and laid in rows with the roots all facing one way. They were then picked up by a small hook and the tops of the beet with the leaves on were cut off. I and another man would put these green leaves into small heaps ready for carting off to be laid out on the meadows for the milking cows to eat. The beet themselves were put into the same sort of heaps to be carted off by horse and cart.

This was the job done by the other men on the farm, who unloaded the carts with what was called a sugar beet fork. This had many tines, all with a small knob on the end to stop pricking the beet. The loads soon formed long high heaps that were wide at the bottom sloping to a point at the top. These heaps were always beside the road so the lorries could be loaded to take them to the factory.

But the pulling and topping of these beet was not done by the farm workers, instead it was done by German prisoners of war, as there was a big camp next to Redgrave Lake on land called The Warren, which was situated between the lake and the A143 Diss to Bury St Edmunds road. They were brought to the fields in army trucks and I think there was about twenty left on this farm, complete with two British soldiers who had a loaded rifle each to guard them. Most of them were hard workers and never tried to cause any trouble. Had they tried to escape I don't think they would have got far anyway as they all had a browny/red battle dress with a big circle on the back of the jacket. The circles would be different colours, red, green, blue and yellow. We had one particular man who had a yellow circle on his jacket. He always worked on his own and would not mix with the other men and neither would he talk us. The guards kept their eye on him and I found out, by talking to some of the other prisoners that he was not a German at all but came from the Ukraine, which was part of Russia.

The army lorry that dropped them off in the morning took some of the other prisoners to another farm but came to pick up the ones from here in the afternoon. Some of them had been farmers or farm workers in their own country so they knew what they were doing. Most of these ones were glad to be out of the war. Like a lot of our own service men they did not want to be there in the first place but had no choice. We would often talk to them as some could speak English. We also caught rabbits which they would prepare and cook for dinner. We also showed them how to catch a rabbit in a drain pipe under a gateway by smoking them out. They would also cook the centre leaves from the sugar beet tops, which were very much like spinach when cooked. Sometimes we would give them apples or pears and the odd cigarette. They always seemed grateful and in return they would bring us small presents like cigarette cases, ash trays, spoons all made from old but clean cocoa tins, also some items made from wood, egg cups and carved items. I can't remember what happened to these things but I now wish I had kept them and kept in touch with the prisoners that we got to know fairly well.

Meanwhile farm work continued much the same as it had the winter before, carting food and litter for the animals. If it was bad weather I had some help. Starting in the early dark mornings the war continued overhead with our aircraft coming home from raids and the American bombers taking off from the local airfields for the daytime raid. It got to the stage where we did not take much notice of all this except for the flares that were fired for one reason or another. Crashes happened sometimes and we watched for anything falling from the sky. Also in the dark mornings the V1's (Doodlebugs) could be seen. With the flames coming out at the back and the loud noise of the motor driving them you could see in which direction they were going.

So things carried on, mainly the same jobs as the years before and I could not see much of a future in this job. The men who were in the Home Guard were getting a bit depressed because of working hard and long hours also doing guard duty some nights and training at weekends. All seemed to be getting nowhere. The threat of a German invasion was fading as Hitler decided to attack Russia but we were still getting air raids. This changed the whole situation.

The Ministry of Agriculture was told by the government that all the restrictions which had been put on farmers had to be reviewed, and as a result some things, like cultivating between the sheaves at harvest, had to be stopped to save tractor fuel and a lot of other jobs were done away with. The potatoes which came for pig feed stopped and therefore the only ones that could be steamed were our own damaged ones, found when the riddling was done on all the farms and that also included what we called chits. These were the very smallest potatoes of them all.

Another thing that was done, instead of mowing around the cornfields with a scythe, the tractor and binder cut round leaving the standing corn one binder width from the hedge, which they then cut in the opposite direction, after the rest of the field had been cut.

It was becoming noticeable that there was a lot more air activity besides the night and daytime bombers. There were Dakotas and Sterlings pulling Horsa gliders and a lot more fighters were doing low level flying, while there seemed to be army about all over the place with their tanks, bren gun carriers and all the other transport used by the soldiers.

On top of being told to produce more food the farm was loosing it labour force as many men were getting called up for National Service. If I can remember right Ling Farm lost two men, Hall Farm lost two men and Beech Tree Farm lost three men. One of them was one that lived in the council house just a few yards down the road from us. I can remember that he came up to the well, which they shared with us, one Christmas morning to get a pail of water (as council houses did not have a source of water in those days) and he said that he had his calling up papers that morning. There must have been a post delivery on that day.

A lot of the ships were not only bringing goods for the war effort, but also farm machinery on what was known as lease lend, including many Fordson Standard tractors and International crawlers. These had four, big furrow drag ploughs. There was one of these crawlers came to Hall Farm. That coupled with many other farms having their shafts moved from horse drawn implements and having metal drawbars fitted showed that the speed of change to tractor working was beginning to be noticed.

Now, with more labour being called up, this left fewer men to do more work. With three men gone from Beech Tree Farm I was asked if I would be willing to go and help out there, but first I had to stop at the Hall Farm to help out with the winter threshing. Because of the work being done there was not enough men left to run our own threshing machine and the corn was badly wanted for bread production. So a threshing contractor was hired to do the job and this was Frank Stevens who had about eight sets of threshing tackles kept on a site with some big building on the corner of the road to Palgrave and Wortham Ling, just over Denmark Bridge. These were all worked by Burrel steam engines and each driver had his own engine to look after which was their prides and joy. The drum and elevator was the responsibility of the other member of the engine crew and that was the man who done the steering. There was always a bit of rivalry amongst the engine crews to keep their engine clean and brass shining. It always seemed to be Frank that brought his engine and crew to thrash at all the farms owned by the farmer I worked for. His men worked, feeding the drum, taking off the chaff and all the other jobs the engine men done. The men from the farm had to work on taking the corn off the drum when the sack was full. This was the horseman's job also; weighing each sack to make sure it was full to the right amount.

The other work was taking the sheaves of corn off the stack and putting them up into the drum. This usually took three men and there was two men making the straw stack. It was usually my father who actually built the straw stacks and sometimes I was told to help him if it was a small stack but if it was a big stack it took two corn stacks to find enough straw for a large size. So in this case it needed three men because it was quite a long way to push the loose straw. The whole secret of working on a straw stack was never to work in a hole so you had to push the straw uphill, which made it very hard work especially if the wind was blowing from the engine end as you not only got the dust from the drum but also the smoke from the engine's chimney. I soon learned that you had to keep straw under your feet and make a solid base to stand on. It did not take long for my father to show me how things were done to build part of the outside walls myself, but for the first stack he made the roof. It did not take long to learn to do the roof as most straw stacks were gable ended.

The other job, classed as a boy's job, was carting the chaff into the barn for the horses' food in the stables. I often had to do this job, which involved a horse and cart and lot of sacks that sugar beet pulp came in. These made ideal chaff bags as they were big and light to handle when empty, but was a very heavy when full, depending what type of chaff was being carted. Oat chaff was light and soft and easy to carry. Wheat chaff was not too bad but barley was quite a nuisance as it was not chaff as such, just sharp, brittle bristles that broke into many pieces when touched and got into your boots, socks and clothes and it took a lot of effort to get them out. A big heap of all this chaff was made in the barn and the big sacks had to be carried up wooden planks and as the heap got higher these boards became steeper. We always tried to get about twenty full sacks on the cart so as to cut down on the amount of journeys made from the threshing to the barn.

The other job done by the horse and cart, which I had to do sometimes, was to cart the threshed corn in special sacks, which were thick and heavy, to the corn barn, which was where the corn of all sorts, which was going to be sold was stored, usually two sacks high. I had some help to lift these onto the cart and, as we did not have a sack lift, this had to be done by hand. The way it was done was like this, as the full sack was standing on the ground there was a man each side (in this case one of them was me) who both bent down with each others arm around the lower half of the sack which was then pushed over into a horizontal position and, with both of us working together, we lifted the bottom of the sack onto the cart. This was completed with a big push on the sack. With a push from the shoulders the sack was upright. Moving it to any part of the cart by putting both arms around it was quite easy.

The worst job about carting corn was putting up in the granary the corn that was going to be used for stock feed on the farm. This was above the cart shed so it was all ready for grinding in the mill. To get this up there it had to be carried up twelve narrow steps without any handrails. This was especially hard with beans because they weighed twenty two stone. Each bag was well over two hundredweight. The secret of this particular job was to get the bag of corn lying horizontal over each shoulder and this evened out the load, but it did play a big part in making your legs ache. There were not any rules in those days and weight or age did not come into it. You had to do what you were told and if you slipped or made a mistake then it was your fault and the only sympathy you got was to be told to be careful next time. It soon made men out of boys.

Back to the threshing, the other time the steam engine came to the farm was at the start of harvest. In the first wheat field to be cut the threshing was done in one corner of the field so the straw stack was built in the field and the sheaves of wheat were picked up straight from the binder onto the wagons without any shocking done at all. The whole idea of this was to have a stack of new wheat straw ready for thatching. Corn and chaff was carted into the barn. Some of the horses were a little uneasy standing next to a working drum while the wagons were unloaded so a heap of fresh lucerne was put down so they could feed. It did not take long to thresh a field of wheat and the engine left to do the same job on another farm. The farm workers always said the best part of seeing the engine pulling all the tackle behind it was when it was going away from the farm. I liked the sound of the drum working with a loud hum with a deeper roar as each sheave was put in, especially in the distance on a clear frosty winter morning and not on the farm that you worked on.

Winters came and went and I kept carting food and litter for the animals and I could see no future in it at all. At home in my workshop I was making various item out of wood, linen horses, egg racks shaped like an big egg with shelves with holes in to hold twelve eggs, to hang in people's kitchens. I had a friend who was an upholsterer and he gave me an opportunity to learn how this was done, how to respring and cover a chair.

In the home one or two things were changing, like the paraffin table lamp, which, unless the wick was kept cut would smoke and black the glass so there was no light from it at all. In its place came the Tilley lamp of which there were two sorts. One was a very smart table lamp with its brass base and stem with a clear glass globe over the top to let out the light, which was very bright compared with the old oil lamps. The other model was the storm lantern which was a much stronger item altogether. The base was very strong and the glass globe was shaped like a big glass jar and this was topped with a vented brown enamel hood. All the base and the metal cage which protected the glass was painted in a gold metallic paint. The workings on both lamps were the same, both ran on paraffin and there were no wicks, but these worked on vaporising fuel. In both models paraffin was stored in the base and both had a pump to push air into the base and form pressure. You knew when there was enough air in with the paraffin because it would not pump anymore. At the bottom of the centre stem there was a tap which could be turned off or on. This had to be off while pumping before it was lit but could be on when pumping while it was lit, if the pressure went down. This could be seen by a small pin which worked inside a small tube, fitted into the base. If the top of the pin was level with the top of the tube this meant there was enough air in the paraffin. At the top of the stem was a mantle. This was like a piece of lace which fitted over the stem. This was like loose material when first fitted but when lit it formed a circular balloon of burnt ash.

There was a bit of a trick when lighting a new mantle and this was to turn the pressure tap on and light with a match. The flames would shoot out the top of the lamp so you had to be a bit careful, but this only happened the first time of lighting but not after that if no damage was done to the mesh mantle. These lights needed hardly any maintenance at all and the only real problem was that the centre stem was hollow but inside of that was a very thin piece of wire with a very sharp point on top and this is where the vaporisation took place with the wire and point and it would in time have soot up all the way up the centre and this would dim the light. A lot of people would buy a complete new stem when this happened which was quite unnecessary and expensive.

One of the workers in the ironmongery shop in Diss told me how to make this thing work without buying a new part, and this is how it was done, unscrew the stem and gently draw the pointed wire out and lay on a solid surface and gently tap the wire with a small hammer and the caked soot will fall off leaving a clean bright wire. Put this back into the stem and screw back into place, light as normal and the light will be as good as new. I could do all this in about ten minutes for which I would charge two shillings and sixpence 12 ½ pence in today's money, but it was quite a lot in those days.

The storm lantern had a lot of different uses as it had a very rigid wire handle over the top of the lamp so it could be hung from a beam or roof of a shed and this is what happened when it was used by poultry farmers. As the war was still on all windows had to be blacked out and as the Ministry wanted more and more eggs, the chickens were let out onto the meadows during the day but kept in the hut at night. So to make the chickens think it was still daylight after being shut up for the night what the farmers done were to put a measured amount of paraffin into the base of the lamp and then pump it up with air. This amount of paraffin would burn for about four hours and then go out, but the air pressure would keep on working until the tank was empty.

At that time the railways and road works were still using the same type of oil lamps that had been used for years, and it was the same in the milking parlours and stables on the farms, the old type of oil storm lantern was being used. It was quite a while before the Tilley lamp took over. I did have a Tilley in my workshop but I had made some wooden blackouts and I could carry on making some small pieces of wood furniture and some upholstery. Besides the ATC kept me fairly busy most of my spare time, but I still found time to help with the garden and sawing some firewood.

It was around about the time I saw an advert in the for sale column of our weekly Friday paper where a man a Mr Batchorler on Magpie Green at Wortham had a box of new carpenter's tools for sale. I had brought several new tools so I was tempted to go and look and see how much he wanted for them. I was amazed at what I saw. He brought out this purpose made box full of all sorts of tools all packed in wood wool which is very messy when moved. And this is what had happened. He had brought this box of tools, which opened on the floor of his lounge and true to form this wood wool went all over the room carpet much to the annoyance of his wife, and with that he said that he would not open the box anymore and this was the reason he was selling the box of tools. The cost of things in those days was only a fraction of what they would cost now but there must have been well over forty pounds worth of tools, as they cost at that time, and what he wanted for them was much less than he gave for them. He would sell them to me for ten pounds just to get rid of them provided I took them away there and then which I did. So I cycled home with this heavy box on the handlebars of my bike with great care and was very pleased with my purchase.

I had brought a good strong wooden bench off a friend who had been to an auction and brought ten of these things with the idea of selling them on at a profit. I paid him ten shillings (50p today). I still have this bench and a lot of the tools today. The other thing that was a must was a decent vice all I had was a small two inch thing that was my father's. So one Friday I had some time off work and went to one of the iron mongers in Diss and bought myself a big four inch vice but the weight of this was far more than I could carry on my bicycle so I had to find another way to get it home. The man in the shop told me to go to the bus and ask the driver if he would deliver it home for me, to which he agreed as he was passing our house anyway.

This bus ran from Botesdale picking up passengers on its way to Diss market every Friday. One stop was Wortham Dick at twelve noon and it did this in reverse at four o'clock in the afternoon, so I was lucky enough to have the vice brought home for me.

Meanwhile there was more air activity going on in skies all around us, both night and day, and on the night of 5 June 1944 it seemed that the sky was full of bombers both going out and returning from raids on the French coast. The next day 6 June 1944 the sky was still full of other planes, of which a lot were the American DC3 Dakotas. I have had several flights in Dakotas from Shepherds Grove so I could imagine what it was like. There was also Stirlings and there again I had flown in those as well, some of which were towing Horsa gliders like what was going on above our heads. This was done by having visits to Shepherd Grove with the ATC. We watched some of these Horsa gliders land and I would not like to have been in them. Also towing gliders were Halifax and Lancaster bombers, besides some American Liberators. Mixed in amongst all these were both British and American four and two engined bombers, the whole lot being escorted by fighters from both air forces. I had never seen anything like it before and I don't suppose I shall ever again.

We heard on the radio that this was D-Day or in other words the invasion of Europe. Nearly all the aircraft had what was known as D-Day stripes on their wings and bodies, which were wide, white painted identification marks. All this air activity went on for several days but what we did not know was what was going on in and across the English Channel, only what we heard on the radio or read in the papers. And all the army had disappeared from its manoeuvres from around this district. I think most people knew that something big was happening. Also the men in the Home Guard, who worked on the farm, were asked to do more jobs that should have done by the regular army, much to their disapproval.

I well remember what I was doing on D-Day there had been quite a dry time during May and into June and most of the ponds around the cow farm were dry and the water in the moat around the Hall was being saved for the horses. There was no water laid on in the countryside at that time. This did not happen till the early fifties so I had to cart water in the metal water cart with one of the older horses pulling it. We had to go to one of the ponds on Beech Tree Farm, a distance of about two miles. All the meadows had water tanks fixed on concrete beds so the cattle could not move them. Keeping one hundred cows from going thirsty was a full time job also filling up some of the tanks for the night had to be fitted in as well, on different meadows than the daytime one. All the water had to be moved by pail, from the pond into the cart and from the cart into the tanks. This task was made a little easier by when I got to the tank I would let the cows drink their fill so that amount did not have to be moved by pail. There was one little bit of danger attached to this job. That was why we used an older horse and this was the red short horned bull as he could not really be trusted when he came to drink. I was not afraid of him and all animals sense that, whatever they are. But my main concern was the horse, had he chose to become nasty.

Summer was much the same as the last, followed by the autumn and winter work. We did use a tractor and trailer for the sugar beet tops and kale and sometimes for the hay and straw. I had heard no more about helping at Beech Tree Farm and I began to think it was not going to happen. So I could not see any future in what I was doing or going any higher up the progress ladder so at this time I began to feel it was time for a change. But to my surprise I got to work one morning and was waiting in the shed for the day's orders with the other men and I noticed that the foreman had left me till last which was most unusual. When he came across to me he said that they really wanted me to work at Beech Tree for the unforeseeable future. In was not unusual to change men about from farm to farm when the amount of work required it.

I gathered my tools, two and four tined forks and headed back up the hill towards the rectory and around the corner past our house, where I called in and told my mother what had happened, and finally arrived at Beech Tree Farm, where the foreman, a man named Vic Hunn, who I knew well because I had been friends with his two sons as schoolboys. I also knew all the men as I had spent a lot of time with them for many years going on to any part of the farm as and how I wished, fishing, birds nesting, gathering nuts and blackberries, skating on the ponds in winter, and playing football and cricket on the meadows, not forgetting the poaching. So I knew nearly every part of this farm.

Now this was very different sort of farm, no milking cows here. But there were fattening bullocks, pigs, chickens and turkeys, reared for the Christmas trade and of course horses, ten of them which I had often ridden in company of some of the workers when I was a small boy. As this was the end of winter and the beginning of spring, most of the ploughing had been done and the land was being broken down ready for drilling but my first day was spent on odd jobs with the foreman, feeding chickens, collecting eggs, chopping up green nettles for the day old turkey chicks. I knew nothing about turkeys at all but I soon found out they had to be kept warm under heaters, hanging from the roof of their shed. These were a special type of Tilley heater where the heat was made to come downwards and then rise up naturally. They also had a habit of dropping down dead for no apparent reason. They also reared their own day old chicks of which a lot were cockerels, for the Christmas trade again.

This was also the time the meadows were being dressed with nitrate to make the grass grow and the fields were having artificial fertiliser drilled on them. This was done by a one horse drill which threw this stuff out very evenly. That was a time before this fertiliser came to the farm ready mixed. There was Sulphate of Potassium, Nitrate of soda, Nitrate of chalk and Superphosate . These all came in two hundredweight bags, which were very thick. These bags were washed out, dried and used for potatoes when they were being riddled. Now all this fertiliser was emptied out on to the barn floor, one sack of each sort on top of each other until we had quite a big heap, then with shovels we had to turn this heap over twice to mix it all together to spread onto the fields. I think for potatoes there was something else mixed in with it but I can't remember what that was. After it was all mixed it was put back into the bags and carted out to the field where it was going to be used. This was a totally different type of work from what I had been doing and I did not mind working in the barn especially as there was a cold North East wind blowing across the fields.

My first experience of using a horse on this farm was in fact carting this stuff out for drilling. The horse I was told to use was one bought from a Diss coal merchant when he sold his business to another firm. She was a smart Suffolk punch called Polly and with her in the shafts of one of Youngs made tumbrels with rubber tyres. She knew quite a lot and was very easy to use I always took her if I could after that. But she had one fault and as this farm also took potatoes to the cafes and chip shops in Diss, everyone wanted to take her and her fault was that once in the town she would stop at every house where she delivered coal, but was very reliable and took no notice of traffic (what little there was) at all.

This was a totally different atmosphere on this farm to what I had been used to. There wasn't the must get done today feeling about this place, much more relaxed and I liked it a lot, plus the fact that I did have the chance to go home to dinner sometimes.

Now the land was being got ready for drilling and I was given the job of harrowing with two Clydesdale horses that had been on the farm for quite a long time, and I was told they had been brought in as a plough team and already broken to all harness. One was a mare called Gypsy and the other was a gelding called Nobby. They worked well as a team, but singly it was a different matter. Nobby was good in a cart but Gypsy hated being in between shafts of any sort. She would run away every chance she got. I think she had been very ill treated some time in her life because if you tried to lead her she would walk with her neck up high and to one side as if she wanted to get away from you and she always had her tongue hanging to one side of her mouth and it looked like someone had at sometime put a piece of wire on her tongue and cut partway through. I don't know how she managed to eat but she did.

Not only did I do a lot of harrowing during drilling but I also bush harrowed all the meadows. I really like doing this as it was just walking behind the harrows without them having to be cleaned at all. This type of harrowing was that the six harrows were each interwoven with pieces of prickly hawthorn cut from a hedge; this levelled the mole hills and pulled out all the dead grass. On a warm sunny morning and the horses knew when to turn, all I had to do was to tell them when to stop and start, coupled with the smell of fresh mowed grass, I thought it an excellent job.

There were some mixed breeds of horses in this farm stable but the main one was the foreman's horse as he was also the horseman and this horse had strong legs as he was half Suffolk and half Shire. He had a dark coat with black main and a very short black tail. He was equivalent to Blossom on Hall farm. This was the one that the colts were broken in with and like Blossom, nothing seemed to upset him. I often took him on single horse jobs, like flat rolling, which was one of the very easy jobs. Also the horseman and I used him on a small Smyth drill for sowing the sugar beet seed, and after they were up, horse hoeing with the disc hoes ready for chopping out.

I can well remember we had him once horse hoeing peas on a very big field, which like some of the other fields around, had a long slope making it a rather hilly area, and on this particular day in early April there was lots of heavy showers. We were half way up the hill and could see a very heavy shower coming from the north, but by the time it reached us it was a really big hail stones that hit us like bullets. So we turned Darkie, as he was called, round to face east and we got underneath him for shelter and he never moved a leg he just stood there and took it all and stopped us getting soaked through.

I liked working on this farm as I was given more opportunities than I had ever had at Hall Farm. I was using two horses to use on different jobs like rib rolling, which was a two horse job. This was a very heavy roll made up of a row of ribbed wheels all fitted on a metal spindle inside a heavy wooden frame. On one side was a pair of shafts and on the other was a round metal ring, into which hooked a ploughing whipple tree for a horse in plough harness. For this job I used Darkie in the shafts and a horse called Stormer in the plough trace. Now he was a very big, heavy horse of no particular breed, with a light mane and tail and a speckled brown coat. But he was very strong and willing horse. He often was used to cart loads to Diss as no one had any trouble with him and he would stand where told too. This particular type of roll with all the wheels dangling together could be heard from a long way off and when moved on the road left a mark on the surface from the ribs on the wheels.

I was also asked if I would help with the chopping out of the sugar beet on what was known as piece work and this was when everyone agreed on a price per acre. I helped the foreman to mark out the acres by using a chain measurement. But I had never done this job before as I had always been carting food and litter for the animals at the Hall Farm. I went down to an ironmonger in Diss and bought a new hoe and handle and made a start under the supervision of some of the other men. The first day was quite good, but at the end of the second day my back felt as if it was breaking, and this is where I learned the secret of chopping out sugar beet which was not to stand up straight on the second and third day. After then, when my back adjusted to the movement it was easy. This is something I remembered whenever I done this job after that. In fact I enjoyed it because the more you done the more money was earned.

But there was other work to be done and I repaired a lot of chicken huts out on the meadows and some had to be given a coat of creosote, a job I liked, and it was not all horse work either but I did help with a lot of horse hoeing, both corn and beet. I also had a chance to drive a tractor as they had a spud wheeled Case and an orange standard Fordson, which I used a lot for carting straw for the pig and cattle yards.

I also had to do some tractor ploughing with a Ransoms two furrow trip plough. Now I had never done a job like this before but what we called setting a top was done by the horseman and a single furrow Ransoms YL plough, pulled by his plough team. Setting a top was done in the old furrow left from last years ploughing and this was what happened. A stick was cut from the hedge, usually a piece of hazel with the bark peeled off, and put in the old furrow at the lowest point which was the centre. Then at the opposite end of the field and in the same furrow just away from the headland and about two yards in, a mark was made with a foot pushing your boot in the soil at right angles to the old furrow. This mark had to be exactly across the way the field was going to be ploughed. And then two more barked sticks were used. This time it was nearly the same as the opposite end of the field. A mark had to be made along the centre of the old furrow again but this time it was about a yard and a half long and a stick had to be put at each end of the mark and bending down to look along these two sticks, the one at the far end of the field should be in line with the other two sticks and not visible from that end behind these two. Now to do this first furrow with a team of horses the tether between the two must be lengthened so you can see all the way down the field and this is where the secret of drawing a straight furrow first time came in. The old horsemen would not tell you this, but when you looked between the horses you took a visual eye of what was in line with all the sticks, such as a thistle, a high piece of grass, a stone or any item that made a straight line. Then getting the horses and plough set in the right position and dropping the foot on the front of the plough to cut out a shallow furrow and the plough line tight so the horses could be steered easily off you went catching each marker as the plough went down the field and turning the white stick over with the front of the plough. Collecting the stick for further use the horses were turned round and ready to go back up the field with each one on their new position each side of the new ploughed furrow, but this time the foot was lifted up a bit so the plough could go in a bit deeper. The return journey was made leaving an open furrow shaped like a 'V'.

The next step was to tie the two horses to the right distance apart for normal ploughing, and lift the foot up high enough so the depth of the furrow was nine or ten inches deep, slightly loosen the plough line and with the furrow horse in its proper position turn the first flag of soil into a practically standing upright angle, and when you get to the end, turn the team round to do the same up the opposite side. This leaves a ridge or a reversed 'V' with a furrow both sides and this is where the front and back right hand tractor wheels run in while twenty yards away the horseman is busy making another top ready for ploughing. After the tractor has ploughed ten yards each side of the first one and turning right each end meant that at the centre of each top became the next furrow, finishing off with a shallow furrow the same as the start of each top. This was quite a nice job to do as if you got tired of sitting down on this model of tractor you could stand up and ride. All the controls of the plough could be operated from the tractor, as the plough had long handles for width and depth but a rope from the plough and tied to the tractor seat was the way of lifting the plough in and out of the ground or tripping as we called it.

This is where I hit a problem. When I came to one end head land which was quite hard going on heavy clay, I turned the tractor and at the same time pulled the rope to lift the plough, which it did and then to my surprise it tripped itself and the plough dug deep into the soil. With this happening while the tractor was turning it pulled the tractor against the bank of a five foot deep ditch and then the bank gave way and fell in the ditch, leaving the tractor hanging with the left hand front wheel with nothing under it at all. I don't know what I though at that particular time as nothing like this had ever happened to me before, but I had to find a way out and get on with the job. So what I done was to take out the pin that connected the plough to the tractor and took the trip rope off the seat and pulled the whole plough drawbar to one side as much as possible. This made room for the tractor to get past so I opened the throttle just a little and engaged reverse gear and slowly the tractor started to move backwards with the left hand back wheel rubber tyre starting to grip the grass verge on the top of the bank. Slowly but surely I was moving backwards much to my surprise but what I had not allowed for was the grip on the rubber tyres were doing the opposite to what they should do and instead of gripping they were actually pushing on the bank. As soon as the front wheel became harder to pull the whole bank gave way again and I was back where I started, only worse because this time the engine stalled and the handle at the front that is used for starting was level with the soil at the side of the bank. So I had no means of starting it again. There was only one answer, get some help. So I had to find the Case tractor and get the driver to come and tow the Fordson out. Which he did quite easily and no damage was done. But I did learn two things from this incident. One was always keep an eye on whatever the tractor was pulling behind it, and two was always leave enough room for turning where ever you were.

Now I liked working on this farm despite most of the jobs were much the same as Hall Farm, but I was given the same responsibility regarding the horses and machinery as any other man on the farm, I helped to walk the fat cattle to market on certain Fridays and even learned which ones to pick out for sale. Usually we took four at a time. There was two yards of fat cattle here. One was at the Barn near the rectory and the other was in some clay lump and pantiled buildings about half way up Marsh Lane, the narrow road that went from the 'T' junction on the Palgrave to Redgrave road and through to the A143 at Wortham. This set of farm buildings were known as The Icca and what the reason for that was I could never find out. Apparently it had been that name for as long as any of the older people could remember. Whether there was ever a farm house there and people lived near these buildings remains a mystery. But one thing both these sets of buildings had in common was they both were built on meadow land and both had deep ponds near them. And both used part of the meadow for a stack yard where the corn was stacked and threshed, leaving the straw for litter in the cattle yards.

I can remember helping to thresh the stacks up at the Icca and cart the chaff home to the chaff house, as it was called, next to the stables at Beech Tree Farm. I did not cart the corn home from there as this was done with the orange Fordson tractor and a tumbrel which had its shafts taken off and a tractor draw bar fitted instead. I had a very quiet horse called Stormer and one of the new Youngs of Diss tumbrels with rubber tyres. The threshing at the Icca was done by Frank Stevens's steam engine so every one had to work very hard. I had to have a big load of chaff sacks on the loads home to the farm because this place was a good mile and a half each way so it was quite a nice long ride with each load.

The meadow had been ploughed up leaving a grass strip from the road to the buildings, due to the way every meadow that could be ploughed to produce food was ploughed up and drilled with crops. I helped to drill these nine acres with peas this particular year using a Smyth drill and two horses.

Another law that came in during the war was that wherever threshing of corn stacks took place a piece of one inch mesh netting that was one yard high was put completely around the stack, engine and threshing machine. This was put up so it could be folded back when the carts went to collect the corn and chaff. This was all held up with lengths of hazel sticks that had been split and cut into one yard lengths and used to hold the thatch on the stacks. The idea of this was that the rats and mice could be caught and killed instead of escaping into the hedges.

I went past the Icca meadow a few weeks ago and was surprised to find that all the buildings had disappeared with the exception of one small clay lump building which was where the corn, meal and hay was kept for cattle food. I had no idea when these buildings were pulled down or what happened to them.

I was tempted to go and see if the pond was still there but somehow I thought it was better not too. I never did like this pond but I can't understand why because as boys we collected moorhens' eggs from the nests in the bushes by tying a table spoon on a long cane. These were very good when fried with a piece of bacon and a round of homemade bread. Some people said that there was some big fish in there, which of course there could have been as this was a big deep pond, but I never saw anyone fish there or know of one being caught. There were some wooden steps down to the water at the nearest point to the building and I did get water out of there at two pails a time for the cattle in the buildings where there was a big tank that they drank from. But as I said before I did not like it. The water always seemed to be very dark and always up to a certain level it never seemed dry and not much weed on top of the water, just some water plantain and a few bulrushes around the sides, no water lilies or anything like that and I can't remember seeing any water boatmen or water beetles in the water (Ugh horrible).

The barn has also gone but I do know what has happened to that but not the year it disappeared. It was brought by a local developer and taken down joint by joint and each part numbered, packed and shipped to America, where the developer took some men over there and rebuilt it the same as it was here in this country. Whether it was made into a house I don't know, but I do know that there was several old barns being exported and rebuilt, the same as the one that was in the meadow near Wortham rectory. But this movement of barns all took place several years after the war finished of course. Up till then they had a double use because after the fat cattle had gone, pigs were reared to fattening weight until after harvest when the yards were cleaned out and the muck was carted onto the stubble fields and the yards were littered down with clean fresh straw ready for the next lot of cattle in the autumn.

However the war was still going on but the big German raids had stopped around this area and most people rarely looked up or took any notice of all of our and American aircraft flying by day and night above out heads. Most people were going to bed to get a good night's sleep. There was a new trick the Germans were carrying out and that was a lone aircraft would follow our bombers home and when they landed at their airfield it would sneak in behind them it would drop some bombs and machine gun the place but I am glad to say that most of those planes never made it back across the English Channel.

On the farm things carried on much the same as the year before and the year before that. The government was urging all farmers to grow more and more with fewer men to do the work. At Hall Farm labour was being taken from Ling Farm to help out. This was still an era where horse power was the main force and tractors were still in the minority, all controlled by the amount of fuel used. Although farming was not rationed, sometimes the tankers did not turn up when they should so the tractors stood in the shed.

At Beech Tree Farm all the hay meadows had been cut and this was where it was different from Hall Farm as there was no hay turning machinery here. All hay was turned by hand with one man and a two tined fork turning a row and so on. All the men who worked here were involved including me. So starting at the outside of the meadow each row was given a shake by the fork and then turned completely over with the bottom of the row now on top to get dried by the sun. It did not take long to get to the centre of the meadow with all these men. I liked the smell of drying hay and as the sun shone it was an enjoyable job. A few days later we all went back into the hay meadows and then working with three rows per man the hay was made into haycocks ready for carting.

Now on this farm unloading the hay from the wagons to put onto the stack was different from the other two farms because here they had an elevator to do this job. This machine I had seen many times before but I had never seen or knew how it worked. This was a very heavy built wooden frame constructed of three inch by six inch and three inch by four inch timber and was quite high. It had heavy, wooden side boards to form the channel where the hay, corn or straw was put in to take it up to the stack. When it was moved from place to place it took one shaft horse and one trace horse to move it and with all the heavy metal cogs and metal driving shafts that the cogs were fitted to, it weighed nearly two tons. The whole thing was made with two halves of which one half could be folded back and dropped so it hung upright at the back which was cranked by a handle turning a worm into a ratchet. As the stack got higher the same method was used to make the elevator higher.

Well this had no engine of any sort but what made it work was good old fashioned horse power and this is how it was done. One of the side frames was made to be removed so that the horse could get inside the frame and from there it was harnessed to a pole with a strap around the bottom of its collar, which in turn had a long strap fitted to the loop on the top and from there the strap looped under the horse's tail. This kept the collar from falling forward. The pole was then able to turn the main big cog wheel, which turned all the other cogs and shafts down to an axle, which turned the wheels on both sides to the chains to the slats of wood and metal spikes that took the hay etc. up the elevator. The side frame was refitted and with the horse walking around in a circle, work could begin.

With the horse restricted to walking like this he was not allowed to stop. If he did the machine stopped and there was a very loud shout from one of the men telling him to start again. If it was a very heavy crop the horses were changed at dinner time. When the stack was completed the elevator was moved to the next one leaving a circle of soil in front of the stack. I helped to build the stacks on this farm as two of the elderly workers took the full and empty wagons from stack to field and field to stack.

Well hay time came and went and harvest arrived in much the same way as at the Hall. I rather liked the harvest as I drove the orange Fordson pulling the binder as field after field got cut and shocked up. Then came the cultivating between the rows of shocks for fire prevention. I helped to build the corn stacks and after the stubble fields were cleared I had to use the horse rake to clear up any loose corn left on the field and one particular sunny morning I was doing this on a very big field reaching from the Marsh Lane nearly to the Long Green to the Church road. All the rakings were left in long straight rows. There was lovely warm sunshine and no wind. I was nearly into the middle of the field when I heard what sounded like a roaring noise. I stopped the horse and turned to look behind me, and I had never seen anything like it in my life before. The whole row of fresh rakings was spiralling round and round and leaving the ground as if it was being lifted. This straw was going higher and higher and still going round and round. As more straw was lifted the higher it went. There was a column of straw as high as the eye could see where it dispersed into a cloud and came down scattering straw over a wide area and dropped to the ground. Then within seconds it all stopped and there was complete calm. This was a big whirlwind and what the local farm worker called a 'Rodger' I had seen small ones before but nothing like this. It was said that this was the sign of good weather but I can't remember if it was or not. It was a long time ago.

I had helped to build nine corn stacks and three hay stacks at Beech Tree Farm which was much more enjoyable work than I had done at the Hall, and so much carting time came round and as so many fields were so far away from the farm we had to have three people driving the full and empty carts of which I was one. We had our change over points and as I was on the farm end my changing point was somewhere along the track in the Home meadow, usually opposite the pond where I nearly drowned when I was a young boy.

The person I changed carts with was an old chap who lived in half of the thatch cottage next to Wortham Dick public house, where he spent as much of his spare time as possible and it was said that he kept a length of rainwater gutter in his bedroom and used it as a goesunder (a pot) by putting it out of the open window and peeing into it. This could have been right as they were a peculiar family. He lived with one of his brothers whose whole ambition in life was to do as little as possible. There was another brother who lived in a cottage in Fersfield and he would cycle over to see his two brothers and when he left he would still be talking very loud when he was going up the hill towards the 1066 road.

Now Jimmy Cox as he was known was a very heavy smoker and rolled his own cigarettes. Well at that time I did have the odd Woodbine as most of us in the ATC did after flying, but in those days cigarettes were made of real tobacco not like the rubbish people smoke today. Jimmy saw me get the packet out of my pocket and said to me, "Why don't you have a real cigarette boy?" and proceeded to make me the biggest cigarette I had ever seen, about as thick as a mans finger and made entirely of Churchman's Counter Shag. I didn't like the look of that at all but did not like to upset the old man so I lit it and had a puff. Well it was the worse thing that I had ever tasted and as we each went our separate ways, as soon as he was out of sight I put this thing out and put it in the mud of a rut made by the cart wheels never to be seen again. The reason I did not want to upset this man was because of what I had seen him do a short while before. He was leading a horse and cart around the back of the barn to get some straw. He had a two tined fork in his hand and a cat sat on the roadway where he was going. He shouted at it to get out of his way but it took no notice, so he got his fork and put it under the cat and threw it up in the air and it landed several yards away onto a ploughed field.

So muck carting finished and the sugar beet season began but here this work was done by the men on the farm and not prisoners of war. This was a piece-work job like chopping out. What the price per acre was I don't know but the horseman did all the lifting and the gang of four men did all the pulling and knocking and laying into rows. The topping was done straight into the carts and there were no heaps left on the ground to be picked up later. I took the empty carts to men in the field and brought the full carts of beet and unloaded these onto clamps on the wide grass banks beside the road, ready for the lorry to be loaded up to take them to Bury factory.

This was a very busy job and if the men had to wait for an empty cart they done a bit of moaning because to them time was money. The cold frosty mornings were the worst because if the beet got frozen they were hard to cut and very often a knife would bounce off a beet and go clean through a glove. A handkerchief was wrapped around the cut and the man carried on. Really wet weather made going very hard as the soil turned to mud and as the carts used the same tracks all the time the mud turned to slurry and was pushed for yards in front of the cart wheels. This was a very messy job when conditions were like this.

At school we were all taught to wash our hands before meals but out here it was a different matter as there were no toilet facilities at all. Most of the old men did not worry about a simple thing like that anyway. From October onwards most of the grass on the banks was wet so this replaced soap and water if you required it too. But using the loo was totally different matter.

Yes you did have running water in the nearest deep ditch you could find, and the nearest thing to toilet paper was a big dock leaf, this was alright until the sharp frosts and gale force north east winds made everything white and very cold. I think this must have been one of the fastest jobs done on the farm in winter. But for all those conditions I never knew of anyone being ill or coming to any harm by it, you just accepted it as a part of life and got on with your work. One thing that was a must though was to avoid the stinging nettles at all cost.

The doodle bugs and V2 rockets kept coming and aircraft of many sorts were flying overhead most of the time except when the weather was so bad flying was impossible and for a while the countryside was quiet and most people had got the idea that the war would soon be over and began to ignore what was going on in the skies above them. I went to one or two parades held in Diss consisting of the army, some bands etc. I remember one parade where people were going round collecting money to buy a Spitfire. If I remember rightly there was enough collected by the people of Diss and the surrounding district to buy one, this sort of thing was going on all over the country.

I helped to drill and harrow the autumn setting of the wheat and winter barley. This was done when the horses were not needed to cart off the sugar beet. The horses at Beech Tree Farm were not taken to any of the blacksmiths in Wortham for new shoes, instead they went to Mr Howells, the Palgrave blacksmith who had a forge on the green (Now a bungalow). They were the family who I was given to understand had been blacksmiths for generations before. They certainly were experts at their job and so were the men who worked for them. I did take some horses to Palgrave mainly two or three at a time; this farm foreman did not like one horse going all that way when it made more sense to take at least two and the reason for that had a simple answer. This blacksmiths had horses coming from the farms in Palgrave, Stuston, Thrandeston and parts of Broome so if you were really unlucky there might be six or more horses waiting to be shod in front of you so you had to stand about and chat with the other men who had brought those horses.

I think that I had mentioned when I was writing about my family that my grandmother at South Creake was a Howell whose father was a blacksmith at Walsingham. Whether they were any relation to the Howells at Palgrave I never found out.

Nearly all my spare time was spent in my workshop and helping in the garden, I bought books on how to make things out of wood, upholstery and carpentry. And one day just by chance the builder/undertaker was putting a pane of glass in a window of the house next door and we had a nice long chat ending up with him asking if I would like to go down to their workshop and help them in the evenings. This was an opportunity I could not miss and I learnt a lot from them. One thing was how to cut a plank of wood so it would bend this was done by making seven cuts one eight of an inch apart and about halfway through the thickness of the wood. This bend was used mainly in the undertaking side of their business. They gave me lots of off cuts of oak, elm and chestnut boards of which I made small pieces of furniture like book ends, wall racks and clothes horses, but one item I made from pine and was always a good seller was an egg rack made like a large egg with shelves fitted across it at intervals with holes drilled in them big enough to take a dozen eggs. One was taken as far away as Tasmania near New Zealand.

I also helped to stain the beams inside the roof in Diss church. This was done by the whole inside of the church being filled with scaffolding so it had to be done very quickly so as not to be there for the Sunday service. They also offered to take me to London which I had never been to before so I gladly accepted their offer. There was four of us all going in one of their cars and when we got as far as Newmarket Heath the car broke down. After making arrangements for it to be picked up and returned to Diss, we walked to Newmarket station and carried on to London by train ending up at Waterloo station. Not knowing very much about London at that time we came out of the station to go on the nearest underground train and I saw this clock on a tower and thought this does not look like the pictures I had seen of Big Ben. I soon got put right on that score. I have been to London several times since but more on that later.

We went to a place called 'Trade' where we all had an excellent meal. This was some sort of business trip which I understood nothing about whatsoever, concerning new uniforms and band instruments. This organisation had branches worldwide and I had the idea that they wanted me to join them but I had no wish to do that but I must admit they did a lot of good for a lot of people. It was getting dark as we used the bus and walked parts of the way back through London to Liverpool Street station where we got on the train to Norwich but we got off at Diss.

The sugar beet harvest finished and all the winter jobs continued like littering the animals' yards so they all had somewhere dry to lie in the winter weather. The usual winter work carried on, hedging, ditching, draining by hand by digging out deep trenches across the fields and laying clay drain pipes in the branch trenches, three inch pipes in the main drain finishing off with a four inch asbestos pipe going through the bank and into the ditch. My job on this work was to have the orange Fordson tractor and cart collect the long sticks cut from the hedging and to lay them along the trench on top of the drain pipes before the trench was back filled. I used this tractor for carting all sorts of things, hay, straw, sacks of milled corn for animal feed. I liked this a lot because the heat from the engine kept you warm.

Then one morning the situation changed when everyone woke up to at least six inches of snow combined with strong winds forming deep drifts in certain places, like gateways to some of the farm buildings. So some of the men had to go out with shovels and clear these drifts so the animals could be fed. Also the sugar beet clamps had to be covered with barley straw. I was lucky as I had to harness up a team of horses and with the foreman took the big heavy snowplough (which was stored at Beech Tree all year round) on to the roads to clear as much snow as possible. Our first trip was down to Wortham church and then on to the school and from there up Wortham Long Green to Speirs Hill and then Magpie Green and back down to the Church. Walking behind this thing kept you nice and warm but there was a seat if you wished to ride, which we sometimes did but this made it harder for the horses. But our main object was to clear as much road as possible in the shortest time taking care not to overwork the horses. We done several more roads out to the village boundaries where we met other ploughs from the surrounding villages doing their roads. But the road we left to last was from the Diss end of the Ling through to the edge of Redgrave village.

Now there was a reason for this which I soon found out. The front area of Redgrave Cross Keys was at that time the only place where we could turn the horses and snowplough round. Once this was done it was time for a lunch and dinner break together. With a warm fire, a pint of beer or two we made good use of a rest after walking all those miles. The horses were given a pail of warm water each to drink to stop them getting too cold. So feeling refreshed we headed back to the farm and left the plough near the road just in case there was another snow fall. But there was still a job to be done before dark. We told one of the other men to brush our two horses down and give them a little extra feed, while we had to harness a single horse and make it pull a very old narrow snowplough around the meadows amongst the chicken huts so the hens could find some grass to eat.

Well we were lucky and winter turned to spring and it was not long before we were harrowing, drilling and rolling and doing all the things that entailed. The meadows beside the fields had to be harrowed and treated with fertiliser and some had to be rolled. The new sown corn soon began to grow and out came the horse hoe to kill the weeds. I can remember we had twelve four inch A hoes on the back bar of the hoe and I was leading the horse, Darky I think it was, and Tom Harbour was guiding the hoe. We were on the field between the Barn and the Wigwam and was changing jobs every now and then.

I was quite happy with this idea and I felt that I was given more chances to learn on this farm, hoping that I could stay here for good, when the foreman came walking across the filed and stopped for a chat and then he said something I didn't want to hear. "They want you back at the Hall", he said "because they are short of labour", and then he told us why. The problem was with the cowmen at Low Farm. The head cowman had shot the second cowman and then turned the twelve bore gun on himself inside one of the sheds. He killed himself but badly injured the other man who did recover but was unable to work for about two months. The cows were milked that morning by the third or reserve cowman and the yardman at the Hall. As all this happened very early in the morning these two men stepped in very quickly so the milk was ready in time for the lorry to collect and take away.

There were lots of police about the farm but they did not get in the way of any work being done. It was revealed that there had been some sort of grievance over one of the men's wives wanting to change husbands, or things like that. Anyhow the farmer was left without two cowmen so I could not really refuse to go back. This was a common problem with cowmen they always seemed to be discontented with something (not shooting of course) and they would always be leaving one farm for another as they knew that not everyone could do their job.

I went back to Hall Farm thinking that they wanted me to feed the cattle and pigs or at least the same sort of jobs which I had done before, but no, what the foreman said to me rather shocked me and that was, "Will you help to milk the cows, one hundred of them, working with the third cowman who knows all the work to be done and how to do it?" My answer to that was "I can't milk a cow" and he said "I know you can." How he knew that I don't know but he was really sure of his facts, and it would be until they got two new cowmen. I would be paid extra with all the milk I wanted to take home, working cowmen's hours which were four o'clock start until eleven o'clock and then home for a break until two o'clock till five o'clock finish with one day off each week. I had known the third cowman all my life as he was the gamekeeper's oldest son, a very quiet man who turned a blind eye to my poaching, which he had known about for a long time. What the foreman did not tell me was the cows were now all milked by machines which made it a lot easier.

I started the next morning and Jack as he was called still lived in the same house with his family on the edge of the Ling so he had to come past our house to work, and if I was not ready he would give a whistle to let me know he was there. Him and me got on straight away and worked well together and as it was springtime the cows were out on the meadows all night as well as daytime. Early mornings were not new to me due to the poaching experience. There was of course a bull with all those cows which was a red shorthorn with a big strong body. I should think he weighed well over a ton and had a mind of his own. The first time I went in to feed him he soon weighed me up and stood looking but would not move so I went round him and put his food in his feeding bin and just walked out. Thankfully he did not seem to mind. We had one particular day when the engine broke down and we had no option but to milk every cow by hand. This made my wrists really ache badly and took a while to get over, but by next day it was repaired and so back on the machines.

A lot of the calves were fed individually from a pail and did not take up too much time. I liked the time off at midday as a visit to Diss was possible but a change of clothes was a must as the working ones always smelled of disinfectant as every precaution was taken to avoid disease.

Time passed very quickly on this job and it was not long before a new couple were living in the house and took over the milking. These were a married couple from Ireland, very hard workers but had their own ideas how to run a milking herd which was not like we done it. I think they upset a lot of the men on the farm so much that some of them would not go up to Low Farm to work if asked to.

I went back to Hall farm and was doing the same old jobs and Jack done some farm work but also helped the keeper when required. I was busy flat rolling one of the biggest fields on the farm in an attempt to flatten as much as possible the ridge that had been made when the potato crop was set. The idea of this was to make the land solid for reridging when the potatoes were growing. This was normal procedure. This was an easy job and it was possible to sit on the frame of the roller and ride if you wished to do so. This was a rather quiet day, warm and sunny. There was some air activity but not as much as other days. I saw one lone Spitfire flying at about five hundred foot high and when it got over Fersfield it went up higher and done a victory roll. I remember thinking that was a bit unusual and then thought nothing more of it.

I stopped the horse and started to have a bit of lunch when I heard Diss church bells ringing in the distance then several village churches were ringing their bells. Even Wortham church with its lone bell started to ring. This was a bit suspicious as this was supposed to be the warning of an invasion, and then the foreman came to where I was working and said that the war was over. Some people thought that things would be back as it used to be overnight when this happened. How wrong they were. Anyhow this was the first time I had ever seen this particular foreman smile and then he said we are letting everyone go home earlier today. I just cannot express how I felt that day I don't think I shall ever forget the date of that day, 8th May 1945. I was seventeen at the time and what did the future hold? I knew this was something that needed a lot of thinking about.

That evening I went down to Diss to meet some pals but got no further than Fair Green. I had never seen anything like it before. There was hundreds of hundreds of people all over the green, singing and dancing and someone had built two massive bonfires, one at each end of the green and as it got dusk they were lit, something that had not been allowed for the last six years. There were fireworks. Where they came from I don't know, and also some one had a very light pistol and was shooting flares up into the sky. Another person had some thunder flash cartridges which when lit made a terrific flash

227

and very loud bang. All these celebrations went on well into the night. At a later date there was a victory parade along Mere Street and a church service of thanks. I can remember very clearly taking our blackout shutters to pieces and using the wood from the frame for something else.

It did seem strange to see the lights on in people's houses and from our house the street lights of Diss could be seen very easily, and also it was nice to see the lights on the vehicles travelling on the roads at night. It must have made it better to see where one was going. It was several years before rationing finished and what changes there were happened so gradual that it was hardly noticeable.

But on the farm things were changing fast as the Government was pressing for more food production and changes were going to be made, but one thing that stopped altogether was the ploughing or cultivating between the rows of shocks on the cornfields. The farmers were getting more money for all sorts of things and for the harvest of 1945 there was a new Lister Blackston elevator. In all its bright blue and red paint it arrived at the Hall. This was worked by a Lister petrol engine which certainly saved a lot of hard work. I think there was one of these delivered to Beech Tree Farm as well. I do know the heavy horse driven elevator was stood up in one corner of the stack yard. What happened to it in the end I don't know, but it was falling into disrepair the last time I saw it.

Well harvest started and I was back to the same old jobs, shocking behind the binder, driving the loads of corn from field to stack and the empty wagons from stack to field, cutting and carting the maize out on the meadows for the cows. There was no suggestion of helping on the stacks. This was very disappointing and I must admit I felt very unhappy and began to think this definitely is not for me. I was doing very little tractor work, I would love to have driven the red crawler tractor but there was no chance of that.

Change of Farm

Out of the blue and at a chance meeting with the foreman from Beech Tree I was told of a small farmer who had sacked his horseman/farm worker for badly treating his pair of horses. This was an old fashioned forty acre small holding farm and I did know the farmer as I have already mentioned about him losing his dairy herd to foot and mouth disease. He did have a local milk round of which we were a customer. I went down to see him about a job, realising that I would be going back several years as he did not have a tractor or many of the implements I had used on the other farms. I had a good look around the place, there was a small thatched barn, two stables and other sheds all built close together. The opposite side of the drive there was two big cart sheds and nearby was a wooden workshop with a big heavy vice and lots of tools for different jobs.

This farmer was a man called Les Cotton or as one of his favourite sayings (once seen never forgotten). He explained to me how he would get help on some of the seasonal work and contractors to cut and thresh his corn. I had seen him lots of times as he was a member of the Wortham bowls club and I think his second home was the Dick pub as he played dominos and cribbage inside that place quite a lot. He would stand out in a crowd as he was a tall man. He always wore a trilby hat and had a long pointed waxed moustache and was a heavy smoker, always Players cigarettes. He was one of the last soldiers around who had served in the army during the Boer War 1899 – 1902, on the Transvaal against the Zulus in South Africa. He told me that on leaving the army it was not his intention to be a farmer. He got a job with Aldrich Bros at the brush factory as a sales rep selling all types of brushes and mats from a suitcase and travelling by train all over the country and then he decided to set up a business on his own and had a brick and tile building built in the garden of one half of Jubilee House in Union Lane Wortham. I think that at one point he had eight woman making brushes for him. But then he got a chance to buy a field next to Jubilee House which he did. Now this field had a gate entrance right on the corner where Union Lane turned before joining Millway Lane complete with a gravel pit. He sold a lot of gravel and sand from this pit.

Then came the change from brush making to farming when he brought some more land and also the farm which was known as Pollard Tree Farm and by hiring some more land this became a forty acre smallholding. He had a pair of horses making a plough team, but had a lot of trouble with the man who used them, He said they would not work well together. He then asked me if I could lift a comb of wheat. Eighteen stone a comb weighed, and he had some stacked up in his barn. So I picked one up off the floor stood it on top of another sack full and lifted it across my shoulders and carried it across the yard and back, then took it back into the barn and set it down where I had got it from. He seemed quite happy with that. Then I looked at the horses.

One was a small Suffolk mare (Darby) and the other one was a big Percheron gelding (Darkie), both very strong horses and the Suffolk was a bit fast at times. I said to him which was the furrow horse when ploughing and he told me that they always put the Suffolk in the furrow. He had a Swootman plough made by Young's foundry in Diss near the railway arch. This plough was a little shorter than the Ransomes YL.

It looked to me as if I would nearly be my own boss as he had more or less retired, just helping when there was a two man job. We agreed on a wage and working hours but I knew that it would not be possible to leave off on time every day, I did not mind that at all and I would be earning more than I was at the Hall. So on the following Friday I gave the foreman a week's notice that I was leaving as I had another job.

Now the fields and meadows on this farm were scattered all around the edges of Wortham Ling and mainly small fields, the biggest one being about fifteen acres. The Monday morning I turned up at this new farm not knowing quite what to expect. I need not have worried as I was made most welcome. First thing was to feed the chickens and there were lots of them all on free range. There were besides a few geese and about thirty Norfolk Black turkeys, all again on free range, wondering around as they pleased but the turkeys were shut up in a pen and shed at night. These were going to be someone's Christmas dinner. There was also about forty light Sussex cockerels in another shed living on straw. There was no free range for them. These were also being reared for the Christmas trade, but these were caponised birds. This was something that was happening all over the country. There was a small pellet injected into their necks and this was supposed to make them bigger and fatter without too much food. When killed in December some of them weighed between fourteen and eighteen pounds, as big as a small turkey.

I noticed that there were five corn stacks and one rather large clover/ hay stack. There were no pigs on this farm which seemed rather strange for a small holding. The reason for this I found out later in the year. Well Les said that we would do some ploughing on a three acre field with a gate opening out into Millway Lane. This was on the opposite side of the road to the fifteen acre known as Long Reeds. This was a long field stretching from Wolsey House to Marsh Lane, but there was one problem with this field as about two thirds of the way down there was an open water course running across from one side to the other, and in the winter this sometimes got flooded also it did not matter which end you went from you were always going up hill. However we got to the three acre field which was clover stubble and had a section that had been ploughed so at that point there was no top to set. We hung the horses on the plough and started off down the field, the Suffolk in the furrow and the grey on the land. He said the person who had been using this team had a job to get the plough to run smoothly. This was really nice land. It wasn't heavy, slightly sand and gravel ideal for ploughing land. He went two or three rounds behind the plough and then told me to have a go and see how well I could do this job. I had not got far down the field when I stopped the horses and said we are never going to make a good job of ploughing like this. Then to my amazement he told me to do whatever I wanted to improve things.

The first thing I done was to raise the foot on the front of the plough to let the plough in a bit deeper – nine inches instead of seven. Then the next thing was to take out the furrow wheel. These were not used on the farms where I worked before. Then Les said that he was going home to dinner. This left me on my own with strange horses and a different type of plough. I remember thinking this set up looks a bit odd and I made up my mind to find out what it was. First of all these two did not look right with the fastest horse in the furrow and she was also the smallest of the two. I also noticed that she was always trying to be in front. This did make the plough pull at a very slight angle which in turn made it harder to hold when working. To me this looked a bit of an oddball team of horses. I had always been told that unless it was a colt being broken in, the biggest horse walked in the furrow. I did not know if this had ever been tried with these two. So I thought I would give it a try.

At least I could control the speed of the Suffolk by using a tie back. This was a piece of rope looped onto the reign of the Suffolk at the top of her collar and then down to one of the whippletrees of the other horse. This rope could be adjusted as required so the two horses pulled together. After I changed them round I found that Darkie would put his foot onto the ploughed land. I did expect him to do this as he had a bit of a problem walking in the furrow as it was quite a job to get one foot in front of the other when there is only nine inches to walk in. It required a lot of patience to train a horse to do what you wanted if it had been taught different when it was broken in. Anyhow I went several rounds of ploughing and they looked a far better team working in that position.

When Les came back from dinner he was really surprised at what I had done but I still felt that there was something that was not quite right. I counted the links of the chains from the hooks on the tees down to the hooks that went onto the plough whippletrees and they seemed alright, all exactly the same length. After checking every other part of the plough at last I found it, the skimmer which cut a small furrow and helped to bury the rubbish in front of the counter were not in line. The counter cut into the soil making it easy for the breast to turn the whole flag over. A small adjustment with a spanner put this right so before we took the horses off the plough that afternoon I had everything going as I wanted it too. I spent a few days ploughing this field and as all the tops had been got ready so the only thing I had to do was to shut the furrows up. I was a bit doubtful about doing this as I had changed the position of the horses and was prepared for one or the other to try to go back to how they had done this job before, but they went very well.

And then there was the headland to plough; now there was two ways of doing this. One year it was ploughed to the hedge and the next year away from the hedge leaving a furrow all the way around the edge of the field. The ploughing to the hedge was the easy one but the other way, a very shallow furrow all the way around the field, this was about four yards away from the hedge and this was the turning area for the horses and plough, measuring out, was mainly guesswork. On this particular field it was to the hedge so it was easy, leaving a shallow furrow all around the field.

What I never told Les or anyone else for that matter was that I had been told a lot about horses from an early age by my father and grandfather. These two seemed quite good together and I was anxious to see how they worked alone. I always carried a special powder in a tin and some lump sugar as a little reward if I thought it was needed. Well Les had some very different views on how he farmed. He did not believe in horse hoeing his barley when it was about four inches high like I had been used to but there was logic in his method though as the whole idea was to leave as much grass in the barley straw as possible after it was threshed. And the reason for this was that every October he would put some iron hurdles across what used to be the cow yard and this formed a cattle fatting yard with a shed both sides for shelter.

There was a cattle dealer by the name of Ernie Slade, who lived in a white brick, slate roofed house at the top of a very marshy type of meadow that stretched from Victoria Road well up past the railway station. It also went from the railway line to Vince's Road. This man was a very good friend of Les and always got him some very good Irish steer cattle which were about half the size that I had been used to, but space was limited so he had twelve to look after and fatten up over the winter months and then sell in the spring at a profit. Most of these were like black and white Hereford polled steers.

This was the reason he would not horse hoe his barley as this was fed to these cattle, besides sugar beet tops, also beet pulp, cattle beet cut up with a special tool, which was two very sharp blades crossed to form four small squares all on a round handle about four foot high. This was lumped onto the beet with a bit of force and so cut the beet into these square pieces. He also had a beet slicer which was a wheel turned by hand and cut the beet into long thin chips, some of which he would feed to the horses as a treat mixed with hand cut hay and straw chaff. He had a hand turned chaff cutter in the barn which we cut our own chaff to mix with that got from threshing the stacks.

Another thing which was done on this farm and I had never seen done before was when he drilled his cattle beet he would mix a small amount of swede seed in with the beet so every so often along the row there were a swede instead of a mangold. He always said that his Swedes would grow big enough for a rabbit to eat out the centre and sit inside the skin. I must admit he did get some very big Swedes.

Growing this barley straw seemed to me to be a rather bad idea as this left the stubble full of grass. But I was proved wrong when I saw how he done the job of getting rid of this grass. It was general knowledge that sugar beet followed barley on most farms, and here again I had never seen this done before and it went as following. When the barley was cut it was cut as low to the ground as possible so the stubble was very low. Then I took the two horses and plough and ploughed the field in the opposite direction, or to put it another way across the furrows so no land was left unturned. This was also done very shallow, no more than three inches or just below the grass roots, so they were turned up on top and dried out by the sun. After a few weeks the whole field was dried out and ready for harrowing. This was done with a set of heavy harrows pulled by both horses but taking their time with a small rest at both ends. This was much harder job than ploughing. After letting the grass and the soil dry out I then went over the whole field again but this time with a set of chain harrows and this rolled all the dry grass out of the soil and lay it on top. We then went with two tined forks and put this dry grass into rows after which we set fire to it and burned it all up. This really was a cleaning operation because at the end we were left with a lot of ash and a weedless soil.

There were no commercial potatoes grown on this farm, just on different parts of a very large garden for private use only. But there was about twelve or fifteen acres of sugar beet as this was a sure income. Another thing about this place being only about forty acres of arable land was that it was impossible to use the four year rotation as was done on many bigger farms. But there was a solution to make this farm, around twenty four acres of arable land bigger, when the government still wanted more food produced.

Les had three meadows across the Ling just into Roydon that had been used when he had cows. He was entitled to the grant for ploughing up meadow land for food production. This land was surrounded by the old part of the river Waveney before the new straight cut of the present river was made and was therefore in Norfolk. Now this soil was very much like the peaty soil of the fenland and would be impossible to plough with horses for the first time. So a local contractor who lived in Snow Street, Roydon was hired to do the job. This man's name was Tom Bryant who had an orange Alldis Chambers tractor on spud wheels onto which he fitted metal road bands to move from farm to farm. Little did I know at that time that in the future I would be living opposite to him for four years.

The plough he used behind his tractor was a two furrow Ransomes drag plough and it could be set to plough deep and turn the grass completely over so it was buried for good, but there was one snag and this was that this soil would not slide along the mouldboard of the plough so he had to spend hours of rubbing the front of the breast with a wet soft red brick to make it shiny. I don't think these meadows had ever been ploughed before, and there were places that were very soft so the tractor was stuck in these many times and this always meant that the plough had to be unhitched and short boards were put under the back wheels of the tractor to get it out of the soft soil of the hole. Then chains were put onto the plough to pull it through these soft spots and then connect up to the tractor drawbar again. Both the tractor and the plough had to be driven over the bridge that formed the gateway onto the Ling every night at leaving off time, because if it was left on this bottomless soil it would have sunk down and the starting handle would be too low to crank and start the engine.

These few acres took weeks to change from grass land to arable as there was also another unexpected thing that kept stopping the work and this was bog oak which was getting caught in the plough and lifting it out of the ground. It was said at the time that some of this had laid in the ground for thousands of years, and also that these meadows were once the very bottom of the Waveney River. Also coming to the surface was the odd piece of old rusty metal and it was hard to find out what it was except for one bit which was shaped like a rusty horseshoe but much smaller and thicker but I did find out what it was. It turned out to be a donkey shoe. I did not know that donkeys had metal shoes but I suppose they must have done. Years before a lot of people had donkeys and carts as these animals would eat almost anything including thistles and thorns so were cheap to keep.

We let this land lay open to all sorts of weather over the following winter to break up ready for spring planting. So some of the fields where corn had been grown during this year would have to have corn on the coming year. To feed this land, in part of the stack yard had been built a very big muck heap which had to be carted onto the field. This particular year it was the turn of the big field called Long Reeds near Millway Lane. Now Les had two iron tyred tumbrels, one being a lot bigger than the other. The big one was pulled by the grey Percheron and the other by the smaller Suffolk. Both horses were very good in the shafts and the cart harness was in quite good order, not tied up with binder string like some small farmers harnesses.

So the system we used to get the muck onto the land was as following. I would fill the first cart with a muck fork. This would normally be the big cart and then take it down the lane, across the Ling and up Jubilee Lane into the gateway which was half down from the top of the field. Here I would lay the muck out in rows of heaps like was done at the Hall Farm. Meanwhile Les would fill the empty cart ready for me to change over with when I got back to the stack yard, and this was continued until leaving off time. It was surprising how much muck we moved in a day just working steadily along all day with just a break for dinner. When we started on the top half of the field we changed the route with the full loads by going up the hill past Beech

Tree Farm and then turned left at the top of the hill. The carts ran much easier on the tarmac roads. Darby the Suffolk pulled a little faster on the road but in all I was pleased with the way they worked. There were two elderly men who helped to spread the muck over the field and when they had done down one side I was ready to start ploughing again, setting the muck skimmer so all the muck and stubble got ploughed in, and the bigger horse in the furrow. I had several days of steady ploughing.

The top end of the field near Marsh Lane had some heavy clay in the soil but apart from that the land was very good ploughing soil. I enjoyed doing this taking great care that all the furrows were straight and level. The weather was ideal and the pair seemed to be working well despite me changing their position. On all farms no two horses are alike and I watched carefully for their own little habits and I began to notice that the grey on certain days did not seem to be working as he should. So I asked Les if he had ever had a problem with this horse and then he said at certain times he had suffered with colic and had spent quite a lot of money on vet's bills.

Now I had known for many years about horse ills and how to cure them as this was something handed down from generations of our family before. The things to look for with colic, which is a very bad pain in its stomach is that the horse would keep turning its head and looking at its stomach. When this happens you must keep the horse walking about and on no account let it lay down. So I said to Les that if he gets colic again to come and get me and I will save you a vet's bill. The following Saturday about seven in the evening Les came up our front path and said the horse had got colic again. By the time I got down to the farm he was lying on the stable floor and looking at his stomach and dropping his head flat on the floor. He repeated this time after time and I could see he was in a very bad way. Now I knew what to do as I had seen this done, but I never done anything like what I was about to do before so I just kept my fingers crossed and hoped for the best. I asked Les to shut all the farm gates and leave the stable door wide open and then keep well out of the way.

I knelt down as near to the horse's head as I thought it safe to go, then putting my mouth as close to his ear as I could I shouted as loud as I possibly could. This took him completely by surprise and with one almighty heave he jumped up onto his feet and through the doorway out into the yard where he went round several times at full gallop. Poor old Les had never seen anything like it before and said to me what do we do now, and my answer was nothing but keep out of his way which he did while I stood in the middle of the yard very still. The horse had a rope halter on but there was no chance of catching him, but he saw me standing still and changed from a gallop to a trot and then a walk and came right up to me and stopped. So I took hold of the halter and spoke to him very quietly and gave him a sugar lump from my pocket and a gentle pat on his neck. After which I gave him a slow walk around our nearby meadow, then a rub down with an old towel to cool him down after which he had calmed down. Then he was put back in his stable where he started to eat some hay. While all this was going on Darby, the Suffolk, was watching over her stable door and got a reward of a sugar lump as well.

The old horsemen of those days kept their secrets very close to their chests and if you were not born into a horseman's family they would not tell you anything. I was lucky in that respect I was always told whatever I wanted to know. This procedure I done on that horse was also done on cows and other cattle and as the small farmers could not afford vet's bills no one said anything about it.

By this time the sugar beet harvest was fast approaching and I began to think how does a small farm manage a labour intensive job like this with the cattle, hens and turkeys to look after besides all the other jobs that we had to do. Also the mangolds had to be got up and stored before the sharp frosts started. We got the beet lifter ready for work by putting on new shares and greasing the wheels. Now I had never seen a beet lifter like this before, which was a Cornish and Lloyd manufacture from Bury St Edmunds. Most of them were a Ransomes YL plough with the mould board taken off and special piece of sloped metal fitted in its place which lifted the beet up after the share had cut the soil under it. But not this implement. It had two metal parts that worked on a squeezing movement, with two triangles shares formed like a long box, each one joined onto a metal arm which the beet went through as they were lifted. The two arms were joined onto a metal frame shaped like a horseshoe which in turn was joined onto a metal frame. To the front was the end to which the whippletrees were fitted for the horses to pull, and the other end was made to fit a pair of wooden handles very much like horse hoe handles.

I found this very easy thing to use as the beet were lifted up high enough to be pulled out of the ground with ease. This was done different to ploughing as two rows had to lay slightly one way and the next two laid the opposite. This made it better for pulling and laying in rows which in turn made it better for topping (Cutting a small piece off the crown complete with the leaves). Some of the leaves were cleared away and the topped beet were put into heaps ready for carting off the field and put into clamps. I never had to do this job as Les had a few regular local women who came and done this for him. That was a relief and then came the carting off for which we used both horses and carts. There again Les had the help of some of his friends from the local farms on Saturday afternoons, my father included. All I had to do was to take the carts to the clamp and unload and then take the empty cart back for a refill but it certainly kept me busy.

I used the horses in the same team position that I used for ploughing, but Darky was giving me a bit of trouble. As a soon as we started across the field he would walk very fast and so pulled the lifter at an angle. I put a tie back on his rein back to the bottom of the trace of the other horse. This slowed him down but he didn't like it. This was a new thing for me and it was hard to find out what caused this. Then I noticed something which was when he walked on bare ground there was no problem. He was calm and steady. So the next time we lifted some sugar beet he started to misbehave again and then the penny dropped. He did not like to walk between the high leaves of the sugar beet. The only way to stop this was to keep him in amongst the beet as much as possible, so I would stop them and give them a rest in the middle of the field and when turning on the ends I would make them stop in the rows of beet ready to move off. It wasn't long before he got used to this and was no trouble at all so off came the tieback and they worked well together.

Then the next job was loading up lorries to take the beet to Bury St Edmund's sugar beet factory. This was done with a specially designed fork shaped very much like a potato fork but not so many tines which curved down from the handle to form a basket like base that held the beet. All tines had a knob welded on each end to stop the beet getting pierced. The lorries that carted these beet belonged to Les's nephew, who started his business at the top of Union lane Wortham, just before or during the war in a small galvanised shed, which served as a garage. I can just remember there being a petrol pump there as well.

These brown painted lorries had some boards fitted over the side boards of the lorry so they could carry a bigger load. They carried about seven tons when fully loaded and took three men about one hour to load at one forkful at a time, a good job for a cold frosty morning. All loads had to have a net over them to stop any beet falling onto the road. I can clearly remember one morning we were expecting a lorry to come for a load and it was later than usual but when it did turn up it was not one of the old ramshackle lorries like we had been loading but a brand new shiny brown articulated lorry with the British Road Sign emblem on each door. The old lorries had been taken over by the government and changed for brand new ones.

There were many firms that this happened to and it changed the whole value of these firms. This articulated lorry meant that the actual trailer was not fitted to the cab as a solid unit but was joined flexibly. This thing looked nice but it had a big snag, it held fourteen tons when fully loaded and it took three men two hours to load. Thank goodness it got the beet moved to the factory quicker so I think in the long run it was to our advantage.

Then I had a few days helping to take the potatoes up from their garden and storing them inside the old cow house in bags. Then I found out about this sort of secret corner in this garden. Les told me that during the war there were many forty gallon drums of petrol stored there, all covered over with turf and branches to hide them from view, and that's how lawn mowers and other machines were being fuelled but what I never found out was where it came from in the first place. It was rumoured that the grey petrol tankers with 'POOL' printed on the side was seen in that area quite often, mostly late at night but I never did see one.

The next thing done on this farm over the winter was threshing the corn stacks. The actual sacks that the corn was stored in were hired from a local sack merchant, who lived in Mission Road in Diss but had buildings beside the Norwich Road in Scole, where his sacks were kept. He made a living by selling and buying Hessian sacks and also hiring out any sort of sack that people wanted. The threshing engine and machines came from some contractors from Cotton near Stowmarket. I was told that a local firm had done it before these people, but on one occasion when they had finished and left the engine and drum on one of the roadways on the Ling one of the workmen had seen something that did not look right. So that night he took a ladder and climbed onto the top of the drum, and he was right because under the tilt over the drum laid three bags of threshed corn. It was well known that this contractor kept chickens and pigs. He never came onto that farm again.

These people from Cotton brought all the men needed to do the complete job and very hard working they were too. My job was to cart the corn from the drum to the old cow house where it was kept till sold, also to cart the chaff into the barn for feeding the horses. I used each horse on alternate days so they both had some work to do. But the engine driver did have a problem getting a steam engine, threshing drum and elevator around in such a small farm yard and was talking about doing what a lot of other contractors were doing at that time and that was to stop using the Burrell steam engine and instead use a Marshal tractor with a winch. At that time the tractors were cheaper to run, no need to get to work earlier to raise the steam.

Winter was coming quickly but the weather was good and I kept on ploughing and we did drill some winter wheat so we had some straw for thatching. Apparently this was done every year. The cattle had settled down in their yard and they were doing well. I did go to Diss and get them two salt licks from a shop that specialised in animal medicines. One was put in the manger of each shed. This was good for them or they would lick the chalk in the clay lump walls of the buildings.

This was my first winter here and Christmas was coming fast, but I was really enjoying it, much easier than I had been used to. Les decided to take his family away for one weekend and left me in charge of feeding all the livestock and he said would I just have a walk round at night to keep an eye on the turkeys and cockerels as there were people about who would notice that the house never had any lights on after dark. So on that Saturday night about ten o'clock with a clear full moon, I thought I would take a look round so walked very quietly around the straw stacks and up beside the house to the back garden where the turkeys were kept in a shed.

The moon was casting shadows of the trees in the garden and everything seemed quiet when to my surprise I thought I saw a shadow move. I then froze and kept still, by that time there was a noise coming from somewhere. So I picked up a short piece of wood and moved towards the turkey shed but keeping in the shadows of some shrubs and then I saw a silhouette of a man standing just a few yards in front of me. I rushed out waving the bit of wood and then I saw him jump away and I thought he was going to run away. Then he spoke and said you frightened the life out of me. I knew this voice it was Les's son in law. We had a laugh and a chat because I did not know till then that Les had asked him to keep an eye on the place as well.

We went round to the front of the house and both thought of the same thing at the same time. The dog had never made a sound. Now this was something I had overlooked. Les had brought him as a pup and he was a real mongrel part Lurcher and part something else, I don't know what, but his scruffy coat made him look bigger than he really was. His home was in one of the cart sheds and at night he was on a long chain that went nearly up to the house's back door. He spent a lot of his time with me, especially when I took the horses out on the meadows for the night. If you did not know him very well or were a stranger coming onto the farm he would growl, bark and show his teeth but anyone he knew he was so docile and gentle you could not help liking him. He knew both of us and that was to reason he did not make any noise that night.

Christmas came and we made an arrangement. I would feed all the stock and collect the eggs on Christmas morning and Les would do it in the afternoon. This worked well all the years I was there. We done some hedge cutting around the new ploughed meadow and made some gateways bigger, took down some posts and barbed wire that had kept the cows in and in general had a good tidy up all round these meadows. We had the soil tested on what to grow on them the first year. Most farmers that were mechanised would grow potatoes on this type of soil because this was a cleaning crop. We could not do this as this was the first time ever these had been ploughed and the soil tests showed there was a infestation of wire worm so the only crop that could be grown was rye and also peas for seed could be grown as these two crops were not affected by wire worms. In fact they helped to get rid of them.

The winter weather had played its part on this soil and there were no clods or clay as this had broken down to a peaty sand. So on February 14th I took the gang of light harrows and the two horses and quickly harrowed what had been the middle meadow of about six acres, after which I started doing my first drilling on this farm, and with Les helping I planted six acres of peas to grow for seed. One thing I remember was that we had drilled about half the field when there was a very heavy snow storm, but we kept going and got the job done.

The next two weeks were spent cleaning out the turkey and cockerel sheds and starting a new muck heap in the stack yard. And then it was time to drill the two other meadows with rye, this was grown under contract to the Ryvita firm to be made into their crispy Wafers. The straw was sold to dealers for the making or repairing of horse harnesses, collars and saddles as it was long, thin and very strong and would pack together tight and solid. This was all new to me as I had never seen or grown rye before. One thing I did notice was that it had a peculiar smell. This soil seemed to suit this crop as once it was up it started to grow very fast and by harvest time the straw was at least six foot high topped with long ears of corn which looked like long thin wheat with very sharp bristle like barley but unlike the barley this was no good for chaff as horse food. When it was ripe to cut I had to mow an area about five feet wide all the way around both fields, and to make matters worse I had to tie the cut corn into sheaves.

We had another farmer come and cut the corn with his tractor and binder. This was a very slow job to do as the straw was longer than the binder and the sheaves it was throwing out were more like an untidy bundle and very awkward to shock. I built the stack when we carted this crop and to my surprise I found it very easy as each sheaf was so floppy that it tied itself together with no fear of moving.

I chopped out all the sugar beet and done all the work required. We did the horse hoeing together and all the corn harvest after we finished the hay cutting and stacking of the clover and meadow hay. And this was where I saw something else that was new to me and this was when the haystack was about half built he cut a big patch of green nettles and put them into the centre of the stack and said that this would stop the hay overheating and catching fire. This was a common thing in those days and many farmers had to cut a stack in half to cool it down.

This had been my first spring and summer and I was happy to do most of the work myself. I was not pushed and was able to chose what day I done a certain job. I had got the horses working as I wanted them. But as I have said we did have some help at the really busy times. I went home to dinner when I could and leaving off time was when the job was done as Les had this policy, for example when we were drilling to stop and finish even if took an extra two hours as this was better than coming back the next day.

Another thing that was new to me was when the headlands were ploughed this was always done by leaving a rounded corner. Now Les wanted to cultivate every inch of land so we would take spades and dig the land what was left to make a square corner. When drilling he would throw a handful of corn into these corners.

After all the stacks had been built a local poultry farmer would come and thatch them in his spare time. I got the wheat straw shook up and wetted ready for pulling the yelms. After a day of helping like this the thatcher asked me if I would like to learn how to thatch, which was a chance I jumped at and it was not long before we had changed jobs and I was enjoying it.

As the year progressed with the same sort of work as the year before, more new cattle in the yard we had made again, beet harvesting, loading lorries with some help from the men and woman, it all seemed to be dropping into place. I started ploughing again but this time we had those extra three fields that had been meadows. The field that had grown peas was nearly clean soil but the other two had the rye stubble to plough in but first of all I had to plough a three acre field near the allotment in Union Lane. The idea was to make the mouldboard and other parts of the plough shiny so the soil would flow and turn over easy. That done I started on those meadows and it all went well on some parts of the land but on other parts it was like peat with no solid bottom under it at all and this is where the plough would sink down so it had to be held with the share pointing upwards which made it quite hard work.

Now dividing these fields were two deep ditches full of stinking red mud, in which grew some reeds with razor sharp leaves, and over the summer there had been yellow water iris growing with the reeds. These ditches joined the river although I never saw any water running in them. Also along these ditches were some lovely old oak trees which must have been hundreds of years old. Between the trees were some hawthorn, hazel and willow hedges which at one time kept the cows in. In due course I got these all ploughed ready for the winter weather. Christmas came with the same arrangement as the last. Turkeys and cockerels were killed and plucked and I went with Les down to Diss with some of these hanging from our bicycle handlebars till we got to the Two Brewers pub where he had customers waiting for them. He then brought a pint of beer and a half pint for me, which I drank and then came home to the farm where I was repairing one of the sheds.

Now Les would go to Diss every Friday and I often done the feeding before he came home so I did know his routine fairly well, which would be pub, Corn Hall, Sale Ground and back to the pub, after fitting in the bank for the wages. Now I though I would go down to Diss for some Christmas shopping this particular Friday so I got on the bus and was shopping for a few hours before catching the bus back home. Now I did not expect to meet Les in Mere Street and he did not expect to see me, so he stopped and said what are you doing here but with a bit of quick thinking I said that I had run out of nails for the building repair. Then he put his hand in his pocket and gave me some money saying here is your bus fare and some for the nails. I was glad he did not ask to see the nails and I got away with that.

I started to plough our Long Reeds field a few days after Christmas and we did have a few sharp frosts but not enough to make the ground hard. We also had some misty days and hoar frosts. These looked nice because everywhere

241

was covered in a thin layer of ice. There was one very bushy elm tree which was in the roadside hedge and it looked a real picture, and when the mist cleared and the winter sun started to shine it would drop shards of ice onto the road. I didn't like the mist much as not only could you not know if you were ploughing a straight furrow it also made the horses give off a misty vapour and their breath came out of their nostrils like a steam train. It would not pay to let them stand still too long so they got cold as they, like us, could easily catch a cold. It was necessary to give them a good rub down with a piece of sacking before giving them a drink of cold water.

Then one day I was busy ploughing and there was a slightly cool breeze blowing from the north but it was comfortable work. The soil was in good condition and I had the plough set so it could be controlled by one finger. The team were walking well and I can clearly remember thinking that if I kept going like this the field should be done in about the next ten days and all the ploughing would be done. I started on the last furrow of the day working from Wolsey House up to Marsh Lane or to put it another way from east to west and that afternoon there was a sunset like I had never seen before and we were going straight towards it. The sun was a big red ball slowly getting bigger and almost crimson as it sank below the horizon.

I got to the top of the field and uncoupled the horses leaving the plough in the ground ready for the next day. That next day never came because when we woke up the next morning everywhere was covered in six inches of snow, which lasted for the next six weeks. During the night the wind had increased and many roads were blocked solid and many men from the big farms were out on the roads digging through high snowdrifts. It was impossible for the snow plough to go out. I know my father and his workmates had to dig out the road from Wortham Church to Wortham School. This winter of 1947 was the worst for many years and it doubled the amount of work we had to do at feeding time for the animals, but we were lucky that there was a well of fresh water which did not freeze over, and we used that for everything.

I walked to work through the snow but we kept busy as it gave us a chance to get a lot of hedges cut that under normal circumstances we would have left alone. I also walked home at dinner time and had a hot meal. Les did not seem to worry about time at all as long as we got some work done. The sacks of corn had been sold to Smiths, the miller at Dickleburgh, and what we noticed was there were a few holes been dug out of the concrete floor next to the wall. This could only mean one thing, rats. These had to be destroyed at any cost. So what we done was to block up all the holes except one into which we poured pails of water and with sticks ready we stood and waited and it was not long before a gurgling noise and then up popped a soaked rat.

A hefty hit with a stick stopped it in its tracks. It was the first of many over a period of days. I think we ended up with ten big and small. After those days we never saw signs of anymore.

The winter weather had its good points as we got forward with some of the jobs that we would have left for later in the year. We cut a lot of barley straw into chaff and stored it for future use which we would normally have done as required. We cut the hedges that were usually left till July for stack bottoms. Some small trees were cut down and replaced the gateposts that were getting in a bad condition. Some muck was carted out from the cattle sheds and put onto the muck heap in the stack yard. All the axles on the carts and drills were greased ready for spring and summer.

And so the snow melted and after a few days I was able to finish ploughing Long Reeds. Other fields became dry enough to harrow and drill. The three meadows near the river were drilled with spring wheat. This was not good wheat land but this was done to obtain subsidy given to farmers by the government for increasing the wheat yield, but at harvest this was not a bad crop after all.

Life was changing on most farms and also on the social circle as more entertainment was allowed and restrictions of travel was coming to an end. I and a friend, who I had got to know because he was the person, other than Father's cousin, John, who would drive the car we hired to take us to see my mother's family at South Creake at certain weekends. This friendship lasted right up to the present day but in those days we would go up to Norwich Speedway at the Firs Stadium on Saturday evenings on a bus hired by a local dear old lady. In fact there were several local lads on this bus and we all became good pals and we often went on this woman's coach trips on Sundays to the coast resorts at Skegness down to Southend.

It was on one of these trips to the Speedway one Saturday night that Darkie had one of his colic attacks and Les had to once again call in the vet who got the horse back on his feet, but advised Les to get rid of him before any more trouble, so this was the news I was greeted with on Monday morning. But Les decided to sell him, so for a short while we were left with only one horse. I tried to persuade Les to buy a Ferguson T20 tractor and its implements, which at that time with its hydraulic arms and top link adjustable plough fittings, also a drop and lift hook, you could pick up a trailer without getting off the tractor seat. But Les was rather set in his ways and preferred to still use horses but I had a nasty feeling that this was too big a cost to lay out at his age. He did toy with the idea for a short while and, as his son in law was a rep for Knights of Harleston and I knew they were David Brown stockist. I reckon he would have got a good deal but this did not happen.

We carried on with work. As we had got well forward over the winter, one

Pollard Tree Farmhouse, The Ling, Wortham, Diss, Norfolk
This was the first house I thatched, when I was eighteen

The horses of Pollard Tree Farm
Darby, Poppy, above and right

day Les said to me, "You have thatched some stacks. Would you like to thatch the house?" Now this was a simple answer to give. But the point was, could I? Never one to turn down opportunity, I said that I would try providing his thatcher, who was retiring, let me borrow his ladders and tools also keep an eye on things so that I'd do it under supervision. He agreed to all of this.

Now where to start was the first problem. I loaded up a cart load of long wheat straw and carted it near the front of the house to be near the well for water and to cut down on the walking with yelms of pulled straw. The next job was a trip to Mr Coe at Burgate, the hurdle maker, who also supplied brooches for thatching. The long ones like we used on stacks and some shorter ones sharpened at both ends which were soaked in water for a few days and then twisted in the centre to make a big wood staple. These were used for decoration by holding the long ones across the thatch on top of the straw. It was a few days and they arrived ready for use.

In the meantime I prepared a bed of straw ready for pulling out the yelms. This was done with a two tined fork by shaking the straw up to what size bed was required. When there was a covering of about six inches, pails of water was thrown all over it. This was done until the heap was high enough to last for a few days. The damp straw stopped your hands from being cut when pulling. Putting the ladder up for the first time was in itself a bit of a dangerous job. Now there was two ways of doing this, one was to put the bottom of the ladder near the bottom of the house and, laying the ladder at right angles, lift the narrow top of the ladder over your head and start walking towards the house, lifting the ladder with each step. Then it came to a point where it was straight upright and by this time you stood holding the rungs just a few from the bottom. This was a very dangerous position as the whole thing could slip and fall over backwards trapping you underneath. No safety helmets in those days. Once the balance was tipped and the ladder fell onto the roof it was up there till the job was done, moving it little by little from front to back, past the chimney on the end very carefully. I was lucky in one way because this house had dormer windows so I had a chance to practice on them first before the main roof.

I got on quite well and I was halfway along the front roof when one morning Les said he had brought another horse from a dealer at Hoxne and this time it was an eight year old Suffolk mare fully broken in to all work. My reaction was that this was good, a Suffolk plough team. That morning a lorry brought this horse up to the farm and when she came out of the lorry I was pleased to see such a smart looking animal. She looked big and strong and had a very shiny coat and a set of new shoes. It was obvious that she had been well looked after. The man said he would stop and see how we got on with her, so for a start we tried on the spare harness, collar, bridle and brechens and they all fitted very well. We put her in shafts of our big cart with no problems, pulling and backing fine. We harnessed up Darby and put them together. They went side by side as if they had known each other for years. We decided that when we started ploughing she would be the furrow horse. I was pleased to have a pair of Suffolks as I always thought they looked better than odd pairs. One thing that both Les and I did not think to ask was what her name was. We both thought he was calling her something beginning with P so with some careful thought we decided to name her Poppy, which she accepted with no problem.

I carried on thatching every chance I could but the hay and corn harvest was fast approaching so I had to leave that to get these done. I built the hay and corn stacks and they had to be thatched as well, but after working on the house these were easy. It was an unwritten law that a man could thatch one stack a day, depending on the size of the stack of course. Some were much bigger than others. With all those jobs finished Les liked to have a stubble fields shallow ploughed but this year with wanting to get the house done before winter, he decided to have the stubble cultivated so he got in touch with a friend who lived at Brome in a house between Brome Grange and the Thranderson road. Owing to expanding business this man said that he had bought a brand new dark blue and orange Fordson Major but he had a problem in as much as he had not got a driver for it. So Les asked me if I would drive it to do the cultivating on our fields. This was a petrol/paraffin tractor and he said that he would bring the fuel for it. Now this was an offer that I could not refuse and I agreed to do the job.

Now this was a time before diesel fuel or batteries and self starters were brought into farming as standard, so this tractor had to be started by cranking a handle at the front and turning the engine over till it fired and started to run for a short time on petrol and then by changing the position of a tap to T.V.O. (Tractor Vaporising Oil). Now I had done all this on the Standard Fordson at Hall Farm. This new tractor arrived complete with cultivator, a Martins nine tine, and working by a trip and rope to the seat. We had a chat with the contractor about the tractor gears and so on. One thing about this tractor was that it had rubber tyres back and front, which made it comfortable to ride.

This was something I had always wanted to do so off I went up the field, after setting the cultivator at the right depth. With the field done one way the next thing to do was to cultivate at right angles to what had been done. The idea was to make sure all the ground had been cut by the tines so no weeds would grow. That field finished I went and done the same with all the other stubbles and finished the job. Then to my surprise the contractor told Les that he had still not got a driver so would he let me do some work for him. So I went onto farms after taking the tractor on the road without a license but in those days no one seemed to worry. With more food produced this was when the police turned a blind eye.

All this done it was back to roof thatching. The weather was good so I finished that. Before we started on the sugar beet there was a field to be ploughed for drilling the winter wheat, so taking the two Suffolks I wanted to see how they worked together. With Poppy as the furrow horse everything was fine until one Monday morning. I thought that I would change the way to the field and we went past some of the houses on the edge of the Ling and as we went past these Poppy started to jump around and I had a job to stop her running away. I noticed that the following days she was no problem it only appeared to be Mondays. The whole thing was solved when one day in Diss a man came up to me and said he broke her in and used her on his farm which he was selling up. He asked me how I was getting on with Peggy, which he said was her proper name. I told him about her behaviour on Mondays. With that he told me the problem. She had been frightened by a passing lorry, which had a tilt flapping about. So after we went past any flapping linen on people's lines I took her closer to the flapping linen each time and in the end she overcame her fear.

Sugar beet season finished and winter came with us doing the same as other years. When the land dried out in the spring we finished the drilling and everything was going well when one day Les came up to me and said he was retiring from farming and selling everything connected with it, including the horses, in about three weeks time at Gaze's sale ground and would I take the things down there for him like carts, drills, harrows also the plough. I was absolutely shocked. I had not expected that. I did not know what to say and for the first time in my life I was going to be without a job. I was not sacked it was just one of those things. As he was beginning to get an old man and all the things that went with it, work was getting slower and he done all the feeding at weekends of the horses, cattle and chickens. I could well understand the situation.

At that time there were plenty of jobs going, all the big farms were turning to mechanisation to work side by side with their horses. We took the two carts filled with the beet grinder, chaff cutter and all the hand items used on a small farm. On the Thursday before the sale I took both horses up to the blacksmiths at Palgrave to have new shoes and their hooves tidied up. The rest of the day was spent cleaning brasses and oiling harnesses and chatting about things we done and I said that I would miss his tales about the Boer War and his time in the army.

The next morning it was time to brush the horses down and comb their tails and manes. At about 11 o'clock I put rope halters on and I led them both together down to the sale ground and handed them over to a man at the sale ground. I must admit there was a lump in my throat as I loved horses and all their little ways. I walked home sadly to the farm knowing I would not see them again and to collect wages which there was little extra in that brown envelope. Les said come in and have a sit down. He poured out two glasses of Lacons Stout and said that he was wondering what sort of job was I looking for. At that point I had no idea. I was surprised at what he said next. He had a drink or two at the pub, the Tumbledown Dick, with his friend, who was the foreman at Beech Tree Farm and they wanted me back because they were short of a horseman, preferably one to break in colts and do ploughing and all the jobs they done, someone who could thatch, for which the pay would be very good.

Now this was something to think about very carefully but first all I decided to have a week's holiday as I had some furniture to make in my workshop and I wanted to get it done. I did go down to Beech Tree Farm to see what the job entailed. They had some new horses and some had gone. What the job entailed was looking after ten horses, starting at five in the morning, brushing and currie combing them down and in general getting them ready for work after letting them out to the water tank for a drink. I could also walk the ten minutes home for breakfast after all this work was done. There was also the feeding and drinking for them at weekends.

I really did not know whether to take this job or not, and then the weekly wages was told to me by the foreman. I never had that sort of money before. There was one big BUT and that was the amount of work to be done. Did I want to work all those hours? I did have a few more days to think about it.

Meanwhile on the social side of things, with my pal Jessie we were going out quite a bit to Norwich speedway on Saturday nights at the Firs Stadium. This was by the bus that the woman at Palgrave organised. We usually got back at Diss at nearly 11pm but the fish and chip shop stayed open for us as there were about thirty six people on that bus so it was worth their while. After about three years the bus was stopped and we never found out why. That problem was soon solved when the vicar of Palgrave said we could borrow his car so we did, and then more people wanted to come so we hired a car from the garage where Jess worked at very cut price. One of the people who came with us was our barber George, then two friends who once joined the Russian Communist Party, but we were all great friends.

There were days at the coast, Felixstowe, Clacton and Southend, by bus trips. It was at Southend that we went on a boat trip up the Medway to the Naval Dockyard at Chatham, while there we saw lots of Naval ships all in what was called mothballing. Then we found out that British Rail were doing special excursion on Sundays from Norwich to Liverpool Street Station, London and stopping at Diss, so four of us decided to go on this. We got to London and using the underground trains and buses we went to see a lot of the sights like St Paul's Cathedral, Westminster Abbey, Big Ben and Tower Bridge and lots of other places. We done this several times seeing lots of places that we had not seen the times before.

Me and Jess, On holiday in London, 1951

Dome of Discovery, More Festival memories

Railway engine for India

249

Both sides of the Festival Crown

A few years later Jess and I had a chance to have a week's holiday in London, staying at No 6. Alder Grove, Cricklewood, the home of the butcher that I done the poaching for. This was at the Festival of Britain time and also the World Speedway Championship at Wembley, which was within walking distance. We went to both. Also lots of other places we had not seen before. We both enjoyed that week with one exception, at about a quarter of mile from the bottom of the garden there was a railway shunting yard so there were train whistles and trucks clanking about all night.

When we came home I had to make a decision what I was going to do regarding work and I decided that I would take the horseman's job at Beech Tree farm. So on the next Monday morning the foreman showed me around and told me what the job entailed. I also had a look at the horses to get to know them. Some had been there from the time I was borrowed from Hall farm. One of things that I notice was this place was going from horse power to mechanisation as they had a new Massey Harris combine coming, which put the corn into sacks. Also one of the new Fordson Majors like the one I was driving for the contractor. There were two new trailers as well. Now this was the time that tractor fuel was changing from T.V.O to diesel and the tractors were doing more and more of the land work. The tumbrels were left in the cart shed, the wagons were stilled pulled by horses, and also the tumbrels were used for the sugar beet harvest. But there were still fields left for the horse ploughing.

Then one day the foreman said to me that this farm was now the one going to be used to break in the two year old colts into plough teams and cart work. This was what I wanted to do so this suited me. I started just too late for the potato harvest when four horses and four carts had been used, but none of these were any of the young horses. Being head horseman I had the best of them all for my plough team, and I done a lot of ploughing with them and a Ransomes YL plough. It was not long before I was told that there was a two year old Percheron gelding coming to the farm from the marshes at Haddiscoe and he had never been handled so was nearly wild.

I came back to the farm with my team from a days ploughing and the foreman met me at the gate and said your new horse is here but there was a problem as he said that the horse had run him out of the yard and it took three men to get him into what we called a loose box. This was a brick shed with a top and bottom door so one half could be opened leaving the other half shut. These loose boxes also had a manger in each. What I done next was to open the top door to see what he was like. The men who helped to put him in the shed said he was a bad horse. In our family there was no such thing as a bad horse just people who made them bad. Well he started to kick the walls and running around snorting, so what I done was to get the brush I used to groom the other horses with and threw it into the manger, then shut the door and left him on his own while I got on with my work.

251

My old stables at Beech Tree Farm, I looked after ten horses here for five years. This is now a modern housing complex.

The horses at Beech Tree

These were the last pair of Suffolk Colts I broke in

Brandy

Whisky

Harvest time break from cutting wheat with Fordson Major and binder.

What happened next the foreman said he had never seen anything like it and he also had been working horses all his life but what he did not know was that my grandfather passed on the knowledge of how to deal with this situation. Never shout at the horse but talk firmly and quietly and it was times like this I always had the feeling he was with me and making me do the right thing. So I took a rope halter with me and went inside the loose box and stood still. I had noticed he was watching and had sensed that I was not afraid of him and within a few minutes I walked straight up to him and talking very quiet I put the halter on him and took him out into the horse yard and walked him around.

If my grandfather could see these so called horse whisperers nowadays who walk up to a horse and then walk away several times and rub a stick with foam pipe lagging across the back of a horse, he would have been very amused. So would the old gypsies and horse dealers of those days. My own personal view is that these people would not do that if there was not a lot of money to be made out of it. There was a well known fact on farms that you never turned your back on any horse until it was broken in or you had formed a trust with it. Well I took him around a meadow with a rope halter every chance I got until one day I went to put him in his loose box. He had calmed down very well and was a quick learner. I thought this is the time to play my trump card so I took his halter off and stood talking to him and gave him a pat on his neck. I put my hand in my pocket and took out a sugar lump and held it in the open palm of my hand. He took this and chewed it up and from then him and me understood each other. I still would not let anyone else near him. Keeping his halter on I tried a bridle on to see if it fitted and it did but I changed the bit from one in two halves to one solid length because these were easier to put in the horse's mouth. He did not like it much but after a while and a lot of chewing he accepted it. He did not mind the blinkers on this bridle so I only left it on for a short while and gave him another sugar lump.

I told the foreman I had got as far as I could alone and this was traditionally now a two man job. There were three plough teams on this farm so I had one of these horsemen to help. His name was Tom Harbour. His father had also been a horseman in his day, and Tom who had worked on this farm ever since he started work, knew a thing or two about horses. He was quiet and steady, just the man to help as he had also done this job before. Now this was a very critical time in this horse's life, make one mistakes and you could do what the old horsemen called breaking the horse's heart. If this was done you might as well sell it as it would never be the same again. The next morning Tom came into the loose box with me as I put the halter on and with me on one side and him on the other we tried a collar on which we done with the collar upside down and then the bridle. So with the chains on the hames rattling it was turned up the proper way. It fitted well. Then we put it on the plough chains with the hooks on chains fitting into a loop on the collar.

The next job was to make him pull a purposely heavy log with the chains on to enable a plough whippletree to be fitted. He pulled this one way and then the other, stopping at both ends after turning, the same as if he was ploughing. And then Tom said we have not given him a name. Well the way he took to all the things we ask of him we decided his name should be PRINCE. He caused no problem as we put him in the shafts of a cart.

Then came the next stage of working with another horse to become a plough team. Every farm had what I will call an anchor horse which was always used to break in colts. In my case it was Darkie, a bit of a mongrel breed and part of my plough team but he knew exactly what to do without being told. So with Tom's help I had a new plough team and Prince had grown from a bit of a handful when he arrived to a gentle giant and weighing nearly a ton.

I took those two lifting sugar beet but this was a slow job with the skeleton of a Ransomes plough and a special share that curved upwards towards the back of the plough to lift the beet out of the soil, and at rows eighteen inches apart and one row at a time, twenty acre field seemed to go on for ever. We had two of the really old horses sold to a horse dealer in Eye who had an abattoir where horses were killed and sent to France for some Frenchman's dinner table. I did not like this much after many years of hard work they did not deserve this. However this made a place in the main stable for Prince. I took him up to the blacksmith's for his first set of shoes which was done with no bother. A lot of horsemen on other farms had heard of him and one farmer actually wanted to buy him.

Then one Saturday morning I had started to lift sugar beet around the headlands of a field up beside Marsh Lane. I had done all the way round three times. Darkie and Prince were working well together and we had just turned the corner the furthest away from the gateway when Prince started to limp and I thought perhaps he had got a stone in the frog of his hoof. This did happen sometimes. I stopped them and lifted his foot up but there was no stone. So off we went again just a short distance and then stop and rested and then went off again until we got round to the gateway. Prince was limping badly and really holding his leg up, and he really was in lots of pain. So I now had a problem should I try and get him home or tie both horses to the hedge and run home to the farm myself? I choose the latter.

I found the foreman who immediately called the vet. We both went back and Prince was standing up but you could see by the ground that he had been stamping around a lot. The vet soon turned up and diagnosed thrombosis in his back leg. He would have to put him down. Now I have done some hard things in my life but this was the hardest. When I saw the vet put a gun to his head and shoot him, I was devastated I was at a loss what to do. The foreman and I stopped there till Mr Last's lorry came and took him away. A bond between man and horse had been broken forever; things could never be the same again. We took Darkie home on his own and the foreman sent another chap with a horse and cart to pick up Princes' harness.

That next Monday morning when I went to feed the other horses there was one empty space in the stable but I had a feeling that all the work put into it not been wasted. I had grown much wiser for it. The little sugar lumps had helped to gain his trust. I had learned a lot and had broken in a horse my way.

But things went on and big changes were taking place, especially in the poultry side of farming. Instead of a few laying hens and a dozen or so cockerels fattening up for Christmas some farmers were keeping hens in what was called deep litter sheds or another way was hundred of birds in wire cages without any room to move around and any eggs laid rolled into wire trays in front of the cages so they could be collected easily.

But it was in the tractor section that the biggest change took place. At Beech Tree the old Fordson major was gone and a new Fordson Major E27N took its place. I don't know what spot this tractor was but every tractor had a coloured spot on the gearbox case under its seat, which told you at a glance how powerful it was. There were red, green, light blue, yellow and orange. This one had a top link to set a plough at any angle, also hydraulic linkage for special lifting implements and also PTO (Power Take Off) to drive the grass mower etc.Bigger ploughs were also being made two, three and four furrows all able to be fitted to the hydraulic arms. This was nearly the end of the drag plough era.

Then we heard some good news that there was an Allis Chambers Model B coming to this farm. This little orange tractor was very versatile because when it came it was complete with an under hung toolbar between the front and back wheels and this meant that it could be used for hoeing sugar beet therefore making it a one man, no horse job. This toolbar could also be fitted with grass mower therefore making two more horses out of a job.

At the Hall Farm the small crawler had gone in exchange for a much bigger more powerful International that could pull a six furrow plough. And there was still a rumour going around that Beech Tree Farm was supposed to have a new Massey – Harris combine but this was not something that could be picked off the shelf as apparently there was a long waiting list so when it was going to arrive no one knew.

Winter was coming quite fast, and we had several sharp frosts and misty mornings. The cattle yards at the barn and the Icca were full of long horned Hereford bullocks ready for fattening up over the winter but I did not have much to do with them. That was the yardman's job. But one job I did have to do every Saturday dinner time was to cut some stuvver hay (clover) and put it in one of the sheds in the horse yards ready to use at the weekend. As the frosts became sharper it was making the beet harder to lift and ploughing by horses on other than stubble land was getting a bit of a problem.

Every morning when I left home to walk to work at five o'clock it was getting darker and colder. Sometimes I would meet an elderly man, called Mr Dade, cycling to work at one of the maltings in Diss. I know who he was as his son was in the top class at school when I was in one of the younger classes. By the time I left school his son was a pilot of a Spitfire during the Battle of Britain. This chap was always willing to walk with me as far as the farm gate. He lived at the top of Wortham Long Green but did not like biking down the main road to Diss. He was in fact a retired horseman so we both spoke the same language and he always told me the same thing. "Get out boy because horses are going to be a thing of the past". How right he was, but I liked hearing his tongue in cheek tales he always told with a sly grin on his face. Like the time he said that he had broken lots of sugar beet forks loading up milk churns on to lorries. I would think it was impossible to even get a churn onto a fork. But he was good company for all that.

It was not always a straight forward walk to work each morning like the time a fox jumped out of the hedge about a yard in front of me and crossed the road and went up through the hedge on the opposite side of the road. On odd occasions you met a roadster (tramp) on his way to get a crust of bread or a cup of tea. These men slept rough in a straw stack or any shelter they could get whatever the weather. These chaps had a code all of their own by laying a twig on the ground in certain directions like three bits of sticks pointing like an arrow meant that they could get a cup of hot tea at this house and so on. As most people had a pail toilet at the bottom of the garden they would not think twice about using that as well. And then there was the farm gate, which every Saturday morning just as I got up to it would bang shut with a rattle and a quiver. It took me quite a long time to find out what caused that. One Friday I borrowed a very powerful torch that shone a long thin beam and took it to work on Saturday morning. I was a long way off the gate when I shone the torch onto it and there sat one of the farm cats which jumped off with one big leap therefore shaking the gate.

But the best thing of all was the chap who was the retired landlord of the Dick and had bought the thatch cottage near the pond. Up the top of his garden was a small round pond in which he kept three geese and a gander. Now this garden was well above the road, divided by a high bank and on top of that was about a two foot privet hedge. The foreman told me one morning that he knew what time I came to work because Dickson's gander made a noise as I went past. So I thought to myself that this is something that needs stopping. So the next morning I walked quietly down to the pond and when the old gander started to make a noise I ran up the bank grabbed a part of the privet hedge and shook it furiously. What happened next took me by surprise. The gander gave one big jump up into the air and then dived head first out of sight into the deepest part of the pond. I waited but he did not come back up and all went quiet and I carried on to work.

About a fortnight afterwards the foreman said Jim Dickson has lost his gander and asked me if I had seen it. Of course I hadn't but about a week later it was seen floating on top of the water with wings outstretched and its head all covered in mud. What had happened was that he had dived so hard into the pond that his head had got stuck in the mud at the bottom of the pond and he could not get out. He never bothered me again.

The winter was getting colder every day and most of the ponds froze over so solid that it would be strong enough for at least three men to walk on this thick ice. So it was decided that we should all help and cut back all the bushes that grew around the sides and overhung the water. This was a big job as it had not been done for years. We done all the ponds belonged to Beech Tree farm and the only other job that could be done in this weather was threshing. So the old Case tractor was brought out and all the corn stacks were threshed, but this time I only had to take the sacks of corn off the drum, weigh them and put them onto the cart ready for someone to take it to the barn. There was no lifting to do because we now had a sack lifter where a bag of corn was stood on the bottom and, by turning a handle, chains would lift the bag up to shoulder height so it could be lifted onto a cart, very much like getting a pail of water out of the well.

With winter starting early and lasting a long time all farm work was being put back and on top of all that we had two weekends of heavy snowfalls but this time the horses stopped in the horse yard as we used the Allis Chambers tractor to pull the snowplough, which was much better for me as all I had to do was to sit on the snowplough seat.

It was well into March when the weather changed and it took a little while for the land to dry out but it did. There were several fields that should have been ploughed but had not been touched so everything that could plough was brought into use, three horse teams, the Fordson Major and even the Case pulled a drag plough. But when it was time for drilling a new bigger drill arrived at the farm in all its shiny red and yellow paint. Now this was a really up to date machine as it now only drilled the seed corn and granulated fertiliser as well doing away with the horse drawn manure distributors. The Allis Chambers pulled this drill which had a disc marker on each side in which the front wheel of the tractor ran to keep the drill joints equal, and on the back was a wide board for a man to ride on to keep an eye on the drill so it did not block up. More horse work had been mechanised.

Spring came and went and then the hay time and by this time the hay turner had been made to be pulled behind a tractor. Another horse job gone.

I was beginning to think that Mr Dade was right in what he said. Then one day I was busy ploughing in a field that had been left for an early crop of next year's wheat when the foreman came up to tell me that I had got a pair of Suffolk colts coming home to be broken in for a new plough team. Well both these horses arrived and as they were two year olds I had quite a surprise. Instead of them being half wild as they also had been out on the marshes, these had been reared by a farmer near Great Yarmouth, who breeds Suffolk Horses on an arable farm to keep this breed going. I am sure they had been handled a lot as they were no trouble with a halter or any sort of harness. So with Tom and Darkie's help we soon had them working. They were quiet, steady and gentle, but the sugar lumps and an apple every so often did help, and it was not long before I had a team of Suffolks working quietly together. They were quick learners.

At certain times of the year there were stag hunts around here. There were some living wild on the farm and they did not take much notice of our horses. One day I was ploughing a field near the Ling when I heard the huntsman's horn blowing on the park around the manor and it was getting closer. I turned the two young horses around at the top of the field so they could see across the Ling, and then I saw three deer running across the Ling towards us. I stood and held the horse's heads. We had named one Whisky and the other Brandy. I stood still talking to the horses when the deer ran up the road beside us and jumped over the hedge, one behind the other, just like a Bambi film. The horses and hounds followed behind making lots of noise. My two Suffolks stood still and watched and I was pleased with that.

Harvest was getting closer and still no sign of the combine so it was decided to cut the corn with a binder. I and one of the tractor drivers took it in turns to sit on the binder and drive the Fordson Major, acre after acre and field after field was cut and shocked, and then came the carting using the horses and wagons and it was my job to stack the corn. That year I built and thatched eleven stacks including hay and clover, a very busy time indeed. Just as harvest was nearly finished the combine arrived also a new baler for the loose straw but there was still a field or two to be harvested at the Hall so it threshed those being driven by the main tractor driver from Beech Tree. Harvest would never be the same again.

It was the same with horse ploughing. We did not plough a whole field anymore just set the tops and shut the furrows. I had ten horses in the stable and not doing anything. I could see no future in this job at all, as the chance to become a tractor driver on this farm was very slim indeed.

In early September 1954 our family had brought a semi-detached house for £600 cash in Union Lane, Wortham, a transaction that took about half an hour in those days. We had moved in and things were changing fast. Unknown to anyone except my parents, besides making furniture and other wooden items in my workshop, which we moved as well, I had been to night school classes at Diss Grammar school every winter for the last four years learning woodwork, building, plumbing and lots of other things. So the next thing I did was to go and see a builder in Diss who offered me a job. So I went to work the next day and gave a week's notice.

This was an end of an era. All my knowledge about horses that had been handed down to me was of no use. I would miss the brass polishing, oiling the harness and painting the hames and other wood parts of the harness. But one thing I would not miss was the boss appearing in the stable early morning and rubbing a white silk handkerchief across any horse at random to see if they had been groomed down properly.

Well the next Monday morning I took a bag of tools to a building in Victoria Road to start a job as a builder. I only knew two of the men but I got on alright with them all. My first job was to help with reroofing a house in Dickleburgh. Carrying five tiles up a ladder onto a roof all day was a bit tiring. Next there was putting central heating in a cottage in the street of that village and then on to the next job, interior decoration to a big farm house in Roydon, fitting skirting in a house in Shelfanger Road. I was enjoying the variety of the places and jobs.

Then the main plumber and I started fitting central heating in an old cottage in Rickinghall Street. This was a real challenge as the walls were stud and plaster and really rotten. Without the modern electric tools this was quite hard, but we did it and, before you realised it, Christmas was upon us.

I went to work on the 24 December as before. Little did I realise how the day would end. At leaving off time this builder came round with our wages and told me and seven others that he could no longer employ us. What a shock. For the first time in my life I was without a job and being Christmas didn't help. Anyhow I had made up my mind not to go back to horses. So on December 27 1954 I set off on my bike for what was called The Labour Exchange in a prefab building along the side of Park Road, Diss and asked about any jobs going in the building trade at that time and I was told there was not, just that at that period it was the policy of local builders to put men on the dole during bad weather.

There was one glimmer of hope on a farm at Goswold Hall, Thrandeston, where I was told there was a vacancy for an all round tractor driver/full maintenance man. So off I went and met an elderly gentleman and started to talk about this job. His son came and we talked about hours, wages and so on. They both said something which I had never heard before on a farm and that was, "Do you mind doing this or that?" They took me around the farm. I was shown the workshop which catered for all sorts of maintenance, building, carpentry and tractor repairs. I was told that one tractor came in for a general overhaul every winter. I said I didn't know if I could do this and the answer I got was that there were the tools and instruction book and a David Brown tractor. I would have the time but they expected it to start the first time after it was put back together. Now this was a real modern farm with several tractors, combine and Land Rover. I asked when they wanted me to start and the answer was, tomorrow 7:15. I did know the lorry driver as he once lived on the edge of Wortham Ling. I had also flown over this place in a B-17 from Brome airfield on the way to Germany one week after the war.

I was there for nine years and they were good to me. Within six months of me leaving all the horses and everything that went with them on all three farms at Wortham had been sold.

The Bad Years

During the late 1920s and early 1930s farming was in a very bad way. The crops were not very good and animals were being sold at markets for very little money. The farm buildings were getting in a very bad state but there was no money to spend on repairs. Even the farm houses were being left to deteriorate, more so the thatched ones which were covered in a thick green moss, as were the thatched cottages in the villages. Hedges were left to grow as farmers could not pay to have them cut and the only thing plentiful was labour as more and more men were coming home from the army after being called up for the 1914-1918 war.

The sad fact was that there was no work for them to do, as the farmers only employed as little labour as possible. Some took to the road in despair, begging for food and drink, and sleeping in any shelter they could find. Others left the area of open fields and fresh air for the dust and dirt of the Yorkshire and Derbyshire coal mines where labour was required. Locally, if you had a job you had to be very careful if you went to a pub in any of the surrounding villages. Beer was only a few pence a pint and men with no work spent a lot of time drinking and became jealous and fights broke out ending with people being chased or even carried back to their own village and dumped inside the village boundary.

Now I was too young to understand any of this or realise how serious things were and a lot of what I have just written was told to me by a man in his middle eighties who was still working full time for a farmer. This old gentleman was a very interesting person but he had the misfortune to lose an eye when he was a boy. He told me that he and other boys were playing around a chaff cutter belonging to a threshing contractor when he slipped and fell onto one of the blades of the cutter which turned and one corner went into his eye. He had not seen with that eye since. I liked to listen to these people and their tales of the hard life they had lived. We both had one thing in common as he had at one part of his life been a horseman and knew the tricks of the trade. One thing he told me that no one else ever had was how to make a horse go to sleep. It was so simple I cannot understand why I had not heard of it before. I can still make that happen, but it was his wish that I kept it to myself.

Despite this man's age he asked no favours and expected to be treated as any other man on this farm. He could and did build corn stacks and hay stacks. Talking to some of the men who worked with him, they said he had a bit of a crafty nature as well, especially at sugar beet chopping out time. He would have his acre the same as all the others, but around about three in the afternoon he would throw his hoe down and say "I've had enough of this!" get on his bicycle and go home. But the next morning, and daylight came early in May, he was there at four o'clock busy hoeing away and by the time the other men arrived he had done several rows and wanted to know where they had been. He was also just as crafty hoeing the beet second time as he would walk yards rolling up his shirt sleeves without the hoe touching the ground at all.

He was also a very strong union man and not afraid to express his feelings about it. He always had the union badge on his jacket and to anyone not a member he would say you accept the pay rises they get you but contribute nothing towards it. In his way of thinking you were getting something for nothing. (I don't know what he would have thought of today's scroungers.) Most men working on farms were members and like him had very strong feeling about it. I myself was for a few years and still have the badge. The whole reason for this was the way some farmers treated their men. If you lived in what was known as a tied cottage, it was impossible to get any repairs done. The farmers had very little money and workers came at the bottom of the list of what they spent it on. I can remember before I started school, my mother getting angry if there was a heavy rain during the day as all the men working outside would get sent home. It was not unusual to see my father come walking up the front path with an old sack tied around his shoulders, soaking wet because there was no work to be done inside in the dry. Despite the fact that the farmer had sent them home this time was cut off their weekly wage.

There were at that time several small farmers going bankrupt. I can remember one farm beside the Wortham to Redgrave road doing just that, so a large herd of milking cows and all that went with the farm was sold,. For some reason these farmers were looked down on and were classed as outcasts. They never got another farm as that was how things were in those days. The amount of men ready to take your job if you left or were sacked was on everyone's mind at that time and for that reason I have heard my father say that people done work which they did not like without question. As I have written before, one particular job that he and another man were told to do, was to walk to Diss Railway station and get on an early train to Stowmarket station. They also had to take a rope halter each because when they got there they had to collect two unknown, unbroken horses. But that was not all. They also had to collect about thirty to forty head of long horned Hereford cattle for fatting up for beef over the winter at the Hall and Beech Tree farms. Why they could not have been brought to Diss station by rail I never found out. However from Stowmarket to Wortham is a distance of about fifteen miles, bearing in mind in those days most roadsides had high hedges but the built up areas of the villages were the worst places and the cattle had to be kept on the move. Now all these animals had been brought by the farmer from a dealer somewhere else in the country and had come a long way by train, so were glad to get out of those trucks and walk about. Also, as these two horses had never been handled before, it was quite a risk to fit a halter on them and then ride them home bareback and keep control of the cattle, but they did and

I can only think that these two men knew something about horses that others didn't. Well the cattle were put in a meadow overnight before going to their winter fatting sheds and the horses were broken in to work on whichever farm wanted them.

One of the biggest employers of men at that time was the railways and some people left the farms to work for LNER as it was then. Every station had its horses. There were two Shires at Diss and they were used for moving wagons about in the sidings. I can remember seeing them moving coal trucks in the goods yard. They knew how to walk on the wooden sleepers to get a grip to start the trucks moving. There were also some cattle pens here and I have seen cattle in them. That was before the war when each platform had a slot machine and a bar of Nestles chocolate could be brought for one penny. Not only were the railways the biggest employers they were one of the richest companies in this area. They also owned lots of land, farms included.

There is one thing that I feel should be told which I remember clearly. It happened during the war about 1944. From where we lived at Wortham the smoke from the steam trains could be seen above the hedge tops, and in the early summer evenings at 10:30pm great clouds of really black smoke could be seen belching up into the sky, travelling from Diss towards Mellis. This was at that time a long slow incline on this stretch of line. So one evening two of us biked to Palgrave and waited on Rose Lane Bridge. We would see the train come through Diss Station and sure enough it did put out clouds of black smoke. We had never seen anything like it before. This was only a little, black goods engine and behind its tender full of coal it was pulling fifty four open wagons full of steel off cuts and drillings. Each wagon was as full as it could be. However many tons that engine was hauling I would not like to guess. This length of line was known for being dangerous and it was not uncommon for trucks to start to roll down the line towards Diss. Most were stopped before they got far but there was the odd one that gained speed before the station staff could stop it but there was a solution as just past the two bridges near Thrandeston Green, where the line runs on top of an embankment, there was a set of points on each line that could be controlled from the signal box at Mellis station. I have heard my father say he could clearly remember when two empty wagons coupled together ran out of control and started to go down the line towards Diss, gaining speed. The signalman put these points into operation and the two wagons left the line and rolled down the embankment into what was known locally as the rod ground, the Suffolk name for an osier bed. How they were got out from there I don't know.

There was more trouble brewing on the farms in the early 1930s, even before I started school and I still remember it well. It was being caused by the other richest organisation which, like the railways at that time, owned lots of land and farms all over the country, and that of course was the church. The reason it was so rich was the fact that every farmer and property owner in the country by law was made to pay the church every year a tenth of their profits if they made any, leaving some tenant farmers with nothing. The church was supposed to give this money to villagers to help with the poor, but they did not do this. Now this had been rumbling on for many years but I was too young to really understand what was going on at that time. But I will write about what I saw and have been told since.

The history of tithe payment goes back many years and in 1650-1660 a group of Quaker farmers refused to pay and had all their livestock taken. Again in 1880s the tithe payment was disputed but it was in 1933, which I can remember, that the farmers had decided to rebel against what they called an unnecessary tax. They formed a group headed by a farmer near Lowestoft by the name of Mobbs and all refused to pay this money.

This was then known as the Tithe War and farmers were taken to court and fined, but they still refused to pay the tithe money. So the police were called in and the farmers had their cattle and pigs confiscated, including Mr Rash who my father worked for. Now this caused great concern within our family as my mother worked for the Rev Moore at the rectory at that time and they did not know what reaction they would get from the people in the village. One thing it did do was to form a closer relationship between farmer and worker. I don't remember how long all this went on for but all the buildings housing cattle and pigs had a guard of police surrounding it and only the stockmen were allowed to go near to feed and litter them. All roads were closed and even the workers were not allowed to cycle to the farms but could walk if they wanted to. As I could understand it, all farm animals were now the property of the government and would be sold at auction to get the money.

I remember one day in particular the roads from Redgrave right through to Palgrave were lined with cars. There were people everywhere and I don't think the police could keep the roads closed. Now I was too young to remember if this was the day the Black Shirts under Oswald Mosley arrived. These people were not invited by anyone but said they had come to help the farmers. These people had black uniforms and tall jack boots and were Fascists from Germany. They had no time for the church and they also helped the farm workers if they could. People soon realised what they were doing and made friends with them. My mother made them cups of tea and I sat at the table with Oswald Mosley several times.

They soon got busy and dug deep, wide trenches across the roadways. They also felled trees and moved the threshing engine and heavy machines into the gateways to the buildings where the animals were kept.

On the day the animals were to be collected my father came indoors and said that the roadway around the shrubby at the rectory was full of red buses full of London policemen, so when the lorries of General Dealers Ltd turned up, which was very early in the morning, they just filled in the ditches and drove across the meadows and loaded every animal they wanted and took them away. No one opposed them at all and at that time the police had no use whatsoever. I can also remember being taken up the Magpie road and seeing big bonfires with guys dressed as parsons on top being set fire to.

After all this the tithe was redeemed and did not have to paid anymore. The house we brought in Union Lane had the tithe redeemed on that. My personal part in this was, when I started work at Hall farm, the job of carting the sand and gravel from the farm up to a site near the road at the Black Sheds, where the cattle had gone from, to build a Tithe War memorial, which is as far as I know still there today. Some of the things I have written about the Tithe War have been taken from an old diary of my parents.

This monument was built by a Mr Potter who was the maintenance man for Mr Rash on all the farms. I remember clearly carting the sand, gravel and cement from Hall Farm to the site with a horse and cart and putting in the cattle shed that was there at that time. This can be seen on the right of the road from Wortham Church to the Magpie pub.

Mrs Rash being held aloft by the farm workers, near one of the many bonfires held in a field near the Hall Farm House. The man at the bottom of the right hand corner of the sign, wearing a trilby hat is my father R V Frost.

Many recall Doreen's 'war'

My call for social campaigner and prolific writer Doreen Wallace to be ushered back into the spotlight she warrants certainly struck a chord with several readers.

Bert Miller of Horsham St Faith was a teenager living at Palgrave at the time of the tithe war. He recalled saddling up and heading for the showdown at Wortham in 1934.

"Preparations had been made to meet the 'invaders'. Traction engines blocked the gateways and ditches were dug at vulnerable points. The highlight had to be the arrival of a coachload of Oswald Mosley's Blackshirts.

"For a while I would assume the barrels at the old 'Wortham Dick' were changed far more frequently than of yore. We never bothered whether 'might was right' or whether the 'baddies' won, but for a while it certainly provided more excitement than Youngman's Saturday night chip van on Palgrave Green," said Bert.

Barbara Scales of Flixton, near Bungay, knew Doreen Wallace in her retirement years.

"Perhaps her association with the Blackshirts may be one reason why she isn't so popular."

They clearly used the Wortham episode as an attempt to gain some credibility as political rebels supporting British agriculture.

There is no evidence that either Doreen or her husband Rowland sympathised with views of the British Union of Fascists, formed by Mosley in 1932, and the Wortham couple insisted the Blackshirts had arrived uninvited.

In her splendid book, Tithe War 1918-1939, The Countryside in Revolt, Carol Twinch points out: "As an exercise in rebellious behaviour, the exploits of the Blackshirts in the tithe war were not entirely successful or fruitful, but their intervention succeeded in bringing the matter to the front pages of the nation's press."

G Went of Bungay told me Cyril Piper had a dahlia nursery at Diss some years ago. He raised several dahlias, one of which was named Doreen Wallace.

"I grew it for many years and I hope it is still going strong somewhere as a fitting tribute to this remarkable lady."

This piece of paper was found with my parents diary, I have no idea where it came from. But it does give a lot of information about the Tithe War; I thought I would save this for future generations.

The Gipsies of Wortham Ling

Wortham Ling in the 1940/50s was an area of about three hundred acres of gorse with open areas of short grass and rushes, surrounded in places by variety of bramble (Blackberry bushes) and wild raspberries. These three hundred acres run beside the River Waveney to the north which divides Norfolk and Suffolk, although. Some parts of the present day river are not the original route it took many years ago, when it turned right just past Sandy Bottoms and went south for about quarter of a mile and then turned east until it joined the new cut of the present river therefore making part of Norfolk into Suffolk but to this day this is still regarded as Roydon.

Now there were two families of gypsies that paid a visit to the Ling once or twice a year. One family, the Gaskins, usually stopped on the grass near where Redgrave road joins the Ling. This family were not as smart and tidy as the family that stopped on a large piece of grass near the Doit Bridge and beside the river. They were the Smyths or the Smiths which ever you liked to call them. They were the much tidier of the two families and all their caravans, horse carts and harnesses were in top condition. Sometimes this family would go past our house after dark with just candle lanterns for light depending on how far they had travelled from that day. By law these people, wherever they stopped, were allowed to stop for one day and one night to rest their horses. No one seemed to mind how long either of these families stayed. Sometimes it was a week or longer.

The Smiths were the family I knew the better of the two, as they would come and talk to me when I was working on the fields near the river. The first thing they done when they arrived, after they had fed and watered and then tethered their horses, they would dig out a circle of turf and stack it up ready to put back when they left. This was the place they built their fire for cooking in a big cast iron pot, held up by metal rods to form a tripod. These rods had hooks on the top to hold the handle of the pot. The water used for drinking came from a land drain pipe that ran into the roadside ditch about three to four hundred yards on the left hand side of the Redgrave road. This water was as clear and cool as that that came out of any well as it had been coming through the soil for nearly two miles away, as far away as Magpie Green in fact. I must point out here that it was very rare to get these two families on the Ling at the same time so they never crossed each other's path.

The washing water came from the river and the washed clothes were put out to dry either laid on a bush or hung from a line from the caravan to a nearby tree. They always seemed to have washing out which was clean and spotless. They had no trouble with pegs of course as they made them themselves from nearby willow shrubs, and it was these they took round to sell to householders.

My grandfather had made his family pegs for years and he did show me what to do. The thin strip of tin that stopped the peg from splitting was part of an old cocoa tin held in place by a brass nail. I did make one or two lots at certain times.

Winter or summer the Smith family always stood in the flowing water of the river and got scrubbed down, even if there was ice on the water. This family had two Reading caravans, a round top (Canvas roof) and one four wheeled flat cart. Each one was pulled by piebald ponies with one spare pony tied to the back of the flat cart when travelling. All these carts and caravans were highly carved and decorated.

The head one of the family, who was a pipe smoking, bearded man in about his middle seventies, came over to see me one day when I was working and asked if they could dig out rabbits from the banks around these fields and I said he could and we got talking and to my surprise he invited me to his caravan to meet his family, to which I agreed. After discussion about how nice their caravans looked he said come down tonight as there is a full moon and I will show you something and this is what it was. He was sitting on a stool by the side of the van. He was painting some of the lines on the woodwork. He had a small tin of yellow paint but no brush. What he had was a piece of young hawthorn, which had been chewed like a brush, and was painting with it. Inside the van I had never seen anything like it, china, brass and glass all shining and spotless. In one corner there was a tall round black stove called a policeman. It was very warm in there but the biggest surprise of all was the big box under the van between the wheels, for in there was a massive dog, which I thought was a Lurcher but I have since found out this could have been a Smithfield. This dog, as I understood it, never saw daylight but was let out at night for poaching rabbits and hares.

These people were the real Romany gipsies trying to keep an old tradition alive as best they could. The local gamekeeper turned a blind eye to this family as did the village policeman. When they left the turf was put back over the ashes of their fire and the whole area was left very tidy and if the grass was not left shorter where the horses had been tethered no one would have known they had been. These people certainly knew a lot about horses and they done all their own shoeing. But one thing I could never understand was why they nearly always travelled by night. I don't know how long ago the last gipsies came onto the Ling. They would not go onto the area near the bridge now as it is all covered in silver birch trees, no grass at all. But the whole place has changed over the years. I often wonder if those people are about in this country now or has their lifestyle gone for ever? I don't know.

Tradesmen that I remember of those early days

Mr Leeks – Diss, had a horse drawn, four wheel, covered in cart, came round twice a week, Wednesdays and Saturdays, selling paraffin oil, bundles of kindling, soap flakes, Lifebuoy Soup, pan scourers, matches, dusters and cleaning cloths.

Mr Buckle – Mission Road, Diss, had a horse drawn, high, two wheeled, open cart, no solid top, just a tilt to cover his goods. He sold much the same, paraffin oil, linen pegs, soup, kindling. He too came round on Saturday afternoons but had different customers.

Coal Merchants

Colliers delivered coal on horse drawn, four wheeled carts in one hundredweight sacks. They had about four of these carts and had a yard and stables beside the goods yard at Diss Railway Station. Delivery day in our part of Wortham was Monday morning. When the delivery men were paid they would give you a coloured ticket to be exchanged at the Co-op for goods to the value of the ticket.

Moys also had a coal yard at the station and two horses and four wheeled carts delivering in and around Diss.

There was also Savills, who had a coal yard at Mellis Station. They had a horse and a big two wheeled cart like a farm tumbrel. They delivered to Wortham and other villages.

Frank Stevens had threshing engines near Denmark Bridge. E Howard, Wortham, threshing machines, tractors, The Brook, Wortham.

Milk Men

G Colman, Ivy House, Wortham, had a pony and milk float, sold milk out of churns also eggs and home made butter.

L Cotton, Pollard Tree Farm, The Ling, Wortham, sold milk door to door from small churns carried on bicycle handle bars.

L Warren, Long Green, Wortham, also sold milk from small churns on bicycle handle bars.

Bakers

Clarke, Long Green, Wortham, delivered by van.

Charlie Doe, Redgrave, had a small van for delivery of bread and

271

cakes in all local villages.

Nightingales, Denmark Green, had shop and café in Mere Street, Diss, or bread and cakes could be collected from bakery.

Corn Merchants

Savills of Mellis had mill at Mellis Station, also delivered meal to farms for stock feed. Chairman, a Mr Clarke, always wore a stiff white shirt collar, a hard man to please.

H Burroughes, Bressingham, Corn and seed merchants.

Mr Kemp, The Windmill, Bury Road, Wortham, Corn and seed merchants and millers.

Fish and chips and Game dealers

Benny Manning, The Ling, Wortham, had a mobile cart pulled around by a heavy cart horse, usually in evenings to different villages.

Sunny Youngman, had a shop next to Cock P.H. by the side of Denmark Green. Very good all one could eat for sixpence, always full up.

Brill, Shelfanger Road, open most evening, tables and chairs to sit inside and eat meal.

Easto, Market Place, Diss, had inside eating area also had an adjoining shop for wet fish sales with big marble slab and open front to see in from the road.

Digby, wet fish and game, same set up for fish, marble slab open front, rabbits and game hung from walls on hooks. This shop was in St Nicholas Street, nearly down to the church.

Butchers

Wells in Mere Street had whole carcasses of cattle hanging inside and outside of shop, also half of pigs hanging on heavy iron hooks, sliding on metal rails, sawdust covered floor. Game and rabbits also sold.

Three Anniss butcher shops in different parts of Diss, all selling the same as Wells and at Christmas they all had turkeys, geese, chickens and ducks.

Wood Merchants

Sweep Bartrum, The Ling, Wortham, bought and sawed up trees and delivered them as cut logs around nearby villages with a four wheeled cart pulled by a very tall horse.

Fruit and vegetables and sweets

Mr Ellis' shop just onto Denmark Green also sold sweets and chocolate, cigarettes and tobacco.

Mrs Hurren, next to Mr Digby's, sweets and every other item that was saleable, stocked from floor to ceiling.

Doubles shop in Mere Street sold everything for smoking, pipes, lighters, tobacco and cigarettes. They always had a Red Indian chief near the door on the outside.

Main Post Office

Was in Mount Street with Sub Post Offices at the top of Victoria Road and on the side of Denmark Green run by a Mr Bowden.

Cafes in Diss

Of which there were two, Mr Gardener of St Nicholas Street and Mr Denny's in Mere Street.

Ironmongers

There was Albrights in Nicholas Street and Aldridge just off the market place, which got burn down one Friday afternoon. I saw lots of fire engines there at the time.

Grocers

Aldridge and Bryant, Nicholas Street, wholesale grocers and wine merchants.

Co-op, Victoria Road and Market Place, they had a delivery service to all the villages around Diss, besides a butchers shop, shoe shop, hardware store, clothes shop and cake shop.

Blacksmiths

Howells of Palgrave.

Garnham, Wortham Magpie.

G Rice, Wortham Long Green.

Builders Merchants

Masons, Victoria Road, Diss.

Bardwells, Church Street, Diss.

Builder and Carpenters

Rackham Builders, Denmark Green, Diss, also undertakers.

Sid Garnham, Bury Road, Wortham.

G Churchyard, Long Green, Wortham.

Chapman – Plumber, Wolsey House, Wortham.

Goddard – Builder, Botesdale.

Potter Bros – Carpenters and undertakes, Long Green, Wortham.

Pubs

The Magpie – Mr Garnham, Magpie Green.

The Dick – Mr Dickson, The Ling.

The Dolphin – Mr Groom, Long Green.

The Cherry Tree, shut before I knew of it.

Wortham Post Office

Postmaster Mr Needham.

Postmen, Lawson Potter and Mr Percy.

Roadmen

Mr Potter, Mr Stiff and Mr Kidgell.

Paperman

Dick Easto, everyday excerpt Sundays.

Diss Cinema

Mr Jones.

Shoe and Harness Maker

Mr Potter, workshop in garden of first house on right round Dick corner.

Ice Cream Makers

Bumshi's, Diss, had tricycle for delivering around villages. also one van.

Walls Ices also done delivery in the same way.

Bicycle Agents

Cobbs in St Nicholas Street, new and second hand bicycles.

Magetts, Victoria Road, Diss the same both done repair.

Barbers in Diss 1940/1950's

Fred Studd

Dan Jones

Youngman's Mill on the Ling, before the big gale in the late 1920s

Youngman's Mill on the Ling after the big gale in the late 1920s

Some Facts and Opinions

As I have been writing this book I have since remembered other things that should have been included in certain parts, like some of the early days when before I started school I would go with mother to the Rectory, where each week there would be a man with a trade bike complete with wicker basket in a special frame on the front and a solid piece of metal under the crossbar and joined to the other parts of the frame. On this metal was some white painted letters against a black background and these letters were WELL'S, THE BUTCHERS, MERE STREET, DISS. Now this man delivered all sorts of meat and sausages that had been ordered by telephone by the rector's wife. One day in conversation with my mother he asked if she was interested in doing some domestic work for the butcher. My mother knew this family as she herself shopped there. As money was short and the wage these people offered was good for those days, the job was accepted.

I had passed this shop at certain times with my mother and being so young one shop was very much like another. When my mother started work there must have been some reason I was not left with these other people, but put in the seat of her bicycle and off I went to Diss. She cycled up Mere Street (it was two way traffic in those days) and arrived at the shop, where her cycle was pushed into a room at the back of the shop, and we went up stairs to the living quarters, which very much like the inside of the rectory at Wortham. The views from the back windows was something I never seen before and I stood and watched the ducks for a long time while mother got on with the cleaning. I went through to the bedroom and there on a table beside the bed was a book and on the front cover was a picture I have never forgotten and this was a human head with all its details of the inside contents, the brain, muscles, veins and even the teeth. As this was all in colour I did not like it at all. But for a four year old boy this was frightening. I don't know what this book was about but who could read a book with a cover like that?

There were other things I remembered from those days like the front of the shop. Open to all the dirt and dust of the street hung the huge carcasses of cattle and pigs also rabbits and, in season, unplucked pheasants and partridges and at Christmas, turkeys, geese, ducks and chickens with the odd woodcock amongst them. I never saw a pigeon either inside the shop or out. I think that the amount paid for them was only a few pence and not very profitable. But on the other hand many a farm worker ate the pigeons they shot. I know we had them quite often and, baked in the oven like the rabbits, they were very good indeed.

Getting back to the shop, as you walked in the door there was a very heavy wooden counter and on top was a set of very heavy scales for weighing meat complete with brass weights for use with the scales. These were all made so they had a handle on top for holding when used. They all stood on the counter with the largest at one end to the very smallest at the other end. The floor was covered in clean sawdust. Behind this counter sitting on a stool was Mrs Wells, a rather large woman, who took the money paid by customers, putting this in an old wooden till. Mr Wells was a tall, stout person, who cut up the meat as required. Around the walls hung on a metal bar were big heavy S hooks holding up the same sort of carcasses as hung outside, and inside these carcasses great lumps of white suet could be seen, from these pieces were cut and sold to the customers requirements. Also hanging from this rail were half a pig carcasses of different sizes, from which parts were chopped off with a cleaver, saw or sharp knife. All this was done on what was called a butcher' block, a very solid, heavy type of bench made from very hard wood with the end grain forming the top. One part of this rail had a section where big bunches of sausages hung to be cut to how many customers wanted.

Another thing on top of the counter was the bacon slicer, turned by hand and it could make a rasher of bacon as thick or thin as wanted. There was also a marble slab behind the bottom of the first window on which oven ready poultry was displayed, also chicken eggs and duck eggs and in the spring goose and turkey eggs. On the walls hung the cleavers and saws, but the knives were on the counter or the block. The sausage making machine was in a room at the back, in which by mixing bread crumbs and meat there must have been hundreds of sausages made with different meats to be sold in the shop.

Now Mr and Mrs Wells employed two men to help in the shop and make deliveries into the countryside on the trade bike and all of them were dressed the same, white clothes and a blue and white striped aprons. My mother worked there for about a year and a half. Sometimes she would bring home what we called pig's trotters. These were part of a pig's leg from the toe up to the first joint and from the meat taken from this leg she made a really good homemade pork cheese. All the family enjoyed it and we never got tired of it.

One winter there was a heavy snowfall so we had to walk from the cottage near the rectory to this shop in Mere Street. It took us longer and the thing that fascinated me at that time was, where the Diss sign is now was a little brick shed and in front of it was a metal topped weigh bridge. I would jump on this to make it move which it did, but I don't remember when this was all done away with and the area was all made solid.

Now these people treated my mother well and I always got a bar of chocolate, but things were changing and the war came. The meat carcasses were not seen outside the shop and all types of stock got smaller. Meat was rationed and coupons had to cut from ration books, which took time, and long queues stretching out down Mere Street were a common sight. This carried on long after the end of the war but one thing that never changed was the very sincere and polite way these people dealt with their customers. But it was not long after this they decided to pack up their business and move on. Where they went too I don't know but I shall always remember Mrs Wells as the woman who had cut off all the ends of her fingers on her left hand with a meat cleaver early in her life.

Early in 1946 this shop was bought by a Norfolk man named Mr Cannell. I think he moved to Diss from somewhere near Norwich. To most people if you lived in Norfolk you were one of them. But there was always some who objected to change and left this shop, my mother included, and went to the Co-Op butchers on the market place. I went with her once or twice, and because these men were employed rather than the owners of the shop, this made the atmosphere totally different. It was more of what do you want rather than what would you like?

Meanwhile big changes were being made by Mr Cannell. Gone were the carcasses from outside the shop, but I'm not quite sure but I think there were still a few on the rail inside. There were other big changes going on inside the shop. The sawdust on the floor was gone and an easy tile floor was laid in its place. The big, heavy, wooden counter went and included with that the weighing machine and brass weights but the same men worked there who had worked for Wells. The name of Wells was taken down and the new name of Cannells was put above the big window in the front of the shop and is still there today. The inside was much cleaner. New machines were put in, and people began to come back when they found out that the service given was even better than it was in the years before. I know mother went back and shopped there and did for the rest of her life. And we still do because the meat, in our opinion, is the best you can buy. Just a few years back this shop changed again and, because of modern Health and Safety Laws, there are now glass fronted and topped cabinets, where the meat is on display on stainless steel trays and ready for use in the kitchen. One big thing I have noticed is that all the different kinds of eggs are gone and only chicken eggs are left and, owing to the change in people's eating habits, there are now small, brown, specked eggs laid by a small bird called the quail. I never had one of these. Also with the change the trade bike went and in its place came a van for delivery around the countryside. One thing I never found out was where the cold store was or where the meat was kept before it came into the shop.

I remember in 1977 Mr Cannell asked me if I would do a job for him. I said yes and he took me to the store room above the shop and those old memories came back as this was the Wells sitting room, which mother cleaned, while I sat on the window sill watching the people in Mere Street. Well I got a man to help me and we took all the materials and tools when the shop was shut on a Saturday afternoon. We also took some food and drink and started work. We worked all Saturday night, all Sunday and Sunday night and finished at 2 am on Monday morning, when we cleaned all our stuff out and everything was clean and tidy by opening time. What a change from the carpets on the floor, the big table in the middle of the room, the heavy armchairs and so on.

I have moved away from 1954 for this part of the story to show how one shop played a part of my and my family's lives as that is how it was then. I suppose this chapter should have a title of 'From sawdust to stainless steel'. Thankfully the name of Cannells is above the shop, which always reminds me of all those things that started with a meat delivery to Wortham Rectory all those years ago.

More Recollections

Not everyone went to the butchers for pork in those days but nearly all the local villages had their own butchers' shops. I can remember one in Redgrave but I don't think Wortham ever had one. The reason for this was that lots of households kept their own pigs for the sole purpose of having a meat supply for the table. I know my grandfather did as there were some clay lump pig sties and chicken runs on part of the Ling in front of their house. I have heard him say that he kept Large White breed of pigs. I can remember these building but never saw any pigs, as this was in the early 1920s. As they killed these animals themselves they would also do almost all of the butchery work. The only exception being the bacon rashers and sausages would be made at some butcher's for a few shillings but I don't know where that was. I can quite clearly remember the big wooden tub which was a big barrel cut in half, which was filled with boiling hot water heated in the copper and used for putting the carcass in and the bristles were scraped off. Nothing was wasted and would last a long time, including the hams, which they cured themselves.

In those days of hot summers lots of meat was salted to last longer but some was done different as it was put in muslin bags and hung down the wall just above the water level where it was cool. This was being done all over the countryside. I know there was someone in Wortham Long Green and also one very old bearded man who lived in one of the houses at the bottom of Union Lane. A lot of people went to him. I sometimes saw him tethering his three goats on the Ling but kept out of his way. This business of keeping pigs for one's own use was always done even through the war years, and I am not quite sure about this but I think you had to give up some meat coupons from your ration book. New laws have stopped this being done at home now.

Grandfather's chickens were kept for eggs, which I helped to collect and there was also cockerels with these hens and each spring eggs would be collected and put under a broody hen for hatching new chicks. There was a few cockerels fattened up for Christmas but the buildings were all pulled down sometime during 1950 and there is nothing left of them now.

Getting back to the late 1920s and as I have said, lots of farmers were going bankrupt and selling their farms, but big changes were on the way unforeseen by the people in the villages. Now a lot of this was the years before I was born and my knowledge has been gained by reading old diaries keep by my parents, my grandfather and other members of the family. There was another way I learned what things were like because as I got older and could walk down to my grandfather's house with my parents for a visit and a chat, once we got inside the living room I was made to sit on a chair and not get off until it was time to go home. So, while they talked and drank glasses of homemade wine, I had no alternative but to sit and listen.

The deterioration of the countryside continued but this did not go unnoticed by people in other parts of the country as, up in the hills of Scotland, farmers left for the fertile land of East Anglia and with them came big herds of milking cows, which gave employment to many of the local men who had lost their jobs on the failed farms. A lot of arable land was drilled with grass and made into new meadows for grazing and hay. Several small farms were made into large farms of one thousand acres and more, but they also knew a lot about growing other crops, in fact they were very good farmers and are still here to this day although lots of herds of cows are gone. One of the things they did was to change the whole business of milk production. Milk churns were still used for a few years but as more and more milk was produced so the industry became more efficient, changing the churns for bulk collection by tanker lorries from the farms.

Now as more cows were being kept more tankers were used and there was a firm at Bunwell, which began to get a lot of lorries on the road and as far as I know it is still there today. What I remember is that most of these lorries with big engines still had to be started by cranking a handle like a tractor and one Sunday dinner time in the 1940s, when I and two other boys were having a shandy at the Dick, one of these tankers came onto the forecourt and the driver came in the pub for a drink. When it was time to go he turned the handle to start the engine, and the whole thing misfired causing the handle to kick back and break his wrist. This was the first time I had seen anything like this happen and I must admit it was scary.

However this new way of the dairy farming was increasing quite quickly as farm after farm changed to bulk collection. There were still the farms that kept one or two cows for their own milk and butter for use in the house. I am not sure when an organisation called The Milk Marketing Board was formed but they built a depot/factory on one of the meadows beside Park Road, which was where the tankers took the milk to from local farms.

As the face of farming was changing and more cows were being kept, so the big flocks of sheep began to disappear. I can't remember what year the flocks from Hall and Beech Tree Farms were put up for sale but they were probably in one of the last big sales held at the Diss Auctions at Roydon Road. The biggest cause for this was fact that wool prices were very low. The shepherds became what were then known as farm labourers, a very different job from what they had been doing. I worked with both of them on some jobs. All the things used on sheep farming and, here again I am not quite sure but I seem to remember, all the netting, troughs and stakes were sold on the same day as all the horses, plus the carts and harnesses were sold and farming as I had known it as a boy was moving into a new era.

This was also the thin edge of the wedge for steam engines, both in the country and on the railways. Most threshing contractors were kept busy because of the need for thatching straw, but were now running their machines by Field Marshall tractors complete with a winch and wire rope for moving drums and elevators in soft ground conditions.

I have already mentioned the meadows between Park Road and the river, but they come up again for an event that I think should be remembered. I saw this happen sometime in the late 1940s and this was the sale of lots of agricultural and other steam engines. Who held the sale I don't know but I clearly remembering seeing all types of engines, Burrells, Fowlers, Aveling and Porter road rollers and many others all fresh from doing the jobs they were made for. Some looked in perfect condition as some owners took more pride in their machines than others, and all were in good working order. I know for certain Mr Rash's Burrell was there, also some of Frank Stevens from Palgrave, besides another contractor from Redgrave who had also changed to tractors. On the day of the sale I heard my father say that people came from all over the country, and as I understand, some of the best engines made a top price of Fifteen Pounds, but a lot made under. Some were brought for preservation and many were sold as scrap, but some farmers hung onto engines and restored them to new condition, and can be sold nowadays for from three hundred to five hundred thousand pounds each.

The same thing was happening on the railways. We still went to Norwich by train and on the right, as the train approached a place named Trowse, there were some big sidings next to the main line. I can remember these sidings being packed full of railway engines all with their tenders standing buffer to buffer. I never had the chance to count all these different types of engine but the whole area seemed full of them, some covered with rust but most were awaiting the scrap man to be cut up. Whether any of these were ever restored I cannot say but the big heavy express engines continued to be used up to and during the 1950s. Some of these thankfully went into preservation for future generations to see.

And still memories come back of what happened many years ago, like in the last years of the war when on certain Friday nights I would get up in the middle of the night and ride my bicycle and push my mother's bike beside me up to Diss Railway Station and meet the 2am train from London, to meet my mother's brother who worked up there repairing bomb damage. He always had a big suitcase with him and as he was staying at ours for the weekend I did not take much notice. This train for some reason was always called The Milk Train but I never saw any connection with milk at all. The big difference was there were very few passengers at all. However he would put the case on the handlebars of the bike and we chatted on the way home.

It was quite a long while before I found out that there was another purpose beside a just a weekend visit to see his sister. No wonder the case was heavy because there were several bottles of whisky inside. Now during the war it was normal for the pubs to run out of beer, due to the fact that so many local airfield personnel, both R.A.F and American Air Force, using them in their free time, also any sort of spirit was sold nearly as soon as it was delivered to most public houses. But the landlords always kept a certain amount of drink back for their regular customers, even if there was a Sold Out sign on the door. I can remember seeing bottles of White Horse Whisky on our table and saw it used for special occasions but what happened to the rest of the drink brought down in the suitcase I never did know but what was certain was that someone was making money from it. Was it the landlord of the Dick or American Service men? This was all very quietly done and even to this day I still have never found out.

Another thing done by the railways in the 1930/40s was to sell off some surplus carriages for people to live in and Wortham had a few of these. There was one beside the road about halfway between the Magpie and the Grove which could be seen clearly, but a few yards away hidden behind a high, thick hedge was another but much older one in very bad condition. When two double dweller council houses were built at the far end of Magpie Green the people from these carriages moved into these houses. Also beside the Low Road, just past the two sharp turns, were two more but these were side by side and therefore made quite a large living area. These two were lived in by a farm worker and his wife. I went to school with their two daughters and our family left our bicycles there when we went poaching on the fen or shooting ducks on the river.

Even more were beside this road as further along on the North side at the far end of a meadow stood another two with some sheds around them. This was the home of the local mole catcher, who went onto most of the surrounding farms to set traps in the mole runs and made a living by catching these animals, skinning them and drying the skins for sale to the fur industry. The ladies of those days were someone important if they had a mole skin coat. I often saw my father and his brother with skins stretched out over flat boards by brass pins being dried for sale. I feel that they and the mole catcher had an understanding that they sold their skins to him. I went up to his home with my father several times when I was a schoolboy. This man was a very tall, upright man, who always wore a trilby hat with a blue Jay's feather on one side. He also wore a thick tweed suit with a jacket made slightly on the large side complete with moleskin collar partly covered by his red handkerchief with white spots. Steggles, as he was known, could always be seen cycling around the countryside with a hessian sack held over his shoulder by a leather strap, and lots of mole traps clipped to his bicycle handlebars and tied to his crossbar was his spud. This was a flat piece of metal about three inches wide with a long hoe like neck to which a handle was fitted. This was used for digging out underground mole runs to make holes to set traps in.

The wives of both these men were part of the workers along side my mother and several other women who done the fruit and potato picking for Mr Rash. There was one more railway carriage that I knew of being used as a house. This was just over the old river bed beside the Ling but just into Roydon. Now this one was different as it had been walled round by weather board and had a metal roof, so it looked like a bungalow and was very smartly painted as well. Lots of villages in those days had these carriages with people living in them, and to a certain extent were better than many houses.

I would like to add here that, in the book written by Richard Cobbold, he shows a picture of a house on the Ling against a background of trees. Nobody I asked, including my family, knew where it was. It appears that the woman who lived there sold tobacco, cigarettes and sweets to the people in that area. Well quite by chance I and another man, who helped me on some jobs at Pollard Tree Farm, found lots of local made, red bricks and some brick footings on a certain part of the Ling.

This person lived in a house near the Dick and kept a lot of tame rabbits for sale at Diss at that time and was very successful with them. So he thought that he would move on and keep some laying hens. He brought about thirty Rhode Island Reds but, as his garden was small, he decided to keep them on the Ling. He brought himself a wooden poultry hut, complete with nest boxes and iron wheels. This was impossible to move by himself so he asked me to help him, which I did and the place he decided to put this hut was in a very deep hole with a gentle slope down one end for the hut to run down. To get to this hole we went off the road onto a wide track past the White House and down beside where the Bartrums cut up their firewood. We followed this track down to a bridge over the old river and just on the left was this big hole. It was not long before the hens were busy scratching amongst the gorse and high grass and laying eggs in the well locked nest boxes.

This was not the only part of the Ling that had hills and holes. There was a part that was on the west of the track from the road to the Beehive Cottages that was pitted with very deep holes and high hills and the cause of this was, according to my grandfather who helped to make these when he first went to work, a certain farmer would let them have horses and carts and they would dig out all the flints and big stones and they would be sold to the Council to make roads with.

Now out in the country it was said that, as the roads were so winding from place to place, they followed old cattle tracks but there was another story and that was the men making the roads always worked with their backs to the wind. There must have been a lot of change of direction of wind according to some of the roads around this area.

There was also another part of the Ling that had been used for an industrial purpose, and this was on the east side of the cycle path running from Union Lane to the corner where the Ling joined the Diss road. This was a large low piece of land which got covered in water every winter and was known as The Swamps, which was at no time much more than two foot deep with nice clear water and the grass could be seen under the water most of the time. This was the ideal place to skate during the very sharp frosty days of those long winters. But how they came there was where my grandfather's knowledge comes in again. The soil here was not soft sand like most of the other parts of the Ling but very heavy clay with small pieces of chalk in it. This was ideal for making clay lumps. I know he helped to make these clay lumps and he also had several wooden boxes about six inches by six inches by about eighteen inches long stored in one of his sheds. These were the moulds in which the clay lumps were made. There was no top or bottom as they were stood on boards when in use.

Now I was told how these were made and it was as following. Clay was dug out with spades and laid on a bed over a large area but was not very deep. Then a thin layer of wheat or barley straw was spread over the top followed by more clay and a repeat of straw and so on, until the bed was made to the required thickness. And then the animals were brought in. Either a donkey or a pony was used and if the clay was a bit hard a small amount of water was used to make it a little more pliable. Then the animal was made to walk on top of it all. Cutting up the straw and forcing it into the clay. This took a long time to do and must have been quite tiring for any animal on a job like this. When the straw was well mixed the clay was cut into pieces by a spade and put into the wood boxes on the board and jammed down tight to get any air out and then left for a short while to dry enough for each box to be taken off and the lump to dry completely. It must have taken a long while to make enough blocks to build a house.

Several houses were built around the Ling and I know for certain the house we brought in Union Lane was, and there was a very good possibility that the clay used came from The Swamps. Each course of blocks was held together by a wet clay plaster without any straw in. Even the chimney on this house was built of clay lump and that was when we found out there a hazard to these buildings. We were unlucky one morning when for some reason the chimney caught fire and the fire engine came and put it out without much mess at all. But to our surprise it came back again about three hours later to check and see if everything was alright and they told us the reason for this was that the straw in the clay lump would smoulder and reignite itself. Thankfully it had not done so here. It was not long after then that all new buildings had to have either round or square terracotta chimney linings.

Most of my young life had some connection with the Ling but my father was actually born in a house beside the Ling and started school at the Ling School but had to go to the Long Green when he was eight as did the rest of his family. The school was a long red brick building on some high ground beside a track from the Dick corner to the Homestead (The old

Union Workhouse) and is just before the first bend in the track. I have heard him say the headmaster was always ready to use the cane but he had one disadvantage, he had one wooden leg and the children would climb over the fence to get out of his way.

When I knew this building it was a private house and was the home of the blind organist, a very clever man by the name of Mr Edwards. He always played the organ at Wortham Church and I sometimes pumped the bellows for him before an electric motor was installed. He was not only an organ player but he also tuned organs at other local churches, it was not unusual to see him walking to Burgate or Redgrave to do some private job. He nearly always walked in the middle of the road as there were not many cars on the road at that time. If he heard anything coming he would stand on one side. I never saw him at any time with a white stick, a very clever man indeed.

Now in the late 1930s early 1940s there was a start of something that, in my mind, should never have happened and this carried on to the early 1950s. The village would never be the same again. What started in the meadows next to the footpath from the church to the Dick, went nearly unnoticed by the people in the other parts of the village and this was some large straight oak trees that must have been hundreds of years old were felled for whatever the reason. The branches were cut for carting away and the trunks were all debarked with the bark stacked in heaps ready for sale to the tanning industry. We did go and fill bags with the big chips cut from the trunks where the direction of fall was cut out. These made good logs for the fire and saved cutting wood with the handsaw.

Unfortunately this was just the start of the country around here, as I knew it, being destroyed. I don't know if the farmer was forced to cut these trees down or what was the reason for it. The next ones to go were four lovely old oak trees growing in the hedgerow next to the road between the Dick and Beech Tree Farm. The same thing was done here with the bark being stripped off and carted away. And there were other trees about the village being felled in the same way but I am glad to say that the same sort of trees beside the road from the church to the Long Green are still there with the exception of one very big tree, whose trunk must have been at least four foot wide.

But the worst destruction of the trees was not in Wortham at all but just over the Waveney into Roydon but this was all part of the scenery as seen from the Ling. It was always a favourite walk on a Sunday morning during the spring to go along some of the foot paths leading down to the river amongst all the gorse, which with a few exceptions was about two foot high and full of lovely yellow sweet smelling blooms. There were a few very tall gorse bushes beside the road edges and some areas also had heather but this was at its best in the autumn. This large area of gorse covered most of the Ling from one end to the other and when the wind was in the west could it be smelt down as far as Denmark Bridge. When it was a sunny morning there were many things going on as we went on these walks and one thing that stood out the most was the skylarks which seemed to be everywhere. They would do a lot of wing flapping and singing, rising up in the air till they were a small moving object high in the sky, and then for no apparent reason they would stop singing and drop to the ground like a stone. But they were very crafty birds as they would land on the ground quite a long way from their nests, and then run very quickly through the dry grass so they could not be found. There were also linnets, finches and hedge sparrows nesting on the Ling and in the hedgerows and woods all around this part of the village. In the wood just over the river were wood pigeons, rooks, jackdaws and a pair of carrion crows, who made enough noise for all the rest put together. Grazing on the grass and free to wander about the Ling as they pleased were the three horses belonging to Ernie Bartrum, the man who sold logs of wood around the district. But the best sound of all was the peal of bells from Roydon Church ringing out over the Waveney Valley.

These walks did not take place every Sunday but mainly at the time when we wanted a haircut because Uncle Ernie, my father's brother, was one of the hairdressers in the village, a trade he learned when he was in the army. The other was a man who lived in one of the Council houses on Magpie Green. If there were others I did not know of them.

Getting back to the wood just into Roydon, the farmer at Grove Farm was a man by the named Briscoe. Uncle Ernie drove his Standard Fordson for him. This orange tractor could often be seen pulling a trailer through the woods and the reason for this was because he kept a big herd of pigs of all ages and sizes running wild in the bushes and trees. Now this wood was full of mature trees, oak, beech, elm, sweet chestnut and silver birch, beside all the undergrowth, and these pigs seemed to enjoy it. With the exception of two small meadows the wood started at the edge of Roydon Fen and went right through to Bressingham Fen with the road going through the middle for the whole quarter of a mile or more. As the bridge over the river was called Doit bridge so the wood was called The Doit. This must have been sometime in the 1950s. I think Grove Farm was sold and the new owners were two brothers who had also come down from Scotland. It was around this time that this wood was cut down. All the big trees were carted away and one or two were left but were very small and are still there today. This left just brushwood and brambles, which after the big caterpillar tractors had bulldozed out all the tree roots, were made into big heaps and with the help of this waste were burnt and all the land was levelled and sown with grass to make meadows, which today are in turn grazed by flocks of sheep or about thirty ponies.

When I worked at Pollard Tree Farm and we worked on the three meadows adjoining the river Waveney, which is the boundary between Norfolk and

Suffolk, this river started as a small trickle in a ditch on the east side of the road from Redgrave to South Lopham, and on the opposite side of the road under the same conditions was the Little Ouse. I did go out for cycle rides with my parents around this area and can remember stopping while on one of these rides and looking at both sides of the road to see where these rivers started, but all there was was just a small amount of water that appeared to be coming up from the ground in a boggy area of soil, nothing spectacular at all.

Now the rivers in those days were under the control of what was known as the River Authority and a very good job they done of it too. Every summer there were gangs of about four men each, all wearing high wanders, they would walk in the water, with two in front cutting all the weeds with a scythe and the two behind getting the weeds out of the water with forks and laying them on the banks. If the river was deep and wide they would use a very special type of saw that could be drawn back and forward from each bank. Normally a piece of wire netting was put across the river at the starting point with the sole purpose of catching any weeds that had been missed by the men with forks.

There was another thing done every three or four years and we would notice the start of this near Denmark Bridge but they always seemed to do this work from the Suffolk side, and this was how it was done. First of all there was some great big eighteen by eighteen timbers arrive presumably from the opposite side of the bridge. There were two different lengths to these, six of these were twenty foot or more long and six were ten foot long and with them came a very powerful blue Ransome and Rapier dragline. This great, tracked machine was made at Ipswich and many of them went all over the world. What the horsepower of the diesel engine was I don't know but the digging bucket, controlled by chains, wire ropes running on pulleys, could hold over a ton when full. Like all rivers the Waveney had ditches and wide watercourses running into it at various points, which this machine had to cross. So the dragline moved the big heavy timbers into a platform on the ground all done by heavy chains. After all the long ones were laid next came the short ones laid end to end with the long ones until a platform of about thirty foot long had been made. With the dragline tracks on top of the platform, dredging of the river could begin. This driver was an expert at his job and each river bank was left with a gentle slope leaving the river wider at the top than the bottom. This was a slow moving job and there was always a high narrow ridge of spoil left along the river bank. As this machine worked its way along our ploughed up meadows we always left all this to dry out for one year and then it could be ploughed along the bottom edge bit by bit until the amount left could be made nearly level.

It was interesting to see what had been dredged up. I found deer antlers, rusty pieces of metal, bones of other animals and quite a lot of big stones including flints, and there were always the shells of massive fresh water mussels, just like the ones found at Redgrave Lake. This big machine continued slowly along the side of the Ling and up to Bressingham Fen and beyond, but where it stopped cleaning out I never did see, but as the river narrowed I should think it was somewhere on Redgrave Fen.

For some reason the fish always seemed to be there despite the fact that the river had been disturbed. There were roach, rudd, eels and a small fawn coloured fish with what looked like whiskers, this was called a gudgeon and was about three inches long, and there always seemed plenty of them. These were the favourite food of the kingfisher, which was always sitting on the trees near the river edge. All the time we collected birds eggs we never got a kingfisher's egg, for the simple reason that they made their nests in burrows in the river bank and were well out of reach of us.

There was always duck and teal swimming along the river, but unfortunately a lot of those got shot as there was never a season to shooting them like there was for game birds. Also there was an odd heron standing in the water waiting for a fish to pass to close. A lot of the trees near the river were Alder, a tree that had small cones like a fir tree. In some places there were several of these trees together to form a small wood, and these were what we called Alder Carrs, a favourite place in the spring for the cuckoo, of which there were many pairs because of being near the Ling this was ideal for them to find another birds nest to lay their single egg. Only once did I see a pair of swans but they did not stay many weeks and even then they spent a lot of time on the meadows and not on the river.

When I was working on one of the fields near the edge of the Ling, I saw a sight that I had never seen before or since. I was busy ploughing with the team of Suffolks and just giving the horses a little break when I heard what sounded like a huntsman's horn, and then along one of the footpaths between the gorse came two men, both dressed in dark green jackets, dark green plus-fours (A type of trouser) with knee high buff woollen socks, heavy leather walking boots complete with deerstalker hats. There was some sort of badge on their jacket but I was not close enough to see what was on these. One was carrying the horn that I had heard. These men had with them twelve beagle hounds. They were a very much like a fox hound only smaller. Not having seen anything like this before I made some enquires and found out that these dogs were used for hunting hares and the men walked everywhere. I would not think that this is allowed now.

After writing about the river there is one more thing that comes to mind of what happened in it during 1946 and this involved the man who helped us at Pollard Tree Farm, when we needed extra labour. He was in the RAF during the war and was posted out to India and Burma, working on Mosquito engines. At one of these places he had the chance to buy a single barrel, six cartridge, sixteen bore shotgun, which he brought back to this country after moving back from the Far East. But this is where he hit a problem. As this was a gun that shot a cartridge bigger than the normal twelve bore shotgun, this was illegal to own in this country unless you had a special license which of course he hadn't. Despite all the problems he managed to bring this gun home to his house near the Ling but it was taken to pieces and hidden in his clothes bit by bit. However this did not go unnoticed by someone in the base he left, as three weeks later his pal who was also demobbed at the same time got in touch with him and told him he could expect trouble. With this knowledge he was one step in front, and this is what he done. He covered every part in really thick grease and wrapped the whole thing in a waterproof covering and took it down to the river, known as Sandy Bottoms, where people could swim as it was very deep. Then nearly out into the middle of the river he dug a deep hole in the sand and put the gun in, covering it over with sand and there it stayed with people swimming over it for about three months. I don't think anything was ever done about it and he took it out of the river bed, cleaned it and licensed it and used it on some shoots he went to.

I did not know anything about this till we were working together one day and he told me all about it.

When he first started work as a part time insurance agent he used a bicycle to do his rounds, but it was not long before he bought a Morris Eight car, which he would let me drive on some of the country roads. I don't know what he done before being in the RAF as I had never met him before he started to work with us, but there was a twist in this tale. As we worked and talked he told me that his family were landlords of the pub in Redgrave, which was the very place we turned the snowplough round, which brings me to write about the weather we had in the 1940/50s.

Winter was really winter and there was nearly always a white Christmas. Some winters were worst than others. Heavy snowfall and very strong easterly winds caused big snowdrifts and most roads were completely blocked. Some as high as the top of the hedges each side. There was no hope of getting the snowplough out, so a lot of the men from Hall Farm had to dig out the road from the church to Wortham Long Green with shovels. Other men from neighbouring farms dug out adjoining roads until it was possible to move from one place to another. But still the animals had to be fed and watered and also they had to have dry straw bedding. This is one of the jobs that took two men to do but travelling to the cow farm was made a bit easier for the horse and carts because the ground was frozen solid and the wind had blown the snow from the fields onto the roads. I was lucky as I was then working on the smallholding and we chose if we worked inside or out.

Then some days it was freezing fog for several days on end, and some days when it was clear and sunny ending up with clear starry nights when the dark sky seem full of little lights and the occasional streak of light from a shooting star. These nights were the ideal time to see the Aurora Borealis (Northern Lights) in all their colours of red, blue, yellow and green all dancing across the sky. When I was very small my parents took me outside to see this phenomenon which to me at that time seemed very scary, but as I got older I saw this during several winters and one particular winter the sky was bright red right over the top of our heads. The very old people said that all the coloured lights was caused by the sun shining on the icebergs in the Arctic but our days at school soon changed that idea but you could not convince these people what it really was. What they believed in they believed in and nothing was going to change that.

But in another way of looking at things this older generation were very clever and wise. They knew how to use things that nature provided, like the cures for any ailment for themselves and their animals. My mother had a cure for bronchitis which had been handed down from her parents. I know what it was because it was done to me and I must say I did not like it much. This was before I started school and I was feeling quite ill so I was put to bed and that was followed by my mother cutting out a heart shaped piece of brown paper and then covering one side in thick layer of goose grease which was put on my chest. Whether this cured the problem I am not sure but one thing was certain, the smell soon made you get better.

Most families made their own white oils (embrocation), as they called them, which cured any joint problem on both man and horse. Now once made this mixture lasted for years and I know some of the ingredients were eggs, turpentine and vinegar. What the rest were I don't know but I do know this was a very effective remedy.

One other thing I found out about the older generation of my younger days was the fact that they could predict the weather to within an hour or so of it happening. They could read the sky like a book and also watched nature's reaction to change. It was first made known to me while I was leading the horse one day in a field of young wheat. The man behind and steering the hoes between the rows was the oldest man on the farm, a man who everyone called Jack and was well over ninety years old and had spent many years of his life working as a horseman on one farm. He would work any day they required him to, just like Grandfather did. Retirement was a word they did not wish to understand. We was working together one day when he said, "Let's get this done boy. It's going to rain within the next three hours." But the sun was still shining brightly, so I was curious to know the reason he said this and then he told me to look at the weeds we were hoeing up. The scarlet pimpernel and the blue speedwell, both tiny flowers, had closed up having been out in full bloom all morning. He was right. By the time we got the horse back to the stable it was raining quite hard. Most of those who worked on the land at that time knew a lot about two things, weather lore and folklore. Now this was a good thing during the war as the weather forecast was not allowed to be printed in the papers or allowed to be broadcast to the people who had wireless sets, which was very few.

More Changes and Recollections

Not every winter was snow and ice. There were a few that were just cold and frosty, sometimes sharp enough to freeze my mother's washing on the line so it was stiff like a board and had to be thawed out before it could be ironed. I suppose one could say this was the first type of freeze drying. Monday was always wash day. It was all done in the copper after the fire had been lit and any rubbish burnt that was not wanted to save on the coal. My parents, like most people in the countryside had certain days for certain jobs. Monday was always wash day, Tuesday a day for ironing if it could not be done on Monday, Wednesday and Thursday carpet sweeping and dusting, bearing in mind most people had to do this by hand, no electricity meant no Hoovers unless it was a hand pushed machine, which would brush the carpets but not collect any dust at all. It was not unusual to see the stiff yard broom being used on the coco matting covering most floors, or a wet mop being used on the lino (linoleum), which covered most kitchen and pantry floors, both of which were made at the Diss Brush Factory which was in fact in Roydon. They made flooring and mats besides brushes. It was possible to go straight to the factory, choose what you liked, pay for it yourself and take it home. This was much to the disapproval of the local mat and carpet retailers as they would rather sell you something from their shops, or at least give you a ticket to choose and collect but not pay for anything. This had to be done through them so they made some money out of you. I could understand the logic of this.

This was not the only way some shops lost trade because there were two other types of selling being done at that time but the war stopped both of those. One was done by a man who came round with a suitcase on his bicycle full of mainly women's clothes. This man was years in front of time because his sole ambition was to sell his clothes as cheap as possible to anyone who was stupid enough to buy from him. He would convince you that his goods were far better than those at the local market and were good value. What he would not say was that his stock was seconds that the factories would not sell to the shops. If anyone bought a coat or dress he would not want paying then but would come round once a month to collect what money you could afford and by that time he would have sold you something else. These people were known to the locals as packmen and were scorned by the majority of people because in those days if you could not afford an item you saved up for it until you could. I only knew of one family that dealt with this man but of course there must have been others.

The other door to door selling was done by two men working together, both these bearded men came from a country that was once part of the British Commonwealth and dressed in that country's fashion. I think that most people treated these men with respect because of what they did. I don't know where they lived but they had a bicycle each and on each pedal rested a massive suitcase held together over the crossbar by a strap. They walked miles pushing their cycles and the cases full of clothes, both men's and women's. They were very polite to people, and would take no for an answer. When one of them came up the garden path complete with a suitcase and you opened the door, their first words were, "You buy necktie", and would then proceed to open the case and show you their goods. I must admit they sold some very nice neck ties and scarves and things like that. Sometimes my father would buy a tie from them, after which they would give him what they called a lucky bean. I could see no difference in that and the ones grown on the farm, but everyone was happy. They had made a sale and you had a tie and a lucky bean. These people were not seen during the war but they did come around again in the late 1940s.

There was one man who made very much of an impact on people's lives and many households were glad to see him and that was the scissor grinder as he was called. He had a tricycle very much like the ice cream sellers with a maroon painted box with gold writing on the front and sides. On top was an emery wheel which he operated by the pedals of the cycle with him sitting on the seat. He would sharpen anything for a few pence each, such as scissors, shears, knives, chisels, and plane blades but not saws. As he was normally paid cash I doubt if he paid any tax but made a very comfortable living. There are others I will explain later which I think should be recorded as they were also part of everyday life at that time.

As I have been writing about winters I should have mentioned the terrific storm and wind of January 1953, when a northeast gale force wind forced a surge of water down the coastline of the North Sea causing the sea wall to burst all along the shores of Norfolk and Suffolk. I am not sure which weekend in January it was but I know for certain it was a Saturday evening and all through the night. And the reason for this was because in the evening I had to go out in the strong wind. What had happened was that my father had been taken ill on the Saturday morning and Mother had phoned the doctor from the phone at the rectory. Within two hours he had arrived and diagnosed the problem. He then left saying that there would be some medicine ready for collection that evening from the surgery.

Now in those days the doctor's surgery was part of the big house opposite the Co-op shops in Victoria Road, and the waiting room was a galvanised building joined to the house. There were always three doctors on duty, one of which was the one that visited you if you could not get down to see them. I feel certain they changed this job so each one was away from the surgery in turn. You did not know which one would visit you until he appeared. The surgery was open six days a week from eight in the morning to seven at night. There were two women who worked there as well. Both could do each other's job. They were both receptionists and dispensers and changed jobs alternating weeks. Going to the doctors then was totally different from what it is now. Then you went down to the surgery, told the receptionist you would like to see a doctor, she would normally ask what was wrong, no one minded this, after which you sat in the waiting room, looked to see who was in front of you and waited. One by one each patient would be called by the doctor coming into the waiting room and asking "Who's next?" until it was your turn. You then went into the room of the doctor who called you, and you then told him your problem. He would then tell you his opinion and how to cure it, writing down the cure either by a medicine or a pill and he would take and give that to the dispenser and you would sit down and wait till it was ready.

The saying around that time was, "Ill, pill, better", which in fact usually worked. Most medicines were in clear glass or coloured bottles depending what the mixture was, and marked in ounces, but also embossed in the glass at the back were dessert and table spoon marks for the amount to be taken. The pills were a small round pink ball with seven (one per day) or more in a round, maroon outside, white inside cardboard box. I had some of those medicines for various illnesses from time to time and I remember there was a red one that tasted very nice and a brown one that tasted like creosote, which I avoided if I could.

Now a lot of things could also be obtained from the chemist, which my family did. Things like Iron Jelloids, a black smooth tablet used for improving iron in the blood, also a buff type of tablet called Zube, for sore throats, Epsom Salts for constipation and many, many more. But, as I have said, lots of people made their own remedies for two reasons, one was their beliefs in things they had done for generations, and two, they could not afford to go to the doctors. In the 1930s well into the 1940s there were charges for seeing the doctor. What I must have cost my family I dread to think, but they managed it somehow. I can remember when I had chicken-pox or measles and had to keep in bed. The doctor would turn up unannounced, which in turn would make my mother go into a flap, as the house had to be spick and span and nothing out of place.

Another thing stands out of my very young days when in Diss with my mother. While we were shopping on one side of the street we saw one of the doctors on the other side, who then came across and asked how the whole family was. That was the sort of people they were. But we must take into consideration that the population was very small and both village and town were occupied with families that had lived there for years. Anyone who moved into the area was viewed with suspicion and it took ten years or more to become a local.

Writing about local brings me to tell about at the time 1930/40s Diss had its own ambulance, which was stationed just up Mount Street next to the Rectory and the meadow that came down to the road. This was a cream coloured vehicle with black glass windows along each side and the back doors. This, like the Diss Fire Engine which was stationed in the council depot in Chapel Street, had a bell to warn people to get out of the way. The ambulance crew lived in both Diss and Roydon whereas the firemen all lived in Diss, many of them coming from the same family.

Getting back to the night of the January storm and gale force winds, I had a hard job to ride a cycle facing the wind, but I had a three speed cycle which meant that to use it in low gear you had to pedal faster but you could get along better. I arrived at the doctor's by going along the road from the Ling to Denmark Bridge because this had high hedges both sides so it was sheltered quite a bit from the wind. I collected the pills and started to come home and tiles were being blown off roofs everywhere. It was dark with just the cycle dynamo light to see by and there was also branches of trees about the road everywhere, but the biggest surprise was when I got back to Denmark Bridge because in the meadow next to the river was a big poster hoarding used for the purpose of sticking what was known as bills. These were big sheets of paper advertising a product such as a beer or a certain make of car tyre. The size of these boards was quite big so most of the posters were made in two halves, and pasted on by a man called a bill poster. His tools were a big pot of glue, a big broom-like brush and a ladder. Well I had just got level with this board when a massive gust of wind ripped all the posters off and like a blanket it went up into the sky. Where it landed I don't know but it completely disappeared. I decided to go home by Palgrave hill and down Millway Lane so the wind was behind me. This was the fastest I had gone on a bicycle for years, no pedalling from Palgrave to Wortham.

The wind kept blowing hard all night and with the beech trees next to our house it was hard to get any sleep. The next morning I went to feed the horses at Beech Tree Farm and there were a few tiles off some of the sheds but the wind had become a strong breeze and the sky was clear, no cloud at all. So after listening to the news on the wireless it was a very serious situation that had happened that night along our coastline and indeed over the other side of the English Channel as well. In certain places the sea was well inland. People and animals of all sorts had been drowned. Coastal roads in both countryside and towns became rivers. The only transport that could be used was small boats, especially for getting people out of their upstairs rooms when all their ground floors rooms were full of water, reaching within a few inches of the ceilings.

Now as we live just over thirty seven miles from the nearest seaside towns of Dunwich and Southwold, nobody expected it to affect us. But it did in an unforeseen way because all the men on the farms not concerned with animals were asked to bring a shovel each and meet a bus at a certain part of the village, from where they were then taken to Sea Palling or some other part of the coast to fill sandbags to fill in the breaches in the sea wall. There was not much work done on the farms for the following two weeks, and some of the tales they told of what they have seen, well it must have been horrible. I am glad that I did not have to go, not that I did not want too, but some of them had to help in burying the dead animals, terrible.

But as winter turned to spring and the two Suffolk colts were working well on every job we gave them, they were quick to learn, and became my plough team. It was plain to see they had been handled a lot but not for work. Then came the date of 8 May and every year despite the weather this was the day the horses were taken from their winter sleeping quarters of the walled-in yard and put out onto the meadows to stay out all night. But whatever the weather had been, it would certainly change from that date and for the next week, cold, misty and damp but it did eventually get warmer. Now this made less work for me, and to see them galloping around the meadow the first time out was a sight never forgotten.

Now one thing that did not change much winter or summer was meals we ate and the time we ate them. Sunday dinner was always the biggest meal of the week, usually a roast of some sort of meat, beef or pork all complete with homemade Yorkshire puddings and our own vegetables from the garden, which did change according to the seasons, all cooked in a Valour three stove burner oven using paraffin soaked wicks to make the heat. Sunday dinner would not be complete without some sort of dessert. This again depended what was fit in the garden, either fruit or vegetables made into pies or in the case of plums it would be with homemade custard. This was after a breakfast of eggs and bacon if you were lucky but only on a Sunday, the eggs fresh straight from the nest of our own chickens. Tea time before the war was a large tin of peaches or pears which cost half a crown, which is about 12 ½ pence in today's money. This was after, garden or water cress or if mother had saved a little extra from her housekeeping money she would buy a large tin of red salmon. All these were made into sandwiches. To me this was the best day of the week as far as food was concerned, but if my parents had not worked hard and saved every penny they could, this would not have been possible.

We always had a cooked tea when we came home from work on weekdays, and both my father and I helped with this when we could, especially if we had been lucky at sea or fresh water fishing. Then Mondays become a fish and mashed potato day instead of cold meat left over from Sunday. The other day that stands out about the country housewives was Fridays, because not only was it market day in Diss, so it was always fish for tea, either herring or mackerel, we had a piece of newspaper to wipe our fingers on when getting the bones out of these, or sprats in season. The type did not come off newspapers in those days.

Most people done their baking on a Friday as well, so it was always fresh bread and cakes for the weekend. I can remember going round to Tom's house when his mother was baking and always got a fresh baked bun these tasted delicious. Some people went out on a Sunday for a picnic. I never did. My parents had enough meals outside during the week.

When the war started our way of eating changed also as rationing was brought in and the big tins of fruit and salmon disappeared never to be seen again. People began to dig up every piece of spare land they had, including lawns, to grow vegetables. Although we did not know it at the time we were living in an organic era. But most farm workers were better off than many other workers because a lot of them had a big pocket in their jackets to put the odd rabbit in, either caught in a net or shot with a catapult. This became one of the main meals for many families and there was always plenty of potatoes and soft fruits which could be bought straight from the farms. I can also remember getting a horse and cart, loading it with half a ton of potatoes and delivering those one hundredweight bags to certain customers in the village.

When the ATC paid a visit to any RAF base on any Sunday, we went into the mess room for dinner, the same as the serving personnel. This was very much like we had at home, the same sort of roast but not as good as home cooking, and here we had to queue up to be served as everything was dished out of big tins because all catering was done for a large amount of people. There was a dessert, apple and custard or something else but choice was limited. There was always the NAAFI to fall back on if you were still hungry. This was really a type of shop where you could buy cakes, sandwiches and sometimes chocolate or sweets.

Despite nearly everything being on ration some things were not. You could still buy fish and chips, fresh fish from the fishmongers open slab, also rabbits, and all game in season from the game dealers who would hang these outside the shop. This of course did not apply to our family. We never did buy anything from a shop that someone else had caught. I should add here other than sea fish, besides the ones I have already mentioned, my mother would, as a treat for my father and me, buy a pint of cockles. That was the way they were sold by one or half a pint. Some other things that were not on ration included a type of cornflakes called FORCE. This was sold in a blue box with a funny looking man on the front, also QUAKER OATS, which was used for making porridge. We often had this for breakfast during those cold winters. Vegetables and fruit, hazel and walnuts were also sold in many shops but anything like the above from foreign countries was not on sale and did not appear till quite a while after the war with the result that a lot of children, six and under, had never seen an orange or a banana. However we did buy a certain type of fine crushed oats for feeding to the rabbits and chickens. This was mixed with boiled up potato peelings and there again fed to them during the cold winter months.

Getting back to the airfield visits, by this time in the early 1940s there was an airfield about ten miles away, some of which had been built by the American Engineers themselves. This caused a lot of interest to the country people for two reasons – one was the massive machines brought over from America to build the airfields and two was the military personnel brought over to use these machines. Most people had never seen so many coloured men before and often went to watch these men working. We had all been taught at school about the slave trade and some older part of our generation thought that was a long way from the truth. Many more came over later as aircrew. In fact they were very brave people, taking into account that the average age of aircrew was at that time only twenty, just a few years older than I was myself.

As each base, as these airfields became known, got operational, either with B17 or B24 bombers, it soon became apparent there was a very big difference between the USAAF (United States Army Air Force) and the RAF. They had better food and clothes, in fact better everything and always seemed to have plenty of money, which was of course dollars. They could not get used to the English pounds, shillings and pence and many of them got ripped off by people who spotted this, in the pubs, shops and by private individuals. One of the things they wanted most was bicycles and anyone who could fit a pair of wheels into a frame and put pedals and chain on could sell these wrecks for pounds more than they were worth. But I know of one cycle dealer who had sold a new bike and took in an old cycle in part exchange. He restored it to new condition including painting and lining it out as new. One day an American airman came in looking to buy a cycle in any condition and was willing to pay for one at any cost. When he asked the price of this restored one the dealer told him. Four Pounds Ten Shillings (£4.10s) which was the same price he would have sold it to an English person. A more honest person it would be hard to find.

One of the main things I remember about American Eight Air Force, as it was known, was not only flying in the B17 Flying Fortress but also the fact that if you had you're ATC uniform on they would let you onto their base and always made you welcome, and if it was dinner time they would let you eat with them. Now this was a real eye opener and you could forget that you were in a ration book Britain. Their steaks were massive, flown in straight from the plains of Texas. This applied to nearly everything they ate. But what surprised me the most was that they had all their dinner on one plate, roast, veg and gravy on one end and dessert of apple pie and custard on the other. This was not the only way of eating brought to this country by the Americans. One thing they done was what they called barbecuing or in other words cooking outside on a grill. All sorts of food was cooked like this, fish, chicken, bacon and sausages. This was all new to us as the only people we knew cooked outside were gypsies and boy scouts. One thing I did really like but would not have known about if I had not been on these airbases, I mean who would have thought of cooking a sausage and then putting it in a bread roll and then of all things putting tomato sauce or mustard on it? This was called a hot dog but I must admit I really liked them. They done the same thing with a round cake of minced beef and called these a beef burger, which was very nice.

These people also had plenty of chocolate and sweets what they called candy and everyone had strips of chewing gum. They became the famous words of the British school children whenever they met the American service men, "Have you got any gum chum?"

They were very good at Christmas time as they gave the school children big parties of food. Some had never seen jelly, ice cream, pineapple cubes, all after turkey and Christmas pudding. They decorated the hall with all sorts of Christmas decorations and coloured lights. They came around the villages with their trucks to pick the children up and return them after the party.

One thing that happened at that time was that Redgrave Hall was taken over as an American hospital so it was a very busy place for quite a long time and we could see all this activity when fishing in the lake and I also had a talk with one of the nurses one day when coming off the Magpie meadow with a horse after horseraking hay into rows. She was riding a bicycle towards Redgrave and stopped and said that she would change her bicycle for a horse any time. She did not like our narrow roads and asked a lot of questions about our farm horses and how we broke them in for work. Before she joined the air force she had ridden horses with her brothers on a very big cattle ranch somewhere in America. I had the idea that she was missing all that, a bit homesick perhaps.

That hall was a lovely old building with some connection with the Horsfall family in time past but sadly, like a lot of other old buildings, after the war it got pulled down and a house now stands it its place. The American airman found that there was very little entertainment out in the country, and, as some of them came from the big cities it was hard to adjust to a country pub or the picture house in Diss so what they done was to arrange dances on the base. They picked up the girls from the surrounding villages by truck just the same as they did the children, but this time they also had the company of some of the married women whose husbands were in the forces. I know of two girls I went to school with married American airmen and became what was known as GI brides.

There was one pub in Diss that no local person would go into because it was a favourite place for some of the rougher type of American. This was a very sombre place, red pammet floors, dark brown bar and seats and had not seen a paint brush for years. This place was called THE SHIP and it was a red brick building opposite the Mere. It had a very bad reputation. There were fights that often spilled out onto the road and there was one man who would tell these people that he would find them girls. He done this once too often because the girl did not come, and he was found lying in the road in front of the chapel covered in knife wounds, of which he died. Thankfully after the war this place was pulled down and one of the first supermarkets was built on this site but is now a bakery and cake shop.

When the Americans left a lot of people lost their cigarette supply. Lucky Strike and Camel had been bought from these men for several years. Also a lot of women did their laundry and earned quite a bit of money.

I don't think any Americans liked our picture house as during their off duty time they went to Norwich, Ipswich and even London. This was always known as The New Picture House as it was built before the war, and I remember my first time going in there to see Shirley Temple in Shipyard Sally. This became the only entertainment for local people for many years. Sometimes there would be long queues waiting for opening time if there was a good film on. The films got changed twice a week. It was Monday to Wednesday, one big film and one small film, with a break between for a short newsreel film and ice cream was sold. There were two showings each evening, one at 6pm and one at 8pm and this was repeated Thursday to Saturday with what was known as a matinee on Saturday morning for the school children. The prices for seats were as following, 2/6 the top third of those the furthest away from the screen, 1/9 for those in the middle of the building and about six rows at the very front looking up at the screen were 1/- each, which changed to 6d for a matinee. The 2/6 and 1/9 could be booked in advance at the ticket office. The very back rows always seemed booked up by courting couples, a bit unfair of them I thought. During the war if there was an air raid on there would be a notice come on the screen, "There has just been an air raid warning sounded. Those wishing to leave the cinema may do so." Not many people did despite the sound of anti aircraft guns and bombs dropping on Norwich. Bicycles were stored in an open shed on the side of the building and there was one big problem with that, as there was well over a hundred on most nights and if yours was at the back you either had to move those in front or wait till they had been taken away by their owners. But I never ever heard of one being stolen. I can just remember the very old cinema which stood where the petrol station is now. It had a corrugated iron roof and sides and was painted dark green. What it was like inside I don't know as I never went into there but I did know one or two people who did and apparently those were the days of the silent films.

After the war many of the airfields were used for other purposes. Some had industrial units, for different types of business, built on the runways and perimeter tracks. Some had great big huts called broiler houses built on them and thousands of chickens were reared in them on wood shavings. These were very quick growing birds as it was normal for them to take about eight weeks from hatching to table.

The whole poultry industry was getting bigger and there were several different ways of keeping them. There were the free range egg producers where hens went where they liked on big meadows but laid their eggs inside the building to be collected by hand from nest boxes. Some other hens were not so lucky; they were kept inside big sheds in what was known as battery cages which were in fact wire prisons as far as the hens were concerned. There were two, sometimes three hens in an area roughly two foot square. Even the bottom was wire mesh. Food and water was outside the cage so the hens had to put their heads through the wire mesh to eat and drink, eggs rolled out at the back into wire trays. This was very cruel way to keep anything in my opinion and only done to get maximum production with as little effort and movement as possible.

In the late 1940s disaster struck the poultry industry in the form of a disease known as Fowl Pest. This wiped out flock after flock with the exception of the free range birds, which for some unknown reason did not seem to get it so easily. It was said that this disease was brought over by starlings from Europe. The government paid compensation for each bird killed and for cleaning and disinfecting the huts. I know of one farmer who took some dead hens from an infected farm and laid them with his free range flock, but his hens never caught it so he missed out on any payment. This appeared again in the 1950s and a lot of birds were killed but this time the government did not pay any compensation with the result that this disease disappeared over night and was never heard of again.

The Destruction Of The Countryside As I Knew It

Just after the war years the government was pushing the farmers to produce more and more food and the industry was being pushed to its limits. There were subsidies for all sorts of work to encourage change. The horses had disappeared from grazing on the meadows and only a few farms kept old traditions alive because they loved horses but were not making much if any profit. Even the horses that pulled the coal carts loaded with one hundredweight bags of coal were replaced with lorries. What happened to them I don't know except for the one I had at Beech Tree Farm, which came from a small coal merchant in Diss.

Some shops in Diss had been delivering groceries by van for many years, like the Co-op red vans and the green and gold vans of the International Stores opposite Woolworths in Mere Street. Even the milk ponies were replaced with milk floats carrying pints of milk in glass bottles.

But the real problem started many years before that. The arable fields had been ploughed by horses and before that Oxen, so the workable soil was only about nine inches deep and a hard layer called subsoil was formed which had been there for many hundreds of years. In the 1930s land was being left to deteriorate. A change was needed. Someone at that time and I am not sure about this but I am reasonably certain it was John Fowler, the same person who made the steam plough engines, made a machine called the Gyratiller. This was a massive machine moving on tracks at the back half and each side like a Caterpillar tractor and it was steered by these tracks. This was also a very high machine with a very big diesel tank on top of the engine. As the driver could not see the front and therefore where to steer to, at the front was a big metal wheel, to which was joined a metal rod. On top was a piece of sheet metal cut out like a double pointed flag and turned whichever way the wheel was steered. The whole machine had a roof over the top like a steam roller. However the back end of this machine was like no other of those days. It had a big circle of steel, to which was fitted eight thick metal tines like a cultivator, all of which were wider than the outside of the tracks. Now these tines were lifted up for travelling and dropped to ground level for working. When working, these tines went in to the soil at a maximum depth of two foot. I was too young to understand the workings of machines in those days but somehow this circle of tines was turned in the ground and mixed all the soil and broke up all the subsoil. This was slow moving and the area worked was small so this was a day and night job, as this machine had powerful lights fitted both front and back. One evening Tom and I heard this machine working on some fields behind Hall Farm. I was seven and Tom was six. We decided to go and see it working so off we went past the church and through the Hall farmyard onto the field. I think we must have been fascinated at what was going on. As it got darker the lights came on casting shadows, something we had not seen before.

St Mary's Church, Wortham

The Font, where I was christened

The Latch (or Lynch) gate at Wortham Church

My parents grave, Wortham Churchyard

It wasn't until one of the men working on the field told us it was ten o'clock that we realised that we had been out later than we should, so we started to run home taking a short cut through the churchyard and I don't know about Tom but I had never been so scared before and was glad to get home. Now this machine done more harm than good as it brought the clay from deep down up onto the surface and nothing would grow on those fields for years.

After the war hedges were being ripped out and ditches filled in to make the working of ever bigger machines easier and the horse had gone for good. The wild flower meadows were sprayed with weed killer to grow better grass for grazing cows which in turn meant more milk. With the ditches filled in some fields became flooded and had to be drained. I think there was a grant for this and this was done by strong tractors working a big wheel which cut out a trench and laid the clay drain pipes end to end on a level surface at the bottom of the trench. I had a tractor and trailer loaded with round stones bought specially for the job of lying on top of the pipes to help with draining. Another tractor with a bulldozer blade on the front pushed the soil back to fill the trench. What a difference from the days when my father done all this work by hand.

Beside all the trees cut down when the airfields were built, wood behind The Grove near Magpie Green at Wortham always known as Tooth's wood, disappeared as did the woods near the rectory, where we done our poaching, beside lots of smaller woods around the village. Nothing was planted to replace any of these. There were two big woods left untouched in the adjoining village of Burgate. These were Burgate Wood and Gittings Wood.

One of these woods had a tale to tell but I cannot remember which one it was because I was only a schoolboy at the time but I can remember my parents talking about it at the time. I have already mentioned about the keeper's house at one end of Redgrave Lake and the keeper for the Squire at that time was a man called Wop Garnham. He would often walk past the school wearing a light mac. His cap would be slightly cocked to one side of his head, a shoulder strap would support a sacking bag on his back and with his double barrelled, twelve bore gun under his arm and his black Labrador dog at his side he would speak to the teachers and children when passing and would also come and have a word or two if you were fishing in the lake. During one of his visits to the woods he found one of the other keepers lying on the ground having been shot by someone. Wop done his best to get help but sadly this was not quick enough and the man died. This then became a murder case and the police had a good idea who done it.

At that time there was a renowned poacher on the Squire's estate, called Joe Whistlecraft, who had a habit of getting caught just before Christmas so he had a Christmas dinner in prison. It was not long before the police arrested Joe because this man had been shot with a four-ten gun and they knew he had one. Joe went through court after court each time denying he had done it. It was said that he had put the gun down a well in a copse beside the Wortham to Redgrave road. No one ever found it and as the murder weapon could not be found Joe was found not guilty and walked away a free man. However there was a twist in this story as Joe was offered a job working for the Squire as, believe it or not, a gamekeeper. A true case of poacher turned gamekeeper.

Still changes were taking place and some were for the better because instead of taking down things some were being put up and these were wooden poles supporting wires carrying electricity both to the farms and private houses. I was still working at Hall Farm at the time. It was around 1946 and big electric motors were being put in. The mill's big Horsby Ruston engine did not have to be started by standing on the spokes of the wheel anymore. Each other machine had its own motor to work it. The wheels and belts were taken down and everything worked with a switch being moved.

The same thing happened at Low Farm, where the dairy herd was kept. The milking machine engine did not have to be started with a crank. This was all done by electric motor, by switching it on. The Tilley lights were replaced with electric lights and for the first time you could really see what you were doing. Water mains came to the villages about 1953/54 and the whole country life was made much easier.

But there were things done, which in my opinion was a big mistake. One of them was The Water Board, as it was known, making people fill in the wells in their gardens by condemning the water as undrinkable, therefore making people pay for their mains water. I never heard of anyone dying through drinking well water. But it was nice to just turn a tap and boilers were built at the back of the fireplaces and people had hot water for a good big bath.

Flush toilets appeared in workers' cottages and the privy at the bottom of the garden disappeared. In all life was made more comfortable. A lot of landlords would not improve their property so many people still lived the old lifestyle. I can still remember the first fast sink I put in Mother's kitchen at 2 Jubilee House in 1954, just after we moved in. She was pleased that washing up did not have to be done in a bowl anymore. I did other things to improve our way of life. I had help and moved my workshop to Union Lane and still made furniture and wood items. It took a long time to make this place like home but we did and were quite happy there.

Characters and Other Things

Some of the things and people of my early years should be remembered. There was the old lady who lived in a caravan opposite Abby Farm at Thrandeston, she walked miles pushing an old pram full of baking tins, pegs and most of the tin kitchen goods of the day, all for sale at her price. As she walk she always held her head on one side and therefore got the name of Wry Neck Alice. My mother would on rare occasions go by train on a shopping trip to Norwich and we get off at Norwich Thorpe station and get on a tram to city centre, one day we went into Woolworths which was in those days a 3d and 6d store and there was this old lady buying tins and so on to resell. Another thing she done was always smoking a curved pipe, but this caused her to come to a sad end, she sat in a chair smoking and fell asleep and the pipe dropped from her mouth and set the caravan on fire, neither her or her caravan could be saved.

Another one who came round in those days was the hurdy gurdy man (Barrel Organ) I was scared of him with his monkey on top, if he stopped outside our house and turned the handle to play a tune I would get under the table. From our front garden the Pulham Airship sheds could be seen quite clearly even during the war. We as a family would cycle around here on a Sunday afternoon and see the big heaps of crashed aircraft as this place was used as a collecting dump; when it was cleared I don't know. And last of all was the Aldrige Brush Factory at Roydon next to Diss, this employed local people, some whole families and made brushes of all sorts, coco matting, floor tiles etc, but its steam hooter could be heard for miles around telling people when to come to work and when to leave off – this is all gone now and the area is full of houses.

Another lot of likeable characters during my school days were three brothers who lived all together in one house on the Marsh at Wortham. I knew them as Al-Jack, George and Dorgy. Now Al-Jack was a thin wirey short man who kept lots of rabbits in sheds and hutches also I think he kept goats on the Marsh itself. I know he kept the churchyard tidy and cut it with sythe each year for hay, going down on his bicycle with a two tined fork tied to it so that he could turn the hay over to get dry and then he would make into hay cocks. Then came the most annoying part of how to get the hay home. Al-Jack had a cart but no horse, now this cart was not a small pony cart but a big wheeled high cart made for a cob or a tall horse. Now I saw this myself two or three times, Al-Jack would get between the shafts and pull this cart empty down to the churchyard and load up with hay which he would then rope on, get back between the shafts and start to pull this load home, with a shaft under each arm he pulled this load up hill all the way from the church to the Marsh where he built a stack. Would anyone do this nowadays I don't think so.

Now George was a tall thickest man always wore a pair of cut down rubber boots, a thick wide leather belt and an old trilby hat with the centre pushed up. He also would stop for a chat and a joke I never saw him flustered or angry. Now Dorgy was totally different person, he was smarter with the clothes he wore, a bit taller than Al-Jack, very quiet man and did not talk much and kept himself to himself. I never did know his proper name or the surname of any of them. Neither did I question how they got the money to live. But they were remarkable people and I think most people in the village liked them.

Now there were things happening in the 1930s during those long hot summer days or rather nights which I did not like to see, and this was the fen fires, instead of the colours of the Northern Lights there was the red glow of one of the fens on fire, as these fens stretched along the Waveney from Roydon to Blo Norton and beyond, to see the high flames and big clouds of smoke and hear the bells of the fire engines going to put these fires out was something never to be forgotten. Sometimes these were set on fire on purpose by people or by internal combustion as the peat under the surface was always smouldering and could break through. And there was another devastating blow for the countryside in the early 1950s as the whole country was swept with a disease to wild rabbits called myxomatosis that was a horrible thing, rabbits lost all sense of direction and just sat still were ever they were. Their heads swelled to nearly double the size and their eyes stuck out and seemed to be weeping down their face. Dead rabbits laid around everywhere, in the ditches beside the roads, and in the woods. Lots of people hit them on the head with sticks to stop them suffering. However some did survive and the rabbit population started to grow back, I have never eaten a rabbit since as after seeing all that I could not fancy it.

I started writing this book with the idea of letting future generations know what life was like in my young days, what we had to eat, how our family lived before my time, the changes over the years and in some parts I got sidetracked when trying to give as much details as I remembered them. I hope people will have enjoyed reading it as much as I have enjoyed writing my part of history, some people have said these were The Good Old Days -Were they I can't decide.

J F Frost

Writing in progress

Should I continue after 1954?
There is a lot more to tell and a decision to be made